CAMBRIDGE WORLD ARCH

THE BRONZE AGE OF SOUTHEAST ASIA

CAMBRIDGE WORLD ARCHAEOLOGY

THE BRONZE AGE OF SOUTHEAST ASIA

CHARLES HIGHAM

University of Otago

CAMBRIDGE
UNIVERSITY PRESS

Published by the Press Syndicate of the University of Cambridge
The Pitt Building, Trumpington Street, Cambridge CB2 1RP, UK
40 West 20th Street, New York, NY 10011–4211, USA
10 Stamford Road, Oakleigh, Melbourne 3166, Australia

Printed in Hong Kong by Colorcraft

National Library of Australia cataloguing-in-publication data

Higham, Charles, 1939–
The Bronze age of Southeast Asia
Bibliography
Inludes index
1. Bronze age – Asia, Southeastern. 2. Archaeology – Asia,
Southeastern. 3. Asia, Southeastern – antiquities.
I. Title (Series: Cambridge world archaeology).
930.150959

Library of Congress cataloguing-in-publication data

Higham, Charles.
The bronze age of Southeast Asia / Charles Higham.
    p.   cm. – (Cambridge world archaelogy)
Includes bibliographical references and index.
1. Asia, Southeastern – Antiquities. 2. Bronze age – Asia,
Southeastern. I. Title. II Series.
DS523.H55 1995
959'.01–dc20   95–39223

A catalogue record for this book is available from the British Library.

ISBN 0 521 49660 8 Hardback
ISBN 0 521 56505 7 Paperback

CONTENTS

ERRATA

Higham *The Bronze Age of Southeast Asia*
ISBN 0 521 49660 8 Hardback
ISBN 0 521 56505 7 Paperback

p. vii, line 8
p. 196, lines 21 and 22
p. 246, lines 23 and 24
In each case, for Ban Chiang Hian *read* Ban Chiang

ILLUSTRATIONS

PREFACE

This book was conceived during a conversation with Robin Derricourt, then in charge of Australian publishing at Cambridge University Press. A previous book of mine, *The Archaeology of Mainland Southeast Asia*, was then looking rather dated and I wished to work on a second edition. He countered by suggesting a new book, and without sufficient thought, I proposed a book on the Bronze Age.

There the idea lay until 1992, when I was able, through my fellowship of St John's College, Cambridge, to enjoy an uninterrupted period for reflection and writing, and access to the University and Haddon libraries. I could never have completed this book without the support of my college, but my debt goes beyond the physical facilities. The range of interests and expertise within the fellowship, and the opportunities to mull matters over, provided me with an invaluable source of help and inspiration. Robert Hinde was able to impress on me the need to communicate one's views unambiguously. I was particularly grateful to Jim Charles for his patience in fielding questions on metallurgy and Peter Matthews for tempering my enthusiasm for the implications of linguistic data. David McMullan and Joe McDermott were always on hand and willing to help with a Chinese caption. Jack and Esther Goody provided their customary insight into social matters and, through their good offices, I was able to enjoy a brief period of writing in their daughters' beautiful farmhouse in Quercy while knowing they were just up the road if I needed help, intellectual or gastronomic.

Many friends and colleagues have been generous in providing me with information and opinions. I would particularly like to thank Ian Glover and Moira Woods in England, and either in person or through email, Robert Blust and Laurie Reid have provided many stimulating ideas on the linguistics. Noel Barnard, Peter Bellwood, Bill Meacham, Elizabeth Moore, Vincent Pigott, Penny Rode, Matthew Spriggs, Magdalene von Dewall, and Peter Wilson have all provided me with advice and help in one form or another.

I shall not forget a train journey I took in the company of Robert Maddin and T. Ko from Beijing to Zhengzhou when I awoke to an early dawn, drew back the curtain in the sleeper and saw that we had stopped at a station labelled Anyang. Not long after, we crossed the Huanghe River and quite apart from the steep learning curve I experienced in my knowledge of Chinese archaeology, I was able to visit the Shang walls of Zhengzhou and stop on the outskirts of the city during evening jogging to watch specialists in a fiery workshop still casting. A few years later, in the company of Wang Dadao and Tong Enzheng, I was able to visit the necropolis of Shizhaishan and examine the wonderful bronzes on exhibit at the Yunnan Provincial Museum. In Beijing, I have been welcomed more than once by Han Rubin and Sun Shuyun to their Department to follow their important work on the analysis of Chinese bronzes. Ha Van Tan, Hoang Xuan Chinh, Vu The Long and Pham Minh Huyen were no less hospitable in Hanoi, and took me to Dong Son, Lang Ca, Co Loa and many other key sites in Bac Bo. In Hong Kong, I have had the pleasure of Bill Meacham's company and his patient assistance in summarising the archaeology of Guangdong has been deeply appreciated. Many Thai colleagues have been generous with their time, none more so than Rachanie Thosarat, whose patience has been extraordinary, and Metha Wichakana.

Writing a book which involves so much primary data in other languages has not been easy, and I acknowledge the help of Yun Kuen Lee and Xincan Chen for commenting on my drafts and helping with information, and Yvette Yeung, Vu The Long, Erich Kolig and Nguyen Kim Dung in telling me what others were saying.

A particular and profound acknowledgement must also be given to Francis Allard. While finishing his doctorate on the later prehistory of Lingnan, he has not only been unfailingly helpful, but has provided me with information he has painstakingly acquired and distilled from remote Chinese sources with a degree of generosity rarely encountered in academe.

To my son Thomas, I give my thanks for his patient assistance with numerous time-consuming requests to help with radiocarbon dating. All dates cited are given as 2 sigma ranges, corrected following Stuiver and Reimer, 1993. I am most grateful to Jane Farago of the Cambridge University Press, and Nick Hudson of N.S. Hudson Publishing Services, for their important contribution to producing this book. Finally, I have once again been fortunate enough to call on the services of Leslie O'Neill and Martin Fisher in the preparation of the illustrations.

All those mentioned have contributed to improve this book, but its faults are mine alone.

CHAPTER I

INTRODUCTION

From their hub in the eastern Himalayas, a series of the world's great rivers radiate like the spokes of a wheel. Fed by the melting snows and augmented in the northern spring by the May monsoon, they have cut through mountain ranges and formed extensive flood plains and deltas in an area which today sustains a sixth of humanity. Enclosed between the Brahmaputra in the west to the Yangzi (Changjiang), we encounter the Chindwin, Irrawaddy, Salween, Chao Phraya, Mekong, Red (Hong) and the many rivers which drain Lingnan and join to form the Zhujiang. In an area where the copious monsoon rains encourage dense forest cover, including triple-canopied rainforest in favoured areas, these rivers have historically provided passage for the movement of people, goods and ideas (Fig. 1.1).

In a previous study, I confined mainland Southeast Asia to the valleys of the lower Red, Mekong and Chao Phraya rivers together with the intervening uplands (Higham 1989). This area could easily be expanded. If, for example, we defined Southeast Asia as those areas affected by the monsoon but excluding India, then we should incorporate Lingnan, that part of southern China comprising Guangdong and Guangxi provinces. There is, indeed, a logical case for doing so: the Chinese only seized this territory under the Qin and Western Han dynasties, and to this day local customs and languages, as well as the habitat, show far greater affinities with the land to the south than with the *zhongyuan,* the Chinese central plains. The southern boundary of China has for too long intruded into archaeology. Chang (1986) scarcely once looked beyond this line in his synthesis of Chinese prehistory and I have been taken to task for the same blind spot but in reverse (Bronson 1989). I will, therefore, cross this particular Rubicon, and include the Yunnan Plateau and Lingnan in Southeast Asia. Burma would be included were there any evidence to cite, and there are also strong grounds for including the areas of eastern India settled by those speaking Mundaric, Austroasiatic languages. This last area will be considered in seeking parallels to the Southeast Asian metallurgical tradition. There is also island Southeast Asia, the extensive arc of islands to the south and east of the mainland, which, hardly experienced a bronze age, and will be considered as a relevant but not integral part of this study.

There are also environmental and cultural reasons for this definition of mainland Southeast Asia. The area defined was subject to the monsoon, although its impact varied with local topography. This involves a sharp distinction between

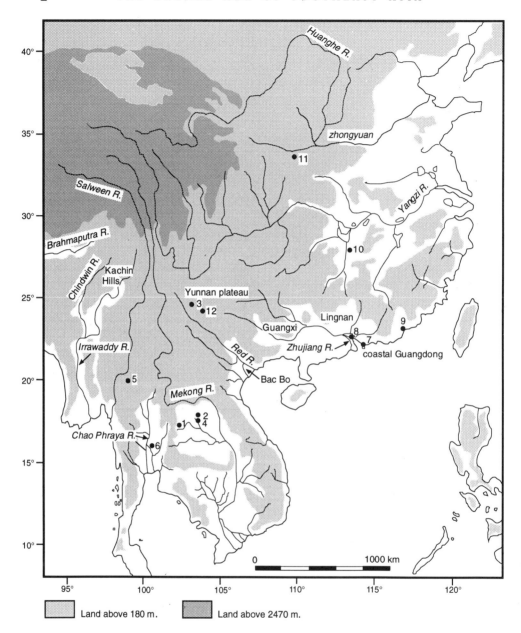

1.1   Southeast and East Asia, showing the principal rivers and locations of places mentioned in this chapter, together with climate stations considered below. **1.** Non Nok Tha. **2.** Ban Chiang. **3.** Wanjiaba. **4.** Ban Na Di. **5.** Spirit Cave. **6.** Chansen. **7.** Hong Kong. **8.** Guangzhou. **9.** Shantou. **10.** Changsha. **11.** Xian. **12.** Kunming.

a wet and a dry season, although the temperature, other than in upland areas, rarely falls below 10°C. The subsistence base in the extensive lowlands, where most bronze age sites are found, was rice cultivation, fishing and stock raising. Only towards the end of the first millennium BC did the Chinese have a major impact in Southeast Asia, and then only in Yunnan, Lingnan and Bac Bo. Most prehistoric people would have spoken a language within the Austroasiatic family, but as we proceed to the northern margins of Southeast Asia, it is possible that Austro-Tai languages were also present.

Essentially, then, Southeast Asia involved Austroasiatic speakers living in a hot, monsoonal habitat with an economy based on rice cultivation. The naturally dense forest cover would have stressed the importance of riverine and coastal movement, and it is along these lines of communication that I have divided Southeast Asia when considering regional cultural developments. There are four principal regions: the Chao Phraya and Mekong valleys, Lingnan and Bac Bo, and the Yunnan Plateau (Fig. 1.1).

The study of prehistory in most of this extensive area has been a recent development. This has resulted in much confusion and controversy: on the one hand, claims based on few or shaky data have been made for the world's earliest agriculture and metallurgy. On the other, the very term 'Indo-China' conveys the manner in which Southeast Asia has been seen as provincial and reliant on the influence of adjacent higher civilisations. This situation, however, has now been redressed, and we can begin to discern a pattern which places Southeast Asia in a prominent position for anyone approaching such issues as the origins and spread of agriculture, or the adoption of metal working, on a broad, comparative front.

The prehistoric sequence

The shallow seas and mangrove shores indented with estuaries which character-ise the coast of tropical Southeast Asia provide the world's richest habitat in terms of biological activity. Although many archaeological sites have been drowned by the rapid Holocene rise in the sea level, the marine adaptation has been documented at settlements on raised beaches. We encounter a pattern which falls into place alongside sites stretching from northern Australia to Japan: rich, coastal foragers, whose settlements were often sedentary and socially complex. In mainland Southeast Asia, the interior seems to have been sparsely occupied by smaller and more transient groups (Fig. 1.2).

There is not yet a consensus on later prehistoric developments and it is necessary to consider alternative explanations of virtually all aspects of the sequence. The origins and spread of rice-growing communities, for example, may have involved an expansionary movement down the river systems from the Yangzi. There may, however, also have been local transitions to agriculture. In the Yangzi Valley, the cultivation of rice was probably under way by about 6500 BC

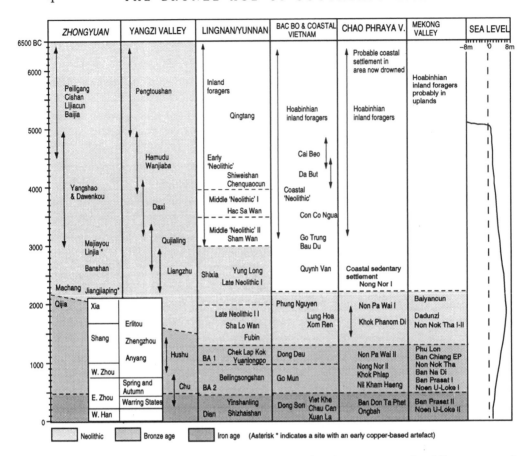

1.2 Chronological chart showing the cultural sequences in the different parts of
Southeast and East Asia considered below.

and assuredly by 5000 BC. Neolithic communities proliferated, and spread
beyond the confines of the Yangzi catchment to the north, south and quite
probably by boat to Taiwan and ultimately, to Melanesia and the Pacific
(Bellwood 1985, 1991). This expansion is thought to have involved languages in
the Austric phylum (Schmidt 1906), which in due course gave rise to Austroasiatic
(AA) and Austronesian (AN) languages. The former are distributed from eastern
India to southern China (Fig. 1.3). The latter are found from Taiwan south into
island Southeast Asia, then to Malagasy in one direction, and Polynesia in the
other. In this overview the expansion of AA speakers followed the lines of least
resistance: the major rivers. According to Blust (1993a), the present distribution of
Vietnamese, Mon, Khmer and Munda languages resulted from the movement of
agriculturalists down the Red, Chao Phraya, Mekong and Brahmaputra rivers, a
process which saw neolithic communities established in our area during the third
and second millennia BC.

While this interpretation is logical and plausible, it is also necessary to consider local and independent developments. We know of many coastal, sedentary communities in tropical Southeast Asia, and it is highly likely that in due course some adopted agriculture. At present, there is no convincing evidence for an independent transition in these groups, but the possibility cannot be ruled out.

In both the Yangzi Valley and Southeast Asia, village communities proliferated and increasing social complexity is encountered (Pearson 1981, Chang 1986, Higham 1989). The almost universal presence of inhumation cemeteries in association with the settlements also reveals that exotic goods were exchanged and employed in mortuary ritual to denote achieved status. In the valley of the Huanghe (Yellow) River, the first consistent evidence for smelting and alloying of copper and tin is found towards the end of the third millennium BC. It will be argued that in Southeast Asia, copper-based artefacts were first locally cast within the period 1500–1000 BC. Some colleagues prefer a date towards the end of the third millennium, others between 2000–1500 BC. This chronological issue will be considered below.

In Lingnan and Bac Bo, the earliest evidence for local casting is found between *c.* 1500–1000 BC, when jades of Shang inspiration were available. The repertoire, which included axes, fishhooks, projectile points and bracelets, copied late neolithic stone and shell prototypes. In this same area, we also encounter a scatter of imported exotic Shang-style bronze vessels, bells and weapons and throughout the bronze age, there was continuing exchange with the *zhongyuan*. The further removed from this contact in Southeast Asia, the less evidence there is for the presence of exotic Chinese bronzes. Yet the same tradition of casting a limited range of artefacts in bivalve moulds recurs in the Mekong and Chao Phraya valleys, and must have been related intimately to that established in Lingnan within the context of exchange with the Shang state.

From about 500 BC, we encounter a widespread cultural change in Southeast Asia which involved the adoption of iron working, a trend towards the concentration of authority in the hands of social elites, a widening exchange network which incorporated greater distances and new products, a marked increase in the range, size and quantity of bronzes and a commensurate growth in the skill of the bronze workers. The range of new items made from bronze, as well as technical changes and innovations, will be considered within these communities. It will be seen that bronzes were used to project the achievements and status of the elite.

Two related issues are central to this study. The first concerns the relationship between the bronze ages of Southeast Asia and of China. Were there two independent and unrelated transitions to metal working, or was one later, developing in the context of the transmission of information? The second, and more interesting issue, is the nature of the communities which adopted metal working in Southeast Asia, how they employed this new medium, and developed it over time.

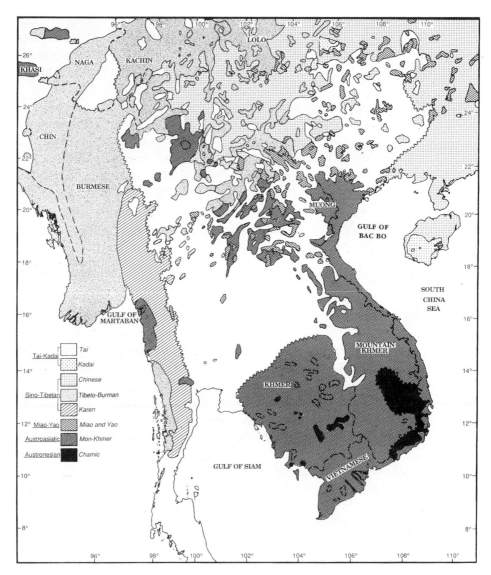

1.3   The distribution of language families and major languages in Southeast Asia (from Bellwood 1992).

The relationship between the bronze ages of China and Southeast Asia has not hitherto been considered in a detailed and objective manner, and this is hardly surprising given the immense area and the difficulties involved in coping with different languages, interpretations, and the confused and controversial issue of chronology. Any such review must grapple with the continuing disagreement over dating the first evidence for bronze in the middle reaches of the Mekong Valley. If it was significantly earlier than that of the *zhongyuan*, or even contemporary, then there is a strong case for an independent origin. If it was later, then the situation changes without ruling out independence. Under these circumstances, it would be necessary to consider the evidence for the exchange of goods, and with them knowledge, between the bronze-using communities to the north and those in Southeast Asia still showing no evidence for the use of metal. This issue turns on the establishment of an accepted chronological framework which, in some areas, remains in the future. It further involves consideration of the mechanisms for the transfer and acceptance of technological innovations.

The second issue also requires a resolution of chronology. Thus, an appreciation of the structure of bronze age communities will vary in line with its duration. As will be seen, there was little evident social change between the neolithic groups and their successors, and bronze was found only sparingly in bronze age cemeteries. At two extremes, we have the option of either a very long bronze age in Southeast Asia, of independent origin, or a briefer period where knowledge of metallurgy was introduced.

Nomenclature

There is no agreed system of nomenclature for the prehistory of mainland Southeast Asia. In the following pages, agricultural communities antedating metal use will be called neolithic and the period from the first use of copper-based artefacts will be called the Bronze Age. We have a wide choice when turning to the complex, increasingly centralised groups evident from about 500 BC. Options include General Period C (Bayard 1984, Higham 1989), Mode 2 (Higham 1983), *Muang* Period (Bayard 1992), the High Bronze Age (Hutterer 1991), the Late Bronze Age (von Dewall 1979), the Iron Age (Penny 1984, Charoenwongsa 1988), the High Metal Age (Ho 1992), the Late Metal Age (Bronson 1992), the Late Prehistoric (Glover 1991) and the Formative (Welch 1985). I have chosen the Iron Age. It is, however, stressed that the Three Age System is used only as a convenient shorthand and with no implications for similarities with other regions where it has been employed. It is also the case that in Yunnan and northern Vietnam, iron was much rarer than in Central Thailand and the Mekong Valley during the period described as the Iron Age. To avoid confusion, however, the term will be used even if iron was later and less abundant in some areas than in others. Since the Iron Age saw a sharp increase in the quantity and range of bronzes produced, this study will cover both the Bronze and Iron Ages.

The Bronze Age: issues and problems

This period is seminal in any consideration of prehistoric Southeast Asia. It opens with the establishment of neolithic communities in a new world of dense forests, broad wetlands during the rains and the long and difficult dry season. By the final act, we can perceive the foundations of the distinct regional states described by early Chinese and Indian visitors, some of which can be traced in an unbroken lineage to the present.

It is also a part of our prehistory which is covered in overlays of confusion and contradiction. It is the intention of this book to strip these away and present a judicious interpretation of the period within a broad, comparative framework. The birth of our understanding of prehistoric Southeast Asia has been difficult and its formative years have seen stunted growth. This has been incisively summarised by Hutterer:

[For many decades,] the scholarly world took it for granted that the indolent spirit of Southeast Asian peoples had been brought to florescence only relatively late by grafting onto it shoots of the more vigorous – and already mature – civilisations of India and China. (Hutterer 1982:559)

He proceeded to urge specialists in Southeast Asia to adopt a comparative approach which would

move Southeast Asia into a meaningful and important place within the history and development of mankind. (Hutterer 1982:567)

This approach contrasts with that recommended by Bayard (1992:17), who has shown concern that the use of terms for ideal social types, such as tribe or chiefdom, might imply too high a degree of similarity with the same term employed in other areas. He advocated the use of the term *ban* to describe autonomous village communities, and *muang* for later, centralised societies. The use of such Thai words is, in my view, inward looking. Should we substitute the equivalent words in Vietnamese or Khmer, or Mon, when considering other parts of Southeast Asia? It is argued that the use of terms known only to native Thai speakers and a tiny group of foreign specialists is likely to marginalise a region which this book is designed to advertise.

Several studies on the nature and development of social inequality in prehistory have recently appeared (Renfrew 1986, Brumfiel, Earle 1987 and Earle 1991). All have in common the absence of any reference to Southeast Asia. This is sensible, and may be ascribed to the overlays of confusion which involve chronology, the nature of the societies which deployed bronze and the myriad approaches to the data within an area of contrasting political ideologies. Any attempt to present an overview of the Southeast Asian Bronze Age soon encounters problems. Publications of relevant material come in many languages: Chinese, Vietnamese, Thai, French, English, Dutch and German. More significantly, interpretations involve distinct, even mutually conflicting, approaches. Chinese scholars, for example, operate within an intellectual straightjacket described by Tong Enzheng:

For the past forty years, Chinese scholars doing research on ancient societies have been forced to tailor their interpretations to a single approved model. This model is the unilineal evolutionary model proposed by the American Henry Morgan in the 19th century in his book *Ancient Society*. As a result of Engels adopting and systematically developing this model ... it was branded with the mark of Marxism and thus above reproach. It was later further simplified and taken to a greater extreme by Lenin and Stalin. After 1949, it became, in China, a sacred formula and rigid doctrine. (Tong Enzheng 1991)

This doctrine required that all societies evolved in a unilineal manner from a primitive band to the final goal of a socialist society. The stage most commonly equated with the southern Chinese bronze age was described as the slave society. So, we find Wang Dadao (1985) interpreting the Wanjiaba cemetery as representing an elite of slave owners, their weapons being required to constrain slaves. The possibility that the wealthy aristocrats used weapons to protect their community from alien aggression and were sustained by consensus was not considered. In Vietnam, the post-colonial period has seen a vigorously nationalistic interpretation of the archaeological record in which innovations, particularly those concerning the Dong Son culture, are necessarily of local inspiration by the ancestors of the present inhabitants.

The Bronze Age in Thailand: a controversy over dates

Archaeology came late to Thailand, and the interpretation of bronze age material became highly controversial when Solheim (1968) announced the presence of a cemetery containing bronze artefacts and their stone moulds at Non Nok Tha, Northeast Thailand. On the basis of two radiocarbon dates, he assigned the bronze to the third millennium BC, concluding that these finds

would mean that bronze was being worked in North-eastern Thailand nearly one thousand years before it is now considered to have begun in Shang China and one hundred or more years earlier than it started in the Harappa Culture of the Indus Valley. (Solheim 1968:62)

A few years later, this chronological issue had been considerably extended. Solheim wrote that a socketed tool dated

from about 3500 BC – the oldest known metal tool coming from Southeast Asia, and the oldest socketed tool yet found anywhere. (Solheim 1972:36)

This claim received support from Bayard (1971), who directed the excavations at Non Nok Tha. When reviewing the situation in 1980, he noted:

Are claims for early metallurgy in Southeast Asia valid? On this question, I can for once give an unequivocal answer: yes. Based on the earlier evidence and problematical chronology of Non Nok Tha there was still room for doubt – not much in my view – although even sceptics were forced to accept the presence of bronze in the area before 1500 BC. But I believe that the recent Ban Chiang evidence makes it highly likely that bronze metallurgy was well developed before 3000 BC. (Bayard 1980:105)

In 1974–5, Gorman co-directed the excavation of Ban Chiang (Gorman and Charoenwongsa 1976). This is an occupation and cemetery site near the headwaters of the Songkhram River in Northeast Thailand. He added further to the controversy by his proposal that bronze at Ban Chiang dated back to 3600 BC, with iron appearing by about 1500 BC.

The results of these claims were predictable: some accepted them with enthusiasm, while they were rejected by others. I was introduced to the area and its prehistory in 1968, when Gorman and Bayard asked me to analyse some faunal material from Spirit Cave and Non Nok Tha. I knew little of the area and found myself part of a team, as for example at the excavation of Ban Chiang in 1974–5, working in an atmosphere of infectious enthusiasm and conviction that indeed we had found remarkably early evidence for bronze and iron. My review of the chronological evidence for the beginning of the bronze age written in 1970 concluded that a date in the fourth millennium BC was the most plausible (Higham 1972).

The blinkers were removed from my eyes in 1981, when I received the radiocarbon dates for our excavations at Ban Na Di, a site located a few kilometres south of Ban Chiang and spanning part of its sequence. These were far later than the claims for equivalent cultural contexts at Ban Chiang, and I knew that our charcoal samples came from *in situ* contexts (Higham and Kijngam 1984). I therefore have considerable sympathy for Muhly (1988), Stech and Maddin (1988) and many others who have found it hard, if not impossible, to penetrate the vapours surrounding Non Nok Tha and Ban Chiang and the attendant claims, a veil which will not properly be lifted until final excavation reports are available.

The hares, however, had been started and the issue generated its own momentum. An article for general consumption published by the Smithsonian Institution declared: 'sophisticated bronze ornaments and pottery have been found dating back at least as far as 3600 BC. The bronzes turning up at Ban Chiang are 15 centuries older than comparable objects found in China' (Mosaic 1977). White's initial re-analysis of the radiocarbon dates from this site provided for a range between 2100 and 1700 BC for the initial presence of bronze (White 1982). In the same publication, Goodenough (1982) attempted to place the site in world ethnological perspective by placing Ban Chiang at the beginnings of the expansion of Austronesian speakers across island Southeast Asia and the Pacific. Goodenough makes no mention of the fact that Ban Chiang lies in the Austroasiatic heartland, an area which has never, to my knowledge, been cited as one which was ever settled by speakers of any Austronesian language.

One direct result of the claims for an early and enduring bronze age tradition has been its projection as being fundamentally different from all other examples of prehistoric societies engaged in metal production. This speculation by White (1982) further bolstered Solheim's proposal that Southeast Asian bronze working is early:

The discovery of a distinctive metallurgical tradition in Southeast Asia at least comparable to that of northern China, if not earlier, has added new pieces to a puzzle of metallurgical origins. (White 1982:48)

But origins were not the only point made by White. She went on to stress, under the heading 'The Peaceful Bronze Age', that this metal-working tradition began and continued in

simple village contexts that derived their subsistence from hunting and gathering and simple cultivation ... no urban, state or military stimulus from within or outside the region is in evidence. No complex, stratified social organisation appears to have been a cause or consequence of the development of metal technology. (White 1982:48)

She consequently stressed that, since this context for metal working did not fit existing theories, new models would have to be developed.

This portrayal of the Bronze Age in Southeast Asia as being set apart from any other received support from Bronson's consideration of the late prehistoric sequence in Central Thailand. When reviewing his excavations at the large moated site of Chansen, he noted of the Iron Age:

The social configuration is an unusual one: a set of not noticeably primitive 'mini-societies' existing side-by-side in a region without important geographical barriers, but in almost hermetic isolation from one another. Such a configuration would seem to preclude the existence of even the most elementary supra-local political structures. Bronson (1979:320)

It is hardly surprising to find Muhly, in a broad survey, identifying Southeast Asia as an exception to a broad pattern. He wrote:

In all other corners of the bronze age world – China, Mesopotamia, Anatolia, the Aegean and central Europe – we find the introduction of bronze technology associated with a complex of social, political and economic developments that mark the 'rise of the state'. Only in Southeast Asia, especially in Thailand and Vietnam, do these developments seem to be missing. (Muhly 1988:16)

There are at least two aspects to this situation which need careful appraisal. The first is the chronological framework. If the earliest bronze working in Southeast Asia falls between 1500 and 1000 BC, then there would be less time in which to fit a long, peaceful bronze age. Second, we must look at the actual artefacts made of bronze, and the contexts in which they were found. Is it, for example, reasonable to view as peaceful a bronze tradition which saw socketed spearheads, axeheads and a wide variety of arrowheads within the repertoire?

In 1983, I suggested that the Bronze Age in Northeast Thailand indeed began about 1500 BC and was centred on autonomous village communities which operated within an exchange network (Higham 1983). This brought exotic items, such as marine shell, marble, slate, ceramics, copper and tin into circulation, some of which were used to denote personal rank as grave goods in mortuary ritual. I described the system as one involving competitive emulation, wherein a community which controlled access to raw materials in demand, such as copper, or the skills required to transform them, such as a potter or lapidary, or was located on a strategic riverine location, would have an edge in the establishment of a social hierarchy involving more than one village. In the sequel, we find just this situation crystallising from the mid-first millennium BC. This book will examine these alternatives.

Chronometric hygiene

It has taken too long for the dust raised by enthusiastic claims to begin to settle, and for further research and more sober handling of the data to resolve this issue of chronology. Spriggs and Anderson (1993) and Spriggs (1989) have done the discipline sterling service in their determination to adopt stringent principles when seeking 'chronometric hygiene'. In a less formalised manner, I attempted to follow the same path in 1983 when reviewing the dating samples from Non Nok Tha and Ban Chiang (Higham 1983). The firm treatment of such charcoal is greatly to be encouraged, for most samples from these two sites are unacceptable because they come from grave fill. I have argued that this source is unreliable on the grounds that charcoal might be relocated from the layers through which the grave is cut, thereby providing a spuriously early date.

Fortunately, the Gordian knot presented by the Non Nok Tha chronology has been severed by the AMS dating of rice chaff from provenanced pottery. The current dating programme on the Ban Chiang mortuary pots, which will also employ this technique will, it is hoped, resolve any remaining controversy over this site. The emerging chronological framework is beginning to form a consistent pattern, and we can move on to more interesting matters. Indeed, recent excavations have made it possible to consider a critical factor, the nature of neolithic societies, and thus appreciate their social and technological complexity. The evidence from these sites will be looked at in some detail, not only because much of the information is not yet widely available, but also because the origins of the Southeast Asian tradition of metal working must be placed within its cultural context. This requirement answers a *cri de coeur* from Muhly. Writing of the haze surrounding the Southeast Asian bronze age, he wrote:

Explaining (or eliminating) this anomalous situation is one of the major challenges of archaeological and archaeometallurgical research during the next decade. (Muhly 1988:16)

This anomaly can be summarised thus: the development of copper and its alloys provides a new, unusual and attractive medium for making a potentially wide variety of goods. It can be cast into ingots and exchanged, or made into ornaments for personal adornment, tools, weapons, or sumptuary goods, such as the bowls and ladles used in feasting and ceremony. Bronze can also be decorated in many ways to add further to its symbolic or ritual value. It can thus play a social as well as a technological role. Renfrew (1986) has explored the social changes which accompanied the adoption of bronze working in various parts of Europe. He has stressed that bronze, particularly when imbued with novelty and rarity, is not only a means of monitoring the achievement of increasingly marked social status by individuals within their community. Its very availability is a means whereby that status is generated.

Central variables in considering the Bronze Age of Southeast Asia

Before distilling a mass of information, it is essential to isolate relevant variables. The first concerns the adoption of bronze casting. If this practice began in the context of exchange between late neolithic communities in Lingnan and the Shang state, what was the mechanism for acceptance, both social and technical, of this innovation?

Whether of independent origin or not, we must then consider the role which bronzes played: did major social changes eventuate, or did this new medium join others in technical and social functions and of itself, show little or no impetus for cultural change. That deep social changes did occur from about 500 BC is undisputed. Earle (1991) has provided a summary of variables which must be taken into account when reviewing the development of centralised, hierarchical societies, and all are germane to this study. We will be considering various regional sequences which display a general similarity: small, autonomous neolithic communities which incorporated copper-based artefacts into their repertoire within the period 1500–1000 BC. Bronzes were rare and no major social changes are seen for a millennium. Then, there were rapid moves towards centralised social groupings, often described as chiefdoms.

The autonomous communities are recognised on the basis of their similar size, the lack of large, superordinate centres and marked status differences between individuals in communal cemeteries. Chiefdoms, however, reveal at least one level of site hierarchy above the local communities, rising to two levels in more complex cases. Elites usually leave evidence of their presence: a special burial place rich in grave goods, a central residence, technical improvements in agriculture.

There are many different aspects of community behaviour, as well as of the environment, which need definition before it is possible to consider how chiefdoms developed. A central group, for example, needs sustenance, and we must therefore review the nature of the habitat, subsistence, and the means for increasing and distributing food. Increased agricultural productivity may be seen in the provision of irrigation facilities, the diversion of metal to new and more efficient agricultural implements or the clearance of forest to improve the habitat for livestock. Recently documented instances of chiefly behaviour stress the importance of providing feasts (Wilson 1988). This is a way of distributing food which creates indebtedness between recipient and donor, and therefore provides a benchmark for social inequality. In the following pages, therefore, it is critical that evidence for such behaviour (for example, the casting of sumptuary bowls, ladles or drinking vessels in bronze) be recognised. The social organisation of chiefdoms can express collective or individualising trends (Renfrew 1974). The former might involve the construction of impressive ritual monuments, the latter would see elite individuals reserving for themselves tangible symbols of status, or impressive and carefully-placed burial monuments. It will, therefore, be necessary to scrutinise the available mortuary record in Southeast Asia for changing burial practices.

The growth in population does not in itself require the development of social complexity, but under certain circumstances, it is a relevant variable. Where a group of people can move away and settle elsewhere, population pressure on resources need not occur. But where such movement is circumscribed physically, by geographic barriers to settlement, or socially by proximity to hostile groups, then the need to take social decisions affecting many local communities is a spur to the development of a hierarchy. This trend is magnified under the threat of a more powerful and predatory polity. It is, therefore, necessary to describe prehistoric Southeast Asian societies within the context of their physical and social environments.

The control of force, whether applied internally or externally, is a widespread phenomenon in hierarchical societies. Metal may be converted into weaponry, and it is necessary to be alert to changes in the variety, abundance and deployment of armaments. A restricted distribution of more effective weapons, such as the long sword, or the embellishment of armour, are likely to reflect underlying social change. This development may also be documented by the provision of moats or ramparts to strategic settlements.

Copper and tin are localised in nature, providing opportunities to restrict access to them. The conversion of both into bronze artefacts is demanding, but in the case of simple trinkets or ornaments, does not require a long apprenticeship or full-time involvement. If, however, the elite seek to restrict access to bronze and have it converted into intricate, large and demanding status objects, then it will be necessary to engage and control full-time specialists. It is, therefore, essential to define the range of bronzes produced in prehistoric Southeast Asia, and the degree of skill required in their creation. Bronze is not the only medium for expressing elite status. Jade, fine ceramics, fabrics and clothing, exotic carnelian and agate, or the accumulation of symbols of wealth, such as cowrie shells, fulfil the same role.

This deployment of bronze and other valuables turns on control. But chiefdoms are historically unstable and order can evaporate. One critical area of control identified by Earle (1991) turns on legitimacy. Stability is encouraged if members of a polity recognise the legitimacy of hierarchical authority. Controlling force is less potent than controlling minds. Recognising the latter on the basis of prehistoric remains is less tangible than cataloguing weaponry, but the presence of ceremonial religious structures, or the representation of ritual directed by elites, are powerful expressions of this variable.

Leach (1954) has contrasted two forms of chiefdom which he encountered half a century ago in the Kachin Hills of Burma. The *gumsa* system operated among the lowland Shan, who occupied river flats and cultivated their rice in fixed fields. The *gumlao* system was found in the surrounding hills, and involved swidden rice. The former was durable, the latter unstable. A critical contributory factor was the permanence and predictability of rice cultivation in the valleys. Earle (1991:10) has stressed that the success or failure of hierarchical societies cannot be understood without reference to the environment within which they operated, and as in the Kachin Hills, it is necessary to appreciate the potential of a people's environment, in terms of soil quality, predictability of rainfall and capacity for intensified production. The location of critical resources, and degree of access to them, must be considered, while the control of natural exchange routes, which in Southeast Asia are usually riverine, is decidedly advantageous.

The social environment is no less important. Population growth within a physically circumscribed region and exposure through exchange or conflict to alien groups has a demonstrable impact on any society. But archaeology provides access to long-term change in prehistory, and one of the most significant issues we will meet is the social organisation of communities which preceded the first use of bronze, and indeed, of the bronze age villages within which social elites had their origins. What Earle calls the 'structural preconditions for hierarchy' will give impetus to the pace of change. We could, for example, reasonably expect hierarchies, and the use of bronze to indicate status, to develop more rapidly where people already acknowledge social inequality than in a conservative gerontocracy.

In following Hutterer's recommendation to set the prehistoric communities of Southeast Asia in a broad, comparative perspective, therefore, it is necessary to examine a number of basic variables. These must begin with chronology, the lens whereby the sequence is focused. But the early adoption of bronze casting must also be considered to a background of the nature of neolithic societies. Only then will we be able to weigh the actual social impact. It will equally be necessary to explore the range of artefacts which satisfied demands, whether social or technological. The means whereby copper and tin were mined, smelted and brought together are critical to an understanding of the bronze age as a whole. What was the scale of production? How was it organised, and how did it change? Indeed, this organisational aspect cannot be considered in isolation from the means of subsistence, the structure of exchange transactions, the development of expertise in working other metals, such as lead and iron, and the impact of the expansion of other cultures into the area.

There are at least five interrelated sources of information. In terms of archaeology, we have many sites, the most common being the inhumation cemetery. Only in a few cases, however, have they yielded all the information we would wish for. In Vietnam and the Yunnan Plateau, some have been extensively excavated but human bone survives rarely. The interpretation of cemetery plans without the gender or age structure of the population encounters limitations. In Thailand, where human remains often survive, excavations have not been as extensive and we lack the spatial variable. In all cases, however, artefacts, including bronzes, were placed with some of the dead, and this is indeed our basic source of information. I will adopt a conventional approach to the interpretation of such mortuary data, acknowledging that the energy expended, including the size of the grave, the nature of any receptacle for the dead and the range of grave goods provides us with a blurred image of an individual's place in the community. Such information has greater potential to provide social information with increasingly extensive exposure of the cemetery, so that spatial differences between groups within a community, or temporal change, can be considered. Where a sample is large enough, it is also possible to refine our appreciation of the variables and their relationships by the application of multivariate statistical manipulations, and these will be applied where appropriate.

Excavated prehistoric settlements in Southeast Asia are very rare, and we must do without any plans of living sites. This is a major lacuna only partially filled, late in the sequences of the Red River valley and Yunnan, by scenes and models which reveal detailed information on domestic buildings and communal activities in settlements, in war, ritual and agriculture. At best, we have some vague information on the size of some settlements, and the energy involved in the digging of moats, reservoirs and defensive walls. The archaeological examination of copper mines began only recently in Southeast Asia, but results have provided us with a wealth of new and vital information on the techniques and organisation of mining and processing.

We can also turn to the bronze, copper, tin and iron artefacts themselves. The choice of what to cast or fashion and the nature and development of the appropriate technology present the opportunity to evaluate the social and technical role of metal. We will find that the range of items was fairly limited during the first millennium of the bronze age, followed by a dramatic expansion which occurred within the context of political centralisation. This trend is further illuminated by a fifth source of information, the Chinese documentary record. This corpus contains a number of references to the southern barbarians, the principal actors in the chapters which follow.

CHAPTER 2

THE DISCOVERY OF THE BRONZE AGE

The existence of a bronze age in Southeast Asia first entered the historical record when the Han Chinese expanded to the south and encountered groups which they described as 'southern barbarians', masters in the casting of bronzes unknown to the Chinese. The *Sui Shu* (History of the Sui), which was compiled by Wei Zheng and covers the years AD 586–617 noted that:

the different Lao tribes make bronze drums, ... before going to war, the chief summons the warriors of the tribe by beating the drum.

The *Man Shu,* which dates to the Tang Dynasty (AD 618–906) described how the southern barbarians beat war drums when in mourning and during feasts (Pirazzoli-t'Serstevens 1979).

The first recorded western description of such drums came in the wake of the establishment of the Dutch East India Company. One of its employees, Georg Rumpf, who lived at Ambon in the Moluccas during the second half of the seventeenth century, heard of the discovery of a large piece of metal, reputed to have fallen from the sky. This was the Pejeng drum (Fig. 2.1). Although Rumpf never saw it, in 1687 he described a second specimen from Serua as an *'ingens et monstrosum vas aereum'* (huge and extraordinary bronze vessel). Some specimens were sent back to Europe, one to the Grand Duke of Tuscany (Bernet Kempers 1988).

Early work in French Indo-China

If the bronze age of island Southeast Asia was first recognised by the Dutch, that on the mainland, excepting the early Chinese reports, was initially encountered by the French, who colonised much of the region in the second half of the nineteenth century.

This process began in Vietnam, the first major military action being directed against Da Nang in 1858 under the command of Admiral Rigault de Genouilly (Fig. 2.2). The admiral subsequently took a bronze drum back to France where, in 1862, it was presented by Napoleon III to the Musée de la Marine in Paris. In 1863, a treaty of protection was signed between the French authorities in Saigon and King Norodom of Cambodia, which involved increasing colonial control. Numerous French settlers followed the colonial presence. In addition to the military, there was the civil administration and others concerned with commerce,

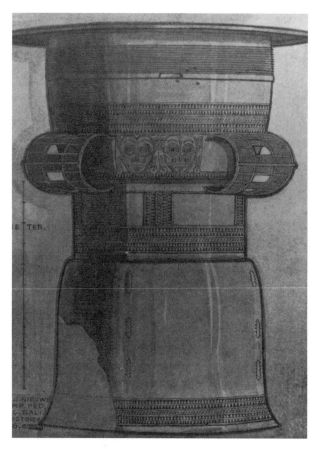

2.1 The Moon of Pejeng, a large bronze drum found in Bali.
It was first described in 1705 by the Dutchman Georg Rumpf, and represents
one of the earliest instances of the recognition of a distinctive Bronze Age
in Southeast Asia. Height: 186.5 cm.

education and health. Some were interested in antiquities, and their concern led
to the recognition of a bronze age in Southeast Asia.

Samrong Sen, the focus of much early attention, is a settlement mound located
in the valley of the Chinit, one of many rivers which flows into the lower Tonle
Sap, or great lake of central Cambodia. It was first examined by M. Roque, director
of the Company of River Transport of Cochin China, in 1876. He found that the
inhabitants would dig for shells to convert them to the lime used when chewing
betel. Their pits revealed a deep stratigraphy of shells interspersed with layers of
flood-deposited sand. The shells represent food refuse from prehistoric occupation, and ceramic, stone and shell artefacts were kept by the diggers as good luck
charms (Cartailhac 1890). Three years later, M. Moura, representative of the
French Protectorate, went to investigate. Floods prevented his excavating, but he
collected some artefacts, including bronzes, from villagers. He took these to the

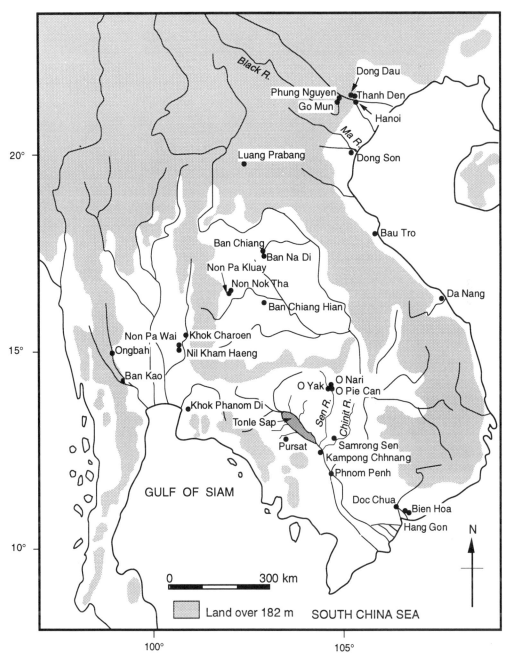

2.2 Map showing the sites mentioned in chapter 2.

Natural History Museum in Toulouse, where they were examined by the director, M. Noulet. Further items were also sent to France by E. Fuchs, a mining engineer and two naval doctors, Corre and Roux.

Noulet published this important new material in the first number of a new publication, the *Archives du Musée d'Histoire Naturelle de Toulouse* (Noulet 1879). He described the polished stone axes, chisels, adzes, bangles and rings, some of the stone originating in Pursat Province, some distance from the site. Other ornaments were fashioned from conus shell, of marine origin. Bronzes comprised three large bracelets, an axe, two arrowheads and a fishhook (Fig. 2.3). The arrowheads were found to have 4.8% tin, the fishhook 4% tin and a bracelet had a tin content of 12%. Noulet suggested that the bronzes and the stone artefacts were contemporary, but in reviewing this publication, Cartailhac (1879) queried the claim, noting that they could have come from different levels. Moura, however, was more forthcoming, suggesting not only that there was a bronze age, but a preceding period of copper as well (Moura 1883:147–8).

The next stage in the examination of Samrong Sen involved Ludovic Jammes, a teacher from Realmont (Tarn). He was employed as the director of the French School in Phnom Penh, just over 100 km to the south. In an article published in 1891, he claimed to have employed the first systematic approach to prehistory in Cambodia, both by seeking a range of sites, and excavating with due attention to stratigraphy (Jammes 1891). He described fifteen prehistoric sites and excavated four. Eight were located on the borders of the Tonle Sap. An-luon-padau is 40 km from Samrong Sen and provided a number of interesting artefacts. Bong-xa and Kop-che were not disturbed by shell diggers, and were described as particularly rich. Kamnianh revealed prehistoric material stratified below Khmer remains of the historic period, and Dat-ho was located on an arm of the lake above Kampong-Chhnang, and was described as being of considerable importance.

Jammes first turned his attention to Noulet's view that the shell layers might be natural flood deposits. He excavated at Samrong Sen to depths of 4–10 m. Here, and at the three other sites excavated, he reported three distinct layers. The lowest contained only stone implements and coarse pottery. The second included some bronze items with stone artefacts and a thinner variety of pottery, while the third he ascribed to a pure Bronze Age with some polished stone artefacts and pottery bearing rich ornamentation. Many of the artefacts were associated with human inhumation burials, the dead having been placed in the middens with no evidence of coffins or grave markers. Some interments had a pottery vessel placed over the face, and some of the pots contained food remains, mainly comprising shells and fish skeletons. There were burials with three or four stone adzes, others with bone or bronze fishhooks. Clay net weights were commonly encountered, one person being buried with about ten, suggesting to Jammes that a net had been placed as a grave offering. He recovered over a thousand shouldered stone adzes in his excavations, and a great variety of stone bracelets and pendants. About eight hundred stone beads were found with one individual. Jammes was also the first

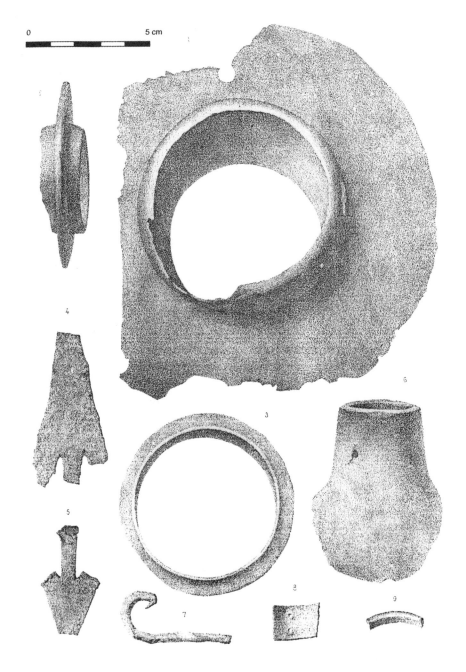

2.3 The illustration of bronze bracelets, arrowheads, a fishhook and a socketed axe taken from Noulet's 1879 publication of artefacts from Samrong Sen, Cambodia.

to note that the stone bracelets were too small to allow removal from the wrist, and he suggested that they had been worn since childhood.

He recovered 40 complete pottery vessels, some of which he illustrated in his report, and noted that all 35 items of bronze were found in the upper layers. Turning to the people and their way of life he speculated on how a community lived at Samrong Sen over so many generations. Clearly, he felt, a location in the vicinity of the Great Lake, with its abundant resources of fish, was significant. Other bones came from deer, cats, cattle, elephant and rhinoceros. The last was the most common, reflecting no doubt the ideal habitat for large herbivores on lake margins. Some rhinoceros skeletons, he noted, were almost complete. The people were tall, and his examination of the long bones revealed evidence for a robust musculature. Some skulls were 11–12 mm thick. In a final and most significant conclusion to his report, he noted: 'Prehistoric Archaeology in Indo-China will provide many surprises'. (Jammes 1891:50)

This report has posed serious problems of veracity and ethics. Several accepted his findings without question. That Jammes had obtained some artefacts from Samrong Sen is not disputed. The Smithsonian Institution in Washington, susceptible to hyperbole, it seems, in the nineteenth as well as in the present century, purchased his collections in two lots in 1890 and 1898. Commenting on these in 1922, the curator of Old World archaeology repeated Jammes's claims unquestioningly, although he was described as Professor L.H. James (Casanowicz 1922). Two years later, we find this same Professor, through Cazanowicz's publication, being cited by Étienne Patte when assessing his own excavations at the coastal midden site of Bau Tro (Patte 1924). It was Louis Finot, distinguished director of the French School in Hanoi, who unmasked Jammes (Finot 1928). Quite apart from his exaggerating the depth and extent of Samrong Sen, Finot naturally questioned the location and indeed existence of the innumerable burials and clear stratigraphy which was now being repeated in the professional literature.

He also followed the path of Jammes's subsequent career. In 1896, we find him editing the *Courrier du Saigon,* and attending meetings of the Société des Études Indochinoises. On 12 February 1897, he communicated to this learned body the recovery of prehistoric skeletons over 2 m long. He subsequently set off on an expedition to resolve a long list of archaeological issues, which lasted all of 20 days before he returned to Saigon on health grounds. There he died in August 1899, leaving the balance of his collections, without any bronzes or human remains, to the Society of which he was a member.

Worman (1949) has described Jammes as 'one of the most shameless prevaricators ever to indulge in archaeology'. He noted that only two of the sites which Jammes claimed to have identified have been relocated, and there are no known plans of any of the burials. Nor is the location of the human remains known. No one else has ever seen them. Yet Jammes must have undertaken some recovery of information at Samrong Sen, and perhaps at other sites. Some artefacts in his collection have been published. Jammes described them at a congress held in Paris in 1891, and several bronzes were analysed and published by Emile Cartailhac, one of the leading prehistorians of the day (Cartailhac 1890). While Jammes's finds might have appeared outlandish to Worman writing in the 1940s, some recent excavations have produced material which is uncannily similar to more than one of Jammes's claims. Thus at Khok Phanom Di, a coastal site in Central Thailand, skeletons were found lying on the back and side by side, associated with pottery vessels, fish bones, shellfish remains and bracelets which would have been too small in diameter for removal. Net weights were found at this site too, though none with burials (Higham and Thosarat 1994). Tayles (1992) has found that some of the males at Khok Phanom Di were well muscled, while a thickened cranial wall is associated with haemoglobin problems and was found in many of the skulls from this site. There are also some very close similarities between the material culture of Samrong Sen and Khok Phanom Di, which was located on the coast of the Gulf of Siam, about 400 km to the west. It is possible that Jammes was economical with the truth, presenting a garbled account of what the shell diggers at Samrong Sen had found, and left the site with another collection of artefacts.

One of the major issues confronting these early investigators concerned chronology, an issue still very much alive. The first contribution was made by E. Fuchs (1883). He noted that Samrong Sen, which covered 300 by 150 m, and rose 5–6 m above the Chinit River at low water, had a clear stratigraphy. The uppermost layer was 80 cm thick, and he interpreted it as a flood deposit of recent date, because it contained modern pottery. These lay over a series of shell lenses from which the material items were recovered. He described these as including adzes of black phthanite, gouges, chisels, pottery vessels bearing hatched and meander incisions, and bracelets of marine shell. On the basis of the rate of sediment deposition at the mouth of the Mekong, Fuchs (1883) concluded that Samrong Sen was probably occupied a few centuries before the Christian era. Apart from rare cases where late prehistoric sites included Chinese imports of known age, dating was largely a question of reasoned guesswork.

These early finds from the sites round Tonle Sap in Cambodia were followed by many others as the French administration became established over a wider area, and specific expeditions sought information on the natural history of the region. One of the most intensive and best-reported of these was undertaken by Auguste Pavie, under the auspices of the Musée d'Histoire Naturelle de Paris. In the introduction to his three-volume report, Pavie noted how the natural sciences in Indo-China were virtually unknown until the early exploratory travels of Henri Mouhot (Mouhot 1864, Pavie 1904). Two members of the expedition directed by Doudart de Lagrée in 1867–8, Joubert and Thorel, studied the natural history of the region they covered when travelling from Saigon into Yunnan (Osborne 1975), while M. Harmand, a naval doctor, initiated the study of entomology in the new colonies. Between 1876 and 1895, however, Pavie and his colleagues undertook a systematic survey of the insects, fish, shellfish and prehistoric remains of Vietnam, Laos and Cambodia.

Massie (1904) was an army pharmacist who assisted the mission from 1888–1892. He was particularly active in the region of Luang Prabang and the upper Black River in Laos and obtained, mainly from local villagers, a collection of bronzes which included 11 socketed axes, a needle and four chisels. He described how a Siamese had found a socketed spearhead at a depth of 4 m, and leaves the reader in little doubt that he recognised the existence of a bronze age in Southeast Asia. Laune (1904) reported finding eight arrowheads and two socketed axes in Laos, and in 1891, Lefèvre-Pontalis (1894) also collected a number of socketed axes, a chisel and a spear in the area of the upper Black River, similar artefacts to those assembled by Prince Henri of Orleans in the same area. At about the same time, M. Verneau described finding two bronze items near the mouth of the Mekong River at Bien Hoa, a socketed axe and a bracelet (Verneau 1904). Most noted that there appeared to be more bronze finds in Laos than in Cambodia and southern Vietnam. In the area of Luang Prabang, Massie (1894) proposed that there were three periods in prehistory, from one characterised by chipped stone to polished stone and finally a bronze age. Pavie (1894) himself summarised the chronological issue with the prescient words: 'Certes, le dernier mot de cette question interessante n'est pas encore dit'.

Lefèvre-Pontalis (1894), when surveying the situation near the turn of century, observed a range of similarities between the bronze artefacts found in the south, mainly in Cambodia, and the Luang Prabang area in Laos. This suggested that there was a common group of people, and that the prehistoric sequence involved a stone and a bronze age. In another area of imperial expansion, Balfour (1901) reported finding a bronze spearhead and a socketed axe in the Shan states of Burma.

The new century was ushered in, at least in terms of archaeology, by expanded research under the auspices of the recently-founded French Institute in Hanoi, the École Française d'Extrême Orient. In 1901 and again twenty years later, Henry Mansuy excavated at Samrong Sen (Mansuy 1902, 1923). His first season added little to what was already known. He purchased a further four bronze items from the local villagers: two bells, a tanged arrowhead and an unidentified piece. He also recovered much pottery, animal and human bone but nothing remotely comparable with the claims of Jammes a generation earlier, even though he removed 400 m^3 of material. The second season, twenty years later, was reported in a handsome publication of the Geological Service of Indo-China. No mention was made of the area excavated, nor are there any plans or sections. Again, he purchased a small number of bronzes, and also reported on a sandstone mould for casting a socketed axe-like implement (Fig. 2.4). There is no report on whether this mould was purchased or found in the prehistoric deposits, but it was, according to Mansuy, the first time such a mould had been found in Southeast Asia, although many similar ones were known to him from European sites.

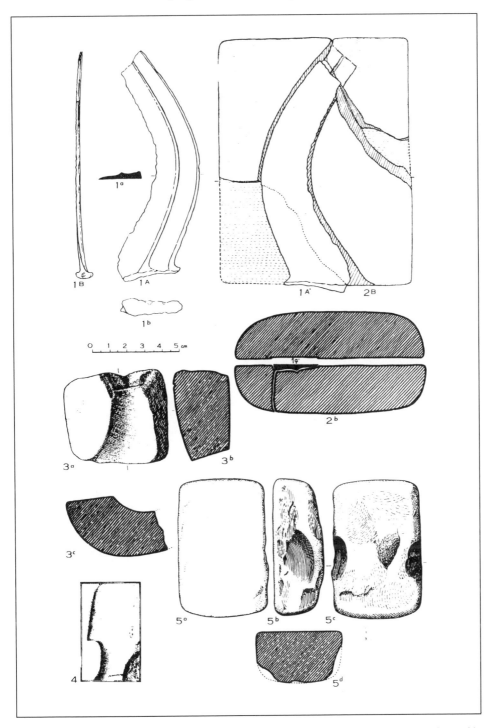

2.4 Sandstone moulds discovered near Mlu Prei (O Pie Can, O Nari and O Yak), Cambodia, by Lévy (1943), and by Mansuy at Samrong Sen (no. 4).

In 1902, an assemblage of 165 large bronze drums was published by Heger, who subdivided them, on the basis of their form, into four types (Heger 1902). The majority came from southern China and the valley of the Red River, but others were from further afield in Southeast Asia. By 1918, the corpus of drums had grown in number to 188, and Henri Parmentier, then working with the École Française in Hanoi, undertook a survey of them, paying particular attention to their form and decoration (Parmentier 1918a). These drums bear decoration which includes geometric designs and scenes depicting a range of activities. They represent one of the finest sources of information on a prehistoric society one could hope to encounter, for not only are the drums the product of masterly bronze casters, but the scenes tell us much of the activities of the people themselves (Fig. 2.5). We see warriors, dressed in combat gear, and engaged in war. This was undertaken from impressive boats, equipped with cabins, fighting platforms and even a drummer to beat a rhythm for the paddlers. He noted the attention paid to birds: we find them represented on the prows, and the warriors wear large plumed headdresses. There are also birds on top of the houses, which were themselves raised on stilts. Another scene shows four musicians playing the drums. They sit on a raised platform, beating drums located below them, although

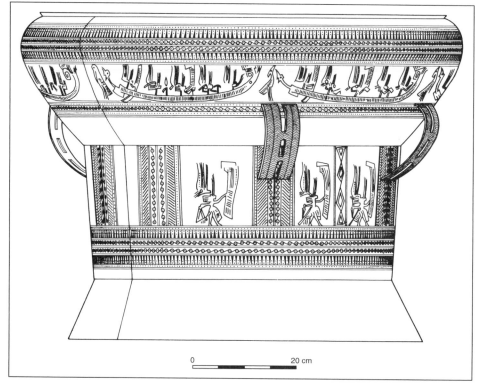

0   20 cm

2.5   The Song Da drum, cast about two thousand years ago, shows feathered warriors on land and water.

on this occasion Parmentier appears in error, for he argued that this scene depicts rice threshing, the rice being stored below in hide containers. Of one issue there was no doubt. The area sustained complex communities by AD 30, the date given on one of these drums commemorating the sixth year of the reign of the Han emperor Wudi.

By the time that Victor Goloubew addressed the issue of the Bronze Age in 1929, he had available not only the growing corpus of drums and associated finds, but also the first results of excavations at the settlement and cemetery of Dong Son. Parmentier had already noted that the decoration on the drums was matched on some of the axes and spearheads which were known as stray finds in the Red River delta area, although none had been provenanced to a particular site. In 1924, following the realisation that many such implements originated in the lower valley of the Ma River to the south, the École Française sponsored excavations at a site on the southern bank of the river near the village of Dong Son. These they placed in the hands of Louis Pajot, a person with no training in excavation, but who nevertheless encountered a number of graves containing bronze artefacts, and a few of iron as well. Some of the bronzes still had fragments of cloth, preserved through impregnation with corroding metal, adhering to them.

Goloubew (1929) catalogued a most impressive series of bronzes. In addition to drums, there were weapons, such as spearheads, axes and daggers, vessels in the form of situlae and bowls and agricultural implements, although whether hoes or ploughshares has not been fully settled. These graves also contained a small proportion of metal artefacts of Chinese, Han Dynasty, origin. These included a mirror and a sword, as well as coins which dated the imports to the early first century AD. He was also able to match some of the weapons, such as the 'pediform' (foot-shaped) axes with implements being wielded on the drum scenes, and on the impressive decorated plaques found in some of the graves. These last items have been interpreted as armour, or more simply, as ornaments worn by warriors of particularly high status. The arrowheads and socketed axes had been cast in a double mould, of a type similar to those found at Samrong Sen. The people in question relished fine ornaments, for apart from bracelets of jade, shell and bronze, there are also bronze belt buckles ornamented with little bells.

The Dong Son bronze workers were also skilled in the difficult technique of lost wax casting, where the figure to be cast was first rendered in wax and surrounded by clay. Wax was then removed and replaced by molten bronze. One product of this technique was a superb figure of a *khen* player, riding piggy-back on another man. A *khen* is a bamboo pipe instrument still widely played in Southeast Asia. People are also portrayed playing on the *khen* on some drums, as members of a musical quartet.

The association of Chinese imports with the Dong Son bronzes may have led Goloubew to stress the importance of northern influence on the bronze industry of the Red River Valley, for he concluded his review by noting that the Bronze Age did not start there until the mid first century AD, and then it was inspired by China.

A more extreme view on the origin of the Dong Son bronzes was propounded in 1931 by the Swede, Olov Janse, on the basis of his analysis of a group of bronze implements held in the Swedish National Museum in Stockholm. He identified what he saw as a number of stylistic similarities with items of European origin, and concluded that the Dong Son culture resulted from waves of influence from the Hallstatt culture of Europe, in conjunction with other sources of influence from the Caucasian region (Janse 1931). This thesis was minutely examined a decade later by Karlgren (1942), who convincingly rejected such extreme diffusionist views and substituted for them a proposed inspiration in pre-Han China. While thus bringing the origins of the Southeast Asian Bronze Age closer to home, Karlgren's claimed parallels in terms of style and motifs are unconvincing at best. Indeed, the answer to this issue lies in seeking local origins through archaeological research.

Steps in this direction began in 1935, when Janse began the first of three excavation seasons at Dong Son. These were reported in 1958, in one of the first publications in Southeast Asia which laid out the excavation area, produced section drawings and presented a full coverage of the finds. The range of artefacts was considerably augmented, and plans of each burial help us to appreciate the wealth of some grave assemblages. Tomb no. 1, for example, was orientated on a north-south axis, and although the bones have not survived because of soil conditions, we know that the body was accompanied by a bronze drum, vase and plate, a few bronze spearheads and arrowheads, three miniature drums, a situla and slit stone rings and nine pottery vessels. Janse concluded that this was probably the burial of a chief. Throughout his consideration of the material culture, we find that Janse was at pains to emphasise the Chinese inspiration he felt lay behind the bronze industry. The bronze spearheads were described as a local development of a Chinese prototype but the arrowheads and axes were 'no doubt of Chinese origin'. Even where bronzes had no possible Chinese prototypes, we still find that the Chinese artisans were at work, satisfying the needs of the local inhabitants. Documentary evidence for Chinese expansion into this area was then supplemented by Janse's recovery of brick tombs of undoubted Han inspiration, but no serious modification was made in Janse's views on the origins of the bronze-working tradition.

Early work in southern China

If the beginning of archaeology in Vietnam owes much to French colonial influence, that in southern China originated in the colonial presence in Hong Kong and the influence of Jesuit missions. The recognition of prehistoric sites began with the fieldwork of Joseph Shellshear, who taught anatomy at Hong Kong University. Together with Charles Heanley, a doctor and geologist, he spent much of his time exploring Hong Kong for prehistoric material between 1925 and his return to Australia a decade later (Bard 1995). Father Daniel Finn (1886–1936) was an Irish Jesuit with a flair for history and languages. After spending some time in Australia after the First World War, he was posted to Hong Kong where he joined the university as a lecturer in geography. He initiated much fieldwork, identifying sites, collecting artefacts and ordering them relative to the finds then being made in northern China and in Indo-China to the southwest. He recovered a large assemblage of bronzes and published them in a series of articles in the *Hong Kong Naturalist* (Ryan 1958). He emphasised the ease of communication, both riverine and coastal, between Hong Kong and the Red River delta and the parallels between bronzes from both areas. At the same time, however, he showed that other bronze artefacts were of Chinese origin or inspiration.

In 1934, Finn met Father Rafael Maglioni, an Italian Jesuit missionary stationed at Swabue, in the Haifeng district about 110 km east of Hong Kong along the coast

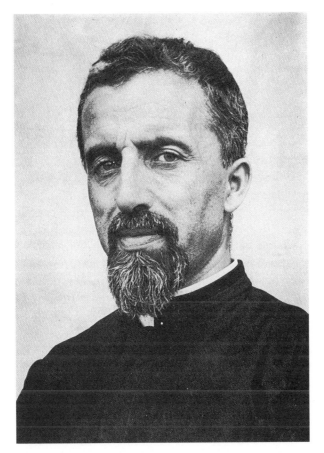

2.6 Rafael Maglioni (1881–1953).
Maglioni was one of the pioneers in recognising the Bronze Age in Southeast Asia. He identified numerous prehistoric sites on the coast of Guangdong Province between 1936 and 1946.
Permission: The Hong Kong Archaeological Society.

of Guangdong (Fig. 2.6). The meeting sparked the latter's interest in antiquities of this region, and forty years later, Meacham (1975a) could write that between 1936 and 1946, Maglioni examined, collected and studied more prehistoric material than any other archaeologist in South China before or since. The area in which he undertook his mission is rich in archaeological sites, and the priest would proceed on his bicycle, equipped with a basket to carry his trowel and screwdriver, in search of new material (Walden 1975). The area had been subjected to deforestation and deflation of the sand dunes, allied with inland soil erosion, exposing many prehistoric sites. He didn't excavate, but collected surface material. Since many sites appeared to have only a shallow stratigraphy, he was then able to consider the associations of finds which formed the basis of his cultural subdivision (Maglioni 1975). He proposed five successive phases, each named after one of the sites he identified. There was a first neolithic, which he dated to 4000–3000 BC, followed by a second (3000–1500 BC) and a final neolithic. These were followed by a chalcolithic and then the Bronze Age. The last phase, best represented at the site of Po-lau, was characterised by a wide range of weapons and tools, some paralleled in the Dong Son sites to the west. While his later periods were dated because they contained classical Chinese imports, earlier dates were more arbitrary, being based on reasoned guesswork.

The early development of archaeology in this area was also stimulated by the interest shown by Walter Schofield, a member of the civilian administration who worked in Hong Kong from 1911 to 1938 (Fig. 2.7, Hayes 1975). He was active in identifying and mapping prehistoric sites, and with his expertise in geology, he suggested that the change in the distribution of bronze age against earlier sites reflected an increase in population and adoption of rice agriculture. He was particularly interested in the sequence of sites in raised beaches, noting the stratigraphical distinction between so-called soft geometric pottery with stone artefacts and the later hard-fired pottery with bronze remains. In 1937, he excavated the site of Shek Pik on Lantao Island, where he found six burials under a cultural layer which yielded bronze artefacts (Meacham 1975b). A gully adjacent to the site contained the remains of six sandstone moulds for casting socketed axes. Three of these are very similar to the specimens found in Cambodia and Vietnam (Schofield 1975).

At the same time that archaeology was beginning in Guangdong and Hong Kong, Madeleine Colani was excavating in the uplands of Laos. She had previously concentrated her research on the rock shelters in the karst hills south of the Red River, but was attracted to Laos by the huge and enigmatic stone jars which are such a prominent feature of this area that it is known as the Plain of Jars. Her excavations revealed prehistoric crematoria in association with a number of cemeteries. The stone jars contained cremated human remains associated with bronze and iron grave goods. The presence of moulds for casting bronzes added to the growing body of evidence for widespread metal working, while the date of the objects in question, although largely unknown to Colani, corresponds with the Dong Son material. Colani (1935) found the closest parallels, at least in terms of cremation, with the many urnfields which had been encountered since 1909 on the coastal tract of central Vietnam. These were first described in detail by Parmentier (1918b). Again, we encounter cremations, this time placed in large ceramic urns, with a range of grave goods displaying contemporaneity with the Dong Son material. In addition to iron, there were also a number of bronzes, including bells and spearheads.

During this same period, Lévy (1943) investigated three sites in the headwaters of the Sen and Chinit rivers, about 150 km upstream from Samrong Sen. He found further evidence for bronze working, in the form of sandstone moulds for casting a sickle and an axe at O Pie Can, in addition to crucible fragments (Fig. 2.4). At O Yak, he reported burials with bronze bracelets, and at the third site, O Nari, he

2.7 Walter Schofield (1888–1968).
Schofield was a pioneer in identifying the Bronze Age in Hong Kong. He is seen here in December 1931 at a site on Tung Kwu Island.
Permission: Hong Kong Archaeological Society.

found evidence for bronze working. By the time that the Second World War slowed archaeological inquiries, therefore, evidence for bronze working in Southeast Asia had been found in the valley of the Red River, along the coast of Vietnam, in the Mekong River valley from its mouth to Luang Prabang in Laos, in the lowlands surrounding the Tonle Sap in Central Cambodia and even at an altitude of a thousand metres in the Laotian uplands. Indeed, prehistoric bronzes had been found in virtually all the areas explored by the French. Only Thailand, never colonised, remained little known, at least in terms of prehistoric bronze working.

The post-war period

One positive aspect of the Second World War in Southeast Asia was the impetus given to air photography. Williams-Hunt (1950) flew missions over Northeast Thailand, and identified many large, moated prehistoric settlements now known to incorporate bronze age layers (Figs. 2.8 and 6.17a). When Worman (1949), writing at the same time, summarised what was known of prehistoric Southeast Asia, however, he was sceptical about the presence of a bronze age there. This view echoed that of Janse (1958), and was again stressed in the influential writings of Coedès (1968).

Post-war research in Southeast Asia, however, has increased our information beyond recognition through more intensive fieldwork. This new wave of activity can be divided geographically into four major areas. Cambodia, for long in the vanguard of research, has been virtually silent. Thailand, however, a late starter, is now the best documented, due to the absence of warfare, training programmes for Thai archaeologists in America, Europe and Australasia, the vigour of the Thai Fine Arts Department and the permission given to foreign archaeologists to excavate. Two regions of Thailand have received particularly close attention: the northeast, or Khorat Plateau, and the Chao Phraya Valley.

In Vietnam, despite the ravages of war, archaeologists remained remarkably active, with important new cultural sequences being recognised in the Red River valley, the lower Mekong area and the coastal plains. Finally, a quickening of research in southern China, particularly in Yunnan Province, provided much new and significant material.

One of the major achievements of the Vietnamese archaeologists after the end of the war against the French was the research they undertook in the so-called Middle Country, the rolling lowlands above the confluence of the Red and Black rivers in the vicinity of Viet Tri. There are numerous low mounds in this area, and in 1959, they commenced a series of excavations at the site of Phung Nguyen, which ultimately uncovered an area of about 4000 m^2 (Hoang Xuan Chinh and Nguyen Ngoc Bich 1978). They encountered a rich material culture in stone, but no bronze. There were, however, numerous other sites belonging to what they have called the Phung Nguyen culture, and eleven of these have yielded small

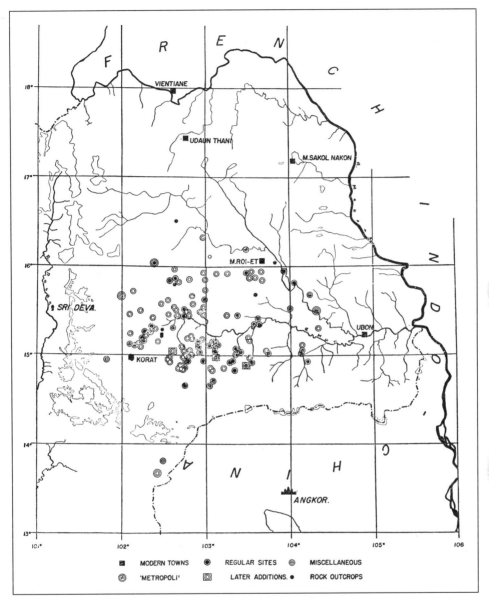

2.8 Map showing the distribution of moated sites in Northeast Thailand, published by Williams-Hunt in 1950. Compare this distribution with that based on more recent surveys (Fig. 6.14).
Permission: Antiquity Publications.

pieces of bronze. Phung Nguyen style ceramics were found in the basal layers of a second important site, Dong Dau. This mound, located about a kilometre north of the Red River, has a cultural stratigraphy up to 6 m deep. It was first excavated in 1965, and again two years later, 550 m² being uncovered. The cultural sequence saw the Phung Nguyen material succeeded by layers in which stone artefacts were copied in bronze (Trinh Sinh 1977). Stone moulds for bronze casting were also found there, together with a radiocarbon date in the middle of the second millennium BC. Excavations at a third site, Go Mun, began in 1961 and furnished a still larger assemblage of bronzes which linked the Dong Dau culture with that of Dong Son. Fishhooks were the commonest bronze item, but there were also numerous socketed axes as well as chisels, spearheads, bracelets and a sickle (Ha Van Phung and Nguyen Duy Ti 1982). The documentation of this cultural sequence established not only a chronological framework far earlier than had been considered possible, but laid the foundations for an appreciation that bronze working might have had both early and indigenous origins in Southeast Asia.

The decade of the sixties saw a blossoming of research in Southeast Asia. In southern Vietnam, Saurin (1963) reported on the site of Hang Gon, where land development three years previously had revealed a prehistoric site covering an area of 350 × 150 m. Four sandstone moulds were found, two for casting the socketed axeheads which had been so well known since the 1870s, and two for casting round-headed pins. At that juncture, Saurin could refer to only five other examples of such moulds in Southeast Asia. A radiocarbon date on the basis of organic material from a pottery vessel at this same site, but in no known stratigraphical relationship to the moulds, was 3044–1745 BC. 1960 also saw the first reports of a remarkable site in northeast Thailand, the village of Ban Chiang (Suthiragsa 1979). The villagers and indeed an official from the Thai Fine Arts Department noted that, particularly after heavy rains, pieces of red-painted pottery would be found on the surface of the mound. In 1967, the Thai archaeologist Vithya Intakosai excavated there, and encountered human burials associated with bronze and iron bracelets, as well as some of the very attractive red-on-buff painted pottery. Further excavations were undertaken in the early 1970s, and in one area 8 × 3 m, Nikom Suthiragsa found deposits about 4 m deep, and reported a skeleton at the very base wearing eight bronze bracelets. At the same time, thermoluminescence (TL) dates on the prehistoric pottery found there suggested extraordinarily early contexts, even back to the fifth millennium BC. In 1974–5, the Fine Arts Department combined with the Museum of the University of Pennsylvania to open two further areas of this site, and in a preliminary publication of initial impressions, Gorman and Charoenwongsa (1976) suggested that the bronzes they had uncovered might, on the basis of radiocarbon dates, have been as early as about 3600 BC. These would have placed them among the earliest in the world and certainly considerably earlier than any bronze items found in the Huanghe Valley, home of the Chinese bronze tradition.

The same part of Northeast Thailand was the focus of a major programme of fieldwork under the direction of W.G. Solheim II, of the University of Hawaii. Following proposals to construct a series of dams on the tributaries of the Mekong, he arranged for surveys to be undertaken in areas threatened by flooding. Test excavations at one of the mounds identified, Non Nok Tha, resulted in the discovery of skeletons with bronzes. Two excavation seasons followed in 1966 and 1968, and a large number of burials were uncovered, about one in twenty being associated with bronze artefacts, in the main socketed axes and bracelets. There were also bronze moulds made of sandstone, of virtually identical form to those recovered from Hang Gon. As the radiocarbon determinations from Non Nok Tha became available, it was evident that the bronze tradition at this site was far earlier, and less complex, than that identified at Dong Son and related sites in Vietnam. There was, however, no clear pattern between the dates and the site's stratigraphy, and clarification of the dating of this and related sites has only recently been settled.

1960 also saw the final season in a five-year excavation programme at one of Southeast Asia's most remarkable sites, Shizhaishan (Fig. 2.9). This is an isolated hill located on the broad lacustrine plain surrounding Lake Dian, in Yunnan Province of southern China. It is linked to the Dong Son area by the Red River. Until excavations commenced there, the region was known to have been occupied during the first millennium BC, because of allusions to the people in official Chinese histories. Some stray bronzes had also been found, linking the area with the Dong Son tradition. All this changed, however, when a royal burial ground comprising at least fifty graves was found on the hill of Shizhaishan.

2.9 Shizhaishan (Stone Fortress Hill), on the eastern shore of Lake Dian, Yunnan.
It was the cemetery for a ruling elite group towards the end of the first millennium BC, and has furnished some of the richest prehistoric graves in Southeast Asia.

Members of what some have seen as the royal clan were buried with an astonishing range of grave offerings. There were drums filled with cowrie shells, models in bronze of battle scenes, the torturing of prisoners and trials, as well as small models of houses recording in unparalleled detail the way of life of people who belonged to this complex chiefdom during the last few centuries BC (Huang Ti and Wang Dadao 1983).

The Chao Phraya Valley has also been a focus for fieldwork from the early sixties. In 1961, a Thai–Danish expedition under the direction of Per Sørensen undertook a series of excavations in Kanchanaburi Province on the western margins of the alluvial lowlands (Sørensen and Hatting 1967). Most attention was given to the Bang mound, near the village of Ban Kao, where a cemetery was encountered. In 1961 and the following year, 44 burials were found. Again, they were associated with grave goods. There were complete pottery vessels, shell jewellery, stone adzes but nothing made of bronze. However, a few fragments of bronze bracelet were found in non-mortuary contexts. The radiocarbon dates from this site suggest that the cemetery was in use by about 2000 BC, while the latest graves date to the period when iron was current in the later first millennium BC. In 1965–6, Sørensen investigated the cave of Ongbah, located upstream of the Bang site. Sadly it had already been ransacked by looters, but it had been a burial site in which wooden coffins had contained a rich array of grave goods, including six bronze drums of Dong Son affinities (Sørensen 1988).

At the same juncture, excavations took place on the eastern margins of the Bangkok plain, in the valley of the Pasak River. Here, at Khok Charoen (prosperity mound), a cemetery was found, and 44 graves excavated. As at the Bang site, no graves contained bronze, though there were many offerings of pottery vessels, stone adzes and shell jewellery. Two TL dates suggest that the site belongs to the late second millennium BC (Watson 1979).

This early period of what might be called the modern era of research into Southeast Asia provided evidence for the widespread presence of bronze casting. There was an early phase when few bronzes of limited forms were found in some of the graves, and a later one when bronzes became very much more elaborate and varied. But several issues were also raised, and these have attracted more recent attention. The first concerned chronology. If the very early dates proposed by Gorman and Solheim were correct, then Southeast Asia would have to be included as one of the very few centres of metal-working origins. Indeed, it would rank with the world's earliest. On the other hand, an initial date for bronze casting in this area in the second millennium BC would place the earliest bronzes comfortably later than those in the Huanghe Valley in China, and a derivation from the north would be possible, at least on chronological grounds. A second and fundamental issue, for those concerned with origins, lay in the finding that all the early phase artefacts comprised an alloy including copper and tin. Local origins would necessarily entail a period when implements were cast from copper alone, with alloys following at a later date. It therefore became clear that the search for such elusive objects of copper was necessary. This issue would be most profitably considered in the same context as tracking down the sources of copper ore, and seeking the early evidence for mining and smelting. Finally, it was important to find more cemeteries away from the mining sites in order to date the inception of exchange in metals and the local casting activity.

The impetus created by the research at Ban Chiang encouraged Higham and Kijngam (1984) to undertake a site survey in the area from Ban Chiang down to the margins of Lake Kumphawapi, one of the bigger lakes on the Khorat Plateau and one which is surrounded by most of the environments one is likely to meet in this region, from the flood-prone clayey soils which ring the lake to the drier middle and upper river terrace soils on slightly higher elevations. Many prehistoric sites were found, three subjected to trial excavations and one, Ban Na Di, excavated extensively in 1980–1. As might be expected in a site located in such a low-lying environment, the stratigraphic sequence, which extended to a depth of 4 m, included a series of lenses laid down by floodwater. These helped in interpreting the site's stratigraphical sequence, while dating was facilitated by the presence of charcoal in hearths, furnaces and as sealing layers in the neck of pits. The two areas excavated had been used as a cemetery, burials being found with a range of bronze artefacts. There were also stone mould fragments and a furnace which was ringed by the remains of crucibles and bronze stains. It had been used to bring metal to melting point before casting commenced. In one area, this cemetery was overlain by a series of furnaces, indicating that this part of the site had been a focus for bronze casting. At a later stage of the sequence, there was a group of lidded urns containing the remains of infants.

Further work on such relatively early sites has been undertaken by Wilen (1989), who has undertaken a site survey and excavations in the Huai Sai Khao Valley. This is located to the west of the sandstone upland known as Phu Wiang, and his work at Non Pa Kluay has added to our understanding of communities familiar with bronze in this area.

When the Khorat Plateau was first evaluated on the basis of air photographs, Williams-Hunt (1950) noted a series of roughly circular, moated sites which were particularly densely distributed in the valleys of the Mun and Chi rivers and their tributaries. These have not received as much attention as they deserve through excavation, but the same team which excavated Ban Na Di also examined the settlement pattern in the region of the middle Chi Valley, and excavated, in a limited way, three sites. The largest of these was one of these moated sites, Ban Chiang Hian. They found a stratigraphic sequence over 5 m deep, with initial settlement probably taking place in the early first millennium BC. A fragment of a pottery crucible with metal staining was found in the lowest level (Chantaratiyakarn 1984).

Evidence for a well-established and widely-distributed bronze tradition during the late second millennium BC has been found in the Red River delta area and near the eastern mouth of the Mekong. In the former area, Ha Van Tan (1991) recovered about thirty pieces of stone and clay moulds for casting bronze axes and fishhooks at Thanh Den. The radiocarbon dates suggest occupation within the period 1500 to 700 BC. The same span has been obtained for Doc Chua to the south, where about fifty clay or stone moulds were recovered. These were involved in the casting of axes, bells, spearheads, harpoons and chisels. It is stressed that these sites lie at some distance from ore sources, and the metal used, it is presumed, must have arrived in the form of ingots from smelting sites.

This brings us to one of the most important developments in the last few years: the discovery of copper mines and smelting sites. As the directors of the Thailand Archaeometallurgy Project, Pigott and Natapintu began excavations at Phu Lon, in Loei Province of Thailand, on the southern bank of the Mekong River (Pigott and Natapintu 1988, Natapintu 1988a). A brief excavation there in 1983 produced a radiocarbon date in the middle of the first millennium BC, encouraging further fieldwork in 1985. The site comprises a hill veined with malachite which has been riddled with galleries and mine shafts. Nearby, on an area known as the pottery flat, there are the remains of mining debris up to 50 cm thick. It contains a number of tools used in crushing and sorting the ore, as well as a scattering of potsherds. There were also ceramic crucible fragments and a piece of a sandstone mould. The distribution of ore-dressing stones in clusters also suggested that people worked their ore in groups. This ore-crushing activity has furnished three radiocarbon dates compatible with use during the first and second millennia BC. The nearby site of Ban Noi has also produced evidence for ore crushing activity, in order to facilitate later smelting, as well as a socketed bronze axe. Its radiocarbon date is in the early first millennium BC.

This evidence has been complemented and expanded upon by the excavations in the Khao Wong Prachan Valley of Central Thailand (Pigott and Natapintu 1988, Natapintu 1991, Bennett 1988). Nine sites within a small radius have been examined, and all reveal aspects of copper working. Khao Phu Kha is a hill containing a substantial copper mine. The ores are malachite and chrysocolla which include up to 10% of copper. Non Pa Wai, located on the flat nearby, is a 5 ha mound most of which comprises the remains of copper smelting and casting. This dense industrial layer overlies a neolithic cemetery dated between about 2300 and 1900 BC. The upper layers, dated to 1400–1000 BC, comprise an accumulation of ore crushing and copper casting debris, including numerous moulds and crucibles. Non Khok Wa is an ore-crushing site and Nil Kham Haeng has deposits of crushed ore and slag up to 5 m deep. The concentration of energy represented in these sites reflects long-term copper working which was under way, according to Natapintu, by 1500–1000 BC. All the stages in copper working from mining to crushing, sorting, the casting of ingots, arrowheads and axes are represented. When linked with sites like Ban Na Di and Doc Chua, it is also possible to follow how ingots were alloyed and cast in settlements far removed from the sources of copper and tin.

CHAPTER 3

THE CULTURAL SEQUENCE IN CHINA

It is a central theme of this book that the Bronze Age of Southeast Asia cannot be properly considered without reference to the technological and cultural innovation and change in the Huanghe and Yangzi valleys to the north. This relationship extends far beyond the simple practicalities of alloying and casting, involving as it does the origins of rice cultivation and the expansion of agricultural communities into Southeast Asia, the long-standing exchange of goods and ideas and the ultimate imperial Han expansion into Yunnan, Lingnan and Bac Bo.

The *zhongyuan* (central plains)

The nuclear area of Chinese civilisation, the *zhongyuan,* is found in the land flanking the central course of the Huanghe River (Fig. 3.1). Zhao Sonquiao (1986) has proposed seven natural divisions within modern China, further divisible into 33 regions. Of these, the North China Plain and the loess plateau represent the area within which early metallurgy originated. Winters in both are cold and dry, but during the summer months, it can be as hot as in southern China. Most rain falls during these warmer months, sustaining extensive agriculture. There are, however, also hazards. Temperatures can change very quickly, and rainfall, which averages 500–800 mm per annum, can be double the mean, or fall to less than 200 mm. The natural vegetation cover on the low, flat plain is a deciduous broad-leaved forest, but hardly any has survived eight millennia of agriculture.

West of the Lüliang Mountains, the loess plateau rises to 1200–1600 m above sea level. Rainfall lessens to 350–650 mm per annum and it becomes increasingly arid and continental as one proceeds westwards. While the vegetation cover on the eastern margins of the plateau remains a broad-leaved deciduous forest, it becomes increasingly steppic to the west.

The climate in this area fluctuated markedly during the Holocene period, a common factor which may well link the transitions to millet cultivation in the Huanghe and to rice in the Yangzi valley. Following the initial establishment of sedentary village communities, however, the economic base of millet cultivation proved sufficiently resilient for these groups to withstand further episodes of climatic change. The area has also undergone major modifications as the Huanghe River has deposited vast quantities of alluvium. When the earliest recorded agricultural communities were being founded, the coast was far to the

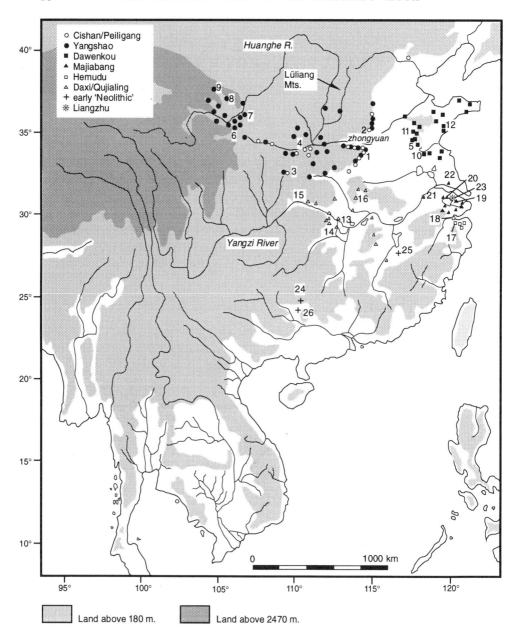

3.1   The distribution of the major Neolithic sites of Central and Northern China.
1. Peiligang. **2.** Cishan. **3.** Lijiacun. **4.** Baijia. **5.** Beixin. **6.** Dibaping.
7. Huazhaizi. **8.** Liuwan. **9.** Yuanyangchi. **10.** Liulin. **11.** Wangyin.
12. Chengzi. **13.** Guanmiaoshan. **14.** Pengtoushan; Huachenggang.
15. Daxi. **16.** Qujialing. **17.** Hemudu. **18.** Linjia. **19.** Songze. **20.** Yudun.
21. Beiyinyangying. **22.** Qingdun. **23.** Sidun. **24.** Zengpiyan. **25.** Xianrendong.
26. Liyuzui.

west of its present position. These sites have been ascribed to four cultures: the Peiligang, Cishan, Lijiacun and Baijia, dated to the period 6500–5000 BC (Fig. 3.1).

The Neolithic prelude

There is some controversy over the environment in which these agricultural communities developed. Ho Ping-ti (1984) has argued in favour of an open steppe with forests confined to favourable lower slopes and along rivers. This open landscape has been reconstructed on the basis of the preponderence of *Artemisia* in the pollen spectra. Pearson (1974), on the other hand, has argued that this plant is a vigorous producer of pollen, which leads to over-representation. Chang (1986), too, feels that the habitat would have been more forested than would seem apparent from the palynological evidence alone. It is, however, generally agreed that the loess soil which is so widespread in this region would have been easily worked, and its properties favoured the cultivation of millet. Hemmed within fairly narrow valley systems, early agricultural sites were occupied over a sufficiently long period for substantial cemeteries to be established.

Peiligang, one of the best known of these village sites, is located on a low hill on the northern bank of the Shuangji River. Excavations in 1979 covered 2175 m². The pottery was mainly plain, and in the rare cases where decoration was found, it involved comb patterns. Although the pottery easily disintegrated when excavated, the remains of a pottery kiln indicates controlled firing. Polished stone adzes were quite common, as were stone sickles with serrated edges. Stone querns were found, raised on four legs. The village cemetery was examined and 116 burials uncovered (Fig. 3.2). They were found in three groups, individuals

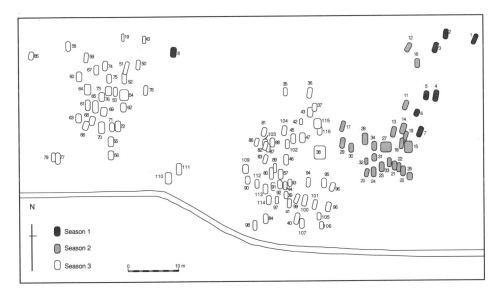

3.2 Plan of the Peiligang cemetery.

being placed on a north-south axis. The single interments were accompanied by grave goods which included pots, stone adzeheads and querns (HATIA 1984). An Zhimin (1980) has suggested that these represent clan cemeteries. This early village community with its cemetery established a form of settlement which was to be followed, with regional variations, down the length of the Huanghe Valley for millennia.

The Cishan site has a number of parallels with Peiligang. It is located on a terrace of the Nanming River. Flat-based pottery vessels, stone adzeheads and querns were found in the excavations of 1976 and 1978, and a considerable number of bone projectile points were recovered (CPAMHP 1981). Zhou Benxiong's (1981) examination of the biological remains has shown that 60% of the bones come from domestic pigs, dogs and possibly cattle, while fishing was an important activity. Walnuts and hackberry seeds were collected, but the mainstay of the subsistence was the cultivation of millet. Chang T.-T. (1983) has described how a wild millet, *Setaria viridis,* grows in northwestern provinces of China. The domestication of this species, and its conversion into *Setaria italica* would have involved increases in plant height, panicle length, a decrease in the tendency to shatter on ripening and increase in grain weight. A second genus, *Panicum miliaceum,* is also native to northern China and was brought into cultivation. The underground storage pits so characteristic of these early sites were probably designed to conserve millet for winter consumption. Some of these pits at Cishan were up to five metres deep.

The material culture from Cishan has a number of parallels with that from Beixin in Shandong (SATIA 1984). Again, we encounter stone sickles, adzeheads and querns along with small spades and shell sickles in a site dated to 5300–4300 BC. Millet husks were also found in a context which antedates the Dawenkou culture of this area.

Agriculture proved a stable resource base for a vigorous and expanding population. As the Huanghe River laid down its vast alluvial plain, so human societies expanded onto the new land created, linking neolithic communities in a network which was soon to extend from Gansu in the west to the Shandong coast in the east. These have been ascribed to two major cultural groupings, the Yangshao and the Dawenkou.

The Yangshao culture

The Yangshao culture was extensive in time and space, dating between about 5150 and 3000 BC. Sites are found in the loess uplands bisected by the Huanghe and its major tributaries, as well as out on the North China plain of river alluvium. There are numerous regional cultures which fall under the Yangshao umbrella, and a single name for all is a considerable simplification (Yun Kuen Lee, pers. comm.). The most interesting from the point of view of copper metallurgy, however, lies in Gansu. Here, there are three successive cultures: Majiayao, Banshan and Machang.

Radiocarbon dates for the Majiayao phase suggest occupation a century or so either side of 3000 BC. The settlements reveal all the basic elements of the Yangshao: houses sunk into the ground and equipped with hearths, a vigorous ceramic industry which saw vessels painted and fired in kilns, polished stone and bone tools, and substantial inhumation cemeteries. Linjia is one of the most significant of these sites (GPMNNC 1984). One storage pit there revealed the economic basis of the community, since it contained 1.8 m^3 of millet (*Panicum miliaceum*). It also yielded the earliest bronze artefact found in the Huanghe Valley, a knife containing 6–10% tin (Fig. 3.3). Copper ores are known in numerous locations from Gansu to Shandong, and while tin is more restricted in distribution, there are sufficient sources to support an indigenous development of metallurgy (Fig. 3.4).

This knife, however, remains an enigmatic object. According to Sun Shuyun and Han Rubin (1981), it was cast in a single mould, but Barnard (1991) has noted that it was cast in a bivalve mould. Some pits from this site also contained fragments of metallic residue. While the metallurgical study concluded that these indicate that local casting was under way, the uncertainty as to what these objects represent encourages caution. They incorporate copper and iron, and are neither slag nor casting spillage. Barnard (1991) prefers to place the knife and associated fragments into a suspense account, pending the recovery of more and better-documented material. The Linjia copper-based knife is, indeed, the only metal artefact found in a site extensively excavated and prolific in cutting implements made from stone or bone.

The three phases of the Gansu Yangshao culture, notwithstanding the metal from Linjia, do not reveal the widespread adoption of copper alloying. This becomes clear when we consider the sites of the Banshan phase, which dates between approximately 2700–2350 BC. At Dibaping, for example, excavations in 1973 uncovered 66 burials, distributed in what look like at least two distinct groups (GPM 1978a). A feature of Banshan graves is their nearly square shape, which accommodated a skeleton in a crouched position within a wooden coffin with the head orientated to the east. The other half of the grave was then filled with painted pottery vessels, each standing upright. The excavators recovered 756 grave offerings, dominated by pottery but including polished stone adzeheads, chisels, spindle whorls and bone beads. But not one item of metal was found. The same situation was found at Huazhaizi, near Lanzhou. Forty-nine burials were found there in 1977 (GPM 1980), again disposed in a wooden burial chamber with pottery vessels and bone beads, but with no sign of copper or bronze.

The site of Liuwan has produced 1500 burials, of which 257 belong to the Banshan phase and 872 to the succeeding Machang phase (2400–2000 BC). There was a variation in the grave goods in the latter group from little at all to a considerable number of vessels, burial 564 having over ninety. Yet despite this unparalleled sample size, no trace of metal was found (Chang 1986). The same situation was encountered at Yuanyangchi, where 189 burials were revealed in an

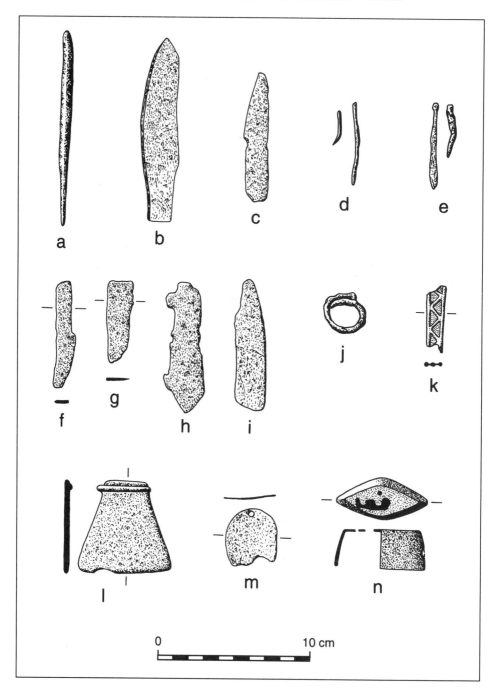

3.3   Copper and bronze artefacts from Qijia and Longshan contexts in the Huanghe Valley.
a. Qinweijia, awl. **b.** Linjia, knife. **c.** Dahezhuang, knife. **d–k.** Huangniangniangtai, knives, awls and a coil. **l, m.** Qinweijia, axe-like object and a disc. **n.** Taosi, bell.

area of about 1200 m². Most come from the Machang but a few belong to the preceding Banshan phase. The burials were laid out in an orderly manner without any clear clustering, but with a number of rows in evidence. Grave goods included pottery vessels, usually placed beyond the head or feet, and stone blades inserted in bone handles (GPM 1982). Only one further metal item has been

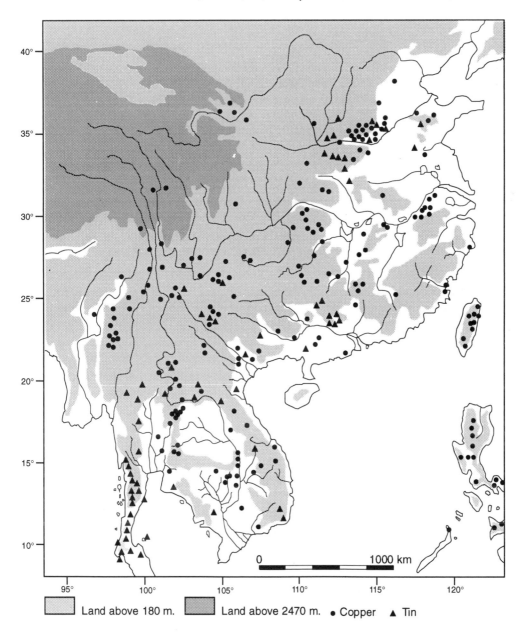

3.4 The distribution of copper and tin ores in East and Southeast Asia.

recovered from the Machang phase, a fragment of a second knife from Jiangjiaping. This has been reported as a copper-tin alloy (Sun Shuyun and Han Rubin 1981).

The Dawenkou culture

In the lower reaches of the Huanghe River, there are numerous sites ascribed to the Dawenkou culture (approximately 4500–2400 BC). The tradition of cultivating millet was continued in this part of the river valley, while the number of alligator bones (*Alligator sinensis*) suggests a warmer climate than at present and a habitat rich in marshes and lakes.

There are many different subdivisions of the Dawenkou culture, but Chang (1986) employs three major periods, an early, middle and late. The first, which is dated from 4300–3500 BC, is represented at the cemeteries of Liulin and Wangyin. The former has yielded 145 graves in five distinct lobes, interpreted as areas for families related to each other within one clan (NM 1965). No area, nor indeed individual burial, stands out as being particularly well endowed with grave goods. Differences were rather expressed between males and females, the former having polished stone adzes and chisels, as well as the remains of dogs, and the latter being more likely to be accompanied by spindle whorls (Pearson 1981). The middle phase (3500–2900 BC) is represented by the early burials at Chengzi, early and middle period burials at Dawenkou and cemeteries at several other sites (Chang 1986). At Chengzi, the middle Dawenkou period graves showed that, with time, interments of men, women and children were superimposed, each person having an individual coffin and grave goods (CAG 1980). With the passage of time, burials became increasingly differentiated by wealth and the energy expended in grave construction. Pearson (1981) has considered these trends in some detail, noting for example, how the average number of ceramic vessels increased from 4.9 to 22.08 between the early and late (2900–2400 BC) phases of the Dawenkou cemetery. This site also shows that there was an increase with time in the proportion of graves containing certain grave goods, such as stone adzes, jade ornaments and stone beads. Some late graves also reached unprecedented levels of complexity and opulence. They contain impressive numbers of jade objects exotic to the area, and although such interments suggest the presence of high status individuals, there is no evidence that members of the higher echelon in society were buried in designated parts of the cemeteries. By the end of the Dawenkou culture, there is abundant evidence for a sharpening in social ranks, the development of craft specialists, as seen in the quality of the ceramics and jades, but not yet any evidence for metal working.

The Qijia culture

Both Dawenkou and Yangshao cultures developed regional variants of what is known as the Longshan culture. In Gansu, the Machang phase of the Yangshao was succeeded by the Qijia culture, which An Zhimin (1980) has described as a regional variant of the Longshan (Fig. 3.5). Four sites have been radiocarbon

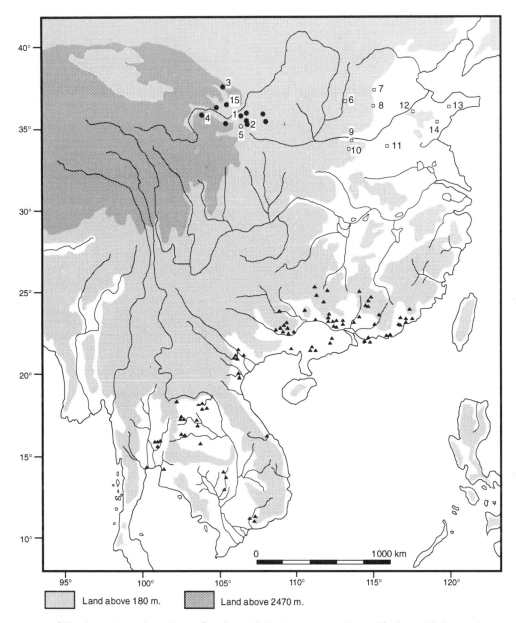

Land above 180 m.   Land above 2470 m.

● Qijia sites □ Longshan sites ▲ Southeast Asian bronze age sites ○ Machang-Majiayao site

3.5 The distribution of sites with early copper-based artefacts in the Huanghe Valley, compared with the location of bronze age sites in Southeast Asia. **1.** Dahezhuang. **2.** Qinweijia. **3.** Huangniangniangtai. **4.** Gamatai. **5.** Linjia. **6.** Taosi. **7.** Jian'gou. **8.** Hougang. **9.** Meishan. **10.** Wangchenggang. **11.** Pingliangtai. **12.** Chengziyai. **13.** Sanlihe. **14.** Chengzi. **15.** Jiangjiaping.

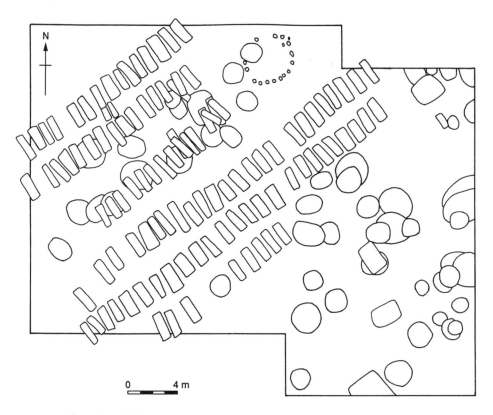

3.6   Plan of the Qinweijia cemetery.

dated, and there are seven available determinations, suggesting that settlement is dated between 2300–1800 BC. Several village sites with cemeteries have been excavated. At Qinweijia, two burial areas were found, the 99 later graves in the southern cemetery being set out in rows with the head orientated to the northwest, while the 29 graves of the northern cemetery are orientated with the head to the west (Fig. 3.6). Polished stone adzeheads, pottery vessels and bone needles and ladles were found in graves, together with pigs' mandibles (GS 1960, GATIA 1975). While most burials are single inhumations, there are cases where a male was buried with a female to one side. There are also a number of storage pits near the cemeteries and under some of the graves. These have yielded copper-based objects: two rings, an awl, axe, finger ring and two thin discs with a hole at one end (Fig. 3.3). The axe and one ring are leaded bronze, but one of the discs is copper with no sign of alloying (Sun Shuyun and Han Rubin 1981). The axe was also worked after casting in a stone mould, by the annealing process. This involved heating and hammering the working surface to harden it.

Excavations at the Qijia site of Dahezhuang in 1960 involved an area of 1589 m², and revealed house remains, storage pits, five stone circles and 82 graves (GATIA 1974). The agricultural basis of such villages is shown by the presence of a pottery vessel in the house, containing the remains of millet. The burials were again laid out in rows with the head to the northwest, but there is less structure to the plan than was seen at Qinweijia. An unusual aspect of these graves is that fully 60% contained the remains of children. In one case, there were three infants in one grave. Bone implements were varied, including spades, spoons and ornaments, while pots were common as grave goods. Ten of the burials included pigs' jaws. A fragment of metal from this site was found to have only 0.02% of tin, indicating that it was made from unalloyed copper (Sun Shuyun and Han Rubin 1981). A flat fragment of copper, possibly part of a knife or spatula, was found beside a house with millet still adhering to it (Fig. 3.3). Other domestic contexts have yielded copper-based knives, chisels, awls and rings (Chang 1986). Two radiocarbon dates in the vicinity of 2000 BC have been obtained from this same house (Fig. 3.7).

There have been four seasons of excavations at the village of Huangniangniangtai between 1957 and 1975 (GPM 1960, 1978b). Square houses, pits and burials have been found, along with the polished stone adzeheads, bone and shell artefacts typical of the Qijia culture. Thirty-two copper-based artefacts were found, not only in the domestic part of the site, but also in some of the burials (An Zhimin 1982–3). They are knives, awls, chisels, a ring, flat pieces of metal and in one case, what has been described as the top of a hairpin. Analysis of a knife and three awls indicated that they were cast from copper with no evidence for alloying (Sun Shuyun and Han Rubin 1981). A copper axe has also been found at Qijiaping, together with a mirror of bronze. A second mirror was found at Gamatai, again of bronze with 9.6% tin content. This came from a burial site which has also yielded copper finger rings.

The Qijia sites reveal, possibly for the first time in a Huanghe context, the presence of metal objects in significant numbers. The chronology of these sites is therefore of some importance. Of those which have yielded metal artefacts, only Dahezhuang has provided radiocarbon dates. The other five dates from Qijia contexts are in general agreement that the culture belongs to between about 2300–1800 BC. An Zhimin (1982–3), however, also stresses that the mirror referred to above is similar to a dated specimen from a late Shang context. Zhang Zhongpei (1987) has subdivided the culture into eight stages, with copper appearing in stages 3–4 and bronze in stage 8. It might well, therefore, be the case that Qijia copper implements belong to the first half of the second millennium BC, with some later contexts extending into the second half.

The Qijia culture was contemporary, some would say part of, a general cultural horizon which extended from Gansu down the length of the Huanghe River. There are several regional groups and virtual unanimity in identifying their origins in the Yangshao cultures or, in the case of Shandong, in the Dawenkou culture. There are few radiocarbon dates from Shandong sites, and they suggest settlement between 2400–1800 BC. The archaeological remains reveal several marked changes in the nature of prehistoric society. Chengziyai is one of a string of walled

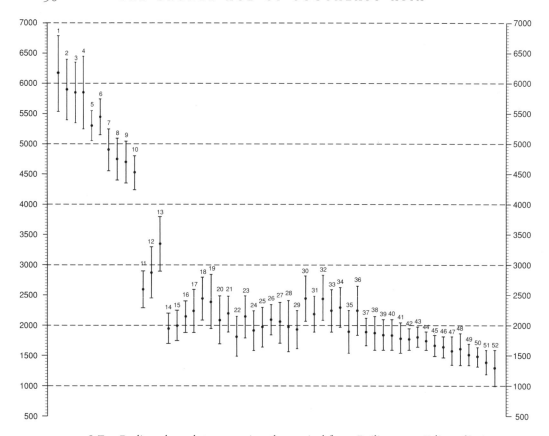

3.7   Radiocarbon dates covering the period from Peiligang to Erlitou (2-sigma corrected range BC). For a comprehensive list, see Chang (1986).
1-5. Peiligang (ZK-754, 434, 753, 571, 751). **6—10.** Beixin (ZK-632, 778, 777, 653, 639). **11-13.** Linjia (ZK-522, 521, 523). **14-19.** Liuwan (ZK-346, BK-75012, 75009, ZK-345, 348, BK-75033). **20-21.** Gaochuding (BK-77053, 77052). **22-23.** Liuwan (Qijia culture) (ZK-347, BK-75010). **24-25.** Dahezhuang (ZK-23, 15). **26.** Qiaocun (ZK-741). **27-29.** Sanlihe (ZK-362, 391, 361). **30-31.** Pingliangtai WB-81-2, 81-3). **32.** Hougang (one of many: ZK-770). **33.** Taosi (one of many: ZK-1086). **34-35.** Meishan (ZK-386, 349). **36-52.** Erlitou (ZK-680, 1082-C, 926, 829, 212/923, 285, 1175, 1178, 1081, 1166, 1176, 928-9, 922/1082, 1078, 930, 1077, 257).

centres located up the Huanghe Valley during this period, and its size, 450 × 390 m, reflects a capacity to marshal a considerable labour force. The wall, set in a foundation trench 13.8 m wide and 1.5 m deep, formerly stood 6 m in height, with a width at the top about 9 m. It was formed by beating loess soil in layers, inclining the wall inward with each increment. This would have involved the movement of about 115,000 m³ of material. Given the defensive nature of such an enterprise, it is not surprising to find that a high proportion of the bone and stone implements at such sites are projectile points.

The Longshan culture

We have seen that late Dawenkou burials were more differentiated in terms of grave wealth and elaboration than earlier ones. This trend continued into the Longshan culture. Chengzi is one of the best-known cemeteries of this period (CAG 1980). Eighty-seven graves were uncovered, which the excavators have divided into rich, small, poor and very narrow groups. The burial layout is also said to comprise three distinct clusters. There are five rich graves, distinguished by a ledge of soil round the coffin for displaying grave offerings. Two were found in the western, three in the northern and none in the eastern cluster. These graves invariably included tall-stemmed cups and pigs' mandibles as grave offerings. The next class also had grave ledges which sometimes included tall-stemmed cups. Some also contained pigs' mandibles. All three clusters included such graves, although there was only a single example in the northern group. There were no ledges and few grave goods in either of the poorer varieties of grave, which formed the bulk of the sample. The excavators see this mortuary pattern as one which involved the change from an egalitarian to a more hierarchical social organisation.

No metal remains were found at Chengzi, but two parts of what may have been an awl have been reported from Sanlihe. Their provenance is uncertain, as they were found 'during sorting and arranging' (Barnard 1991). These have been analysed by Sun Shuyun and Han Rubin (1981), and found to contain between 20.2–26.4% zinc. The combination of copper and zinc produces brass, an alloy which is found late in the Chinese sequence. Shuyun and Rubin, however, have noted that the ceramics of the Shandong Longshan culture were made under technically sophisticated conditions within closed kilns. They also found that mixed copper-zinc ores are present in the area. Their experiments with smelting such ores produced brass, the proportion of zinc varying between 4–34%. There are no practical impediments to the casting of the brass awl at this period, although it was surely unintentional and the planned production of this alloy only occurred much later. Barnard (1991) advocates extreme caution in viewing these brass objects as relating to the Longshan culture, particularly in the light of their dubious provenance.

The Longshan sites in the middle reaches of the Huanghe River and its tributaries provide similar evidence for structural changes in the organisation of society. Several walled settlements have been examined, Pingliangtai being one of the best known. The site covers over 5 ha, with the walls enclosing an inner area 185 by 185 m in extent. There were entrance gates on the northern and southern walls, a drainage system, and one of the pits contained 'verdigris-like dusts, possibly remains of copper metallurgy' (Chang 1986:207). There are two radiocarbon dates from phases III and IV, falling between 2400 and 2200 BC.

Hougang, about 250 km to the northwest, was also walled with the same stamped earth construction as has been found at Pingliangtai and in Shandong.

Wangchenggang is a fourth walled settlement, the defended area covering 7580 m². Further vestiges of stamped earth were found in the central precinct, with human, possibly sacrificial, skeletons within the layers. Chang has suggested that these were house foundations for the upper echelon of the Wangchenggang community, a group which was acquainted with copper metallurgy, for a fragment of a bronze vessel containing copper, tin and lead was found in a period IV pit there. A radiocarbon date from this period has been obtained: 2878–2104 BC. This harmonises with the two dates obtained from earlier contexts at this site and suggests that the casting of a bronze vessel was within the compass of the bronzesmiths by the beginning of the second millennium BC.

Some sites also grew very large. Remains at Taosi cover an area of 300 ha. There is a large cemetery there, of which more than a thousand graves have been excavated (Shanxi-ATIA 1980, Chang 1986). They were placed in an orderly fashion, but they also overlie and intercut each other. Again, there are different grades of mortuary wealth, and some evidence for spatial clustering into two or more groups. Nine are outstandingly rich, containing up to 200 offerings which include jade rings and axeheads, musical instruments including a wooden drum with a crocodile skin cover and handsomely-painted pottery (Pearson and Underhill 1987). In all cases where the primary interment can be sexed, the person was a male. There are eighty graves in the middle division and hundreds of poor interments. The former contain sets of pottery vessels, jade axes, tubes and rings, and pigs' mandibles. The latter have few if any grave goods. Chang (1986:277) has concluded that this important assemblage reveals how wealth was concentrated in only a minority of the burials. Males in large and wealthy graves also appear to have been associated with two medium-sized graves containing the remains of women. The drum and music stones also appear in early historic texts as royal symbols. In this vast assemblage, only one metal object was found, a bell comprising copper with a 1.5% admixture of lead (Fig. 3.3). It was cast around a central core, a technique not previously reported from this area. A human bone from this burial has been dated to 2615–1890 BC.

Further evidence for metal working has been found at Meishan. This site has provided a sequence which saw two phases of the Longshan followed by the succeeding Erlitou culture (HATIA 1982). A substantial domestic area ascribed to the former has been uncovered, which includes house foundations, stone, bone and shell implements. Among them were two crucible fragments with metal still adhering to the interior surfaces. This comprised 95% copper, and the finds are dated to 2290–2005 BC.

These Longshan sites might be earlier by a century or so than the Qijia sites to the west, but there is a consistent thread of evidence for knowledge of copper smelting and alloying with tin and lead. The presence of a copper-zinc alloy is seen as more likely to reflect the unintended selection of a particular ore source, if these finds are properly provenanced. Chang (1986) has listed several cultural changes which characterise this Longshan culture in all its regional expressions.

We find, for example, the presence of large settlements containing areas defended by substantial walls. These were contemporary with a marked increase in the number of arrowheads of stone and bone. There is evidence too, for violence in the sacrificial victims found within the walled precinct at Wangchenggang and the concentration of skeletons in a well at Jian'gou. Cemeteries contained few very rich graves, some moderately wealthy ones and many poor interments. The rich individuals, however, were still interred in the same cemetery as other members of the community and the layout of graves suggests more than one social group, perhaps related by close affinal or consanguinal ties, within the community as a whole. Some of the goods found in the richest graves match early historical descriptions of royal regalia. Jade artefacts requiring much labour in their manufacture were encountered, and these reveal a common ritual basis to communities up the length of the Huanghe and its tributaries. Some of the pottery vessels also suggest the presence of full-time specialists.

The historical period

We have reached the stage in the cultural sequence in the Huanghe Valley when early written records make their first contribution. These date from the fourteenth century BC, when dynastic records were maintained, on silk and bamboo, by specialist scribes. None has survived from this remote period, but inscriptions cast on bronzes have, and these record military campaigns and other events which involved a central court society, such as treaties or appointments to offices. Oracle bones are a second source of information. These record the questions and sometimes the answers put to oracles, and later retained in royal archives. The topics treated concern the rhythm of central court life: the giving of gifts and listings of offerings made in mortuary rituals. Economic life outside the court centres is not mentioned. Many such early records were lost, and others deliberately destroyed. But in about 100 BC, the *Shi Ji* was compiled.

The *Shi Ji* presents one of several versions of three early dynastic sequences. The Xia involved seventeen kings over a period of 471 years, the Shang 29 over 496 and the Zhou, 37 kings over a 867 year period from 1122–256 BC. The Zhou sites concentrate in the west, Xia in the middle and Shang in the east of the Huanghe as it traversed the loess highlands and so into the broad alluvial lowlands (Fig. 3.8). Chang K.-C. (1983) has stressed that these three polities should not be seen as successional, but rather as contemporaries and competitors, each developing from one of the regional groupings of the Longshan culture. The degree to which they succeeded each other in a political and dynastic sense reflects the respective military success as the Shang overcame the Xia, only in turn to succumb to the Zhou.

Harmonising physical remains with this historic framework has been one of the major contributions of archaeological research in China during the last 70 years. This has seen the identification of Shang royal centres at Xiaotun near Anyang, Erligang, Zhengzhou and Shixianggou at Yanshi (Zhao Zhiquan 1985). However,

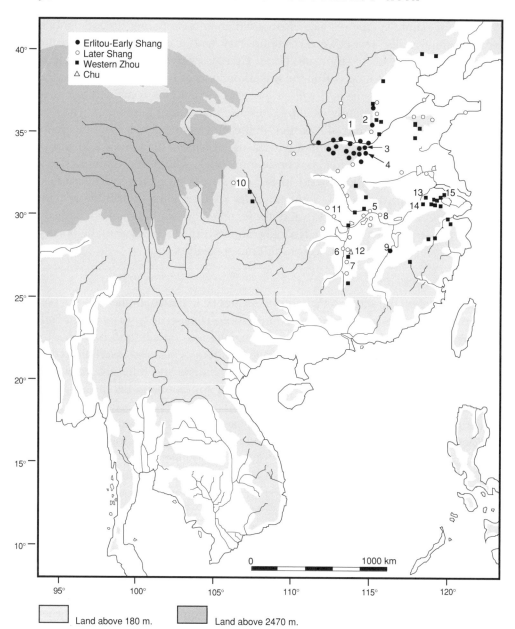

3.8 Distribution of the principal Shang and Western Zhou sites.
1. Zhengzhou. **2.** Anyang. **3.** Yanshi. **4.** Erlitou. **5.** Panlongcheng. **6.** Ning-xiang. **7.** Liling. **8.** Maojiazui. **9.** Xin'gan; Wucheng, **10.** Sanxingdui. **11.** Zhaojiahu. **12.** Changsha (Chu). **13.** Beiyinyangying. **14.** Taigangsi. **15.** Sidun.

in a situation where there was a local evolution from Longshan foundations, identifying the precise stage in a site's development as being the remains of the Xia Dynasty has not been easy, and some controversy has ensued. Nevertheless, a pattern has emerged, and it is relevant to the theme of this book.

Radical changes: Erlitou

Much of our appreciation of this period results from the excavations at Erlitou (EATIA 1974, 1976, 1980; Zhao Zhiquan 1985). This site was first recognised, in a specific effort to identify the archaeological remains of the Xia dynasty, in 1957. Excavations there began two years later, and investigations continue. There are four phases in the sequence, found in a stratigraphic deposit 3–4 m thick. The cultural remains cover an area of 300 ha.

The two early phases are, unfortunately, not as well documented as one would wish due to the intensive later developments. They are closely related to the Longshan culture of Henan, revealing, for example, the same stamped-earth foundations as have been found at Wangchenggang. Stage II bronzes were rare, comprising awls, knives and the bells, which came from complex composite moulds. Early burials match quite closely those described for the Longshan culture. People were interred in individual graves with a range of grave goods which included pottery vessels, stone and shell artefacts and some jade ornaments. Zhao Zhiquan (1985:298) also reports that bronze bells were found in some of the larger graves. These contrast with the fate of some of the dead, who were disposed of in refuse pits. Industrial activity is indicated by the remains of pottery kilns and crucibles for pouring bronze. There is also a range of implements used in agriculture and fishing. Domestic stock included cattle, pigs and sheep. The radiocarbon dates suggest that initial settlement occurred in the vicinity of 1900 BC.

The third phase saw a number of portentous cultural changes which continued into the fourth. Two palaces were constructed. The walls of the first are approximately square, each measuring 100 m in length. A central hall dominated the enclosed space, which looked out over an open courtyard. The hall covered 30.4 × 11.4 m, and the roof was supported on 22 columns. Access to the enclosed courtyard, which covers half a hectare, was by three entrance passages, each flanked by rectangular chambers. A second, smaller palace has also been excavated. Outside these palaces, there are the foundations of houses which presumably belong to the lower classes. The southern area of Erlitou also contained a bronze-working atelier, marked by crucibles and casting residue.

Burials described as 'medium and small elite graves' (Zhao Zhiquan 1985:291) have been found outside the site perimeter. They were placed on a north-south alignment, the dead being interred in a painted wooden coffin. Offerings included bronze cups on tripod legs (*jue*) bronze dagger axes (*ge*), a battle axe (*qi*) and jade ceremonial axes (*yazhang*) of the form found at Phung Nguyen and Xom Ren in Bac Bo, knives, tablets or sceptres, cylinders, dagger-axes and tubes (Fig. 3.9).

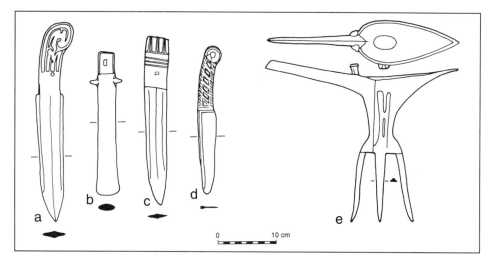

3.9   Bronze artefacts from Erlitou.
a–c. Halberds. **d.** Knife. **e.** *Jue* cup.

The metal items were cast from tin bronze, some having small amounts of lead as well. The cups were cast with two-piece moulds. Bronzes were also found in non-burial contexts. These include adzes, chisels, battle and dagger axes, knives and a series of circular discs and plaques embellished with turquoise inlay. All belong to periods III–IV.

Irrespective of whether this site should be ascribed to the Xia or the Shang, or indeed to both with a break between phases II–III, the fact is that at Erlitou, we encounter the transition to a society based on the central walled palace, a core element in historic Chinese civilisation. The bronzes and jades from later Erlitou reflect an interest in ritual, feasting and display, both in the court and in war. The *Shi Ji* described the walled town as the fundamental unit of Chinese states, and it now has archaeological confirmation at Erlitou between 2000 and 1500 BC. Moreover, the quality of the bronzes reveals the development of a series of techniques which herald the specialised products of the Shang. We find, for example, the use of piece moulds (Fig. 3.10), the application of cores to the interior and the feet of containers, the casting on of handles and provision of grooves to receive turquoise inlay (Barnard 1991).

Erlitou was not the sole example of this phenomenon: many other sites of this period are found in western Henan and southern Shanxi provinces (Fig. 3.8).

The Shang Dynasty: Zhengzhou and Anyang

As has been noted, early historic records referred to 29 successive kings of the Shang Dynasty, which succeeded the Xia rulers as the dominant political force in the middle reaches of the Huanghe River. The capital was moved five times between various centres. In 1950, one of these, known as Xiao, was identified within the limits of the modern city of Zhengzhou. While Shang sites are

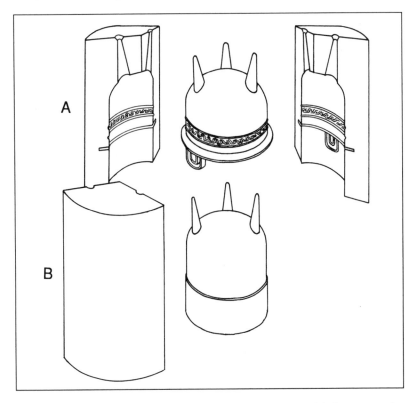

3.10   The clay core and outer clay segments of a piece mould illustrating the technique used to cast Shang and Zhou ceremonial bronze vessels. Based on an illustration in Blunden and Elvin (1983:77).

distributed there over an area of 25 km², the heart of the complex was a walled city covering approximately 318 ha. The walls of Zhengzhou attained a maximum width at the base of 22.5 m, and the highest surviving section stands 9 m high. If these dimensions were typical of the whole, it would have involved moving and shaping about 1.5 million m³ of soil. This is 12.5 as much as the walls at Chengziyai. The interior of the walled area at Zhengzhou also contains stamped earth foundations for buildings ranging considerably in size, the largest yet identified measuring 1000 m² (An Chin-huai 1986). One such foundation platform supported rows of columns, each spaced two metres apart, for a substantial building. Jade and bronze hairpins, An Chin-huai noted, concentrated in this part of the enclosure, suggesting that the highest rank in Zhengzhou society lived within.

Specialised workshops were found outside the walls. Two involved bronze casting. They yielded much bronze detritus, crucible fragments, slag, and ceramic moulds which had been used for casting bronze vessels as well as tools. There was also a workshop specialising in ceramics and bone working. Bone arrowheads were made in the latter, with human bone among the raw materials.

Four distinct cemeteries have been investigated and what have been described as medium and small graves identified. Many contained bronze vessels, jade and pottery offerings. A cache of bronze vessels has also been found outside the city wall, one specimen, a *ting* tripod, weighing 86.4 kg. These contrast with the considerable number of partial human skeletons found disposed of without ceremony in rubbish pits.

Anyang, a late Shang Dynasty centre

Although Zhengzhou has provided evidence for early writing, it has not yet yielded a royal cemetery or evidence for the use of horse-drawn chariots in warfare. These have been identified, however, in the late Shang centre found to the northeast of the town of Anyang. This complex, which covers about 24 km², was identified through the discovery of inscribed oracle bones at the village of Xiaotun. It is the ruins of the Shang capital of Yin. Twelve kings are recorded as having ruled from Yin, and their massive tombs have been found at the royal necropolis of Xibeigang. The mortuary area is but one precinct in this extensive complex, which also includes royal palace foundations, bronze and bone workshops and clusters of houses.

Approximately 2500 burials have been examined, divided into several distinct complexes. Yang Hsi-chang (1986) has ascribed these to the royal necropolis, aristocratic lineages and lineage cemeteries. Unfortunately, the outstandingly large royal tombs have suffered from looting, but at least their location and scale can be assessed. There are two sectors, a western and an eastern. The former comprises eight tombs with descending ramps giving a cruciform shape, the latter has four. The eastern sector also contains numerous sacrificial pits involved in ancestor rituals. The royal graves took the form of a rectangular subterranean chamber, approached from four sides by descending ramps. In the case of tomb 1217, the burial chamber covered an area of 330 m² and was 10 m deep. In 1976, a relatively small tomb was discovered intact in the cemetery at Xiaotun. It has been ascribed to Fuhao, a consort of the King Wuding, and the wealth of grave goods, which included over 440 bronzes and 590 jade items, hints at the scale of the contents which went with the much larger interments. Nine further graves have been found in this group and two of these have been excavated (AAT 1981). Burial 18 is located 22 m from the tomb of Fuhao, and was found intact. The coffin and mortuary chamber were made of lacquered wood, the latter with black designs painted on a red background. Four human sacrificial victims were found between the coffin and the walls of the mortuary chamber. Grave goods comprised four pottery vessels, 19 bronze weapons, 24 bronze ritual vessels, 11 jades, 28 bone artefacts and four cowrie shells. Thirteen of the bronze vessels were inscribed, identifying the owner as Lord Ziyu, whose name appears on the oracle bone inscriptions as a member of King Wuding's lineage. On the other hand, the human remains are probably female, and the mortuary enclave could have been reserved for royal wives.

Between 1969 and 1977, excavations proceeded in the western cemetery at Anyang (AAT 1979). These uncovered 939 inhumation burials, distributed in eight groups, each having sub-groups numbering between ten and forty graves. The standard procedure was to bury the dead in rectangular graves, contained within a wooden coffin or, in some cases, a coffin placed within a second wooden chamber. The corpse was accompanied by a range of grave goods, usually numbering no more than five items, of which pottery vessels predominated. Some burials, however, might have over a dozen grave offerings. In contrast to the massive concentration of bronze and jade in the elite burials, only 67 of the 939 graves in this cemetery complex were accompanied by bronze artefacts, which included beakers, cups and tripod vessels, as well as weapons. The last items, such as arrowheads, axes, spearheads and halberds, were restricted to males. Other offerings were made of jade, bone, lead and shell, and many burials included cowrie shells. Thirty-five of the bronzes bore inscriptions thought to name different lineages, and these concentrated in different sectors of the cemetery. The excavators have suggested that the lineage sectors were further divided into members of the same family. The cemetery was in use during the reigns of nine kings at Anyang.

Yang Hsi-chang (1986), in considering this assemblage, has suggested that there are five different types of burial. The richest is set apart by the presence of a ramp leading down to the mortuary chamber. All have, unfortunately, been looted, but it is still evident that they contained sacrificial human victims, as well as many bronzes and horse-drawn chariots. The second group, of which there are about twenty examples, comprise relatively large mortuary chambers, but without a tomb ramp. There were human sacrifices, and bronze vessels. The sixty graves in the third group have a few bronze vessels, no sacrificial victims, and usually lack an outer chamber to contain the coffin. The vast majority of graves fall into the fourth group, in which no bronzes have been found, and the body is contained within a wooden coffin with one or two pottery vessels. About ninety of the burials lacked any grave goods.

In terms of spatial distribution, it is notable that wealthy graves clustered together. Four tombs with ramps were located in a row along the northern edge of the third sector. One of these was equipped with a chariot and horse. There was another such cluster in the southern edge of the seventh sector, where burial 93 had a ramp. To the west lay a row of five further large graves, although none had a ramp. Nevertheless, there were two pits containing chariots and horses. Twenty metres to the north was a concentration of 27 relatively poor burials. Such a distribution has encouraged Yang Hsi-chang to suggest that there were differences in wealth and rank within family branches of the same lineage. Again, it is likely, to judge from the distribution of the wealthy and poor, that some lineages were more highly ranked than others. The formality of the cemetery contrasts with the disposal of what Chinese archaeologists refer to as slaves: they were interred with little ceremony, and more often than not with no grave goods, in refuse pits.

The Zhou Dynasty

Although the traditional date for the advent of the Zhou Dynasty, 1122 BC, is unlikely to be strictly accurate, there is no doubting the fact that a new line of rulers succeeded towards the end of the twelfth century. They ruled successively for about nine centuries, but the relocation of the capital from near Xian to Luoyang in about 770 BC marks not only the transition from the Western to the Eastern Zhou, but also the increasingly sacred and ritual rather than political role of the Emperor. The Eastern Zhou itself is divided into two periods, the Spring and Autumn (770–475 BC) and the period of Warring States, which ended with the final conquests of the Qin emperor in 221 BC.

There are two issues which are of direct concern to this study. In the first place, the Shang bronze casting tradition continued to flourish, although as is always the case, there were changes in style and taste. Second, it must be appreciated that the Zhou, even during the apogee of their power, never directly controlled the area nominally within their boundaries. Rather, great overlords who acknowledged the supremacy of the central ruler, exercised considerable local sway which, as the Eastern Zhou progressed, saw the development of increasingly independent states. Three of these, the states of Chu, Wu and Yue, brought civilisation close to Southeast Asia. Chu, centred in the area of the middle Yangzi River, was particularly prominent in influencing through the demands of trade and territorial ambition, the northern reaches of Southeast Asia.

Summary

Considerable advances have been made in our understanding of early bronze working in the Huanghe Valley since the sophisticated Shang tradition seemed to appear without local antecedents. The earliest items are two bronze knives from Majiayao and Machang contexts in Gansu. The former is enigmatic, at least as far as its chronology is concerned, because it appears to date almost a millennium earlier than any consistent evidence for copper working in this region. If bronze working was present by 3000 BC, it doesn't appear to have been adopted in Gansu or elsewhere for many centuries thereafter. We have to await the Qijia culture of the same region before encountering consistent evidence for the development of a copper and bronze casting tradition.

Of the four Qijia sites which have been dated by radiocarbon determinations, only one, Dahezhuang, has also yielded metal objects. An Zhimin (1982–3) has further suggested that later Qijia sites might well overlap with the early Shang period. The artefacts in question can be divided into tools and ornaments. The former comprise knives, awls, one implement shaped like an axe, and one socketed axe from Qijiaping, the site which gave its name to the culture. Rings, a possible pendant, and a mirror have also been found, the last being very similar to Shang specimens. Some artefacts were made of copper, others contained sufficient tin to be classified as bronze. Casting was made in a double mould, and some of the implements were cold hammered and annealed. An awl from Qinweijia, for example, bears hammer marks and metallographic analyses have revealed internal structures aligned along the direction of the working of the piece after casting. The Qinweijia axe was also annealed to increase its hardness.

There is some evidence that later Longshan contexts in the middle and lower reaches of the Huanghe incorporated knowledge of bronze casting, but the number of cases is very low, compared with the number of burials which have been excavated. Some controversy surrounds the integrity of these Longshan finds, particularly the brass awl from Sanlihe. Yet some knowledge of copper working and alloying, albeit not yet a significant element in the technology of the Longshan culture, appears to have been present by 2000 BC.

The clearest evidence for the establishment of a local bronze industry, and its increasing proficiency, comes from Erlitou. In terms of metal artefacts, the material from the first two phases recalls Qijia types. This is not surprising, given the fact that the radiocarbon chronology of Erlitou suggests initial settlement in the vicinity of 1900 BC. The significant break came with the third phase, when the range of metal artefacts and the skill of the bronzeworkers reveals a major advance. In addition to the familiar knives, awls, chisels and bells, we find bronze *jue* cups cast in clay piece moulds. These elegant little vessels, each standing on a tripod, represent the beginnings of a tradition of casting ritual vessels in bronze which was to become the hallmark of the Shang industry, and represent one of the supreme achievements of the bronzeworkers art.

The increase in the scale of bronze working as the Shang civilisation developed is perhaps best illustrated by comparing the facilities for casting found at Zhengzhou and Anyang. Barnard and Sato (1975) have described a large crucible from the former as having a capacity of 72 kg of molten metal. A giant crucible reconstructed from Anyang would, if full, have had a capacity of 1650 kg, or over 1.5 tons of metal. This might seem extravagant were it not for the fact that a bronze cauldron from tomb 1004, in the royal necropolis, weighs 879 kg. And this was but one of the many forms of ritual or ceremonial vessel cast in bronze in the Anyang workshops to accompany the weapons of war and horse trappings which were found in the higher-ranked graves. Indeed, together with jade and chariots, bronzes symbolised high social status at Anyang. The energy employed in mining, smelting, moving and casting reached levels surely unmatched in the ancient world. Moreover, this continued unabated during the succeeding Zhou Dynasty.

The Bronze Age in the Yangzi Valley

The Neolithic prelude

The Yangzi Valley witnessed the development of agriculture within sedentary communities at about the same time as in the Huanghe area to the north. The principal difference was that, in this milder and wetter environment, rice took the place of millet. The Yangzi Valley falls within a zone of subtropical mixed evergreen and deciduous forest, and incorporates a series of extensive lakes which provided a low-lying aquatic habitat ideally suited to the cultivation of rice (Zhou Songquiao 1986).

This is not the place in which to consider in detail the timing and context of the origins of rice and millet cultivation in China. The broad pattern, however, presents intriguing similarities with the contemporaneous changes noted by Bar-Yosef and Meadows (1995) for the Levant, where they traced the increasing reliance on cereal crops in conjunction with climatic change. In Southeast and East Asia, climatic fluctuations had an increasingly significant effect as one moves northward from the equator. The changing climate in central and northern China, identified on the basis of pollen cores, glacial advances and retreats, loess deposition and lake levels, shows that from about 11,150 to 10,400 BC, the temperature rose by about 7°C. From 9000 to 8000 BC, there was a sharp

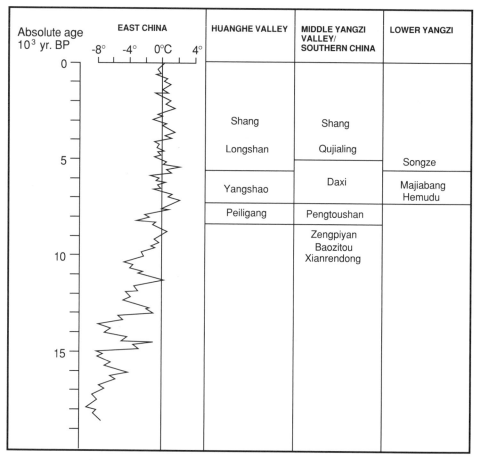

3.11   The changes in the mean annual temperature of eastern China relative to the present figure, set against the cultural sequences.

deterioration, known as the Younger Dryas, which involved increasing cold (Zhou *et al.* 1991). This in turn was followed by a marked warming from 8000 to 6500 BC, and then a succession of fluctuations between relatively warm and cold conditions (Fig. 3.11). During the particular warm phase dating from 8000 BC, a number of open and cave sites in southern China were occupied. Xianrendong, for example, was a riverine site from which aquatic resources were exploited. The occupants also made cord-marked pottery, although no one has suggested that agriculture was involved. At Liyuzui, a number of human burials have been found within the occupied cave. Eighteen flexed burials have been examined at Zengpiyan. Chang (1986) has suggested that these sites represent broad spectrum foragers, who took advantage of the warm conditions, and would have encountered wild rice growing even as far north as the Yangzi Valley (Fig. 3.1).

Both in the Huanghe and the Yangzi valleys, the ensuing cold phase coincided with the first village communities. It has been suggested that this change to settled agriculture represents an adaptive response to the impact of a sharp climatic deterioration (Higham 1995). There followed a long sequence of what Chang, K.C. (1986) has described as Neolithic cultures which span at least 5000 years from the earliest sites which show settled agriculture to the first evidence of bronze working (Fig. 3.12). Pengtoushan, a site located on the northwestern shore of Lake Dongting in the flat, marshy reaches of the middle Yangzi, has provided the earliest evidence for a settled village community and rice remains there are relatively abundant as temper in the pottery vessels (He Jiejun 1986, HAI 1990, Yan Wenming 1991). This site, which covers about 1 ha and rises to a height of 4 m, was excavated in 1988 over an area of 400 m². The foundations of four houses were traced, and 19 human burials were found, some with pottery vessels as grave goods. The inhabitants also used pendants of siltstone, but polished stone adzes were rather rare. It is also interesting to note that no artefacts thought to have been used to cultivate rice, such as sickles, hoes or spades, were found, although they are common in later sites. The radiocarbon dates are not easy to interpret because they provide a spread from 9000 to 5500 BC (Fig. 3.12). The majority fall between 7500 and 6500 BC, and at this juncture, it is noted that this is the earliest evidence for rice from archaeological contexts. It is not yet known whether it came from a wild or domesticated plant. In the marshy habitat reconstructed for the site, rice could well have been collected from wild stands. Nevertheless, Pengtoushan and other similar settlements in the middle Yangzi area evidence a novel and most significant settlement form, the small permanently occupied village.

The subsequent cultural sequence prior to the first evidence for a knowledge of copper-based metallurgy in the lake region of the middle Yangzi incorporates four stages: the lower Zaoshi, Daxi, Qujialing and Shijiahe cultures. The radiocarbon dates for the Daxi culture, most of which come from Guanmiaoshan, suggest settlement between 4500 and 3300 BC. Li Wenjie (1986) has proposed that the culture can be divided into four phases. The earliest sites concentrate in the vicinity of the northwestern shore of Lake Dongting and the flat lands surrounding

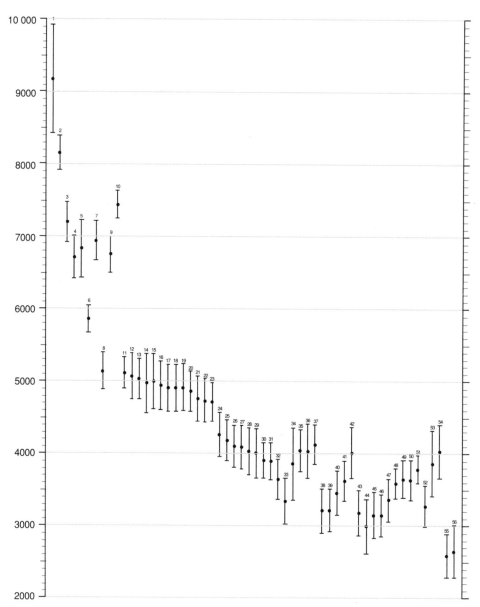

3.12   Radiocarbon dates covering the principal Neolithic sites in the Yangzi Valley
(2-sigma corrected range BC).
1–10. Pengtoushan (OxA-1280, BK-87002, 87050, 89016, 89018, OxA-1274-
5, 1277, 1286, 1282). **11–33**. Hemudu (BK-75075, 78104, 78114, 78109, PV-
47, ZK-590, 263-2, 263, BK-78101, 78111, WB-77-1, BK-78115, 78103, 78106,
78105, ZK-588-9, PV-28, BK-78110, 78117-8, 78058, ZK-587). **34–38.** Songze
(ZK-438-0, 55, BK-79004, 79003, ZK-437-0). **39–43.** Qingdun (Majiabang
culture: WB-78-8/9, ZK-582, WB-78-7, WB-80-46). **44–46.** Xuejiagang (Majiabang culture: WB-80-47, 80-45, 80-46). **47–54.** Guanmiaoshan (Daxi culture:
ZK-832, 891, 685, 831, 994, 991-2, 892). **55–56.** Qujialing (ZK-124-5).

the junction of the Han and Yangzi rivers, but later sites reveal an expansion of the area settled by sedentary rice farmers.

Domestic buildings have been identified at a number of Daxi sites. Houses were constructed of clay strengthened by the addition of plant remains, such as bamboo, reeds and rice husks. The wealth of rice remains, taken in conjunction with the preferred location on spurs commanding low-lying wetlands, affirms that the proliferation of Daxi sites in the middle valley of the Yangzi was based on the cultivation of rice. The diet was supplemented by domestic cattle and pigs, and doubtless by fishing as well. It is noted that a kiln for firing pottery vessels has been found at Huachenggang (HPM 1983).

Daxi is late in the sequence, and 208 graves have been excavated there (MSP 1981). There are some changes in burial practice between the two mortuary phases, early examples being buried in a flexed, later ones in an extended position. Graves were dug just large enough to accommodate the body. The early graves were accompanied by a range of offerings in which pottery vessels were relatively rare, but tools, such as stone chisels and adzes, bone awls and clay spindle whorls were frequently found. In later graves, pottery vessels tended to replace tools as the most common grave offerings, and there were more items of jewellery, particularly stone and jade bracelets and necklaces.

The principal differences between the Daxi and the succeeding Qujialing culture lie in the changing forms of the pottery vessels. There is also continuity in the plant-tempered clay used for building materials and the stone and bone implements used. Huachenggang is one of many sites which has cultural remains from both, stratified one above the other. The 96 Qujialing graves excavated there showed a common orientation, with the head usually pointing to the east, and the graves laid out in rows. The late graves, of which there are 16, belong to a nebulous entity known as the Hubei Longshan or the Qinglongchuan III culture. According to Chang (1986), fewer than 20 sites are in question, and none has been adequately investigated or reported. This gap needs to be filled, because the fertile plains of the middle Yangzi subsequently saw the development of the Chu civilisation. Excavations at Chengtoushan, located on the northwestern margins of Lake Dongting, have added much to our knowledge of the settlement forms of the Qujialing culture (He Jiejun 1995). Large walls of stamped earth enclose an area of 8 ha, within which secular buildings and over 500 burials have been excavated. The site, which is one of several such walled towns now known from this cultural context, included some unusual features: a wooden bridge over a stream, human sacrificial remains under the walls, the remains of a roadway two metres wide, a wooden oar and the remains of rice, gourds and walnuts. A group of eight kilns for firing pottery vessels have been found in the lower layers, which have been ascribed to the Daxi culture.

There are four Neolithic cultures in the lower Yangzi Valley which preceded the appearance of bronze. The earliest is called after the site of Hemudu, where the lowest of the four layers has been dated to *c.* 5000 BC. Hemudu is located on the southern side of the estuary of the Hangzhou River. It was a community of rice farmers which occupied a low-lying, lacustrine environment (You Rujie 1976, ZPM 1978a, Zhou Jiwei 1981). Agricultural implements include scapulae, perforated for hafting as spades. Working edges have been worn smooth through use. The lowest level also yielded a large sample of rice remains. The inhabitants were most proficient at wood-working, the remains of their pile dwellings revealing mastery of making tongued and grooved and mortise and tenon joints as well as wooden pins or dowels to join lengths of timber. The stone adzes and chisels used in this endeavour have also been found, together with the wooden sleeves into which they were hafted. Bone awls and needles evidence a weaving industry, and pottery vessels were formed into a wide range of shapes.

Most of the animal remains from the lowest layer are fragmentary, but 47 species have been identified. The swampy habitat is further seen in the range of fish and water birds represented, including the egret, crane, duck and cormorant. David's deer (*Elaphurus davidianus*), water buffalo (*Bubalus* cf. *mephistopheles*), water deer (*Hydropotes inermis*) and the alligator (*Alligator sinensis*) all indicate hunting in a marshland habitat, although the buffalo may, along with the dog and pig, have been domesticated (ZPM 1978b).

North of Hangzhou Bay, and particularly in the margins of Lake Taihu, we encounter sites ascribed to the Majiabang culture. The earliest dates for these villages correspond with basal Hemudu, the latest dates being about a millennium later. There was much in common between the two in terms of habitat and material culture, although the Majiabang houses were built at ground level. Villages were built on elevated ground, and were foci for hunting in the surrounding marshes, the raising of domestic pigs and cultivation of rice. Some cemeteries have been found, corresponding to the widespread tradition of inhumation burial. Those from Yudun (Yu Su 1978) were orientated to the north or northeast, and were accompanied by grave goods which were not by any means abundant. At Majiabang itself, burials were clustered together and some were superimposed. Grave goods comprised pottery vessels, tools and ornaments (CPAMZP 1961).

Songze, excavated in 1974 and again two years later, revealed a sequence which began with the Majiabang culture, proceeded through the Songze and finished with the transition to the Liangzhu culture (SMRPC 1980). A pollen core taken from the site's vicinity reveals a sharp increase in grass pollen and a decline in the oak (*Quercus glauca*) which may well correspond to forest clearance and cultivation of rice at initial settlement (Wang Kaifa 1980). The climate as represented in this diagram was warmer and wetter than at present during the Majiabang culture, but became cooler and drier during the Songze culture, for which there are radiocarbon dates in the vicinity of 4000 BC.

The cemetery at Songze, of which 97 graves have been uncovered, belongs to the Songze culture itself. Although recalling a number of features of the preceding Majiabang material there are also significant changes. These are seen in the

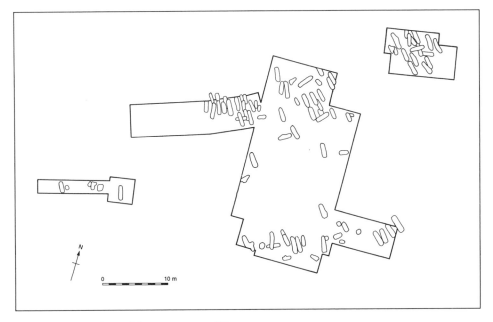

3.13 Plan of the cemetery of Songze.

treatment of the dead. Majiabang burials were often found with the body prone and with few grave goods. At Songze, the dead lay on the back, in rows and clusters (Fig. 3.13). They were accompanied by many more offerings. Women in particular were buried with jade pendants, slit rings or with pieces of jade in the mouth. There was also a growing disparity between richly-endowed graves and those with few offerings.

The same situation has been encountered at Beiyinyangying, where 225 graves have been excavated. These contained many offerings, usually placed beyond the head and feet, and including flat axeheads with a hole bored through, presumably to assist hafting. This method is illustrated in a clay model of an axe from Qingdun (NM 1983). It shows three perforations in the haft to facilitate lashing it to the head. Stone chisels and knives as well as pottery vessels were also counted among the grave goods. Ornaments, such as beads, pendants and rings were made from jade and agate, and their distribution in the cemetery suggests that some individuals were significantly richer than others (NM 1958). At Qingdun, graves were interred in clusters and rows with the head pointing to the east. Individuals were interred on their backs, and grave goods were set out round the lower legs. Burial 17, for example, contained ten pottery vessels, a perforated axe, two flat axes and a chisel. Excavations at the 6 ha site of Xuejiagang have uncovered 103 burials, some of which were associated the jade rings, pendants and tubes. The range of pottery forms is considerable, and quality of production high. So too are the stone implements found in the graves, one stone knife being just over half a metre long (APAT 1982).

With the Liangzhu culture of the third millennium BC, which developed from the Songze, we encounter a similar quickening of wealth and social differentiation as in the contemporary Longshan cultures in the Huanghe Valley to the north. Indeed, the distribution of Liangzhu sites is virtually contiguous with the Longshan sites of Shandong (Fig. 3.1). Still firmly based on rice agriculture linked with fishing and the raising of domestic pigs, cattle and sheep, the Liangzhu cemeteries reveal that certain individuals were given special treatment in terms of grave goods. This is most clearly seen at Sidun, where a young man was interred with a rich array of jades. There were 24 rings and 33 tubes (*cong*). These represent a considerable investment in time and energy, particularly when it is realised that they were carved with animal mask and bird designs similar to those which recur later on early bronzes in the Huanghe Valley (NM 1981, 1984). The pottery forms from Liangzhu burials also hint at increasing concern for display, particularly the decorated lidded bowls on tripod legs and cups on high-stemmed pedestals. The initial use of bronze within the lower Yangzi Valley clearly involved communities already well used to the employment of rare goods in denoting the status of the deceased.

The Bronze Age in the Yangzi Valley

In the Huanghe Valley, there is a consistent thread of evidence for a local origin of copper-based metallurgy which received much stimulus when it was employed by emerging social elites at such palace centres as Erlitou. This contrasts markedly with the situation in the Yangzi Valley, where the first bronze objects came later, and reveal stimulus from the north. The middle reaches of the river, where the Han has its confluence with the Yangzi, are rich in agricultural potential due to the extensive, well-watered lacustrine soil and a summer climate conducive to rice cultivation. Since the Han River links the Yangzi and Huanghe catchments, it is hardly surprising to find that this lake region was early in receiving northern bronzes (Fig. 3.7). At Panlongcheng, for example, Shang-style bronze vessels, halberds, knives and axes characteristic of the Erligang phase have been recovered. The vessels can only be inspired from Shang sources (Chang 1986). Further examples of Shang-inspired but locally produced ritual vessels have been found in Hubei at Ningxiang, in the form of an elephant at Liling (Xiong Chuanxin 1976) and Maojiazui (HuAT 1962). The last site contained the wooden foundations and walls of rectangular buildings as well as bronze arrowheads, knives, axes and a tripod jug.

The quantity and style of the bronzes found at Wucheng on the Gan River in Jiangxi, together with the stone moulds, indicates a Shang-inspired school of metal working but with local stylistic input (Chang 1986). The same pattern has been identified during recent excavations at nearby Xin'gan, and these have added a new dimension to this issue. Xu Pingfang (1992) has described the tomb of a very high status person, perhaps even the ruler of a local polity. He has stressed the Shang affinities of the bronzes, but also noted local styles and preferences, as well as the casting of items not found in the Shang repertoire. Located about 50 km southwest of Lake Poyang, the tomb included many items wrapped in silk, while others were deliberately broken before being stacked within the grave. Apart from the numerous ritual vessels, there was a bronze stepped anvil weighing 20 kg, and the earliest identified bronze socketed ploughshares. The application of bronze to agriculture as well as ritual and warfare is also seen in the socketed shovels, and brings into focus the fact that at Tongling, the earliest copper mine yet identified in China dates back to this period. Numerous jade items were also recovered, including knives, spearheads and rings. This tomb has been dated to late Middle Shang, and therefore overlaps in date an even richer and indeed extraordinary discovery to the west.

Sanxingdui is a large walled and moated city located just north of Chengdu in Sichuan Province. Its occupation covers the period between 1700 and 1100 BC (Bagley 1988). The walls enclose an area of 2.6 km² and are disposed in a trapezoid form, those on the east being 1.8 km in length. The labour force needed must have been considerable, for the foundations were 40–50 m wide at the base and 20 m wide at the top. There was a central wall with two flanking walls on each side, and they were made of stamped earth construction. A moat, linked to the adjacent river, lay in front of the outer wall. Two ritual pits have recently been excavated within the city precinct. The first measures 4.6 × 3.4 m and is 1.64 m deep, the second is slightly smaller, measuring 3.5 × 2.3 m with a depth of 1.5 m. Both were sealed by a layer of stamped earth, below which were the carefully layered remains of ivory, bronze and jade artefacts thought to have been placed there after their use in some form of ritual activity associated with an ancestral temple. Thousands of items have been recovered from them, including bronzes, jades, ceramics, ivories and artefacts of gold (Fig. 3.14; Bagley 1988). An examination of the bronze vessels from this site reveals a wide range, including urns, vats, jars and ewers. It has been proposed that wine and ritual were important aspects of life in this centre (SPCRAC 1987)

While contemporary with the Shang civilisation of the Huanghe Valley, many of the bronzes from Sanxingdui are unmatched outside Sichuan, not only in terms of the cast objects themselves, but their scale. One of the most remarkable recovered was a tree, cast in sections for ease of assembly. It stands 3.8 m high, and its branches bear fruit with birds feeding. A coiled dragon slumbers around the trunk. The largest human figure stands life-size on a podium to a total height of 2.62 m. Cast in a single pouring, the statue weighs over 180 kg. There are numerous other human figures, some crouching, some in the form of masks, others showing strange transformations into spirit-like beings. Dragon or tortoise motifs cast on the head have been found, recalling those cast onto Shang ritual vessels. The largest bronze human mask is colossal: 1.38 m wide, 65 cm high and with eyeballs which project out 16 cm from their sockets. There are fewer bronze ritual vessels than in Shang contexts, but some are cast in the form of animals or plants: there is a dragon, tiger, snake, bird, cockerel and fruits. The more conventional vessels, hardly numbering more than ten, recall those of the Middle and Late Shang of the Central Plains. Others recall those of the middle Yangzi and southern Shaanxi, but there is no doubting their local manufacture for there are regional characteristics too.

The bronzes were layered, above and below ivory and jades. One layer of the former comprised many tens of elephant tusks. Over 100 objects in gold were also found, including the sheet gold covering of a staff 1.42 m long. These, not to mention the thousands of stone and ceramic objects, indicate a society which disposed of very considerable power and energy, not only in the provision of the defences, but also the organisation of bronzeworkers who had the skill and resources to cast reputedly one of the tallest bronze human figures known in the ancient world (Fig. 3.14).

Chang (1986) has suggested that the many bronzes of Shang and Western Zhou inspiration in the Yangzi Valley represent the adoption by the local inhabitants of bronze as a medium for expressing status. This is one strand in the development in the middle Yangzi area of the Chu state, which reached its apogee in the period of Eastern Zhou. At Zhaojiahu, 297 burials were excavated, the sequence illustrating a development from Western Zhou to Chu. Over 1000 Chu graves have been excavated at Changsha and, although preservation has not been good, those with the grave protected from water by a layer of clay provide some indication of the energy expended on the larger interments, some of which were equipped with access ramps as in the Shang cemetery at Anyang. Twenty-one well-preserved graves were found at the bottom of rectangular shafts filled with rammed soil. The walls contain niches for placing offerings. The corpse was enclosed in a wooden coffin made of mortise and tenon construction, and may also have been laid on a wooden bier bearing open-work decoration. Three mortuary phases have been identified, corresponding to the Warring States period and early Western Han. Eighty-two bronze swords were recovered, some in lacquer sheaths, and halberds bore the characters of an undeciphered script. There were also bronze vessels and mirrors (HPM 1959).

The initial use of bronze in the lower Yangzi Valley also seems to have been a response to northern stimuli. In Anhui and Jiangsu provinces, Zeng Zhaoyu and Yin Huanzhang (1959) have reported 159 sites which have been ascribed to the Hushu culture. The sites again congregate on slightly elevated ground adjacent to low-lying river flats. They contain pottery decorated with impressed geometric designs, a style widespread down the eastern seaboard of China south of the Yangzi Estuary. Several sites have also yielded bronzes. At Suojincun, for example, knives and fishhooks have been recovered. Beiyinyangying has furnished the remains of pottery crucibles (Chang 1986). Twenty-nine bronze items were found at Taigangsi. These early bronzes probably reflect contact in one form or another with the Shang, and the presence of crucibles in small village communities indicates that we are by no means restricted to exchange to account for the presence of bronze.

a   b   c

3.14 Three bronzes from Sanxingdui. **a.** Bronze figure, 2.62 m high. **b.** Bronze head, 47 cm high, **c.** Bronze head, 29 cm high.
Sources: **a** and **c**, a leaflet describing the material from the Palace Museum, Beijing, 1987; **b**, *Orientations*, December 1987:51.

Summary

Agricultural communities are found in the Yangzi and Huanghe valleys by 6500 BC. There was a proliferation of sites, based on rice cultivation in the former area and millet in the latter. Over four millennia, there was a marked increase in social differentiation, seen in the development of sumptuary goods, particularly ceramics and jade jewellery, and their restriction to a limited number of individuals. The development of rice cultivation in the Yangzi Valley took place among people who spoke languages within the Austric phylum. Expansionary movement downstream over the millennia saw the establishment of sites such as Hemudu, and the occupation of Taiwan by speakers of a language or languages within the Austronesian family. There was also expansion upstream which ultimately saw the development of Austroasiatic languages. The Brahmaputra, Salween, Mekong, Xiangjiang, Ganjiang and Red rivers then opened the way to the occupation of tropical Southeast Asia and eastern India.

Towards the end of the third millennium BC in the Huanghe Valley, objects of copper and bronze were found in growing numbers. The range of artefacts is distinct from those found rather later in Southeast Asia. During the early centuries of the second millenium BC, a series of particularly large defended sites were constructed, and these have furnished a small but consistent body of evidence for a knowledge of bronze working. By the third phase at the palace centre of Erlitou, dated to about 1700–1500 BC, sumptuary items of bronze, including vessels cast in piece moulds, were in use.

The conversion of bronze into items of ritual and display rapidly accelerated during the period of the Shang civilisation (1766–1122 BC) and the scale of production rose to include specialised full-time metal workers, and presumably a well organised system of copper and tin mining and smelting. The use of the bronze was adopted in the states which developed during this period in the Yangzi Valley, a trend most clearly documented at Sanxingdui (13–12th centuries BC). This city, located north of Chengdu in Sichuan, was a centre of bronze production and is strategically located for communication with Southeast Asia via the Lancang-Mekong, Ganjiang, Xiangjiang and Red rivers. Over many millennia, these great rivers had provided conduits for the passage of people, goods and ideas.

CHAPTER 4

SOUTH OF THE MOUNTAINS

Lingnan and Bac Bo

Lingnan is the name given by the Chinese to the 'land south of the mountains', as indeed, viewed from the *zhongyuan,* it is. Bac Bo is the Vietnamese name for the lower valley and delta of the Red or Hong River. The latter flows from the northwest through precipitous uplands to its flat and extensive delta, while the many rivers which drain Lingnan enter the South China Sea 600 km to the east. There is an extensive coastal shelf, which was inundated progressively during the Holocene rise in sea level (Huang Jinsen 1984, Yang Huairen and Xie Zhiren 1984). The nature of the communities which occupied this drowned region is unknown, but many prehistoric sites have been found on raised beaches formed when the sea rose higher than its present level. Nanhailand, the name given to the drowned continental shelf by Meacham (1983, 1985) is seen as the territory from which the earliest archaeologically visible coastal population originated. The marine-estuarine habitat is one of the richest known in terms of self-replenishing food resources. With the establishment of a higher sea level, the region would have had a relatively narrow coastal plain backed by forested uplands. The major deltas would have been far less extensive than they are at present. The climate of ing season for rice, and a cooler dry season (Fig. 4.1). Described in broad terms as tropical, it provides a sharp contrast with the equally hot summers but much colder winters which characterise the Yangzi Valley. The continuous growing season in this tropical region encourages a luxuriant vegetation, many of the tree species being evergreen (Tregear 1980).

Bac Bo centres on the broad lower plain of the Red River after it leaves the confines of the Truong Son Cordillera (Fig. 4.2). This chapter will include the valleys of the Ma and Ca rivers to the south, in order to cover the area which witnessed the development of the Dong Son culture. The Bac Bo plain owes its formation to the silt brought down by the Red River, and has traditionally, and in terms of folklore, been the heartland of the Vietnamese people from the third millennium BC. Today, it comprises 54% of agricultural land in northern Vietnam and 70% of all crop production. Its climate is singular due to its maritime setting. Winter begins in December, with the onset of the northeast monsoon. Daytime temperatures average 10–15°C. January is the coldest month and has either a dry cold or a cold drizzly climate. The temperature rises slightly in February and there is usually more drizzle, but in March and April, the Siberian high pressure area loses intensity and it becomes warmer. This signals the beginning of the rice planting season which is well underway in May, when hot tropical winds originating in the Bay of Bengal reach the delta. The southeast monsoon reaches its peak between June and July, when very hot conditions coincide with heavy rains. The karst uplands which fringe the delta and coastal plain carry a dense, canopied forest where damp and misty weather prevails and trees grow to a great size over many centuries. The oldest *Terminalia* tree recorded, for example, has lived for over a millennium.

This area is critical in appreciating possible relationships between Southeast Asia and the expansive Neolithic communities, and later the states, of the Yangzi and Huanghe valleys. Two north-flowing rivers provide natural routes for the exchange of goods, ideas and the movement of peoples between Lingnan and the Yangzi Valley. The Ganjiang empties into Lake Poyang, the Xiangjiang into Lake Dongting. In reviewing the prehistoric sequence, we will encounter several periods when local and northern, alien traditions met.

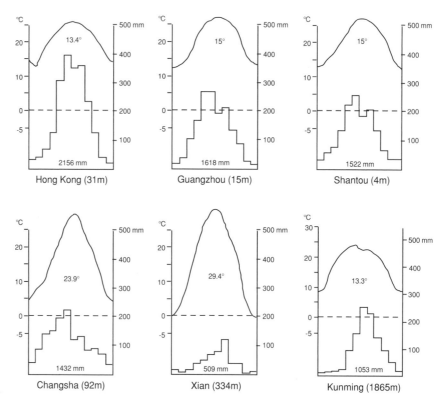

4.1   Climate data illustrating the differences between sites in Lingnan (top row) with Yunnan (Kunming), the Yangzi Valley (Changsha) and the *zhongyuan* (Xian).

For locations, see Fig. 1.1. The climate becomes more extreme as one proceeds in a northerly direction.

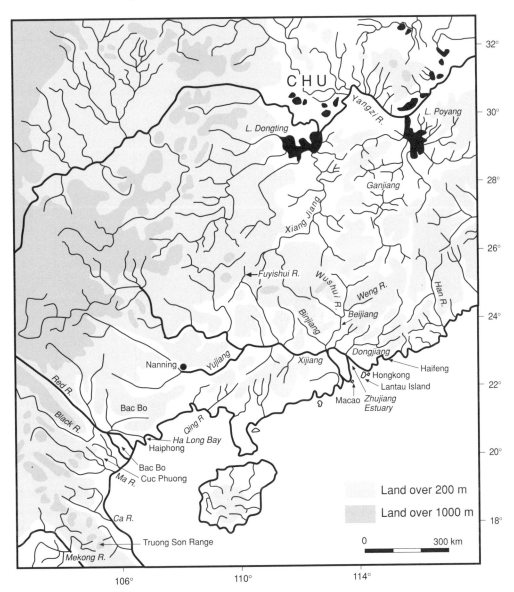

4.2   The location of the principal places mentioned in chapter 4. Lingnan is
dominated by the Yujiang, Xijiang and Zhujiang rivers.

Because the unfolding pattern is complex, it will be briefly summarised
(Fig. 4.3). Both Chinese and Vietnamese archaeologists have long employed the
term 'Neolithic' to describe the communities which occupied this area from the
early Holocene to the Bronze Age. There are three subdivisions: the Early, Middle
and Late. This nomenclature recognises that pottery and polished stone implements were present for millennia, but it rests uneasily with the lack of any
convincing evidence for agriculture or animal husbandry until the Late Neolithic

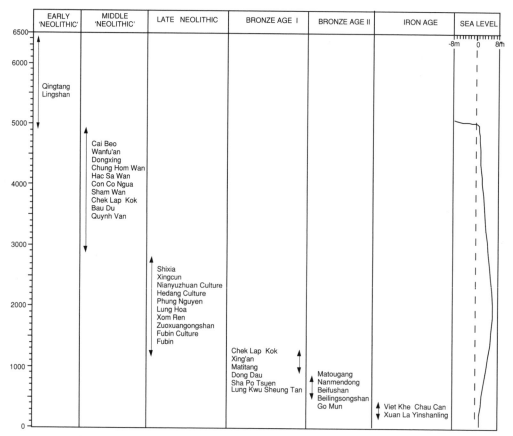

4.3   The principal elements of the cultural sequence in Lingnan and Bac Bo.

in the third millennium BC. It is argued that the numerous coastal communities in question involved foragers who settled for months if not years in this rich coastal habitat. The first evidence for rice comes from sites strategically located south of the riverine route from the middle Yangzi Valley, and the material culture clearly relates to the cultures of that region. It will be argued that rice cultivation was introduced into Lingnan through this expansionary movement.

The bronze age has two distinct strands. A small but growing corpus of jades and bronzes dating to the late Shang and Western Zhou periods have been found in this area, some in Late Neolithic contexts. The exotic bronzes include bells and vessels. Although the chronological context of the initial evidence for local bronze casting is still slightly blurred, it is evident that small axes, arrowheads, fishhooks and spears were being cast at about the same time or slightly later than the contexts within which we find Shang jades. These first local products copy those long since made locally in stone or bone. With the Spring and Autumn and Warring States periods, when the Chu civilisation represented a potent force in the mid-Yangzi Valley, we will again find much evidence for exchange between the two regions which on this occasion involved not only sumptuary bronzes but also iron tools and weapons.

Affluent foragers

Until about 5000 BC, Lingnan and Bac Bo incorporated extensive coastal plains. Thereafter, the sea covered this terrain, and rising higher than at present, formed a series of raised beaches. In consequence, our knowledge of the prehistoric sequence up to 5000 BC is confined to the inland adaptation while settlement on the raised beaches after this date provides evidence for coastal occupation as well (Fig. 4.4). It is surely the case that the latter represents a very long term pattern

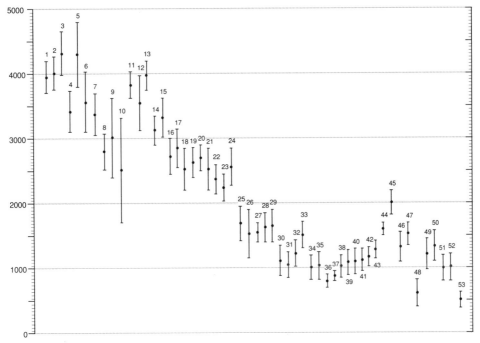

4.4 Radiocarbon dates for the Neolithic and Bronze Age of Lingnan and Bac Bo (2 sigma corrected range BC).
1. Haideiwan (HAR-2522). **2-7.** Yung Long (HAR-54626-7, 60313, 60315, 62188-9). **8.** Sai Wan (Har-6). **9.** Chung Hom Wan (I-8827). **10.** Sham Wan (R-4585/1). **11-13.** Fu Tei (R-42857-8, 63461). **14-15.** Kwo Lo Wan (R-45150, 60795). **16-18.** Shixia (Bk-76024, 75046, 75050). **19-24.** Yung Long (B-5424-5, 60312, 62190, 62218-9). **25-28.** Trang Kenh (Bln, Bln, Ariz, Bln). **29.** Dong Dau (Bln-830). **30.** Doi Giam (Bln-1409). **31-33.** Kwo Lo Wan (B-45149, 46868, 60794). **34.** Lung Kwu Sheung Tan (Beta-40993). **35.** Sha Po Tsuen (Beta-54251). **36-39.** Tung Wan Tsai (Wk-3487, 3486, 3482). **40-52.** Thanh Den (Bln-3263, 3262, 2981, 2953, 2955, 2954a, 2957, 3261, 2956, 3264, NZ-6387, 6372, 6354). **53.** Tra Kenh (ZK-307). **54.** Go Vuan Choi (Bln-894). **55-56.** An Son (Bln-2091/1, 2091/2). **57.** Go Mun (Bln-1278).

which saw reliance on the rich resources of the tropical coast. Many regional coastal groups have been described as Neolithic. While there is much evidence for the use of pottery and the polishing of stone implements, no biological evidence for agriculture has been identified until the third millennium BC. This does not rule out the possibility of plant manipulation, such as removing the competitors of a favoured species, but the remains of shellfish, fish remains and other faunal remains point overwhelmingly to foraging. Nor is there any reference before the third millennium BC to the use of rice chaff to improve the qualities of potting clay. The received sequence until about 2800 BC incorporates an Early and a Middle Neolithic and in describing it, it is stressed that the communities, particularly those occupying the coastal habitat, are better conceived as affluent foragers rather than agriculturalists.

The potential of the coastal environment for a subsistence strategy based on fishing, shellfish collecting and foraging for appropriate plant food has been demonstrated by the ethnographic research in the Andaman Sea of Rogers and Engelhardt among the Chaw Lay (Rogers and Engelhardt 1994). These people remain dependent on fishing and collecting, and their settlement pattern involves both semi-permanent and temporary sites recognised on the basis of the accumulation of shell middens, postholes for house supports and compacted surfaces created by domestic activities and the passage of feet. The food obtained from the forest fringe, particularly the coconut palm and certain mangrove resources, supplements the diet of fish. Shellfish collecting is an essential component in the diet for its predictability when fishing is ruled out by the weather or seasonal deficiencies. Their studies have pinpointed the navigational skills and expert seamanship of the Chaw Lay, and the considerable distances over which they range, both factors likely to facilitate the rapid exchange of goods and information.

Affluent foragers until 4000 BC (Early Neolithic)

The tradition of foraging in inland sites assuredly had its roots in the upper Pleistocene, for at Dushizai and Huangyandong, there is abundant evidence for hunting and gathering in a habitat which included access to rivers or lakes (Fig. 4.5). No pottery has been found at either site (Zhu Feisu 1984) but some stone tools have polished edges. Sites of similar antiquity belonging to the Hoabinhian tradition of Bac Bo have been dated at Xom Trai and Lang Vanh (Ha Van Tan 1994). From about 5000 BC, we encounter a tradition of making pottery and polishing stone adzes in the earliest available coastal sites. Shiweishan and Chenqiaocun, for example, include round-based pottery vessels fired at a low temperature of the order of 680°C. Pottery and polishing have also been recovered in a series of inland rockshelters known as the Qingtang sites (Zhu Feisu 1984). Lingshan County in the upper valley of the Qing River also includes a series of small rockshelters which contained a few pieces of cord-marked pottery and flaked stone implements (Meacham 1978). To the east in the Weng

River valley, there are further caves in Wengyuan County (GuPM 1961). Animal bones were associated with flaked stone implements, and a few ground and polished stone tools were found with fragments of cord-marked, burnished and net-impressed pottery.

Affluent foragers 4000–2800 BC (the Middle Neolithic)

This second phase is recognised on the basis of a marked increase in the number of sites, which are distributed on raised shorelines and alluvial river valleys. The former reveal a sophisticated bone and shell industry, and pottery became more abundant. Some polished adzes were now provided with shoulders to assist in hafting (Zhu Feisu 1984). Perhaps the best-known sequence has been found at Xiqiaoshan, a volcanic hill on the margins of the Zhujiang Estuary (GuPM 1959, Yang Shiting 1985). The lower slopes are rich in prehistoric sites, and although none reveals a deep stratigraphy, there are sufficient differences between the assemblages to suggest a sequence (GuPM 1959, Meacham 1978). One site, for example, had no ceramics nor polished stone implements, and has been ascribed to the earliest occupation of the area. Eight later sites contained the same sort of flaked stone scrapers, adzes and choppers as were also found at Cai Beo, 600 km to the west. Some also show an interest in edge grinding and polishing. The pottery, which was tempered with sand, was plain or decorated with incisions, cord marking or basket impressions.

At Wanfu'an, on the opposite side of the Zhujiang Estuary, two shell middens have been examined. These have a stratified sequence which begins with a stone industry recalling the flaked implements from Xiqiaoshan. The pottery also has marked affinities with the early material from that area. The shell middens at Dongxing are located on a raised beach, the sequence beginning with a layer containing flaked stone implements and some pottery. The next stage saw the introduction of polished stone tools. Pottery was thick, described as coarse and was decorated with cord marks, incisions and basketry and mat impressions. There were some bone projectile points, awls and needles (GuPM 1961). Sites to the northeast near Chao'an, on the Han River delta, were also located on raised beaches between 19 and 30 km inland. These reveal a similar material culture to the Dongxing sites: flaked pebble choppers, scrapers and points, some partially polished stone adzes and points and pottery tempered with shell or sand. Decoration included red slipping, cord marking, burnishing and incising.

This period in Hong Kong begins with a phase of painted pottery described by Meacham (1994) as the Chung Hom Wan or Middle Neolithic (MN) I. The stratigraphic distinctiveness of this period was settled with excavations on the western side of the Zhujiang Estuary at Hac Sa Wan on Macao, and this has been confirmed at Chek Lap Kok and Yung Long on Hong Kong. The radiocarbon determinations from recent excavations date this period to 4100–3600 BC. It was followed by a change from painted to incised pottery characteristic of MNII and dated from 3600 to 3000 BC.

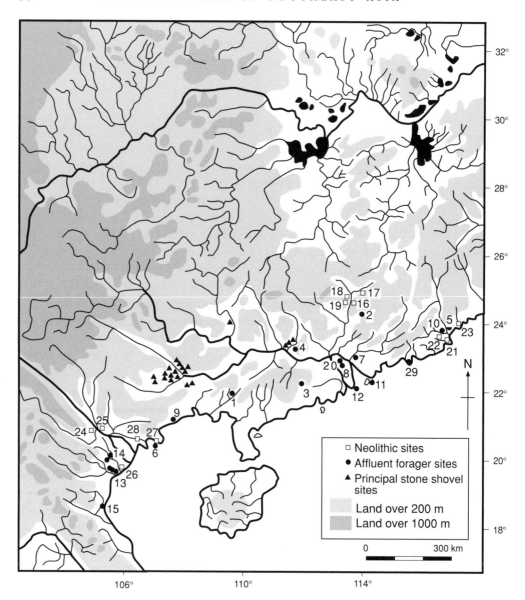

4.5 Sites of affluent foragers and the Neolithic in Lingnan and Bac Bo.
1. Lingshan County. **2.** Wengyuan County. **3.** Dushizai. **4.** Huangyandong.
5. Shiweishan. Chenqiaocun. **6.** Cai Beo. **7.** Wanfu'an. **8.** Xiqiaoshan. **9.**
Dongxing. **10.** Chao'an. **11.** Chung Hom Wan, Chek Lap Kok, Yung Long,
Sham Wan. **12.** Hac Sa Wan. **13.** Da But, Con Co Ngua, Go Trung. **14.** Xom
Trai, Con Moong. **15.** Quynh Van. **16.** Shixia. **17.** Xincun. **18.** Chuangbanling,
Niling. **19.** Nianyuzhuan Culture. **20.** Hedang. **21.** Zuoxuangongshan. **22.**
Futoubu. **23.** Dingdapushan, Tazaijinshan. **24.** Go Bong, Phung Nguyen.
25. Lung Hoa. **26.** Hoa Loc. **27.** Ha Long. **28.** Trang Kenh. **29.** Son.

In 1971, an important multidisciplinary excavation was undertaken at Sham Wan on Lamma Island, Hong Kong (Meacham 1978). The site was situated on a sand bar which formed between the main island and an islet following the rise and then fall of the sea level between about 5000 and 3000 BC. The initial settlement, in what would have been a mangrove-lagoonal habitat, belongs to the MNII Sham Wan phase. It contained pottery and many polished stone tools. The former includes fine paste so called 'chalky' bowls and dishes, but is numerically dominated by a coarse cord-marked ware, in which quartz and sand were abundant. Meacham (1978:127) has suggested that this material might have been present in the clay naturally. Vessels were made by the paddle and anvil technique. After cord marking, a curvilinear decoration was applied with a toothed implement. Some reconstructed pots reveal round-based vessels with an everted rim which is very common in Southeast Asia. Charcoal stains on the bases show that they were used for cooking. Residue analysis to determine what was cooked is most desirable.

Adzes are the most common form of stone tool in the earliest layer at Sham Wan. Most had a trapezoid outline and sub-lentoid cross section (Meacham 1978:184). There were also three shouldered adzes. Grooved polishing or grinding stones used to fashion and sharpen such adzes were abundant. Flaked tools without polishing were also common, and have been described as picks, choppers and scrapers.

There are several sites in the Hong Kong area with material comparable to the MNII horizon at Sham Wan. These confirm the coastal orientation and fourth millennium date, Chung Hom Wan having provided a radiocarbon date of 3400 BC. Maglioni (1975) also identified a number of similar sites during his surveys in Haifeng. He suggested a date between 4000 and 3000 BC for his so-called Son assemblage. Settlements are located on raised beaches at a similar elevation above sea level as Sham Wan. The pottery at Son itself has the same chalky incised wares as at Sham Wan, together with cord marking under incised wavy lines. There are many flaked stone tools and the polished adzes are similar to MNII forms.

Recent excavations on Chek Lap Kok have provided new and important information on the MNII (Meacham 1994). At Kwo Lo Wan, for example, numerous postholes, pits and hearths were encountered in a site which must have had a marine orientation. Specific stone-working areas were found, and among the material culture, there was a considerable number of small polished stone adzes which may well have been resharpened over a long period until their size ruled out further use. Seven pits were found to contain offerings in the form of polished adzes, pottery vessels (some of which could be reconstructed) and a polished quartz slotted ring. These have been interpreted as burials, although as is so often the case in this area, organic remains, such as bone, have not survived. This makes it particularly difficult to assess economic aspects of these MN sites. Were they occupied by sedentary fishing and foraging communities, or was there also an agricultural component to subsistence? Some of the pebble grinders found could have been used for food processing, and the analysis of possible residues might be one avenue for further progress on this elusive subject. Following his consideration of all relevant sites, Li Guo (1994) has suggested that these communities were involved in broadly based foraging, with a marine orientation, rather than agriculture.

Several regional groups have been identified on the raised beaches to the southwest (Bui Vinh 1991). They have many variables in common but also their own distinct characteristics. From north to south, we begin on the islands of Ha Long Bay, and in particular the site of Cai Beo. The interesting point about the first of the three phases of development at this site, is the similarity between the flaked stone tool industry and that identified in the upland Hoabinhian cave sites. There is also an abundance of pottery, decorated with basketry impressions. Ha Van Tan (1994) reports that the ceramic vessels were rather crudely made and fired at a low temperature. During the middle phase, axes with shoulders were encountered, and these were often polished on both sides but not to the extent of removing all the flake scars which result from the initial shaping of the implement. This trend towards polishing the surface of axes continued into the third phase. Dating the sequence is based on five radiocarbon dates, of which at least two, with readings in excess of 40,000 years, are unacceptable. Ha Van Tan cites a date of 4609–4352 BC for the base of the middle layer as being the most likely to be accurate.

This is supported by the dating of related groups to the south. The sequence in the lower Ma Valley, for example, begins with the site of Da But, followed first by the material from Con Co Ngua and finally, that from Go Trung. With time, these sites were located progressively closer to the modern shore, probably as a result of progradation and a lowering of the sea level. Da But was first examined by Patte (1932). He encountered twelve burials in which the body was interred in a seated position, accompanied by pottery vessels, shell jewellery, stone axes and red ochre. It is not a large site, covering only 50 by 32 m, but attains a depth of 5 m. The deposits largely comprise shellfish from an estuarine habitat. Pollen also indicates the presence of saltmarsh nearby (Nguyen Dich Dy *et al.* 1980). Bui Vinh (1991) has described more recent excavations, from which it has become clear that the site was the scene of domestic activities. There are hearths, much pottery and animal bones. The pottery is described as being coarse and basket-impressed, the clay being tempered with laterite. Some of the stone adzes were polished and these, together with the pottery, are closely paralleled in some of the rock shelters in the outliers of the Truong Son range to the west, such as Con Moong and Xom Trai in the Cuc Phuong region. According to Vu The Long (1979), some of the animal bones come from a bovid of domestic size. The five radiocarbon dates suggest occupation within the period 4500–3700 BC.

Con Co Ngua covers 2000 m², and like Da But, contains burials in a seated position. Basal shellfish indicate a continuation of the maritime adaptation, but in the upper layers, they ceased to be found, suggesting that occupation continued after a fall in the sea level, or coastal progradation, had seriously altered the environment. It is in this later context that Bui Vinh has noted a series of significant changes in material culture. These, dated to about 3500 BC, included net sinkers and stone hoes, as well as bones ascribed by Vu The Long to pig and water buffalo of probable domestic origin.

Go Trung is located to the east of Con Co Ngua and Da But, and excavations there in an area of 170 m² reveal continuity, although the site has been dated at least 500 years later than Con Co Ngua. The excavators also recovered pestles and mortars, net sinkers and the remains of sea fish.

The Quynh Van culture sites concentrate in the lower reaches of the Ca River, about 100 km south of Go Trung. While the mortuary ritual of seated, flexed burials recurs, the stone industry differed from the Da But–Go Trung sites, for no edge grinding was encountered. Pottery was found, however, mostly decorated with comb impressions. The radiocarbon dates for this site indicate settlement *c.* 2700 BC. Later sites in this region, however, saw the development of edge grinding and the manufacture of stone hoes. Further south still, we encounter the same flexed, seated burial tradition at Bau Du, which was located in a coastal, probably estuarine setting. Despite its relatively late dates of 3030 and 2510 BC, no pottery or ground stone tools were recovered. Indeed, the flaked stone tools are very similar to those from the upland Hoabinhian sites.

Vietnamese archaeologists have sought the origins of these coastal communities in upland Hoabinhian contexts. But surely, the most likely antecedents lie on the submerged coastal shelf. Sites on raised beaches are small: 0.2 ha for Con Co Ngua, 0.16 ha for Da But. While the excavators describe the sites as Neolithic, there is no evidence for the cultivation of plants such as rice. As is well known from the Japanese Jomon sites, pottery, polished stone tools and cemeteries can well develop in rich coastal habitats without the presence of agriculture. We are faced with two possibilities. These sites might have been occupied by sedentary foragers, who took advantage of the rich resources to be found on a mangrove-fringed shore punctuated by estuaries. Some groups might have begun gathering and ultimately propagating rice, a trend which would have been encouraged by environmental unpredictability. Progradation or major flooding could have been stressful. There are signs that these communities enlarged the scope of their material culture: hoes and pestles and mortars hint at the possibility of rice cultivation, but do not demonstrate it.

The first rice farmers (Late Neolithic)

We have seen that Lingnan is linked with the Yangzi Valley by the Ganjiang and Xiangjiang rivers, the former flowing north into Lake Poyang, the latter into Lake Dongting. The headwaters of the Beijiang, which flows south, are a bare 20 km from the Ganjiang, thus providing a link between the rich and innovative agricultural communities of the Yangzi and the extensive river valleys of Lingnan.

It is hardly surprising, therefore, to find compelling evidence for intrusive settlement in the Beijiang Valley from the north, involving sites which provide unequivocal evidence for the cultivation of rice.

The principal site is Shixia, a 3 ha mound with three cultural phases. The lowest, dated between 2850 and 2500 BC, incorporated a cemetery in which 108 burials have been excavated. The rite, extended inhumation with the head normally pointing to the east, incorporated the placement of grave goods and the use of fire which has scorched the grave walls. Offerings include pottery vessels in a wide range of forms some of which find precise parallels in contemporary Liangzhu culture sites to the north. The stone implements and jewellery also recall northern, Liangzhu forms particularly the stone *cong* tubes and bracelets, pendants, hairpins and slit rings. There are several similar sites in the general area, including Xincun, Chuangbanling and Niling.

The sequel to this intrusive settlement in the upper Beijiang catchment is seen in the sites of the Nianyuzhuan culture, represented at several sites including the middle layer of Shixia itself. Here, we find modifications in the mortuary ritual, but also an element of continuity. The 32 burials of this second phase are still found orientated on an east-west axis, and extended inhumation remained the norm. Grave goods included fine ceramic vessels, decorated with a great range of impressed designs, but the exotic stone ornaments are lacking. One of the important points about this culture, represented at several sites, such as Nianyuzhuan itself, Pushaoshan and Zoumagang, is the recovery of oval or round kilns for firing the fine, thin-walled pottery found as grave offerings. The stone industry, too, shows considerable refinement in the manufacture of projectile points, adzes, chisels and spearheads.

This intrusive impetus did not, as far as is known, reach the coastal tract, where we find strong strands of continuity meshed with a number of new features. Hedang, which gives its name to a group of sites in the Zhujiang Delta region, saw a continuation of the exploitation of marine resources in association with pottery impressed with geometric designs. Firing temperatures were in excess of 1000°C. The site includes thick deposits of shell and dates to the late third millennium BC. It has yielded 77 inhumation graves, in which males were interred with polished stone adzes, females with spindle whorls. Tooth evulsion was common. Some very fine ornaments were also recovered, made from ivory, as well as exotic stone bracelets and slit rings. There was also a vigorous bone industry, which produced hairpins, needles, awls and weaving shuttles. A fortuitous find at Maogang included the remains of domestic wooden structures nearly 15 m in length, which were rectangular, and raised on wooden piles. The degree to which these people incorporated rice agriculture into their subsistence activities, however, is not known and Zhu Feisu (1984) has adroitly pointed out that this innovation appears to have been slow to develop in such coastal, estuarine contexts. Li Guo (1994) has further suggested that there may well have been an increasing trend towards agriculture, but not at the expense of exploiting the marine habitat. He also suggested that rice cultivation would in all likelihood have been derived from a northerly source, presumably incorporating such sites as Shixia. Radiocarbon determinations place this culture in the period 3000–2000 BC.

This Late Neolithic period clearly encompassed a series of regional traditions, none of which was more tightly distributed or singular in its characteristics than the 'stone shovel' sites of southern Guangxi (Allard 1995). These large and enigmatic artefacts, the largest of which stand up to 70 cm in height, were often made of stone unsuited to any possible agricultural or industrial function. Groups of shovels were commonly found interred in pits, positioned vertically. No associated settlements have been found and ritual activity of some form is the most likely explanation.

In Hong Kong, the Late Neolithic (LN) has been subdivided into two phases. LNI, named after the site of Yung Long, is again characterised by geometric decoration on the pottery, imparted by a carved paddle and a decorated anvil. It has been dated from about 2650 BC (Meacham 1993). Excavations have uncovered graves on a north-south orientation, containing pottery vessels and slit stone rings. Jadeite ceremonial axes suggest to Chiu (1993), the development of a strong ritual element by this juncture. The ceramic assemblage developed into the classic soft geometric or LNII, which belongs to the first half of the second millennium BC. Excavations at Sha Lo Wan, a promontory commanding views across the Zhujiang Estuary to the mainland, have revealed an occupation site of this period (Chiu 1993). As in the preceding phases, there are ovens, postholes and much pottery. Spindle whorls and net weights attest a textile industry and fishing, and there were numerous stone adzes and projectile points. Excavations at Tung Kwu have also exposed a LN occupation containing much soft geometric pottery and utilised stone, but again, insufficient organic material to illuminate the subsistence base (Kelly 1975, Meacham 1975c). Late Neolithic occupation even extended to islets, such as Sha Chau, as small as 7 ha (Frost 1975). In addition to the typical LN pottery at site 56.1 on the western edge of this island, excavations revealed the local manufacture of stone rings.

The Hanjiang Estuary and its riverine hinterland in eastern Guangdong saw a cultural sequence not dissimilar to that recognised in the Xijiang catchment to the west. Over the period from approximately 3000 to 1500 BC, Zhu Feisu (1984) has described three phases, named after the sites of Zuoxuangongshan, Wugongshan and Houshan. We again encounter settlements located on the coastal fringe and on raised ground adjacent to the main rivers, and the local firing of pottery impressed with geometric designs. The middle phase at Futoubu has also yielded sophisticated kilns used over a lengthy period of time for firing pottery vessels, and the local stone industry flourished, providing polished adzes, arrowheads, knives and awls. The last phase saw a locally distinctive pottery form, a jug in the shape of a chicken.

The Fubin culture

The sites ascribed to this culture are pivotal in our understanding of the Late Neolithic in Lingnan because the presence in graves of exotic stone artefacts which, along with glazed pottery and incised symbols, allows us to relate the sites to the late Shang and early Western Zhou dynasties, that is a couple of centuries either side of 1100 BC. They follow the later Neolithic sites just described, clustering in the valley of the Hanjiang, the adjacent coastal plain and into southern Fujian Province, with a preferred location on low hills. Pottery vessels predominate among the grave goods, and there is also a new range of highly sophisticated stone weapons and ornaments. Among the former, the *ge* halberd is most informative, because it provides parallels with related weapons from the *zhongyuan*. The presence of glazed pottery bearing incised symbols or numbers also indicates relations with communities in Jiangxi Province (Allard 1995). Jade rings are also found, and to judge from the variation in the size of the grave and the quantity of offerings among the 22 interments at Wanglan, these late Neolithic communities displayed an element of social ranking. This same tendency was noted at Tazaijinshan, where the richest and largest grave also occupied the summit of the hill. This particular grave, number 1 among the 16 excavated, involved considerable energy: it measures 4.2 × 2.9 m, and the base is 3.6 m deep. It is also one of eight equipped with a ledge running round the basal part. Ceramic vessels predominate among the 36 grave goods, and there are also three *ge* halberds, but while contemporary with the vigorous and long-established Shang to early Western Zhou bronze tradition, no grave at the site has yielded any bronze artefacts. There is some doubt over the context of a bronze *ge* halberd from the nearby site of Dingdapushan, found in association with a Fubin style stone adze, but in the other Fubin sites, we find the same situation: ceramics and fine stone artefacts which indicate some form of relationship with complex societies in the *zhongyuan,* but no metal.

The Phung Nguyen culture

A thousand kilometres to the southwest, we meet the delta of the Red River and the Phung Nguyen culture. As with the Fubin sites and Shixia, this represents a marked departure from the earlier pattern of settlement. Sites are located on slightly elevated terrain commanding stream valleys above the confluence of the Red and Black rivers. There are three phases, based on changes in pottery typology, which Ha Van Tan (1991) has dated between the end of the third millennium BC and about 1500 BC. The earliest, Go Bong phase, is characterised by pottery decorated with burnished areas interspersed with incised bands filled with fine impressions. Spirals and 'S' motifs were popular. This technique was modified by the second phase, the decoration being more formally applied but still retaining the spirals and 'S' motif. The infilled bands became less popular with the final phase and incised decoration now took the form of straight or wavy lines.

Only eleven late sites of the 52 examined contained bronze, and no recognisable metal artefacts have been found. The fragments were, however, made of a tin bronze.

Excavations at Phung Nguyen covered 3960 m², and despite this extensive area opened, no bronze was encountered. The rich material culture included over a thousand adzes or adze fragments. Most were quadrangular in cross-section and rectangular in form, but there were also four shouldered specimens and stepped adzes have been found which recall South Chinese forms. Stone bracelets were particularly abundant at Phung Nguyen, the 540 specimens being divisible into eight types (Nguyen Ba Khoach 1980). There are also a few stone arrowheads and a bone harpoon.

The degree of skill associated with the manufacture of stone jewellery is particularly clearly seen at Trang Kenh (Nguyen Kim Dung 1990). The pottery relates to the late Phung Nguyen styles. At this juncture, it is recalled that some sites of this phase have revealed a few fragments of bronze, and Trang Kenh is interpreted here as one belonging culturally to the terminal Neolithic. Located near the coast at Haiphong, excavations have revealed a wide range of nephrite ornaments, including bracelets and beads, as well as the chisels, drill points, saws and grinding stones used in their manufacture. The radiocarbon dates accord well with the received chronology of the late Phung Nguyen culture, the pooled mean for the four dates being 1679–1514 BC.

Although no burials were found at Phung Nguyen, Hoang Xuan Chinh (1968) has uncovered twelve at Lung Hoa. These had been excavated up to 5.2 m into the ground and were provided, as at the wealthy Fubin sites, with ledges (Fig. 4.6). The offerings in two graves included stone bracelets, beads, earrings, adzes and pottery vessels, but others only contained pots and adzes. The excavators have suggested that this may reflect differential social ranking, although a larger sample would be necessary to examine this issue further. A stone *ge* halberd from burial 9 is a form which can be paralleled in the Fubin sites, such as Tazaijinshan and Yuanguang (Fig. 4.7). Similar, albeit larger examples, are known from Sanxingdui in Sichuan the occupants of which were in contact with the later Shang sites of the Huanghe Valley, where there are jade and bronze examples of this type of halberd. Murowchick (1989) has argued that the presence of such similar artefacts at the same period is most unlikely to result from independent development, and favours exchange contact to explain the presence of the Lung Hoa example. This is not the only instance of contact between the Phung Nguyen culture and Shang China. Ha Van Tan (1993) has described a series of jade *yazhang*, or ceremonial knives of a singular form from Phung Nguyen and Xom Ren (Fig. 4.7). These are precisely matched in the Zhujiang Delta area, at Sanxingdui, Erlitou and later Shang sites and must surely represent imports from the Huanghe Valley (Tang Chung 1994; Fig. 4.8). The dating of the latter sites fits well with the available radiocarbon dates from Bac Bo. Such exchange with the contemporary Neolithic sites of Lingnan, which reached ultimately to Sanxingdui

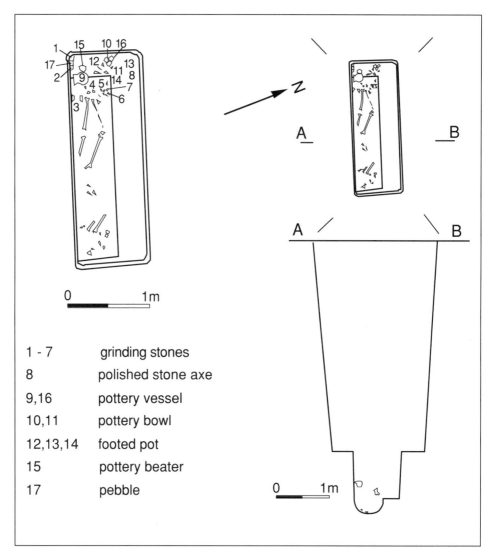

4.6 The cemetery of Lung Hoa contains a series of deep inhumation graves with ledges.

and Anyang, could also have introduced knowledge of the properties of copper and tin.

The Phung Nguyen culture probably became established within the period 2500–2000 BC, and available radiocarbon dates suggest that its late phase was developing into its successor, the Dong Dau phase, from about 1500 BC. Ha Van Tan (1980) has identified parallels in material culture between the Phung Nguyen and the coastal Hoa Loc and Ha Long cultures, both of which succeeded the earlier Quynh Van and Bau Tro cultures on the littoral of the Gulf of Bac Bo. He has ascribed these to exchange contacts.

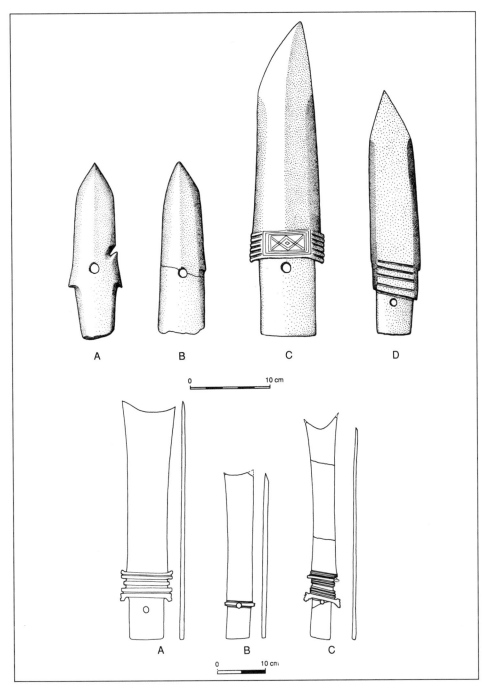

4.7 Stone artefacts from Lingnan, Sichuan and the *zhongyuan*.
Top row: halberds from **a.** Lung Hoa. **b.** Tazaijinshan. **c.** Sanxingdui. **d.** Erlitou.
Bottom row: jade *yazhang* blades from **a.** Erlitou. **b, c.** Xom Ren.

The Bronze Age

By the middle of the second millennium BC, we can recognise a series of regional settlement concentrations from the Hanjiang to the Red River deltas (Fig. 4.9). They have a number of features in common. While there remained a distinct coastal orientation, there was also a preference for the establishment of small villages in the inland river valleys. These communities cultivated rice and maintained domestic stock. They also included skilled workers of clay and stone. The former employed enclosed kilns and their fine wares were fired under controlled conditions at high temperatures. The latter made tools and ornaments of high quality, some of which were used as mortuary offerings. The burial technique, extended inhumation, saw a considerable expenditure of energy in the provision of deep graves equipped with ledges, and containing impressive sets of grave goods. These sites have in common a further variable of critical importance. They include jade artefacts which have their closest parallels in later Shang contexts to the north. There can be no doubt that coastal and riverine exchange placed these late Neolithic communities in touch with one of the most sophisticated bronze traditions in the ancient world.

That bronzes travelled the same routes is clearly evident in the recovery of stray finds, the distribution of which again stresses the importance of riverine communication. Perhaps significantly, one of the earliest specimens, a *you* vessel ascribed on the basis of its dragon design to a later Shang context, has been found at Xing'an, almost literally on the watershed between the Xiangjiang which flows north to Lake Dongting, and the Fuyishui, which flows south to the Xijiang (Fig. 4.10; Liang Jingjin 1978). A similarly exotic dragon-phoenix design was identified on a halberd from Xinjie, located in the same part of northeastern Guangxi (GXBWG 1984), while Huang Zhanyue (1986) has noted that the *nao* bell from nearby Zhongshan has close parallels in Hunan. Both these last finds date to the Western Zhou period, as does a probable copy of a *yong* bell from Mei'ershan (Fig. 4.10). Further downstream, at Matitang, a stray *lei* vessel incorporating dragon designs has been recovered, a vessel virtually identical to one from Wushi, in southern Guangxi (GXBWG 1984). The location of Xing'an and Xinjie indicates the most likely exchange route for a marked concentration of early exotic bronzes, or local imitations of exotic forms, northeast of Nanning. It may not be coincidental that the bronzes are found in the same general area as the Late Neolithic caches of stone spades.

The pivotal location of Shixia, however, should not be overlooked, and indeed the upper layers, likewise belonging to the Western Zhou and Spring and Autumn periods, have yielded a significant range of bronzes including a short sword or dagger, an axe, awls and scrapers. These stray finds and the upper context at Shixia suggest a vigorous exchange network linking Lingnan with the Yangzi Valley and ultimately, with the *zhongyuan*. Yuanlongpo, a most important cemetery near the Wuming River valley northeast of Nanning, provides us with

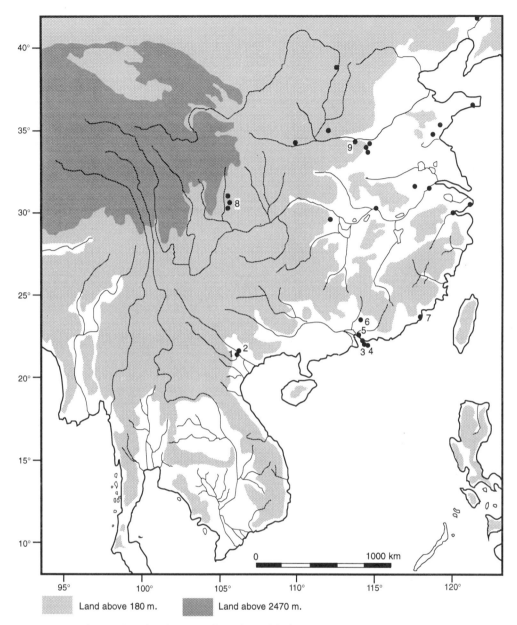

4.8 The distribution of *yazhang* blades.
1. Phung Nguyen. **2.** Xom Ren. **3.** Lamma Island. **4.** Lantao Island.
5. Dongguan Cuntou. **6.** Zengcheng Honghualin. **7.** Zhangpu Meili.
8. Sanxingdui. **9.** Erlitou.

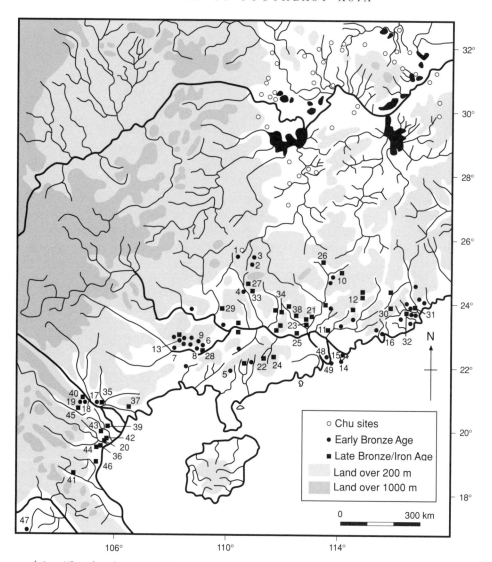

4.9 The distribution of Bronze and Iron Age sites in Lingnan and Bac Bo,
together with that of major Chu centres.
1. Xing'an. **2.** Xinjie. **3.** Zhongshan. **4.** Matitang. **5.** Wushi. **6.** Mei'ershan. **7.**
Tongmeng. **8.** Luxu. **9.** Dabeimiao. **10.** Shixia. **11.** Meicun. **12.** Sanwucun.
13. Yuanlongpo. **14.** Lamma Island. Tai Wan. Sham Wan. **15.** Shek Pik. Kwo
Lo Wan. **16.** Polau, Gebui, Ng Fa. **17.** Dong Dau. **18.** Thanh Den. **19.** Go
Mun. **20.** Quy Chu. **21.** Matougang. **22.** Nanmendong. **23.** Niaodanshan. **24.**
Beifushan. **25.** Beilingsongshan. **26.** Dagongpingcun. **27.** Yangjia. **28.**
Weipocun. **29.** Xia'neicao. **30.** Bayushan. **31.** Miantouling. **32.** Goushipushan.
33. Yinshanling. **34.** Liyangdun. **35.** Co Loa. **36.** Dong Son. **37.** Viet Khe.
38. Tonggugang. **39.** Chau Can. Xuan La. **40.** Lang Ca. **41.** Lang Vac. **42.**
Ngoc Lu. **43.** Hoang Ha, Song Da. **44.** Quang Xuang.,Nong Cong. **45.** Ban
Thom. **46.** Dong Hieu. **47.** Ban Chiang. Ban Na Di. **48.** Doumen. **49.**
Apowan, Tangxiahuan.

glimpse of the role bronze played in mortuary rituals in the early centuries of the first millennium BC (GXBWG 1988, Allard 1995). Unfortunately, the excavation report does not provide the detailed information from each of the 350 burials uncovered, but it is still possible to obtain some valuable results.

The mortuary ritual involved inhumation in individual graves, some of which were provided with a ledge or a side chamber. A wide variety of grave goods was encountered, about 10% being bronzes. Already, these provide a portent of the warfare which was to dominate later bronze assemblages in this region: the items include spearheads, axes, arrowheads, and daggers or short swords. A ritual or

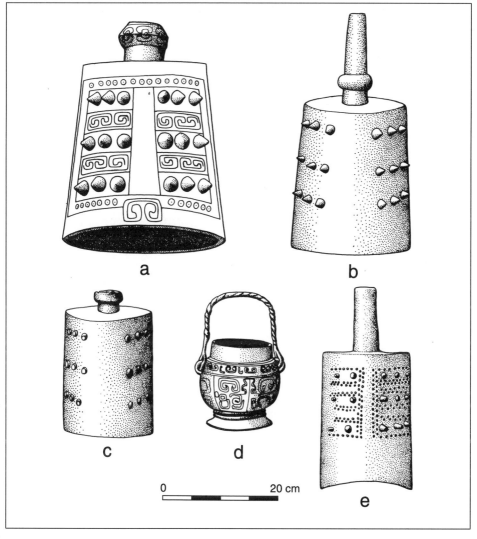

4.10 Early exotic bronzes in Lingnan.
a. *Nao* bell from Zhongshan. **b.** *Yong* bell from Dabeimiao. **c.** *Yong* bell from Tongmeng. **d.** *You* vessel from Xing'an. **e.** *Yong* bell from Mei'ershan.

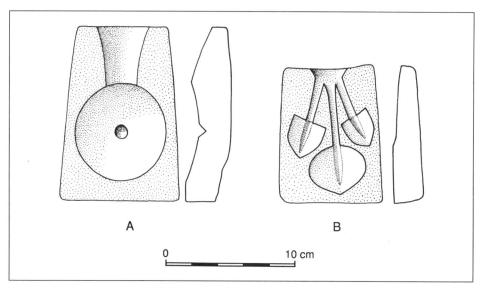

4.11   Sandstone moulds for casting a disc-like object with a raised centre and projectile points from Yuanlongpo.

festive element is also seen in the vessels, at least two of which were probably exotic, and there are also knives and a fragment of bell. The division between imported and local bronzes is facilitated by the recovery of some twelve stone bivalve moulds, some of which were broken probably as part of the mortuary ritual (Fig. 4.11). These were intended for casting *yue* and *fu* axes, *dun* (the tubular cover at the end of a spear), knives and arrowheads. Many jade ornaments were also found as mortuary offerings, and fragments of lacquer indicate some elaboration in the manufacture of coffins. Allard (1995), when summarising this site, has stressed the likelihood that there was some form of social hierarchy, for burial 147 was not only one of only sixteen equipped with a ledge, but it also included a probably exotic *you* bronze vessel, was particularly large and contained more than the usual number of grave goods. It is not, however, possible to probe further and seek evidence for or against the presence of ascribed rank rather than achieved status through personal endeavour.

The period which saw the arrival of exotic bronzes from the *zhongyuan* and the middle reaches of the Yangzi saw, in the context of the Late Neolithic, the beginnings of a local tradition in casting which involved the production in bronze of a limited range of artefacts long since rendered in stone or bone. These comprise arrowheads, axes, fishhooks and spearheads. This regionally distinct tradition, which developed in Lingnan in the context of imported later Shang bronzes, has long been recognised. Thus the conjunction between hard geometric pottery and bronze in Hong Kong sites was noted during the 1930s, for Finn (1958) discovered six axes during his excavations on Lamma Island, four of which were socketed and cast in a bivalve mould. He stressed their affinities with axes found in Vietnam, Laos and Cambodia, noting in particular similarities with those from Samrong Sen. Fishhooks, leaf-shaped knives and arrowheads matching those from Sham Wan have also been found at Man Kok Tsui on the southeast coast of Lantao Island (Watt 1968), but one of the best-known bronze assemblages comes from Tai Wan, about 1.5 km north of Sham Wan. Finn (1936) has described two socketed spearheads from this site, as well as a socketed axe, both of which he compared to similar examples from Bac Bo. One of the spearheads, for example, had the same two slots on the socket as are regular features on examples found to the south.

In 1937, Schofield excavated at Shek Pik on Lantao Island (Meacham 1975b). Although not in stratigraphic contexts, he found six bivalve sandstone moulds for casting socketed axes, three having clear parallels with those from Vietnam and Thailand. The hard geometric layer at the site also furnished a few bronze items. The 1971 excavation at Sham Wan encountered bronze fishhooks and arrowheads, the alloy including about 10% of tin. More recent excavations have clarified the chronology of the Bronze Age in this coastal region (Meacham 1993). There are three determinations from Kwo Lo Wan and one each from Lung Kwu Sheung Tan and Sha Po Tsuen. They suggest the establishment of bronze casting by 1300–1000 BC. Research at Kwo Lo Wan has also added considerably to our knowledge,

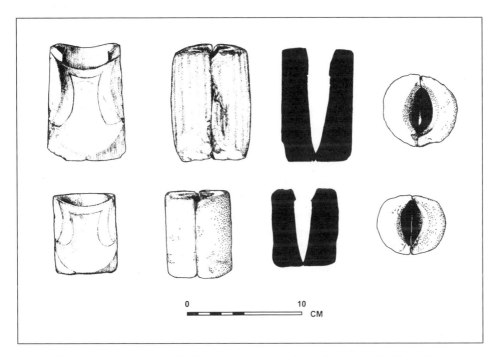

0   10
CM

4.12 Sandstone moulds for casting socketed axes from Kwo Lo Wan, Hong Kong. *Upper:* burial 1. *Lower:* burial 2.
Permission: the Hong Kong Government and the Lord Wilson Heritage Trust.

because burials were identified and the cultural context, dated by three radiocarbon dates between 1300 and 1000 BC (Meacham 1994). Two of the eight burials, which were orientated on a north-south axis, contained bivalve sandstone moulds for casting socketed axes (Fig. 4.12). Other offerings include hard and soft geometric vessels, slotted stone rings of marble and agate, and two bronze projectile points. A further sandstone axe mould has been recovered from Tung Wan Tsai, associated with three radiocarbon dates derived from shell. These range between 1701 and 927 BC (Rogers *et al.* 1995).

Similar material has been found on the mainland nearby. Maglioni (1975) named his Bronze Age phase after the site of Polau, which he discovered in 1940. Several of his sites, examined on surface surveys rather than through excavation, revealed bronze artefacts and evidence for local casting. At Gebui, for example, he recovered the mould for casting a socketed axe. Two further moulds were found at Polau. Ng Fa yielded a bronze bodkin and socketed axe, a socketed spearhead and a chisel. More recent excavations have added to this repertoire, sandstone axe moulds having been recovered from Tangxiahuan, Doumen and Apowan (Li Yan 1995).

The Early Bronze Age in Bac Bo

Exactly the same sequence and chronological framework has been identified in the lower Red River valley. The first bronzes were found in contexts which were receiving exotic northern jades. A few pieces of bronze have been found in some late Phung Nguyen sites, but the following phase, named after the site of Dong Dau, saw a virtually identical range of bronzes and the same casting technology to those found in the Zhujiang Delta area. There is a reasonable corpus of radiocarbon dates for the Dong Dau phase (Fig. 4.4). Most come from Thanh Den, a site with a relatively shallow stratigraphy, and evidence for casting in the form of moulds and melting furnaces. Two of the dates from Thanh Den seem aberrant (Anon 1990), particularly when compared with those available from the later Phung Nguyen contexts. The remaining eleven suggest that bronze working was established within the period 1500–1000 BC, a context which corresponds well with the available dates for virtually the same industry in Hong Kong.

Dong Dau is located just north of the Red River 35 km east of Phung Nguyen. It covers about 3 ha and has a cultural stratigraphy between 5 and 6 m deep. Its basal layer contains late Phung Nguyen pottery, but thereafter the assemblage developed into the Dong Dau culture. Sites are distributed in the same general area as Phung Nguyen settlements. While the pottery continued to be incised with a series of curvilinear lines originating in the Phung Nguyen repertoire and the stone adzes and points continued from local prototypes, there was a flowering of the local bronze industry. Dong Dau and Thanh Den have provided sandstone moulds. Artefacts made from a tin-copper alloy included axes, chisels and arrowheads, socketed spears and fishhooks (Fig. 4.13). The analysis of a sample of 22 Dong Dau bronzes has revealed an alloy similar to that in use in northeast

Thailand at the same juncture in that no lead was employed. Tin levels, however, appear to have been rather higher with values varying between 6.8 and 28% and averaging 11%. The same alloy was used for the axes, spearheads, points, fishhooks and the bracelet analysed, but three arrowheads were made from a most unusual alloy comprising copper and between 2.9 and 6.5% antimony with no tin (Trinh Sinh 1990). Small clay-lined furnaces have been found at Dong Dau and Thanh Den, which were probably used for melting copper and tin before casting.

Ha Van Phung (1993) has identified three phases of the succeeding Go Mun culture, largely on the basis of the rim typology, the earliest being best represented in the upper layers at Dong Dau. Go Mun itself, where the second and

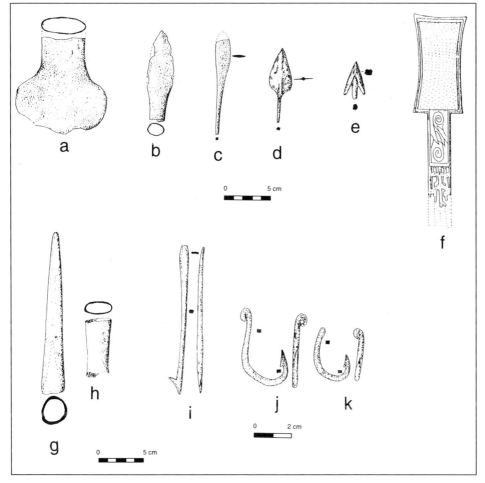

4.13   Bronze artefacts from Dong Dau.
          a. Socketed axe. **b.** Socketed spearhead. **c–e.** Arrowheads. **f.** Implement of
          unknown function. **g.** Socketed point. **h.** Socketed axe or chisel. **i.** Barbed
          point. **j, k.** Fishhooks.

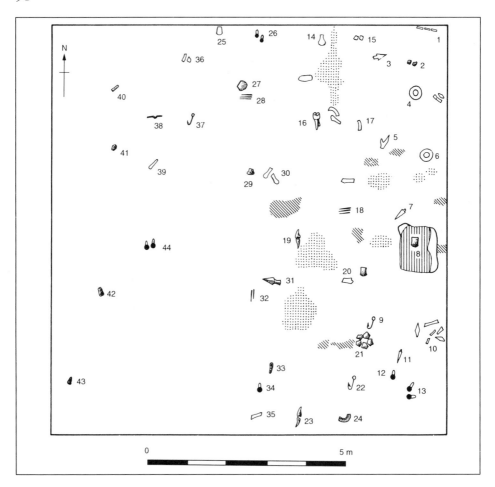

4.14   The distribution of artefacts, including bronzes, from an excavation square from the 1965 season at Go Mun.

1. Wooden spear. **2, 12, 13, 26, 29, 33–4, 40–4.** Bronze waste or fragments. **3.** Bronze tool. **4, 6, 17, 24.** Stone bracelet. **5.** Antler. **7, 11, 31.** Bronze spear. **8, 20, 25.** Stone axehead. **9, 22, 37.** Bronze fishhook. **10.** Potsherds and bronze tool. **14.** Pottery anvil. **15, 27.** Potsherds. **16, 19, 23.** Teeth. **18.** Bronze needle. **21.** Pottery vessel. **30.** Bone. **35–6, 39.** Unknown. **38.** Bronze vessel base.

third phases are present, is located just above the confluence of the Red and Black rivers (Ha Van Phung and Nguyen Duy Ty 1982). Excavated between 1961–71, its particular interest lies in the fact that, unusually, bronzes have been found in non-mortuary contexts. Moreover, the excavations covered various parts of the site, and therefore provide a spatial dimension to the location of bronzes (Fig. 4.14).

The excavations covered 1500 m², and the squares were spread over the central and southern parts of the site. But all yielded a similar variety of bronzes, and finds from one of the 1965 squares revealed a considerable density of bronze finds within a stratigraphic build-up which barely exceeded a metre in depth. Although stone adzes and bracelets remained abundant, the assemblage from Go Mun reveals a proliferation in the range and the function of bronzes. These can be considered in four distinct categories: decorative, utilitarian, ritual and for use in conflict (Fig. 4.15).

Bracelets were cast, but only three were encountered, a marked contrast to their predominance in bronze assemblages from the mortuary contexts west of the Truong Son Range. It is most significant to find bronze being employed in agriculture and industry. The Go Mun sample includes a sickle and five socketed hammers. There are also fishhooks, awls, chisels, axes and knives. Two fragments

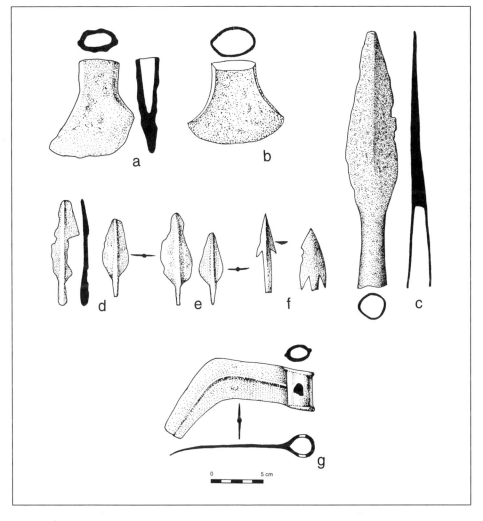

4.15 Bronzes from Go Mun.
    a, b. Socketed axes. **c.** Socketed spearhead. **d–f.** Arrowheads. **g.** Sickle.

spearhead and arrowheads when bronze remained scarce suggests the presence of conflict rather than hunting. Trinh Sinh (1990) has reported on the results of a spectrographic analysis of five Go Mun bronzes, and has found that, as with the Dong Dau material, a tin bronze was used in casting axes and spearheads, while one arrowhead lacked tin, but included 2.1% of antimony. Slit stone earrings are also found in Go Mun contexts, of a form paralleled in earlier Phung Nguyen and Dong Dau sites (Ha Van Phung 1993).

A similar, albeit not so well-documented sequence, has been reconstructed in the valley of the Ma River to the south. Pottery decorated in a similar manner to that of the Phung Nguyen culture has been identified in sites of the Con Chan Tien stage (Ha Van Tan 1991). The industrial technology of the succeeding Dong Khoi sites was still based on stone implements, and although corresponding chrono- logically with the Dong Dau culture, Ha Van Tan has not mentioned any bronze items from this stage. These came in the ensuing Quy Chu stage, when the familiar arrowheads, fishhooks, socketed axes and spearheads appeared, along with crucibles. These sites are thought to have been contemporary with the Go Mun phase to the north (1000–600 BC). Similar crucibles, along with reported bronze spades and hoes, have been recovered from Ru Tran in Nghe Tinh Province, again thought to correspond to the Go Mun phase. Further to the south still, Nguyen Truong Ky (1991) has identified two phases in the Ca Valley which correspond to the sequence in Bac Bo. The Den Doi phase corresponds with Phung Nguyen, and the Ru Tran phase with the Dong Dau and Go Mun phases.

The establishment of the State of Chu

During the Western Zhou perod, the State of Chu was established in the middle reaches of the Yangzi Valley only 500 km to the north of Lingnan. Some idea of the scale of this polity is seen in the investigations at Ji'nan, the former capital. Substantial earthen walls inside a moat follow a rectangle covering 1600 ha. A constant water supply was obtained from the river, which flowed through the city by its own gateway (HuPM 1982a, 1982b). The remains of a palace, houses, wells, specialised tile kilns and two copper smelting furnaces, not to mention numerous graves, reflect a powerful and vibrant civilisation which was influential on the bronze age communities which lay along its southern periphery, both in presenting a military threat and, if later trends are a guide, in its demands for luxury goods, such as pearls, rhinoceros horn and plumage. Allard (1995) has persuasively argued that the concentration of rich graves in the region where the Xijiang, Beijiang and Suijiang rivers converge above the delta represent the rise of local leaders involved in exchange with the Chu State. *Yong* bells were popular in central Guangdong, sets of three and seven respectively coming from Meicun and Sanwucun in the Dongjiang Valley (Xu Hengbin 1984). A grave at Matougang, which dates to the late Spring and Autumn period (550–early fifth century BC), includes on the one hand, bells and vessels of Chu type and probable origin, together with bronzes of local inspiration (GDWGW 1963, 1964). Among the latter, we find four bronze staffs embellished with cast representations of human

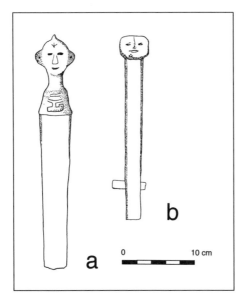

4.16   Bronze human-headed staffs
Left: from tomb 1 at Matougang (height 42.5 cm); *right:* from Nanmendong
(height 24 cm).
Permission: The Art Gallery, Chinese University of Hong Kong.

heads. Weaponry included short swords, lances and axes. A second grave, which belongs to the early Warring States period, was equipped with a particularly rich assemblage of bronze weapons, including 22 arrowheads.

A further set of four human-headed staffs were also recovered from a large and opulent grave at Nanmendong and again, bells and vessels were either imported from the Chu state or represent proficient copies (GuPM 1983). The single grave investigated at Niaodanshan was of considerable size, measuring 5.7 × 3.5 m and incorporated the remains of a wooden coffin (GuPM 1975). Dated to the fourth or fifth centuries BC, the grave goods are dominated by weapons and vessels which represent ritual or sumptuary activity. The latter include Chu forms, as well as a bell. The four human-headed staffs are again encountered and on this occasion, we can gather an impression of their ritual status, since they were placed facing each other in each corner of a northern chamber of the grave (Fig. 4.16; GuPM 1975). At Beifushan, the set of four human-headed staffs recur in a large and richly furnished grave which included numerous weapons, vessels and jades (GuPM and LDWHJ 1986).

The richest burial in this area is located in the Xijiang Valley at Beilingsongshan (GuPM and CBZC 1974). It stands apart from all others on account of its size (8 × 4.7 m), and the opulence of the grave goods. Over 100 bronzes were found, among which arrowheads predominate. There are also two swords, and a spearhead. The set of vessels include some almost certainly cast in the Chu area the most impressive being a decorated bronze jar inlaid with silver (Fig. 4.17). A set of four human-headed staffs were present, and it seems that the wooden coffin had been decorated with bronze plaques. Other grave goods included jade and gold ornaments.

While the concentration of these rich interments is found in the fertile and flat lands commanding the approaches to the delta, bronze age occupation during this period was also flourishing in the routes to the Chu domain to the north. In

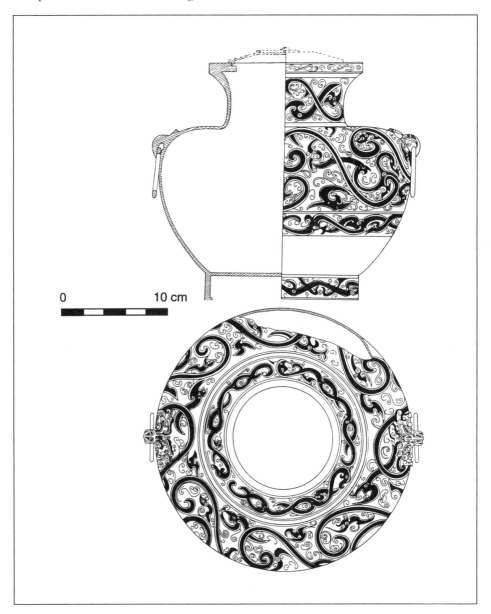

4.17   Bronze jar with silver inlay (height 22 cm) from the big tomb of Beilingsongshan.
Permission: The Guangdong Provincial Museum.

the valley of the Wushui River, for example, we encounter the extensive cemetery of Dagongpingcun. The mortuary sequence here covers the late Spring and Autumn to the Warring States periods (LCR 1989). Bronzes were few in the seven graves of the former period, burial 40, for example, described as typical by the excavators, provided a single bronze halberd. Later graves tended to have more bronzes, including weapons and vessels.

In a westerly direction the same contact with Chu is represented at Yangjia, where northern vessels and *yong* bells have been recovered in association with weaponry and, on this occasion, bronze staffs with animal rather than human heads (GXBWG 1973). Further assemblages in Central Guangxi have been found at Weipocun and Xia'neicao, although the concentration of sites found in the immediately preceding phases is missing. The picture presented by these as being significantly poorer than those above the delta recurs with three sites in eastern Guangdong, Bayushan, Goushipushan and Miantouling (Qiu Licheng and Li Xiongkun 1988). Only one bronze, a sword, was found in the Goushipushan grave. When turning to the distribution of the bronze staffs with either human or animal heads, we find that the former concentrate in central Guangdong, the latter in Guangxi. Allard (1995) has suggested that these may either have been symbols of office or high status. In sum, we find that rich burials and Chu imports concentrate above the Zhujiang Delta, an area which commanded riverine and maritime exchange routes to the Chu state.

Bronze technology

The techniques employed in Lingnan show a combination of bivalve moulds of distinct southern tradition, and the incorporation of piece mould technology from the *zhongyuan*. Xu Hengbin (1984) has described a series of analyses undertaken on Lingnan bronzes including bells, vessels, weapons and ornaments, and the results illustrate beyond doubt that, as the first millennium BC progressed, bronzes of very considerable sophistication were cast. The skill of the specialists is seen not only in the techniques and post-casting treatment, but in the careful choice of alloys and the combining, as for example with the swords, of different alloys to obtain desirable qualities. The admixture of tin varied between the hilt and blade of some swords, to impart a sharp and hard edge to the latter, but both hardness and strength to the former after they had been joined by fusion welding. Annealing was applied to bronze weapons to enhance their strength. Bells and tripods were made of a ternary alloy including lead, tin and copper.

The Iron Age

In the Yangzi Valley, iron made its appearance towards the end of the sixth century BC, cast iron objects having been found at Changsha and Nanking (Ko 1986). The mortuary evidence suggests that the initial use of iron in Lingnan belongs to the mid to late Warring States period (from about 350 BC). Iron was notably absent from all the sites described above, but at the cemetery of Yinshanling, it is possible to consider a cemetery which reveals not only a continued exchange relationship with the Chu, but also the employment of a range of iron artefacts as grave offerings (GZAR 1978). Although this cemetery has been affected by mining activity, 108 intact or nearly intact graves have been unearthed (Fig. 4.18). They are rectangular and varied considerably in terms of size, the provision of a waist pit, presence or absence of a pebble layer at the base and construction of an earth mound (Fig. 4.19). Very few bones survive, ruling

4.18   The plan of the cemetery of Yinshanling.

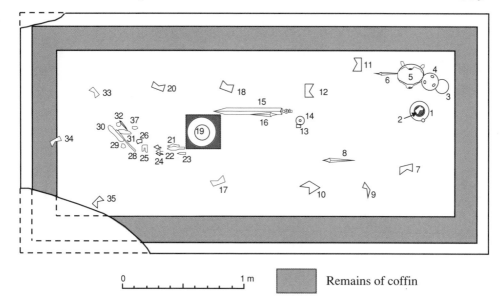

0 |_____| 1 m   [■] Remains of coffin

4.19   Burial 108 from Yinshanling.
1. Pottery tripod *guan*. **2, 7, 9–12, 17, 18, 20, 33–5.** Bronze coffin rivets.
3. Ceramic tripod *he* lid. **4.** Ceramic tripod *he*. **5.** Bronze *ding*. **6, 8.** Bronze
spearheads. **13.** Bronze staff head. **14–16.** Bronze swords. **19.** Ceramic *bu*
in waist pit. **21, 23–4.** Bronze arrowheads. **22.** Iron scraper. **25.** Iron hoe.
26. Bronze *dun*. **28.** Iron chisel. **29–31.** Whetstones. **32.** Iron axe.

out the identification of age or sex of the interment, but 59 different categories of
grave goods have been identified, including ten forms of pottery vessel, clay
spindle whorls, three forms of bronze vessel and bronze swords, arrowheads,
spearheads, halberds and battle axes (Fig. 4.20). Allard (1995) has suggested that
some such weapons may have been imported from the Chu state to the north.
There are also bronze tools, including axes, chisels, scrapers, drill points and
knives, bells, ladles, belt buckles and the singular animal-headed staffs. Iron
offerings include spearheads, axes, adzes, knives and scrapers. Whetstones were
common, and grave goods include some items of jade.

When compared with many contemporary cemeteries in the tropical river
valleys to the south, one is particularly struck by the quantity of bronzes, and the
abundance of weapons. In order to identify possible social groups and relationships between the graves spatially and chronologically, various statistical analyses
have been applied to the Yinshanling graves (Allard, Higham and Manly 1995). A
principal component analysis shows that certain artefacts are distributed in a way
which is significantly different from what might be expected if grave goods were
found at random. These are the animal-headed staffs, iron scrapers, bronze
swords, lances and arrowheads, spindle whorls and whetstones. When individual
graves are plotted on the basis of their principal component scores, we find a large
concentration with a small number of outliers. A consideration of the former was

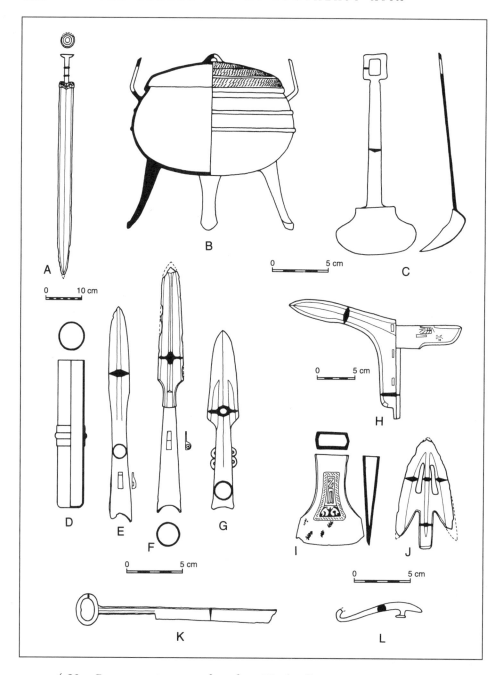

4.20   Bronze mortuary artefacts from Yinshanling.
a. Chu-style sword, burial 108. **b.** Chu-style *ding* vessel, burial 22. **c.** Ladle, burial 119. **d.** *Dun*, burial 4. **e.** Spearhead type VI, burial 24. **f.** Spearhead type III, burial 4. **g.** Spearhead type V, burial 155. **h.** Halberd, burial 4. **i.** *Yue* axe, burial 8. **j.** Arrowhead, burial 151. **k.** Paring knife, burial 74. **l.** Belt clasp, burial 98.

undertaken by contrasting the distribution of graves with spindle whorls and those with swords, because these artefacts are never found in the same grave. It was found that, although not visibly distinct, they are nevertheless complementary in distribution. It is considered highly likely that spindle whorls were associated with women, and swords with men.

If this is so, then other grave goods found in these groups are intriguing. With women, we find many iron spades and certain styles of pot. Putative male graves have weaponry, whetstones and a near monopoly of the six animal-headed staffs. When we turn to the actual size of the graves, most have an area of less than 4.5 m², but of the eighteen graves which exceed that area, eleven are male and seven, female. All but one of the assumed Chu imports are with male graves, eight of which fall into the large group and nine into the group of small graves. It is also notable that five of the six graves with animal-headed staffs also contain Chu-style bronzes.

Despite this apparent dichotomy between large, rich and small poorer graves, there is no lobe or enclave of graves reserved for the former. This spatial separation of the elite became apparent a few centuries later at Shizhaishan and Lijiashan on the Yunnan Plateau (see p. 142), but at Yinshanling, it seems more likely that we can recognise a trend towards the establishment of elites which, to judge from the weaponry and iron tools, took place in a milieu which involved both warfare and considerable concern with efficiencies in food production. In place of the earlier ostentation in displaying exotic Chu items, as seen at Beilingsongshan, we see graves with assemblages of tools and utilitarian vessels. Allard (1994) has suggested that leaders were now concerned with more mundane activities, agriculture and defence, than with display.

A comparison between Yinshanling and Liyangdun, a second cemetery with graves belonging the late Warring States period, emphasises an element of regional variation (Yang Shiting *et al.* 1991). Almost thirty graves have been exposed at the latter site, but none includes Chu imports, there are no ceremonial staffs, relatively few bronzes and jades, and only one grave includes an iron spade.

The end of the prehistoric period in Lingnan is illuminated by historic references. Xu Hengbin (1984), quoting *Huainanzi*, noted that 'army groups were sent along five routes by the First Emperor of Qin to conquer the Lingnan region, one route was to the capital of Panyu'. This occurred towards the end of the third century BC. There are further references to Panyu in the *Shi Ji* and *Han Shu,* where it was described as an emporium which sent north 'pearls, ivory, rhinoceros skins, fruits and cloth' (Xu Hengbin 1984:84). This centre, located it is thought to command the Zhujiang Estuary, provides a strong indication of the complexity of Lingnan society on the eve of conquest. Two centuries were to elapse before the tide of Chinese expansion reached Bac Bo, and in the later Dong Son culture there, we can treat another vibrant society which confronted imperial ambition.

The Iron Age in Bac Bo

There is no specific evidence for dating the first iron in Bac Bo. The second half of the first millennium BC in this area saw the development of the Dong Son culture, and it was during this span that iron came to be employed for weapons and tools. Since there are some cemeteries containing rich burials but no remains of iron, it is considered probable that this metal became known at about the same time as in Lingnan. Certainly some of the iron implements closely resemble those from Lingnan. These include spearheads and spades (Fig. 4.21).

Chinese histories and other tracts, as well as surviving Vietnamese legends, provide a misty glimpse of events in Bac Bo during this period. The latter place the kingdom of Van-lang and the Hung kings with remarkable precision between 2879 and 258 BC, when the kingdom of Au-lac was founded by Thuc Phan. The archaeological record reveals that from at least 2000 BC, Bac Bo was occupied by village communities which undertook rice cultivation, raised domestic stock and

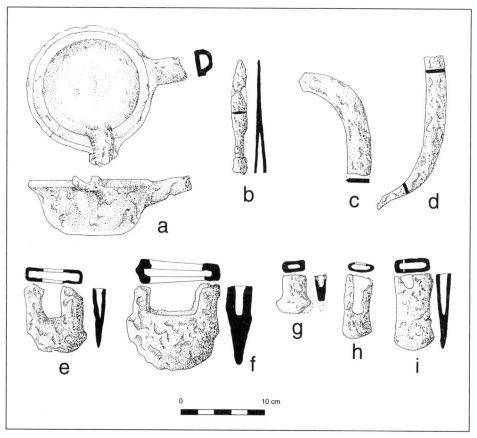

4.21   Iron artefacts from Dong Son contexts in Bac Bo.
a. Bowl. **b.** Spearhead. **c, d.** Knives. **e, f.** Socketed hoes. **g–i.** Socketed axes.
Permission: Ha Van Tan

showed a considerable interest in acquiring exotic goods. From the middle of the second millennium, these included locally cast bronzes. Within this context, it is important to note that the very name of this mythical kingdom derives from a phonetic translation into Chinese of the word *vlang* or *blang* (modern *dang*), a large bird in the Austroasiatic Viet language. The Hung kings chose a water bird as their totem. Again, the important centre of Me Linh is located in Bach Hac district, the latter meaning white heron. Hong Bang, the clan name of the Hung kings, is the name for a heron (Nguyen Phuc Long 1975). The importance of the wading bird, and indeed the Austroasiatic language employed, will take on further significance when we turn to the decoration on the bronze artefacts of the Dong Son culture, and consider its ultimate origins.

The Au-lac kingdom was centred at Co Loa, the ramparts of which dominate the flat plain north of Hanoi. It was of short duration, for the last three centuries BC saw the expansion of imperial Chinese interest in this region. We learn from the *Shui Jingzhu* by Li Daoyuan (died AD 527) of the Chinese perspective on this, the southern extremity of their empire (Taylor 1991). This author, drawing on earlier and for the most part lost sources, took as his theme the passage of the Red River from the Yunnan Plateau to the sea. He described many fabled animals, their amazing properties and activities, but Taylor (1991) has also commented on an interest in the political and economic organisation of those living in the Red River Valley. The kingdom of Au-lac lasted only until 207 BC, when a southern Chinese warlord, Zhao Tuo, established the new kingdom of Nam Viet, which itself endured until the area was received into the Han Empire in 111 BC. A Chinese administration, however, was not immediately put in place. Rather, local leaders were granted authority in return for acknowledging Han dominion.

This situation lasted until a rebellion led by Trung Trac, an aristocratic woman from the region of Me Linh. With troops drawn from Sichuan who came down the Red River, the Chinese general Ma Yuan suppressed the rebellion and established a new system of commanderies (provinces). Li Daoyuan drew on an earlier and now lost source when he described the local Lac lords, prior to Ma Yuan's arrival, as owning irrigated rice land. If these reports have a historic basis, and there is no reason to set them aside, then we might expect the archaeological record to provide evidence for considerable social complexity, and political centres of some size, dating from the later first millennium BC. This received early recognition from the French archaeologists based in Hanoi. Parmentier (1918a), following Heger's consideration of the corpus of drums, described their growing number and wide distribution. He took particular note of the decoration, particularly the representations of boats, plumed warriors, houses and birds.

Dong Son

By the time that Goloubew (1929) reviewed the material, Pajot had excavated at the eponymous site of Dong Son. In 1924, the École Française had sponsored diggings there, and Pajot encountered numerous graves containing many bronze and a few iron artefacts. The former included drums, armaments, agricultural implements, vases, situlae and human figures. These were found with Chinese imports: a Han bronze sword, a mirror and coins dated to the early first century AD. Goloubew noted that some of the axes found in the graves were of the same form as those brandished by the warriors depicted on the surface of the bronze drums. He was also able to observe that the use of bivalve moulds to cast the vessels and arms were similar to a clay axe mould discovered by Colani at the site of Ban Gian. He suggested that some of the decorated bronze plaques were made for great chiefs, a finding supported by other sumptuary goods recovered by Pajot, which included jade, shell and bronze bracelets, bronze belt buckles with bells and decorated drinking vessels.

Goloubew was most interested in the representations of human figures. His consideration of this aspect of Dong Son metal working included a review of the Ngoc Lu drum, found in 1893 and a century later, still one of the finest examples known. The tympanum was decorated with many people, including a man playing a *khen,* a set of pan pipes still popular in Southeast Asia. He was also able to refer to bronze statuettes of men wearing earrings and bracelets, with their hair plaited. Rather than seeking remote origins of this rich culture, Goloubew suggested that the local people during the first century AD initiated a bronze industry under strong Chinese influence.

The Swede, Olov Janse contributed to the debate on the Dong Son Bronze Age when he considered the range of axes, spearheads, daggers and hoes or ploughshares. He found that these were not matched in northern China, but rather identified parallel forms in Europe (Janse 1931). This proposed western origin was also supported by Heine-Geldern (1951), but Karlgren (1942) followed Goloubew in seeking local origins under Chinese influence, and suggested parallels with Chinese motifs and artefacts over the last few centuries of the first millennium BC, thus considerably expanding the duration and lengthening the initial date of the Dong Son culture compared with that advanced by Goloubew.

Janse expanded our knowledge of this culture by excavating at Dong Son between 1935–9. His report described the uncovering of graves in different parts of the site, which lies on the southern bank of the Ma River. The first two included bronze drums, a bronze situla containing a socketed spearhead, a vase, stone rings and ceramic vessels. Unfortunately, soil conditions prevented the survival of bone. In his locality 6, Janse (1958) found a further six graves, and grave goods included Chinese coins, bronze spears, a casting sprue which indicated local bronze working and the central cores from stone bracelets, suggesting local manufacture. In 1936, he encountered wooden foundations of houses, along with many potsherds, net sinkers and animal bones. One house support survived to a length of 4.5 m. The general cultural stratum also contained numerous slit stone rings and a few iron objects.

Janse provided a detailed description of the mortuary goods. The largest spearhead reached 44 cm in length. Another had a bronze socket and an iron blade. He described the arrowheads as of undoubted Chinese origin. Swords were rare, but one was bimetallic, having a bronze hilt and an iron blade. Despite ascribing the axes to Chinese inspiration, he could find no northern parallels for the situlae, nor for the richly decorated bronze plaques. Beads of carnelian, agate and rock crystal, however, indicated participation in an exchange network for which the riverine location would have provided strategic advantages.

Janse couched his interpretation within a model of local stone age people of Indonesian or Proto-Malay stock who received Chinese influence from the third or fourth centuries BC. Chinese bronze workers introduced metallurgy, satisfied local needs and, in the case of the situlae, imitated local baskets in metal. Some groups, he suggested, moved south to establish what became the Cham civilisation. Karlgren (1942) identified a series of Chinese imports in association with Dong Son bronzes, including Wang Mang coins, a first century BC mirror and a pre-Han sword. His conclusions saw the Dong Son culture as an indigenous phenomenon under strong pre-Han and Han influence.

These interpretations, all of which rely in one form or another on foreign inspiration, have now been modified following intensive research by Vietnamese archaeologists. They have produced compelling evidence for local origins, the most immediate sources being the Go Mun phase in the Red River delta, the Quy Chu in the Ma Valley and the Ru Tran phase in the Ca Valley. The presence of crucible remains in all three phases indicates the widespread presence of bronze casting during the early centuries of the first millennium BC and some products of this industry anticipate the major changes which characterise the Dong Son phase. In all these regions, the Dong Son phase proper saw a startling increase in the quantity and variety of bronzes being cast.

Most evidence for assessing the Dong Son culture comes from cemeteries, although Co Loa has been examined archaeologically. Unlike the Yunnan Plateau sites, however, no cemeteries have been excavated over a sufficient area to provide us with evidence for the spatial distribution of graves. Lang Ca may be an exception, but no cemetery plan is available.

Four cemeteries stand out because of the survival of coffins cut from tree trunks. All lie on the fringes of the lower Red River delta in a habitat which must formerly have been low lying, and probably close to the then coast. These are Viet Khe, Chau Can, Xuan La and Minh Duc.

Viet Khe

Viet Khe has produced the richest assemblage. It is located on the southern foot of a hill overlooking the Hoa River in Haiphong Province (Fig. 4.9 site 37; VMH 1965). Five wooden coffins have been excavated, each being orientated on an east-west axis and at least two pairs being in a linear configuration. The largest, burial 2, was 4.76 m long, but unfortunately no human remains were found. The report does not make it clear which items were located in each of the coffins, but there is little doubting the abundance of bronzes. Thirty-one pediform socketed axes with oval sockets were found, as well as two axes of symmetrical but flared blades and rectangular sockets, and two further examples with almost parallel-sided blades. Unlike many Dong Son examples, the Viet Khe pediform axes bear little decoration. Three varieties of chisel were recovered with wide, pointed and small-gauge working ends. While some of these axes and chisels would doubtless have been used to fashion and decorate wooden structures, there was also a range of bronze weapons. Three types of socketed spearhead were catalogued, two forms of socketed arrowhead, daggers with blades up to 20 cm long and a sword nearly half a metre in length. Four ring-handled knives are of Chinese origin or immediate inspiration.

Bronze vessels are perhaps the most impressive aspects of the repertoire at Viet Khe. Of these, the *thap,* a tall vessel with slightly tapering sides and strap handles, is the largest and most richly ornamented. Standing 37 cm high even in its broken

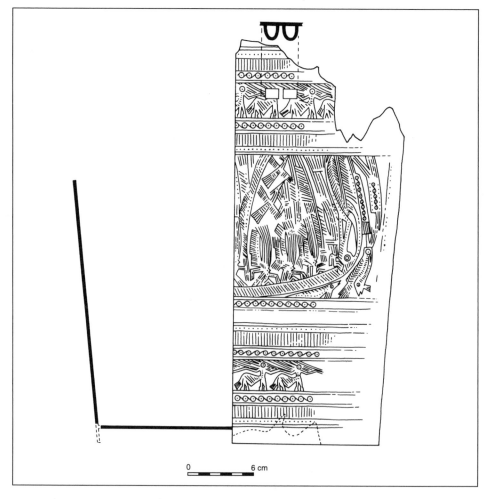

0   6 cm

4.22   Bronze *thap* from Viet Khe.

condition, it bears panels of decoration which vary between geometric and spiral motifs and scenes of plumed warriors on land or on boats. The boats are associated with birds and fish (Fig. 4.22). The *tho* is a bronze vessel with outward sloping sides standing on a low pedestal. Some have an everted lip. An example from Viet Khe stands 22.5 cm in height and was ornamented with rows of geometric and spiral designs. A second also bears rows of decoration but lacks the everted lip. It is just under 18 cm high. The *binh* is a globular vessel on a high pedestal. It has two handles and a lid embellished with geometric decoration (Fig. 4.23). One of the three specimens stood 21 cm high and reached a width of

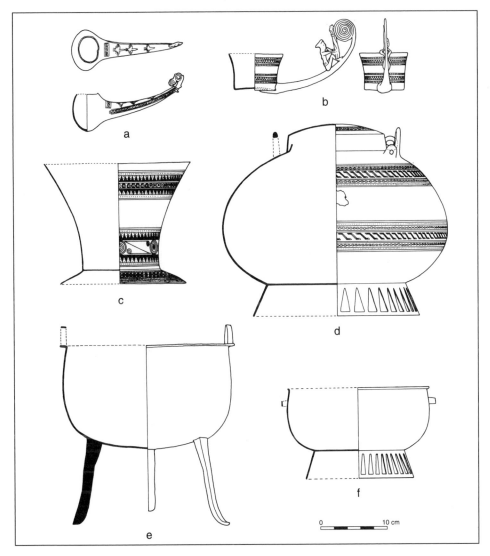

4.23 Bronze vessels from Viet Khe.
a-b. Ladles. **c.** *Tho.* **d.** *Binh.* **e.** *Dinh.* **f.** *Au.*

24.7 cm. There was one example of the *au,* a handled basin raised on a pedestal (Fig. 4.23). The *dinh* is a basin on tripod legs similar in many respects to the Chinese *li*. The *khay* is an unusual artefact in the form of a low tray with broad handles, again decorated with triangles and spirals, while the *am* from Viet Khe, a spouted vessel rather like a kettle, was damaged and as far as can be seen, undecorated. Finally, there is a set of decorated bronze ladles, each about 20 cm long. One was ornamented with flying birds and geometric designs, the other had also the figure of a man playing a *khen* while comfortably seated on the handle.

Musical instruments at Viet Khe are represented by a small drum, with a tympanum 23 cm wide bearing a design of a central-rayed sun surrounded by a panel containing four flying birds. The mantle survives only as a fragment which contains a bird within a panel demarcated by decorated bands. There was also a variety of bells, some with decoration of clearly local tradition, another with a distinctly Chinese form.

The circle as a decorative motif was not confined to bronze. A fragment of leather was also found ornamented in this way. The coffins also contained wooden hafts for spearheads, impressions of matting on soil, and items of lacquer, cloth and basketry.

Three radiocarbon dates have been obtained from the coffin wood which, allowing for the possible use of old trees to manufacture coffins, indicated that a date of 500–300 BC is likely, and would confirm an impression that Viet Khe might be earlier rather than later in the Dong Son sequence. The bronzes, for all their numbers, are not lavishly decorated, the drum is small and has simple ornamentation, and the cemetery has not produced any iron. Most bronzes fall within a local repertoire, but a significant number also parallel closely artefacts from Lingnan. These include the *dinh* tripod, ring-ended paring knife and bronze sword, the *dun* or spear embellishment, some of the spearheads and arrowheads (Fig. 4.24). These recur at Tonggugang (Guangdong) and Yinshanling (Guangxi), sites dated to the Warring States period (475–221 BC).

Chau Can

Chau Can (Ha Son Binh Province) was opened in 1974, and eight log coffins were recovered, of which two were in very poor condition and three others incomplete (Luu Tran Tieu 1977). They lay in a row with the head orientated to the south or southeast and contrast with the Viet Khe graves in several respects, although the single acceptable radiocarbon date of 530–197 BC taken from coffin wood suggests that the two sites were contemporaneous. The graves at Chau Can are smaller and the grave goods fewer, but an unusual number of wooden artefacts survive. There are no bronze vessels, drums or bells. Burial 3 contained the remains of a probable female, interred with a spearhead at the right upper arm, a pediform bronze axe still mounted on its haft by the right leg, a wooden implement by the head and the wooden haft for a spear by the left leg. Fragments of material, probably clothing, were found over the chest.

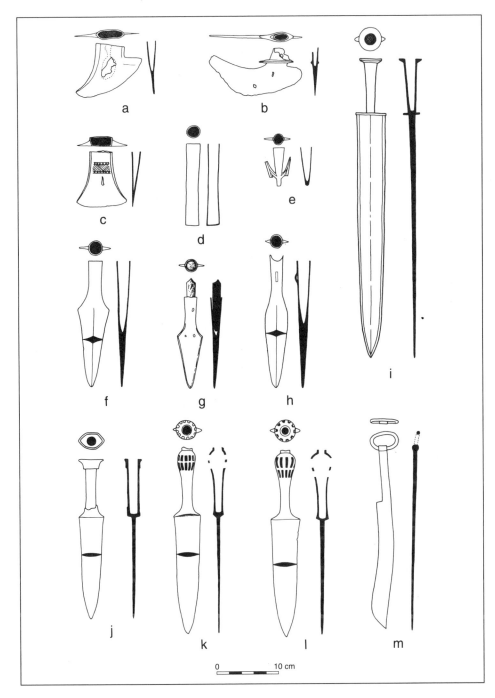

4.24 Bronze weapons from Viet Khe.
a–c. Socketed axes. **d.** *Dun* counterweight at butt end of spear shaft. **e.** Arrowhead. **f–h.** Socketed spearheads. **i.** Sword. **j–l.** Daggers. **m.** Ring-handled paring knife.

Burial 4 contained a male skeleton with a set of grave goods over and beside the ankles: a spear with its wooden haft, a wooden ladle, a pottery vessel and ceramic tray and a bamboo implement of uncertain use. Burial 6 had few human bones, but the preference was to place grave goods by the feet. In this case, we find a gourd ladle, wooden tray and a globular pot while fabric was present over the chest and abdomen, and basketry impressed on clay was found beyond the head area. More such fabric covered the chest of burial 7, with more beyond the feet. Another globular pot and a wooden tray had been placed over the ankles. Burial 8 contained a piece of a wooden tray, and a wooden artefact in two sections, one of which slotted into the other, and which probably represents a hafting device. The bones lay under a fabric shroud.

The Chau Can coffins were smaller than at Viet Khe, and the grave goods lacked the bronze vessels, ladles and the musical instruments which reflect a sumptuary or ritual element in the Dong Son metal industry. The axes and spearheads lacked decorative elements and the few pots were of simple, globular form. The report refers to earrings made of a tin-lead alloy, but even given the remarkable survival of a range of organic offerings, personal ornaments were few. We are left with the impression that there were considerable differences in access to the services of full-time metal workers between the communities of Viet Khe and Chau Can.

Xuan La

Xuan La is located only 10 km from Chau Can, and the seven coffins excavated there in 1982 provide a useful indication of basic similarities, but some changes, in material culture between them (Pham Quoc Quan and Trinh Can 1982). Two of the Xuan La burials contained Chinese coins of Wang Mang, which allow us to date the site within or later than the Xin Dynasty (AD 9–23). The burial rite remains similar, the body being interred in a wooden coffin with grave goods beside the body, by the ankles and beyond the head. We are again reminded how much we might have missed in less protected graves, for a rich assemblage of wooden artefacts has survived, including human figures on the coffin lids.

Burial 1 was found with a wooden tray in the ankle area, two bronze socketed axe heads, three axe hafts, a wooden stick and a section of bamboo (Fig. 4.25). There were also four pottery vessels and 36 Chinese coins beside the left hand. In the case of burial 2, the skull lay over a bronze *chau* vessel, and a wooden human figure had been placed at the left shoulder. A large, circular wooden tray lay over the knees, next to a bronze *thap*. This stands 22 cm in height, and was decorated with three rows of geometric and spiral motifs. A socketed bronze pediform axe lay beside the right hand. Burial 3 included three small ring-footed pottery vessels within the coffin and three more outside it and beyond the head. The skull lay on a group of socketed iron spades virtually identical with those from Yinshanling, with a further group by the left elbow making nine in all. There was a socketed bronze spearhead and an arrowhead by the left hand and a

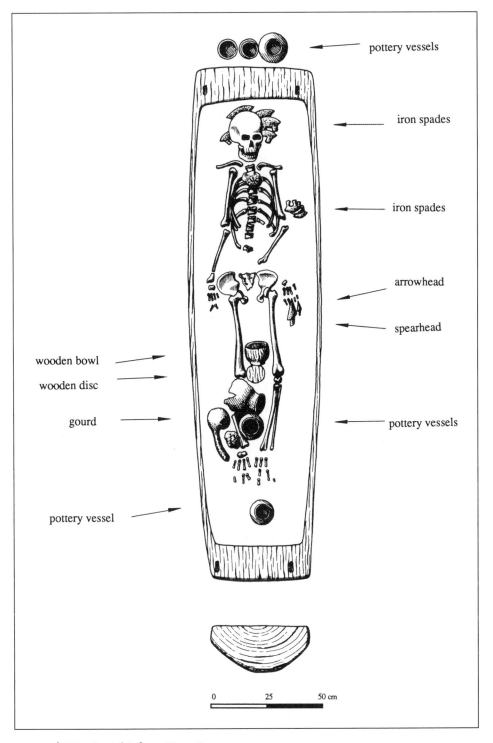

4.25 Burial 3 from Xuan La.

wooden disc between the knees. A round lacquered box lay beside the right ankle. Nine further iron spades were found in burial 4 and a considerable variety of other goods including a bronze bowl in the skull area, a wooden axe haft, eight coins, a socketed iron axehead, three pottery vessels, a wooden disc and three wooden containers.

The burials from Xuan La allow us insight into the range of wooden artefacts selected for mortuary use: bowls, discs, hafts, boxes and figurines. Despite the presence of iron hoes and axes, and the relatively late date of the site within the Dong Son phase, the quantity of bronze fell far short of that found at Viet Khe. Although a number of small bronze vessels were found, the graves lack a number of weapons and ritual or sumptuary items found, for example, at Dong Son. There are no drums, halberds, daggers, plaques or ploughshares. The cemetery seems rather to represent a provincial Dong Son community, remote from the main centres of wealth and display.

Minh Duc

The same might be said of the seven boat coffins examined at Minh Duc. Again, grave goods included lacquerware and clothing or shrouds, in addition to pottery vessels and exchange items. Bronzes include one axe, two spears, a basin, a *thap* tripod and a *binh* container. One iron hoe was discovered, as well as a wooden haft looking very similar to that from Doc Chua, a wooden tray, and four human figures (Bui Van Liem and Pham Quoc Quan 1991).

The burials at Dong Son

The relative paucity of these sites is best illustrated by comparing the Xuan La and Minh Duc graves with some recovered at Dong Son itself. This site was strategically placed at a crossing point of the Ma River, only about 15 km from the present shore. Excavations by Vietnamese archaeologists have shown that the site was in use as a settlement and a cemetery over many centuries. Ha Van Tan (1980) has outlined three phases. The first equates with the Go Mun phase in the Red River Valley and is characterised by few bronzes in graves belonging to the period 1000–500 BC. During the ensuing Dong Son phase, the number of bronze items increased considerably. The third phase saw the introduction of Chinese imports and belongs to the first millennium AD.

Unfortunately, the combination of enthusiastic digging by Pajot in the 1920s, more careful work by Janse in the 1930s and further scientific research by the Vietnamese rules out an overall cemetery plan. We know from some crude sketches published by Bezacier (1972), which are presumably based on Pajot's notes, that some graves contained miniature and full-sized drums, ornamented body plaques, *tho* situlae, ploughshares and weapons: swords, daggers, spearheads and axes. A similar range of finds was encountered by Janse, who noted the presence of Chinese imports and a range of ornaments in exotic stone. Chu Van Tan (1973, quoted in Ha Van Tan 1991) has attempted to quantify the variation in the wealth of graves through time at Dong Son by dividing them into three groups. Poor graves have no or few grave goods, which might extend to a pottery vessel or two and some stone earrings. A medium grave has one or two bracelets, not more than four bronze artefacts and/or one of iron and some pottery vessels. The rich graves have a range of bronze vessels, a drum, at least three iron implements, and bronze tools and weapons. He considered a sample of sixty graves of phase 2 and 26 of phase 3. About a quarter of all graves in both phases are classified as poor. Thirteen out of sixty phase 2 graves fall in the medium category, but during phase 3, there was only one medium grave. Half of all graves in both phases were classified as rich. There was, then, no significant change between the two, and fully half of the graves were wealthy. These figures, sadly, mean little without a spatial dimension. Were these rich graves concentrated in one part of the site? Was there evidence for an upper social echelon at Dong Son?

Lang Ca

This same unsatisfactory state of affairs is found at other Dong Son culture cemeteries. Lang Ca is located just above the confluence of the Red and Black rivers near Viet Tri. A single radiocarbon date from coffin wood suggests contemporaneity with phase 2 at Dong Son (382–195 BC). We read of 309 graves there, but there is no cemetery plan nor list of graves with their contents. Trinh Sinh and Ngo Si Hong (1980), however, have referred to some evidence for the presence of relatively rich graves in part of the cemetery. Burials in the eastern sector had few if any grave goods, while those in the western area were much richer, and disposed of 85.8% of all bronzes recovered. One grave seems to have belonged to a specialist bronze worker, because he was interred with the tools of his trade: ceramic moulds for casting an axe, a spearhead, sword hilt and a bell. The associated crucible could have taken up to 12 kg of molten metal (Fig. 4.26).

The list of the 217 grave goods reveals a remarkable predominance of bronze artefacts. This number seems very few given reports of over 300 graves. Weapons dominate the bronze assemblage, there being 62 spearheads, 36 axes, three knives and six daggers. Some were ornamented with geometric designs and scenes of deer, dogs, and people in boats. There are also bronze vessels, including four *thap* and four *au,* a miniature drum and six bells. Only twenty pottery vessels are reported, and no iron was encountered. This conforms with the absence of iron from Viet Khe and Chau Can, and offers a marked contrast with its abundance at this juncture in Central Thailand. One of the moulds was designed to cast a sword hilt, and it is possible that it was intended to cast it onto an iron blade. If so, it would suggest that iron, during the period represented by the Lang Ca cemetery, was still very rare.

Lang Vac

Lang Vac is located in the valley of the Ca River, and Vietnamese excavations there have uncovered over 100 graves with a full range of Dong Son bronzes. A final

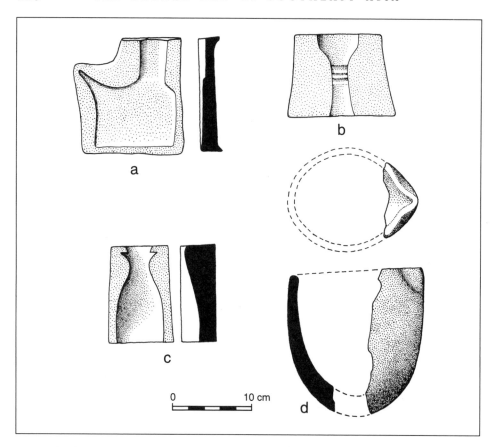

4.26   Moulds and a crucible from Lang Ca.
a. For an axe. **b.** For a sword hilt. **c.** For a bell.

excavation report is awaited with much interest and at present no cemetery plan
is available, although an area of over 600 m² has been excavated even before
renewed excavations by a Japanese team in 1990. A rich assemblage of bronzes
has been reported (Ngo Si Hong 1983). Among tools and/or weapons, there was
a variety of socketed axes, including a novel form, sometimes decorated with
geometric designs, with flaring sides (Fig. 4.27). Hoes and fishhooks and a chisel
were also found, but one of the most intriguing aspects of the assemblage of
bronzes is the abundance of daggers. Of the nearly fifty examples, some are richly
decorated with human figures as hilts. In one case, we can clearly see the man's
bracelets, earrings, patterned loincloth and the long plait of hair held in place by
a headband. In a second example, two men stand back to back, their heads joined
by the figure of an elephant. There are also two bronze swords, one reaching a
length of 43.5 cm, and four socketed spearheads. A crossbow trigger indicates a
knowledge of Chinese weaponry.

Bronze bracelets and armlets were also abundant, some embellished with small
bells, while both miniature and full-sized drums were recovered. One of the latter,

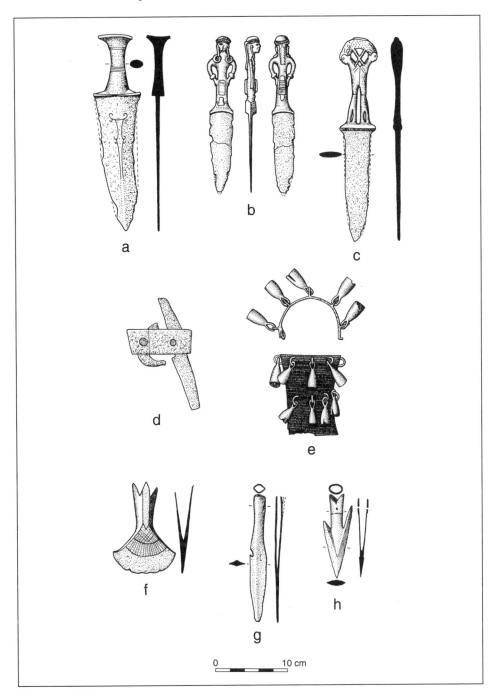

4.27 Bronzes from Lang Vac.
a–c. Daggers. **d.** Crossbow trigger. **e.** Bracelet with bells. **f.** Socketed axe.
g, h. Socketed spearheads.
Permission: Khao Co Hoc.

which stands 27.8 cm high and has a tympanum 37.7 cm in width, was decorated with flying birds, bulls and boats, in addition to bands of geometric and curvilinear motifs. Boats and birds are likewise found on the mantle of a second large drum found in burial 3. Burial 4 in the same part of the site included a particularly large example, standing almost half a metre in height and again decorated on the tympanum with four birds ringing the rayed sun. The four birds reappear on yet another example, but on this occasion half the size of the previous drum. A damaged drum with four cast toads on the tympanum was found in burial 42, and the use of animals as decorative motifs occurred, even on miniature drums and figurines. Among the latter, we find an elephant with two birds perched on its back. The stone and glass jewellery was also abundant, but pottery vessels were plain and dominated by round-based and footed bowls.

Some of the wealth of this site, as well as its remote inland location, might be due to its proximity to a source of tin. Two radiocarbon dates have been reported. One, at AD 850±80, is clearly too late. The other suggests occupation in the first century BC and seems more realistic (83 BC–AD 225).

Co Loa

When, according to folklore, Thuc Phan defeated the last Hung king in 257 BC and founded the kingdom of Au Lac, he chose Co Loa as his capital. This huge site dominates the northern floodplain of the Red River and its size reflects the manpower and energy available to the new ruler. There are two outer sets of ramparts and an inner, rectangular citadel. The outer rampart has a circumference of 8 km, and was punctuated by guard towers. The ramparts still stand up to 12 m high, and are 25 m wide at the base. It has been estimated that over 2 million m^3 of material were moved in constructing the defences, which also involved moats fed by the Hoang River.

Excavations have revealed Dong Son style pottery stratified under the walls, while a chance find within the defences involved an outstanding drum which contained a hoard of bronze objects (Nguyen Giang Hai and Nguyen Van Hung 1983). Such hoards are very rare in Southeast Asia, indeed this one may be unique. It provides us with a glimpse of bronzes which were in circulation presumably during the last couple of centuries BC.

The drum itself is one of the largest recovered from Bac Bo, standing 57 cm high and with a tympanum 73.6 cm in width. It weighs 72 kg. The contents included about 200 bronzes, including 20 kg of scrap pieces from a variety of artefacts (Fig. 4.28). The ploughshares, of which there are 96, dominate numerically. There were also six hoes and a chisel. A wide variety of shapes was evident in the 32 socketed axeheads, including a boat-shaped example virtually identical to the clay mould found in the bronze worker's grave at Lang Ca. There were also sixteen spearheads, a dagger and eight arrowheads. One spearhead is of particular interest because it was bimetallic, having an iron blade on a bronze socket. Again, this technique was reflected in one of the Lang Ca moulds.

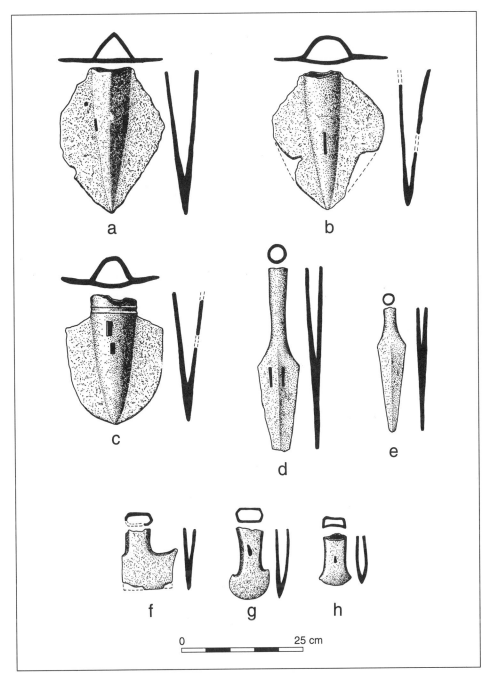

4.28   Bronzes found inside the Co Loa drum.
a–c. Socketed hoes or ploughshares. **d–f.** Socketed axes (cf. **d** with the mould illustrated in figure 4.26a). **g, h.** Socketed spearheads.

Dong Son ritual

The lack of any extensive information from excavated settlements in Bac Bo, while not as serious a problem as on the Yunnan Plateau, is still an impediment to our understanding of the settlement pattern and domestic life. However, it is possible to turn to scenes on the drums and large bronze vessels, as well as to bronze plaques and figurines, for some indication of the appearance and activities of the Dong Son people.

The Ngoc Lu drum is one of the most important in the corpus of Dong Son specimens, because it is well preserved and richly decorated (Pham Huy Thong *et al.* 1990). It was discovered accidentally in 1893 in Ha Nam Ninh Province southeast of Hanoi. The tympanum, unusually, bears three concentric panels of human or animal scenes interspersed with bands of geometric or circular motifs. The innermost panel is the most interesting because it is decorated with human figures enacting what looks like a ceremony involving the drums themselves, other musical instruments and rice preparation (Fig. 4.29). The two outer panels are decorated with friezes of deer, hornbills and crane egrets.

The inner panel repeats itself, although there are minor differences. The scenes are subject to more than one plausible interpretation, but there can be little doubting the importance of a row of plumed figures, probably male, led in one case by a man holding a spear with the point directed to the ground. Behind him follow five more men, two at least playing musical instruments – a *khen* and perhaps cymbals or bells while the others hold what look like wands in the left hand. They wear a form of kilt and high feathered headdress incorporating a bird's head. In front of the leader, there is a structure raised on stilts with either decorated timber walls or some sort of streamers held at the eaves. A kilted figure within plays on a board of gongs, there being two sets on each side of the chamber. He or she does not wear the feathered headdress; nor do three people beyond the house, two of whom have long flowing hair, while the third has the hair tied in a bun. One is chasing away a hornbill, the others are threshing rice with poles which are decorated with streamers or feathers. A house is seen beyond them. It has decorated posts raised at a sharp angle above the ground, from which streamers dangle. The gable ends are decorated with stylised birds' heads. There are three seated figures within, probably playing drums. Beyond and possibly attached to the house, there is a raised platform with a streamer flying from a pole at one end. A standing and three seated figures wield large upright poles which they seem to be bringing down to strike a row of four drums positioned below.

Beyond them, the scene is repeated, but with one or two variations. The drums in the first frieze are all the same size, in the second their sizes are graded. One cymbal or gong player uses one baton, the other has two. On one platform, all drummers are seated but on the other, one is standing. There are two people in one house but the other has three. But the scene is an integrated one and most commentators agree that it represents some sort of festive or ritual occasion. The row of musicians and men wearing elaborate headdresses are processing in a formal manner, possibly in a dance. Music to a rhythm of drums, and the threshing of rice, play important roles. The feathered men contrast with the other participants in their dress: most of the latter, judging from their long hair and different dress, are women. Nor should the decoration on the mantle be overlooked, for here again we encounter plumed warriors in a procession of elegant pirogues with decorated timbers. Birds' heads are found on the end of their headdresses, the stern and prow of their boats, on poles standing on the edge of the raised platforms, and even on the end of the rudder. There is a cleft prow decorated by carved birds and an eye, and a tasselled streamer swings below. Warriors also hold spears, axes and a bow.

This scene of musicians, feathered men and rice processing is repeated on other examples, and its meaning was clearly widely appreciated. The Hoang Ha

0   5cm

4.29   The tympanum of the Ngoc Lu drum.
Permission: The Vietnam Social Sciences Publishing House, Hanoi.

drum, found in Ha Son Binh province in 1937, had an outer panel of crane egrets
and an inner one showing essentially the same procession, albeit with some
minor differences (Fig. 4.30). Four feathered men in line carry spears, and are
followed by two musicians. Someone is beating a drum under the eaves of the
raised house, and there is nobody to frighten away the bird from the rice
threshing. The boats on the mantle are very similar, down to the cleft prow, archer
on the raised platform and a drum within. But it lacks the dog. In the case of the
Co Loa drum, we find that there are only two spear-wielding warriors but the
musical ensemble now comprises three players. A drum lies on its side under the
eaves of the house and an additional long-haired person has joined the rice
threshers and appears to be winnowing grain into a bowl. It is also possible to see
that the four drummers on their platform are alternating their beat: two are in the
act of striking the tympanum as the other pair raise their batons.

0   5cm

4.30   The tympanum of the Hoang Ha drum.
Permission: The Vietnam Social Sciences Publishing House, Hanoi.

A fourth example, the Song Da (Moulié) drum, was found last century in Ha Son Binh province (Fig. 4.31). In this case, there are four sets of processing feathered men rather than two, and each set comprises three or four people none of whom appears to be carrying a weapon. Instead, their posture suggests a march or a dance. Only one couple processes rice, and there is no cymbal player. Yet the basic elements remain in place, as with the boats on the mantle. The Quang Xuong drum from Thanh Hoa Province may be a late or provincial example. It is smaller than the previous ones, and the scene on the tympanum is so stylised that, without clearer examples for reference, it would be difficult to interpret.

Large drums with such detailed scenes are an exception in Bac Bo. Most examples have simpler decoration with fewer representations of people. The Ban Thom drum for example, has an inner panel comprising four houses and plumed individuals standing singly or in pairs (Fig. 4.32).

0   5cm

4.31 The tympanum of the Song Da (Moulié) drum.
Permission: The Vietnam Social Sciences Publishing House, Hanoi.

Pham Huy Thong *et al.* (1990) have divided the Heger 1 drums into five major groups, and imply a chronological succession. Their earliest, group A, comprises the set of large and richly ornamented drums just described. Group B drums are smaller and nearly all have a group of flying waterbirds as the dominant motif on the tympanum and geometric designs covering the mantle. Group C has a central panel on the tympanum made up of a row of plumed warriors inside a second panel of flying birds. Cast toads line the edge of the tympanum while the mantle was ornamented with stylised boats or geometric designs. In the case of the Dong Hieu drum, there are 32 such warriors and on the Nong Cong drum, there are 26. One of the problems with this sequence from large and richly decorated to small and more simply ornamented drums is a lack of contextual evidence. Most of the drums were recovered without associated dating material.

Illustrations of ritual or festive scenes, while best represented on drums, are

0   5cm

4.32   The tympanum of the Ban Thom drum.
Permission: The Vietnam Social Sciences Publishing House, Hanoi.

also found on other bronzes. Perhaps the best example is a magnificent *thap* from Dao Thinh. These lidded vessels are restricted to Bac Bo, and the Dao Thinh specimen stands 81 cm in height. The decoration on the lid resembles that on the drums, centred on a rayed sun and panels of flying crane egrets. But it is also embellished with models of copulating couples. The body of the vessel has concentric bands of rectilinear patterns and linked circles, but the central theme is again a flotilla of boats. In one, the warriors are standing, and holding weapons which include the battleaxe. One individual, lacking a plumed headdress, is seated and might represent a paddler. The boat in front contains seated figures with rather small headdresses. A flock of birds flies overhead, and one has alighted on the prow. The boats on the *thap* from Viet Khe includes one group of warriors with enormous feathered headdresses, one of whom stands on a platform.

Decoration was also extended to some armaments. A boot-shaped socketed axe from Ha Dong, for example, was ornamented with a small boat with a split prow, two standing figures above two deer and a set of geometric designs. A pediform axe from Dong Son has two plumed warriors on the blade and curvilinear ornament on the haft. Halberds, which have their origins in China, are rare in Dong Son contexts, but carry local ornament and were surely locally cast. An example from Dong Son shows a crocodile stalking a small quadruped. A second example from Nui Voi was decorated with birds and an elephant.

Dong Son bronze technology

The techniques employed by Dong Son bronze workers reflect both a continuation of earlier methods and marked innovations in techniques and scale. The fortunate recovery of a set of moulds and a crucible from Lang Ca shows that the traditional method of casting in a bivalve clay mould continued. Two layers of clay were used, a rough outer shell and an interior layer of fine clay into which a copy of the object was impressed. Exactly the same layering has been observed on the remains of clay moulds for the lost wax casting of bracelets from layer 5 at Ban Na Di. One of the Lang Ca moulds was designed for the handle of a sword, and might well have been destined for a bimetallic weapon, the blade being of iron. The Lang Ca crucible was much larger than the specimens from the Khorat Plateau, being able to take a maximum load of about 12 kg of molten metal. It had also been used before burial, for the interior was encrusted with copper scoria.

Murowchick (1989) has undertaken an atomic absorption analysis of seven bronzes recovered by Janse at Dong Son. He found that the chosen alloy now involved three constituents, copper, tin and lead. Other elements, including arsenic, were present only as traces. The same ternary alloy has been identified by Diep Dinh Hoa (1978) for spears and an axe from Chau Can. It is rather unusual to find high quantities of lead in weapons: figures of 12–13% lead have been found in two Dong Son daggers and a spearhead. A bowl included 4.5% tin and 12.91% lead which is more easily understood, for while tin imparts hardness, lead facilitates casting. The spears and daggers show that after casting, they were annealed and hammered to harden the cutting edges. Trinh Sinh (1992) has identified a major change in the range of alloys which distinguished the Go Mun and Dong Son phases, stressing in particular the widespread use of lead. But there were also ternary alloys of copper, tin and lead, copper, arsenic and lead and four alloys which involved four elements, such as copper, arsenic, lead and tin. Of the 556 items which he subjected to analysis, he found that 67 had been cast from unalloyed copper. Artefacts in this group included ploughshares, axes, spears, drums, vessels, daggers and arrowheads. Tin was present in traces up to 0.62% and lead was found up to 0.78% (Trinh Sinh 1992).

The casting procedure for the great drums and vessels was, of course, much more complex (Fig. 4.33). Most investigations, which involve drums from Guangxi Province, Bac Bo and Bali, are in broad agreement on the techniques which were employed (Bernet Kempers 1988, McConnell, Glover 1988–9 and Barnard 1996). It was first necessary to produce a central clay core. This was probably hollow to minimise weight and ease its manipulation. Separate clay pattern moulds would then be prepared, circular for the tympanum and rectangular for sections of the mantle. The surface of this clay received ornamentation in more than one way. It could be impressed with a pattern mould to create the panels of geometric ornament, or for more individual motifs or decorative elements, it could be incised with a stylus. An artist, for example, could incise into the clay the warriors, houses and birds within panels prepared by the use of a compass with a stylus at one end. This pattern mould would then have been filled with molten wax, such that the wax filled and duplicated the chosen decor.

It would then have been necessary to transfer the sheets of cooled wax to the clay core, having first placed bronze spacers strategically into the wax until they reached the surface of the pattern mould. Once the wax was in place, it would have been possible to add any further decoration, either with a stylus for negative impressions, or with thin strips or coils of wax for relief forms. This procedure resulted, in effect, in a wax drum over a clay core. Investment of the wax in a layer of very fine clay followed before the assemblage was covered in a coarse clay coat. It was then necessary to melt out the wax, and preheat the clay mould. It was at this point that the bronze spacers fulfilled their intended purpose by keeping the inner and outer moulds apart. The critical point was then reached for the pour, in the case of larger examples, of nearly 100 kg of molten bronze into the adits to reproduce in metal the wax image of the drum.

This is a task demanding both artistic and technical skill of a high order. It is difficult to envisage any other than full-time specialists being able to undertake such a casting. Indeed, von Dewall (1979) has suggested, on the basis of the halberds, spears and axes from southern China and Bac Bo, that there were local workshops of specialists which, while subscribing to the same technical tradition and many common artefact forms, were employed for their decorative motifs and styles.

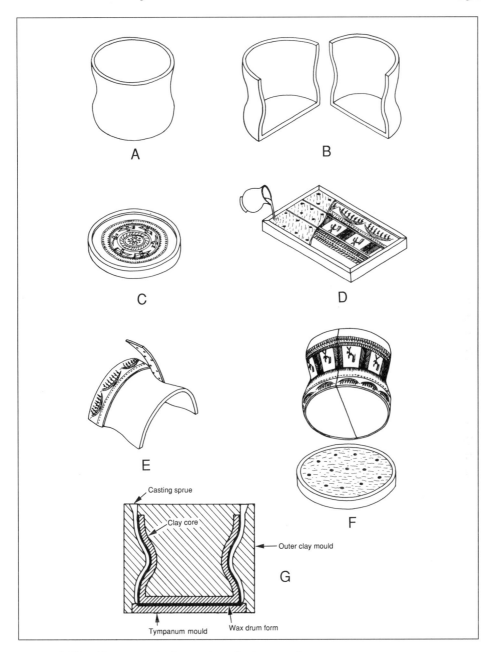

4.33   The stages in the casting of a bronze drum.
a, b. A clay core is produced. **c, d.** Wax is poured onto decorated clay. **e.**
The sheets of wax are lifted and placed on the clay core. **f.** The two halves
of the core are then placed over the similarly produced mould for the
tympanum. The assemblage is then invested with an outer clay mould and
the wax replaced with molten bronze. **g.** The metal runs down the casting
sprue, which is a narrow conduit seen in cross section.

The Dong Son culture: discussion

The archaeological and written sources agree that the last few centuries BC witnessed marked social differentiation in the lowland plains of Bac Bo. The former includes the great centre of Co Loa and rich cemeteries, the latter refer to a king, a marquess, administrators, princes and princesses, male and female servants (Ha Van Tan 1991). We also read of Lac lords owning good agricultural land and using water control based on tidal flows to augment production.

It is now clear that this major social change had its origins in local segmentary village communities like Dong Dau and Go Mun. But the Dong Son culture also developed within the wider context of numerous other such groups in the provinces of southern China. While displaying individual characteristics, it also participated in a broader movement to complexity. This may be seen, for example, in the role of metallurgy. While many of the items cast represent a local tradition, the range of bronzes is paralleled elsewhere, and this exchange of ideas occurred alongside that of a number of bronze artefacts. A comparison between Dong Son bronzes and those recovered from Warring States period graves in Lingnan shows that knives, armaments, scrapers, *dun,* and decorated socketed axes have much in common.

A glance at the bronze working tradition of the Dian aristocrats also reveals both common factors, and some consistent differences. In terms of the former, we find that bronzes were designed to fulfil several cultural objectives. Perhaps the most obvious of these is to enhance effectiveness in war. The artefacts in question include socketed spearheads, arrowheads, halberds, daggers, swords, crossbow triggers and some of the socketed axes. Spearheads, arrowheads and axes have local antecedents, but it is possible to trace the other weapons to Chinese origins. With the exception of crossbow triggers, however, they were adapted and modified to local tastes. We can also see some of the weapons in use, for example on the boat platforms. Methods of warfare must also have had local characteristics: we find no evidence for cavalry in Bac Bo.

The bronze workers were also called upon to cast ritual and sumptuary goods. There was a range of local forms of bronze vessels, including the lidded *thap,* situlae, tripods and decorated ladles which suggest that feasting played a role in the life of the aristocracy. To these we must also add the hallmark of the Dong Son repertoire, the great bronze drum. There is a considerable literature on these (Bernet Kempers 1988), and many interpretations have been offered for their use and the scenes they bear. For our purposes, it is sufficient to stress that the casting of a drum weighing in excess of 80 kg called on specialised skill of a high order, and their decoration reveals a ritual life calling on music, rice processing, impressive costumes including feathered headdresses and the use of boats. The houses and boats were themselves elaborately decorated, and birds, particularly varieties of waterbird recalling the crane, heron and egret, are prominent. Bernet Kempers (1988) has noted a description of a Muong funeral witnessed by

Goloubew before the Second World War. These people lived in Thanh Hoa and Ha Son Binh provinces, and Goloubew described:

The family drum preceded this procession in great pomp, carried by servants in mourning dress and escorted by several men holding long plumes in their hands. The sorcerers followed in Indian file, quite like the persons on the Ngoc Lu drum... (Goloubew 1940, tr. Karlgren 1942)

Bernet Kempers then noted how the Woni of southern Yunnan, during funeral rituals, 'beat drums and shake hand-bells. They stick pheasant tails on their heads and dance. They are called "those who disperse the spirits".'

It is quite possible that the drum scenes represent funeral rites, in which context the herons would symbolise longevity and the boats may be carrying away the dead spirit. But many alternatives are possible. We may be witnessing fertility ceremonies at the onset of the rains, or celebrations of victory in combat. Yet one point is beyond reasonable doubt: participation in ceremonials was part of the aristocratic society of Dong Son. Bronzes and exotic stone ornaments were also worn. We can see this in the figurines which have survived, and in the ornaments themselves, not least the plaques which have been interpreted as armour or as purely decorative devices.

Nor was agriculture overlooked. An aristocratic elite in lowland Southeast Asia cannot maintain itself for long without a willing group of followers and retainers, and they must be provided for. So bronze workers were called upon to cast heavy socketed ploughshares, hoes and sickles. They also became familiar with the properties of iron. Vietnamese archaeologists are firm on the point that iron was cast (Ha Van Tan 1991) rather than forged. This situation would involve the introduction of the technique from China, where iron casting was widespread. In the Mekong Valley and Central Thailand, in contrast, all the iron hitherto analysed was first smelted, and then forged. The Dong Son smiths were adept at manufacturing bimetallic spears and daggers, where the blade was iron, and bronze was cast onto it to form the hilt. They also made spearheads, bowls, axes and spades of iron, and some found their way, as at Xuan La, into graves as mortuary offerings. Again, close similarities with those found in Warring States period cemeteries in Lingnan are evident.

One of the problems faced when considering the Dong Son culture is that it is divided from its contemporaries to the north by the modern boundary between China and Vietnam. The interpretation of its development and status has, therefore, been prone to nationalistic bias. On the one hand, origins might be seen as Chinese and on the other, all innovations of note occurred in Vietnam. Did drums have their origins, as the Chinese would claim, on the Yunnan Plateau in the context of sites like Wanjiaba? or are Heger 1 drums, as Pham Huy Thong (1990) urges, correctly defined as Dong Son drums which developed in Bac Bo?

Arguing over such alternatives obscures the situation revealed by archaeology. What we encounter is a series of increasingly complex polities on the southern margins of the expanding Chu, Qin and Han states. During the last three or four centuries before their absorption by the Chinese, they developed increasingly centralised social structures which in purely subsistence terms, were raised on the production and deployment of agricultural surpluses. These were used to sustain the central aristocracy and their retainers. Among the latter, we find warriors and specialist artisans. One of the tasks allotted the bronze workers was to produce the goods which were used to arm the warriors and signal the high status of their leaders. Seeking the origins of this trend and the associated changes in material culture in one or other particular region misses the point. Changes were taking place across much of what is now southern China and the lower Red River Valley by groups which were exchanging goods and ideas, and responding to the expansion from the north of an aggressive, powerful state.

Summary

Lingnan and Bac Bo are pivotal in any attempt to integrate the Bronze Age of Southeast Asia with the beginning and development of metal casting in the *zhongyuan*. It is argued that until the early third millennium BC, the inhabitants of Lingnan remained affluent foragers, often occupying rich coastal habitats. It is quickly conceded, however, that further research might still identify local trends towards plant cultivation and animal husbandry. Following a long sequence of agricultural communities in the Yangzi Valley, in which rice and domestic stock were economically important, there is some evidence for an intrusive movement south into Lingnan via the linking river systems. At Shixia, the arrival of rice farmers is dated to a century or two after 3000 BC. There is no evidence for a major expansion encompassing the coastal region, but the possibility of local foragers becoming familiar with rice cultivation and even adopting it cannot be ruled out. By the late third and early second millennium BC, it is possible to discern a series of regional groups which displayed considerable expertise in the manufacture and firing of pottery vessels which involved closed kilns and the control of heat. These communities, which maintained large communal inhumation cemeteries and interred the dead with both pottery and high quality stone ornaments, also became familiar with exotic jades which find their closest parallels in the later Shang contexts to the north.

There is also a growing body of evidence for exchange in a few exotic Shang and Western Zhou bronzes, which date to the late second millennium BC. It was at this very juncture, that the local communities began to cast their own tools and weapons from bronze. The axes, fishhooks, spearheads and arrowheads, never found in abundance, have local prototypes in stone and bone. Two possible interpretations are posed: did this industry begin in the context of exposure to exotic bronzes, or was it an independent development with local origins in Lingnan, Bac Bo, or indeed in some other part of Southeast Asia?

In the sequel, further exotic bronzes reached Lingnan through exchange with the Chu state of the middle Yangzi. Dated to the Spring and Autumn and Warring States periods, the Chu sought exotic southern goods which gave, according to Allard (1994), rising local leaders the opportunity to prosper through the control of the sources and exchange routes. We find a number of impressively rich graves during this period, equipped with Chu vessels, bells, and arms in bronze.

Probably during the fourth century BC, iron joined bronze in the local repertoire, and at Yinshanling, we find that some graves were differentially large and richly equipped with grave goods. But the most illuminating evidence for this period comes from Bac Bo, where the Dong Son culture rose and flourished during the second half of the first millennium BC before succumbing to Chinese imperial expansion.

CHAPTER 5

SOUTH OF THE CLOUDS

The Yunnan Plateau

The Red River links the flat deltaic land bordering the Gulf of Bac Bo with the Yunnan Plateau (Fig. 5.1). Much of this area is covered by steep, thickly wooded uplands, but in Yunnan, which means 'south of the clouds', there are also a number of lake basins and of these, Lake Dian is particularly well placed, not only to take advantage of the natural communication route afforded by the Red River, but also to maintain easy contact with Guangxi and Guangdong to the east and, via the Jinsha River, with Sichuan, the middle Yangzi area and ultimately, with the *zhongyuan*. The upper reaches of the Red River also lie within 50 km of the Lancang which, to the south, becomes the main branch of the Mekong. In a region where river transport was critical in exchange, Yunnan is nodal.

The increased altitude and latitude combine to form a quite different climate from that encountered in the Chao Phraya, middle and lower Mekong and lower Red River valleys. Gone is the heat, and the sharp distinction between wet and dry seasons. The temperature range at Kunming varies between about 10°C on the coldest day, and 20°C on the hottest. Rainfall averages 1000 mm per annum, enough for rice cultivation on the lacustrine soils, and grass growth for raising cattle, sheep and horses. But this is also a land of lake basins hemmed in by uplands. There are no extensive river plains which characterise areas to the north and the south.

It is also a region renowned for mineral resources, with copper, tin and lead deposits found both in Yunnan and the lower reaches of the Red River above the delta (Fig. 3.5). No mining sites corresponding to Phu Lon or Non Pa Wai have been identified, but several copper mines dating to the first millennium BC reveal the scale of this industry in adjacent parts of China. The best known is Tonglüshan in Hubei Province, where mining activity commenced at least by the eleventh century BC (Du Faqing 1980, Du Faqing and Gao Wuxun 1980, Zhu Shoukan and Han Rubin 1981 and Zhao Baoquan *et al.* 1986). Extensive shafts and timber-framed tunnels follow ore veins. Initially, ore was brought to the surface by hand, but by 500 BC, winches were used and some shafts, which reached a depth of 20 m below the water table, required elaborate drainage. Since the smelting facilities incorporate stone anvils and pounders, it is apparent that ore was locally crushed and concentrated. Technological advances in the second half of the first millennium BC included gravity separation of the ores in a wooden container. A smelting furnace dated to about 800 BC stood 1.5 m high and had a hollow base,

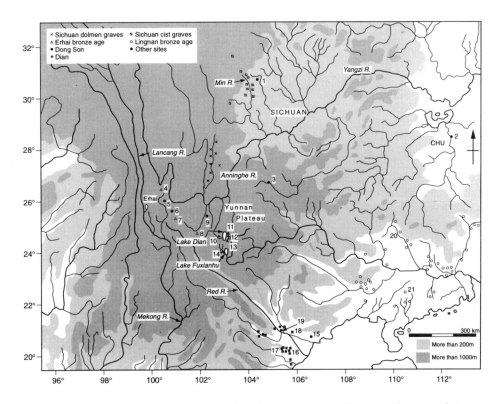

5.1 The distribution of prehistoric sites on the Yunnan Plateau relative to Lingnan and Bac Bo.
1. Sanxingdui. **2.** Changsha. **3.** Liujiagou. **4.** Aofengshan. **5.** Haimenkou. **6.** Baiyancun. **7.** Dabona. **8.** Wanjiaba. **9.** Dadunzi. **10.** Taijishan. **11.** Tianzimao. **12.** Shibeicun. **13.** Shizhaishan. **14.** Lijiashan. **15.** Viet Khe. **16.** Chau Can. **17.** Xuan La. **18.** Co Loa. **19.** Lang Ca. **20.** Yinshanling. **21.** Tongshiling.

probably to counter damp and maintain heat in the chamber above. Two tuyères maintained a constant flow of air. Malachite was the principal ore, and iron ore served as a flux.

There are several other mining sites in southern China. Tongshiling, for example, located in Guangxi province 700 km east of the lower Red River Valley, reveals extensive mining activity including shafts, galleries, slag remains and ingots dating to the late first millennium BC (Murowchick 1989). Given the quantity of bronze encountered during the Iron Age on the Yunnan Plateau, the discovery of similar mines there will surely follow appropriately directed fieldwork.

This region was settled by rice cultivators by the late third millennium BC. Baiyancun is located only 60 km east of a tributary of the Lancang (Upper Mekong) River, close to the headwaters of the Red River (Fig. 5.1). Excavations have revealed a stratigraphic sequence 4.35 m deep, divided into two phases

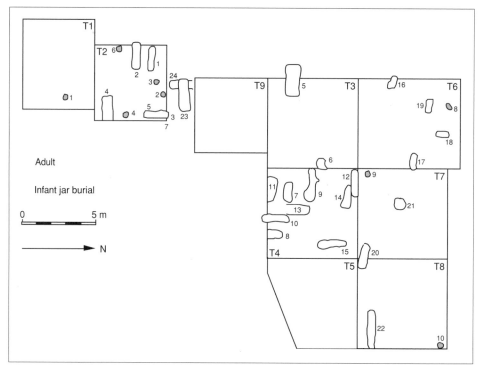

5.2   Plan of the cemetery of Baiyancun.

(YPM 1981). The foundations of eleven houses have been identified, and a cemetery of at least 34 burials. The latter were orientated with heads to the north or the east. Their layout suggests the presence of two clusters, in which there is at least one double burial (Fig. 5.2). Unusually, there are no grave goods, and many of the skeletons lack a cranium. The pottery was decorated with parallel incised lines infilled with impressions, a technique with parallels in Phung Nguyen and many other sites to the south, and the single radiocarbon date of 2462–2014 BC indicates contemporaneity with early Phung Nguyen and Non Pa Wai. The closest parallels to the pottery decoration strongly suggest close links with communities down the Red and Mekong rivers.

   The same may be said of Dadunzi (YPM 1977). This settlement covers 0.5 ha, and excavations in an area of nearly 500 m² have revealed fifteen house plans and 27 burials in the cemetery. Houses were orientated on a north-south axis, and superpositions indicate some length of settlement, the subsistence base of which included rice cultivation and the raising of domestic stock. Adults were buried in an extended position and infants were interred in jars. There was no preferred grave orientation, and the infant jar burials were not regularly placed in association with adult burials. Once again, the pottery was decorated with infilled incised bands and the single radiocarbon date of 1684–1261 BC falls within the chronological range for this tradition to the south.

No bronze was found at either site. Indeed, only two sites in Yunnan have been cited for early evidence for copper or bronze, and neither stands close scrutiny. Haimenkou in northwestern Yunnan contains pine house foundations in addition to a large assemblage of faunal remains, pottery and stone artefacts (YPM 1958). In addition, 26 copper or bronze items have been recovered. The problem is that their relationship to the stratigraphic sequence and the single radiocarbon date of 1409–1127 BC is not established. The assemblage includes many items which fit easily into the range known from the Mekong Valley sites, particularly the sandstone mould for casting a socketed axe head, several axes, bracelets and fishhooks. The awls and a possible knife, however, are not matched to the south. X-ray fluorescence analysis of these items shows that two awls were made of copper, but the majority comprise a tin bronze and one fishhook was made of a lead copper alloy. Murowchick (1989) has suggested that the decoration carved onto the surface of the stone axe mould has close parallels with a ploughshare found at Dabona and an axe from Jiancun, both dating to the fifth–fourth centuries BC. A date within the first millennium BC for the context at Haimenkou which has yielded these bronzes is suggested.

The Iron Age of the Yunnan Plateau

When turning to the Iron Age of the Yunnan Plateau, we have the benefit of contemporary Chinese accounts. Foremost is the *Shi Ji* (Records of the Historian), compiled by Sima Qian (145 to *c*. 90 BC), a court historian who wrote on a number of distinct themes which include the 'South-Western Barbarians'. He described a number of polities, stressing the importance of Yelang, Dian and Qiongdu. These incorporated agricultural settlements under a central authority. While Sima Qian referred to numerous such groups, he noted that only the rulers of Dian and Yelang had received royal seals from the Han emperor, and therefore a firm link with the empire to the north.

The contemporary historic records make it clear that southwestern chiefs commanded considerable force. Sima Qian tells us that in 109 BC, Emperor Han Wudi initiated the subjugation of the Dian polity. The King of Dian sought protection among his allies, but finally submitted and received his gold seal. At that juncture, the newly created commandery of Yizhou, within which Dian falls, comprised 81,946 households and a population of 580,463. This, however, was not the end of the matter, for four years later the populace rebelled, followed by a further insurrection in 86 BC. In 81 BC under Emperor Han Zhaodi, a conference was called to consider the situation in the southwest, and according to the *Yan Tie Lun* (Debate on Salt and Iron, a treatise on the problems of government by Huan Kuan), there was a classic problem of control over guerillas: 'if we pursue them, they flee, if we attack them they scatter'. This view is echoed in the *Hou Han Shu,* the History of the Later or Eastern Han compiled by Fan Ye (AD 398–446), who noted that the area was very rich, but given to war, including head hunting.

Such accounts describe polities with acknowledged leaders, accustomed to

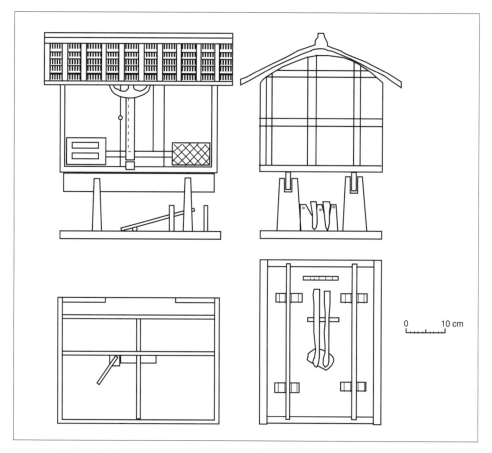

5.3   Clay house model from burial 24 at Liujiagou.

warfare but dependent on agriculture and stock raising. These groups are often distinguished in Chinese accounts by their hair styles. It seems likely that we have encountered societies with centralised authority, dense populations and much warfare between each other and with the expanding Han empire. What of the archaeological record?

Yelang

Yelang is the polity which attracted most interest from the Han. This may reflect its proximity to the empire in western Guizhou. The archaeological examination of Yelang has involved the cemetery of Liujiagou (GuiPM 1986). Between 1976-8, 208 graves were uncovered in an extensive cemetery. They were divided into two groups. There were 39 in the smaller, distinguished by their location, size and the opulence of grave offerings. There are two spatially separate rich lobes. Graves are indeed impressively large, and the interior furnishings included wooden supports for a single or sometimes a double coffin. Burial 8, for example, includes two chambers reached by a ramp, the total length being 8.1 m. It is

4.7 m wide and 2.8 in depth. Burial 10 also has a ramp leading to a chamber 6.25 × 3.6 m, and 1.9 m deep. They include numerous grave goods, many of which were imported from western Han, such as the circular bronze mirrors and coins. There are also clay house models which show a structure with a pitched roof and central ridge, several rooms and a work space under the floor, which is raised on stilts (Fig. 5.3). These large, richly furnished tombs belong to an aristocratic group dating to the last couple of centuries BC.

The dense concentration of graves to the south are smaller. Their distribution suggests some clustering and common alignments, some being set out in rows. These have been dated both typologically and on the basis of radiocarbon determinations from about the fourth to the first centuries BC. They lack coffins, but some impressive bronzes and other items were encountered which reveal the presence of conflict (Fig. 5.4). Twenty individuals were buried with the head over a bronze cauldron or a drum, and there were many bronze halberds, arrowheads, hoes, bells and bracelets. Some graves also contain Han imports as well as

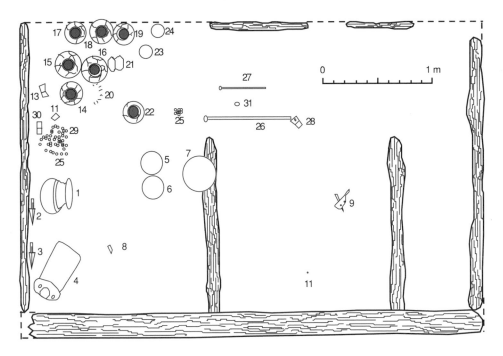

5.4a   Burial 21 from Liujiagou.
   1, 20. Bronze *fu* vessel. **2, 3.** Bronze spearheads. **4.** Ceramic well-shaped object, used as a temporary frame when building a well or as an integral part of a well. **5, 6.** Ceramic *bo* bowl. **7.** Bronze *pan* plate. **8–9, 29.** Bronze crossbow mechanism. **10, 12–13, 28.** Bronze chariot wheel end pieces. **11.** Inkstone, of shale, for grinding pigment. **14, 15–19, 23–4.** Ceramic *guan* vessel. **21.** Bronze *jiao dou*, a heating implement rather like an iron. **22.** Ceramic *yu* vessel. **25.** Bronze *wu zhu* coins. **26–7.** Iron knife. **30.** Bronze *dun*. **31.** Bronze bubble-shaped nail.

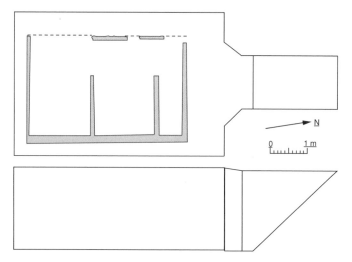

5.4b   Plan and elevation of Burial 21 from Liujiagou.

bimetallic swords and iron spades and knives. While the majority of these graves are thought to antedate the rich set to the north, some were contemporary with them.

The Dian culture

Dian is a second polity identified in Chinese historic sources and was centred on the margins of Lake Dian. Several cemeteries have been investigated, but no settlements are known.

Shizhaishan

Shizhaishan (Stone Fortress Hill), the best known site, rises 33 m above the surrounding lacustrine plain one kilometre from the eastern shore. It covers an area of 10 ha, and has attracted both settlement and use as a cemetery over many centuries. Its location contrasts with the sites in Central Thailand and the Mekong Valley, because the relatively narrow flat plain round the lake soon gives way to rugged uplands, and the amount of good low-lying land suited to agriculture is constrained.

Excavations there in 1954–60 uncovered 48 burials dating to the last few centuries BC (YPM 1956, 1959, Rudolph 1960, Pirazzoli t'Serstevens 1974). About half are outstandingly rich, and we will first review the mortuary ritual represented and the range of grave goods provided. The rocky surface of the hill meant that graves were fitted where possible into hollows between major rock outcrops. An east-west orientation was preferred, and rectangular graves were cut between 4 and 5 m long, about 2 m wide and which reached a depth varying between 0.9 and 2.85 m. These formed a tight group with as little as a metre separating some graves (Fig. 5.5). The base was flattened and ash laid as an insulation against

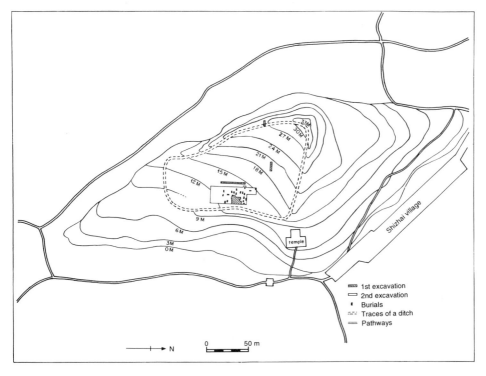

5.5 Plan of the prehistoric necropolis of Shizhaishan.

damp. Fragmentary wooden coffins have been recovered, that for burial 6 being 1.7 m long, 84 cm wide at one end tapering to 66 cm at the other. These had been lacquered in red and covered with designs in black. The coffin rested on wooden planks lacquered in vermilion, green and black. Few human remains have survived. The skeleton in burial 8 had been laid on the back with the head to the west. Burial 21 contained a person also laid supine and holding the wooden handle of a halberd. The individual in burial 9 had been injured before interment, perhaps during war.

The dead were laid out in a wooden coffin which usually contained offerings. A range of other goods were placed round the coffin. Burial 6, for example, was interred in a grave measuring 4.2 × 1.9 m (Fig. 5.6). The disposition of the coffin fragments indicated that it contained, apart from the human remains, numerous beads of turquoise, agate and gold, a bronze mirror, jade rings, a sword with an iron blade, bronze hilt and a gold scabbard and finally, a gold seal bearing the inscription in seal script which reads 'The seal of the King of Dian'. The northwest corner of the grave contained a group of bronze drums and cowrie containers in the shape of a drum. A bronze figure of a man holding what some have called a sunshade stood on top of one of the drums (Fig. 5.7). Tong Enzheng (1991), however, has persuasively argued that he holds a ceremonial staff symbolising the status of the dead. A set of bronze vessels had been placed in the centre of the

5.6 Plan of burial 6 from Shizhaishan.

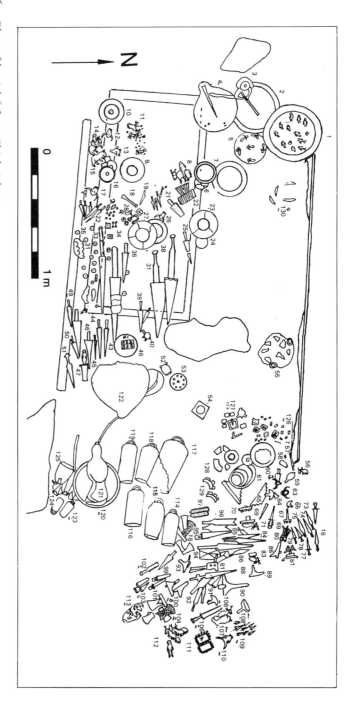

1 Cowrie container made from two drums, the uppermost being decorated with a battle scene. 2, 5 Cowrie container. 3–4, 121-2 Human figure holding a staff ending in the form of a parasol. 6 Fragmentary implement. 7 Small cowrie container. 8, 13-15, 17, 30, 41,107, 111, 113 Decorated plaque. 9, 16, 24, 42,129 Belt ornament. 10 Gold bead and button. 12, 26, 63, 110 Cattle figurine. 18 Socketed knife. 19 Knife. 20 25, 73, 84,6, 99 Spearhead. 21, 29, 39, 43-4, 48-51, 68, 72, 74-9, 92 Sword. 22 Model of a house. 23, 27, 128 Jade armring. 28 Horse and chariot fitting. 31 Agate bead and button. 32 Gold bead. 33 Iron sword with golden scabbard. 34 Golden seal of the King of Dian. 35-8, 102 Bimetallic (bronze and iron) sword. 40 Wine container. 52 Bell. 53 Footed incense cup. 54 Brazier. 55 Mixing jug. 56-7, 65 Fragments. 58 Human skull fragment. 59 Round axe (*qh*). 61 Tripod (*fu*) and two cups (*pan*). 62 Two stands. 64, 66, 106 Battle axe (*yue*). 67, 83, 132 Shaft-hole axe. 69, 103 Hafting iron. 70-1, 82, 89-90, 95, 100-1 Halberd (*ge*). 80 Fish staff head. 81 Iron spear. 87. Crossbow mechanism. 93, 98, 104 socketed axe. 94, 123-4 Hoe (*chu*). 96 Pronged weapon. 97 Mace. 105 Sword with golden scabbard. 108 Mushroom-shaped implement. 109 Arrowhead. 114-9 Set of bells. 120 Cowrie container. 125 Large bell. 126 Fragment of jade. 127 Horse trapping. 130 Two gilt cup handles. 137 Jade armring.

Permission: Yunnan Provincial Museum.

grave, with the remains of a decorated horse harness. The northeast corner was filled with many bronze weapons, including halberds, swords, spearheads, maces, axes, arrowheads and crossbow trigger mechanisms. Another drum was found in the southeast, bearing an identical figurine to that in the northwest, and alongside lay a bronze ploughshare, hoes and spades and six bells set out in two rows of three.

Pirazzoli-t'Serstevens (1974) has considered the arrangement of offerings in the rich graves and suggested that they can be divided into four groups. The first has four burials of which she has cited burial 16 as an example. Orientated east-west, the offerings include a row of bronze drums and cowrie containers at the western end. A table in front of them bore a bronze sword. Axes, halberds and jade rings were found at the southern end and the northern side included a bronze axe, two wine containers and a set of panpipes. The second group is considerably richer. Burial 3 measured 3.2 × 1.5 m and reached a depth of 2.55 m. The western end included an iron sword in a golden scabbard and the northwest corner was reserved for drums and cowrie containers. Again, one of the former bore a large bronze figurine. Two pairs of ceremonial maces and two pairs of bronze forks with wooden handles were found on the northern side. Other grave goods included twelve bronze swords disposed round a bronze vase, a bronze bull's head, aligned beads of gold, agate and turquoise, circular and rectangular bronze ornaments, axes and halberds. The interior of the coffin contained a bronze mirror

5.7   Bronze figure of a tomb guardian from burial 6, Shizhaishan. Height, 38 cm. *Permission:* Yunnan Provincial Museum.

5.8   Bronze halberd from burial 13 at Lijiashan, showing a widely-used human
head-hunting motif on the hilt. Length, 25 cm.
Permission: Yunnan Provincial Museum.

and ten bronze swords, agricultural implements, bronze fish, spearheads, and
dagger ornaments.

The third group of burials includes burial 6 while the fourth, which comprises
only two graves, furnished few grave goods. Burial 8 includes four caches of
Chinese *wu zhu* coins belonging to the Western Han dynasty (206 BC–AD 8). A
feature of the second grave in this group, burial 12, is the number of pottery
vessels.

On the basis of the changing typology of grave goods and the presence of
artefacts with parallels or origins in the states to the north, the graves at
Shizhaishan have been divided chronologically into four phases. Phase 1 is
marked by flat-handled swords without hilt guards and spears and axes with oval
sockets. But the graves also display considerable sumptuary wealth: there are
drums, cowrie containers, maces, halberds, and wine vessels. No graves of this
period contain iron. There is some controversy over the dating of this phase,
because at the related site of Lijiashan, wood associated with similar items has
been dated to the fifth century BC. But the wood might have been old before it
was used, and this fifth century date has not been widely accepted. The second
phase is securely dated to the second century BC (Pirazzoli-t'Serstevens 1988). It
sees the first bronze agricultural implements, and square-socketed spears and
axes. The third phase belongs to the end of the second and first centuries BC and
witnessed the influx of many Han items including mirrors, vessels and coins. Iron
weapons, including spears, swords and halberds often with bronze handles also
appear. The fourth phase belongs to the first century AD.

Pirazzoli-t'Serstevens (1974) has divided the bronzes from the twenty graves
excavated in 1966–7 into weapons, tools of production, ornaments and ceremonial vessels. Weapons predominate. There are 266 arrowheads, 229 spearheads and 214 swords. Bronze workers also made a range of different types of axe
and halberd, maces, forks and crossbow triggers. The principal types of weapon
may be subdivided on the basis of form into numerous varieties, many of which
were decorated. This involved figures of people and animals in the round, and

both animal and geometric motifs. A scene of warriors with the severed heads of captives recurs on the blades of axes and halberds (Fig. 5.8). It is also evident that some, at least, of the warriors wore bronze armour. Representations of battles, dancers and musicians show participants wearing a circular belt ornament, and

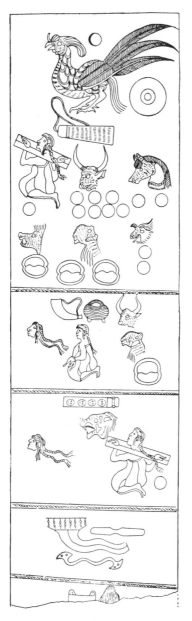

5.9 Bronze plaque from burial 13 at Shizhaishan, showing a phoenix, human captives, cowrie shells, livestock, and a possible numbering system. Height, 42 cm. *Permission:* Yunnan Provincial Museum.

5.10 A battle scene on top of a bronze drum used to contain cowrie shells from burial 6, Shizhaishan. Total height including drum, 53.9 cm. *Permission:* Yunnan Provincial Museum.

numerous examples have been recovered from Shizhaishan. These were cast from bronze and embellished with jade, turquoise and agate. Other ornaments include jewelled bracelets and belt clasps. Bronze was also converted into tools for agriculture and production. There are socketed ploughshares weighing up to 1.6 kg, hoes, spades and sickles. Wood-working was facilitated with axes, adzes, chisels and a saw.

Pottery vessels are rare, but many sumptuary bronze vessels were placed in graves. These indicate the consumption of much wealth in mortuary ritual, but the clearest example of this practice is seen in the provision of drums and cowrie containers. The latter often take the form of drums, with the tympanum replaced by a circular sheet of bronze bearing scenes of aristocratic activities. Historically, the cowrie shell was used as a form of currency in Yunnan and these drums were filled with them. Pirazzoli-t'Serstevens (1992) has suggested that these shells, most of which probably originated in the Indian Ocean, were not used as currency during the period of Dian, but were rather hoarded by the elite as a symbol of high status. This possibility is supported by a bronze plaque from burial 13, which bears a series of illustrations in panels which are thought to symbolise wealth. Apart from cowries there are slaves, cattle, a horse and various other animals, and even a possible simple form of symbolising numbers (Fig. 5.9).

The Shizhaishan cemetery was reserved for the highest social echelon and the provision of sumptuary grave goods was seen as a central part of their mortuary ritual. But the consummate skill of the specialist bronze smiths has provided further insight into the world of Dian by recreating scenes of war, ceremony, feasting, agriculture and gift giving. These scenes are so dynamic and detailed that we are virtually invited to participate, to enter people's homes, to feel the danger of battle and solemnity of ritual. The bronze specialists cast individuals, buildings, animals and artefacts and welded them to the surface of cowrie containers to depict events known to them. Rarely is a prehistoric society represented with such clarity.

A cowrie container from burial 6 depicts a battle involving 22 miniature soldiers, each standing about 6 cm high, and five horses (Fig. 5.10). There is a melée involving vicious hand-to-hand fighting. A mounted warrior wearing armour is plunging a spear into the back of a man who lies prone in the dust. Another horseman spears his adversary, who has fallen off his bolting horse. A foot soldier holds a spear with one hand and a shield with the other. Another prepares his crossbow. Two bound captives are guarded by a soldier wielding a sword. We can see the attack, duels, killing and captives. The different hair styles of victor and vanquished show that Dian won the day.

A similar scene is found on a cowrie container from burial 13 (Fig. 5.11). The battle is dominated by a gilded horseman depicted larger than life, wearing a helmet and armour. He charges into battle, wielding his spear and with a sword at his waist. Already, the severed head of a victim dangles from the bridle, and a

5.11 A battle scene from the lid of a cowrie container from burial 13 at Shizhaishan. The central figure is gilded. Diameter, 30 cm.
Permission: Yunnan Provincial Museum.

5.12   Detail of the battle scene from the lid of a cowrie container from burial 13 at Shizhaishan. A Dian warrior is seen in the act of decapitating his adversary. Note the gilded leader on horseback, equipped with bronze armour, and the headless corpse. Diameter, 30 cm.
Permission: Yunnan Provincial Museum.

naked, headless corpse lies beside him as he prepares to spear a second enemy who looks up, prostrate and defenceless. Two men with plaited hair carry shields and are defending themselves with swords against their helmeted assailants. A third plaited individual is running away from two pursuers, one of whom is carrying a severed human head in his left hand. To the left of the central gilded leader, a soldier has grasped the right plait of his adversary and has his foot firmly planted on his victim's back as he prepares to decapitate him (Fig. 5.12).

Huang Ti and Wang Dadao (1983) have suggested that these were battles between the people of Dian and the Kunming. They have drawn our attention to a passage from the *Shi Ji* which describes the latter as 'great robbers and murderers'.

The fate awaiting captives is revealed in scenes of torture and execution. A gilded belt ornament no more than 9 cm high shows two armoured soldiers each carrying a severed head, escorting a woman and child, together with plundered stock: a cow, a sheep and a goat.

The most complex of all scenes on cowrie containers comes from burial 12. It is dominated by a central dais under a steeply pitched roof at the head of which a seated person, larger than life, presides (Fig. 5.13a). He wears ear rings, large bracelets and a round ornament on his chest. Two rows of men sit before him, five to the right and three to the left. Some hold drinking vessels, others have placed theirs on the ground. Behind them and on the edge of the dais, 16 drums have been arranged in a row. A servant brings sustenance while mounting the steep access stairs, and containers of food are set out below (Fig. 5.13b).

A crowd has gathered round the dais, and many animals are represented (Fig. 5.13c). A tiger feeds on a dog, another is tied to a post. A woman feeds a pig and another gives snake meat to a peacock. An ox lies in front of the slaughterman, who brandishes his knife while a sheep and pig await their turn. A man carries a large fish, and there is much evidence for feasting as Dian women prepare and serve bowls of food. The concourse also involves sacrifice. A person

5.13a Cowrie container from burial 12 at Shizhaishan. A raised structure dominates a scene of feasting and torture. A leader seated centrally on the dais is receiving homage. Total height, 53 cm.
Permission: Yunnan Provincial Museum.

is tied to a post, another has already been partially consumed by a snake. A man is beating on a drum, one of four suspended from posts.

The attention to detail and the variety of activities suggest that we are witnessing an event of some moment. A meeting between people of high status under the direction of a highly-ranked man is taking place on the platform, and there is much feasting and music associated with the sacrifice of two victims. Huang Ti and Wang Dadao (1983:218) have suggested that this scene depicts a ceremony involving the swearing of allegiance between the leaders of different communities. They have cited historic texts which describe the importance attached to such alliances, and the associated ceremonial. The sacrificial victim has been tied to a pillar, which contemporary Chinese sources describe as a *she* or altar to the Earth God. A second pillar has two entwined snakes coiled round it. Mythologically, snakes were seen as spirits closely associated with the earth. The *Zhou Li,* which was compiled during the Han Dynasty, describes Zhou and

5.13b   The cowrie container from burial 12 at Shizhaishan reveals numerous activities surrounding the events on the raised dais. Note the number of drums. Each human figure stands between 12–14 cm in height. *Permission:* Yunnan Provincial Museum.

5.13c A close-up of the scene on the cowrie container from burial 12, Shizhaishan, shows a large receptacle for cooking, the servant climbing the ladder to the dais, and a crowd involved in food preparation. Each human figure stands between 12–14 cm in height.
Permission: Yunnan Provincial Museum.

possibly some Han Dynasty rituals, which incorporate the sacrifice of animals during important ceremonies.

This scene, therefore, probably represents ceremonies associated with a significant meeting to swear alliance. It involved feasting and sacrifice accompanied by music in a formal context, surrounding a central dais. To judge from the variety of costumes and hairstyles, several communities are represented.

Two further tableaux involving human sacrifice have been associated with sowing and the harvest. In the first, which comes from burial 20, centre stage is taken by three drums of diminishing size, one placed over the other. Thirty-two people take part. A decapitated victim, lies on the ground. Another is securely tied to a post (Fig. 5.14). Two men bear a woman seated in a sedan chair. She is gilded, and has a bevy of attendants. Another group of women carry sacks, baskets and agricultural implements including socketed hoes. The relationship between spring sowing and human sacrifice is apparent in rites which, according to the *Chun Qiu* (Spring and Autumn Annals), were presided over by women.

5.14   A scene involving human sacrifice from a cowrie container recovered from
burial 20 at Shizhaishan. A victim is tied to a post, and in the distance, three
drums are placed on top of each other. The container is 30 cm high.

The symbolism of the snake and pillar is seen again in a scene from a cowrie
container in the form of a drum from burial 1 (Fig. 5.15). It involves 51 individuals
engaged in various activities round the central pillar. There appear to be three
sacrificial victims. A woman is tied to a post, another person has one foot in a set
of stocks and a third kneels, with hands tied behind the back. An element of
formality is seen in four rows of women, each carrying an offering in a basket. A
highly-ranked woman is borne by four men in her sedan chair, followed by
servants. She is looking ahead and upward, but to her right, there are four women
with baskets containing fish and meat. Huang Ti and Wang Dadao (1983:226)
have interpreted this scene as a sacrifice to celebrate a successful harvest, the
snakes round the central pillar representing 'the generative power of the earth'.
Supporting evidence comes from the *Li Ji* (Book of Rituals), which links the
agricultural round and the seasons with the hibernation period of snakes.

The side of a cowrie container from burial 12 shows the harvest being brought in. Women carry sacks of rice to a storehouse, some with two sacks balanced on their heads. Others carry empty baskets, but one has three full sacks in her basket. Tong Enzheng (1991) has interpreted the scene as one depicting the collection of rice in a central repository and its subsequent redistribution.

A variety of costumes and hairstyles are represented on a cowrie container from burial 13 (Fig. 5.16). A drum was provided with a flat, circular top around which process several people with animals. The workmanship is of the highest quality and provides a clear view of the clothing and appearance of each person. To judge from dress, bearing and personal ornaments, the file includes people of differing rank. In one group of four, for example, the first two are clad in tunics and trousers and each wears a sword. They are followed by a porter without a sword, and the last in line is virtually naked and leads an ox. A second group of three also has a man with a sword in front. He is wearing a cape, trousers to his knees and a long shirt. He is followed by two porters. Neither has a sword. A man with a sword and hair tied in a double topknot then comes into view, followed by an attendant carrying a large basket on his back out of which emerges the leg of a pig. The next man has his hair in a double plait like the victims of the battles

5.15 A scene to celebrate a successful harvest from a cowrie container found in burial 1, Shizhaishan. Note the woman carried aloft on a sedan chair. A person in the foreground is working the soil with a hoe. Height, 30 cm. *Permission:* Yunnan Provincial Museum.

5.16   A procession set out on top of a cowrie container from burial 13, Shizhaishan. Height, 39.5 cm.
Permission: Yunnan Provincial Museum.

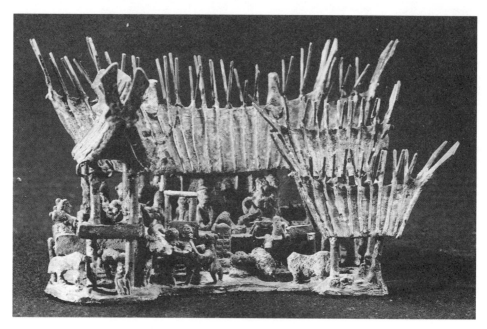

5.17   Model of a house from burial 13, Shizhaishan. A festive occasion is in progress. Height, 11.2 cm.
Permission: Yunnan Provincial Museum.

described above. He has a sword and wears a long, elegant gown. His retainer has a similar hairstyle and leads an ox. Again, they are followed by a well-dressed man with a sword and a follower holding a flat object over his right shoulder. The last group involves a leader wearing large earrings, a hat and a decorated gown. He has a sword, as does his groom, who is leading a horse.

The members of each group reveal different hairstyles and dress. In each case, the leading person has a sword and is followed by a retainer or retainers in charge of an animal or carrying some other object. The *Hou Han Shu* (History of the Later Han) describes how the members of the Kunming tribe wore their hair in plaits whereas the Dian preferred a topknot. The procession could, therefore, represent tribute missions from different groups to the Dian paramount. Some were Dian people, others were alien.

The Dian bronze specialists cast house models of such clarity and detail that we have a rare, possibly unique, opportunity to consider domestic architecture and activities. The largest is a multi-roomed *ganlan* building, which comprised decking raised on pillars under a steeply-pitched wooden roof (Fig. 5.17). Despite its tiny size – the maximum length is 17 cm and it stands 11.2 cm in height – this model provides a wealth of detail. The main room has a mezzanine floor giving access to a balcony, on which sit two women. An interior niche contains a human head. Three men are sitting round a table, and a cauldron with a ladle is positioned in front of the wall niche. Someone is cooking, another man appears to be drinking from a wine cup. A couple copulate in a dark corner. Four men sitting outside are being served drinks. Domestic cattle, pigs and horses shelter under an outer platform, and three men are dancing to the music of a flute. Burial 3 has provided a second, smaller house. It has a narrow roofed area which only partially covers a raised floor. A tethered horse and sleeping groom are seen outside (Fig. 5.18). Once again, a wall niche contains a human head, and the head of an ox has been affixed to the exterior wall. The main platform supports twenty party goers, all of whom are, to judge from their hairstyle, Dian people. Food is laid on a table, and on the outer balustrade. There are joints of pork and beef. Some men dance, others beat drums. On the ground outside, cooks prepare food, and cattle watch curiously from under the platform. It looks as if some form of celebration is in progress.

A third house model was found in burial 6 (Fig. 5.19). The pillars and boards are decorated with linear and curved designs and a snake is modelled on the stairway. Cattle are stabled beneath, and a niche on the outer wall encloses a human head. Food is liberally disposed on plates on top of the balustrade, and on the ground outside, three people are cooking, one blowing on the charcoal within the stove.

Huang Ti and Wang Dadao (1983) have stressed a common theme in these three domestic scenes. Feasting and drinking take place around the central human head in the wall niche. High status people are being waited on, servants prepare food. One visitor appears to have arrived on a horse, and his attendant

5.18   A house model from burial 3, Shizhaishan, showing a feast. A groom sleeps
beside a tethered horse to the right of the house. Height, 9 cm.
Permission: Yunnan Provincial Museum.

waits outside. There is music and dancing to the sound of drums and flutes. We
are once again reminded that, according to historic accounts of the people living
in this region, feasting was common practice, and guests reciprocated in their own
homes at a later date.

The picture presented by these tableaux can be supplemented from a variety
of sources. The drums and containers, for example, were themselves decorated
with scenes, and these include hunting and representations of large and
impressive war canoes. Shizhaishan is, after all, located close to the shore of Lake
Dian. Less well known are the scenes shown on belt buckles. A gilded example
from burial 13 shows a musical ensemble and a group of singers, all of whom

5.19 A house model from burial 6, Shizhaishan, showing feasting. People in the left foreground are preparing food, a dog guards the entrance and joints of meat are laid out around the balcony. Height, 11.5 cm.
Permission: Yunnan Provincial Museum.

wear the circular belt discs and, during their performance, have put their wine flasks on the floor beside them (Fig. 5.20). Tiger hunting was popular. A belt buckle from burial 17 shows a group of hunters spearing a tiger, which is being savaged by hunting dogs as it kills one of the hunters, its jaws tightly gripped on the man's throat (Fig. 5.21). Burials 3, 6 and 7 have yielded almost identical buckle ornaments which show a bull fight. Rows of spectators look down as the bull charges through a portal below them (Fig. 5.22).

Shizhaishan was the royal necropolis of the Dian polity. Before assessing the wealth of information obtained, however, it is necessary to consider other sites in the Yunnan lake region. To what extent did the mortuary ritual of Shizhaishan stand apart from that represented at other cemeteries? Four further sites which have been subjected to extensive excavation are found on or near the shore of Lake Dian: Tianzimao, Shibeicun, Taijishan and Lijiashan.

5.20   A group of musicians and dancers are seen on this gilt buckle ornament from burial 13, Shizhaishan. Height, 9.5 cm.
Permission: Yunnan Provincial Museum.

5.21   A buckle from burial 17 at Shizhaishan, showing a hunting scene. Height, 11.5 cm.
Permission: Yunnan Provincial Museum.

5.22 A buckle from burial 6 at Shizhaishan, showing a crowd watching a bull fight. Height, 5.6 cm.
Permission: Yunnan Provincial Museum.

Tianzimao

Tianzimao is located about 30 km north of Shizhaishan, and excavations in 1979–80 uncovered 44 burials (Hu Shaojin 1984). Their distribution indicates a tight group with little evidence for intercutting, centred upon one very large grave (Fig. 5.23). The orientation was east to west. The absence or rarity of human remains seriously limits the social information available, but the inventory of grave goods from each burial reveals much variability in wealth and the range of offerings. Burial 41, the largest, has attracted much interest because of the opulence and variety of its grave goods, and the detail available for the mortuary rites of a person of considerable social standing. Two radiocarbon dates from the wood used in the grave (770–90 BC and AD 60–350) indicate that the cemetery may be dated between 300–100 BC, or contemporary with Shizhaishan. This grave measures 6.3 × 4 m, and reached a depth of 4 m. A ledge towards the base marked the edge of the coffin chamber, and supported a row of timbers (Fig. 5.24). Grave goods were found below this platform, and upon it. The lower chamber, which was lined with a wooden floor, supported a coffin about 2 m in length, containing the remains of an adult and a child. Many offerings were found in association, including bronze vessels, a drum, and many bronze weapons. There was also a bronze drum containing the only iron object found in the site, a scraper, and a bronze headrest. A group of spears had been placed at the eastern end and numerous decorated circular plaques were recovered.

The platform still bore traces of the mats which covered it, over which had been

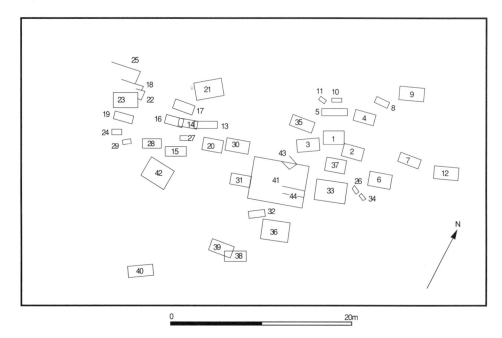

5.23   The plan of the cemetery at Tianzimao.

placed further bundles of offerings, which had been wrapped in silk or placed in boxes. The list includes eighteen swords, spears, plates of armour, belt discs, ladles, and agate and jade jewellery. Over 10,000 malachite beads were recovered. The bronze weapons and vessels are notable for their elaborate decoration (Figs. 5.25a, 5.25b and 5.25c). We see cattle and boats, while the halberds are often decorated with a motif interpreted by Murowchick (1989) as a head-hunting scene.

Other graves are considerably smaller, although some still contain a number of bronzes. Burial 33, for example, adjacent and to the east of burial 41, contains a drum, a cowrie shell container ornamented with models of cattle, small bronze bells, a circular belt disc, daggers, spears and items of jade jewellery.

With the exception of burial 41, for which a complete inventory of mortuary goods is unavailable, the interments at Tianzimao have been subjected to a series of statistical analyses. Multidimensional scaling has separated three groups of graves from the majority, which have relatively few grave goods. The first, represented by burial 33 in figure 5.26, is very rich indeed. Burial 41 would, if included in the analysis, lie even further from the main group. Burials 11, 12, 19 and 21 all contained spindle whorls. Dian scenes show women in weaving scenes, and these graves were probably, therefore, those of females. None of these graves contain any weapons, but pottery vessels are present in all but burial 11. There are other graves with spindle whorls, but little else, and they appear in the large central cluster of poor graves. Three graves are separated by high negative values for axis 2. This reflects the presence of exotic stone jewellery.

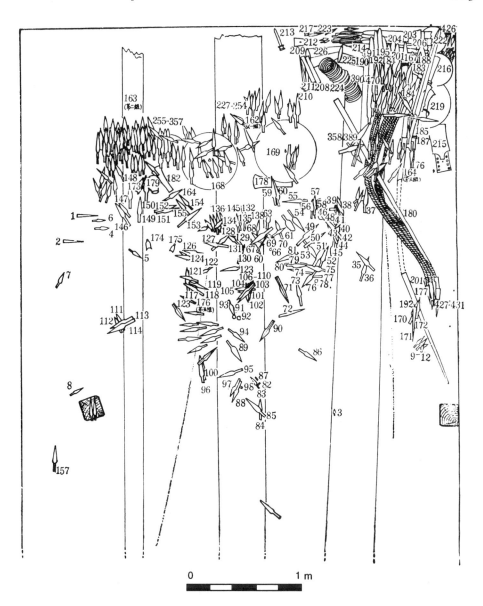

5.24 Burial 41 at Tianzimao.

1, 2, 156, 171, 177, 180, 427–31. Bronze *zun*, a bronze artefact placed at the butt end of a *ge* dagger axe. **3, 217, 223, 426.** Thirteen bronze arrowheads. **4–12, 23, 35–155, 157, 162–5, 167, 170, 172, 176, 183–202, 227–424.** Bronze arrowheads (n=351). **13, 166, 212, 215.** Bronze axes. **14–22, 24–6, 178, 182.** Bronze hoes. **27** Bronze sword. **28–30.** Round, hollowed-out tin ornaments. **31–4.** Agate beads. **158–161.** Bronze drums. **168–9, 216, 219, 222.** Shield ornament. **173–5.** Bronze bells. **179.** Ceramic *guan* vessel. **181.** Two bronze *yue* axes. **203–7, 214.** Six bronze *ge* dagger axes. **208–9, 213.** Bronze chisels. **210–1.** Unnamed bronze artefacts. **218.** Pottery sherd. **221, 225–6.** Bronze arm armour. **224.** Bronze bracelets (n=79). *Permission:* Publications Department, Kexue Chubanshe.

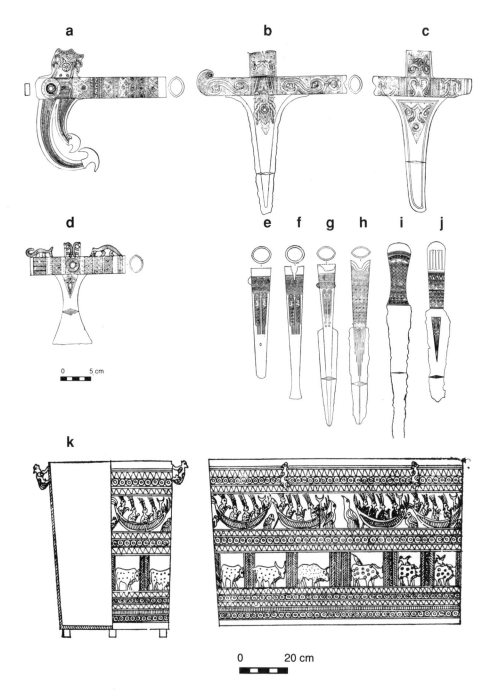

5.25   Bronze artefacts from burial 41 at Tianzimao.
a, b. *Ge* dagger axes.   **c, d**. Shaft-hole axes.   **e, f**. Socketed axes.   **g, h**.
Spearheads. **i, j**. Daggers. **k**. Situla decorated with cattle, birds and warriors
in boats.

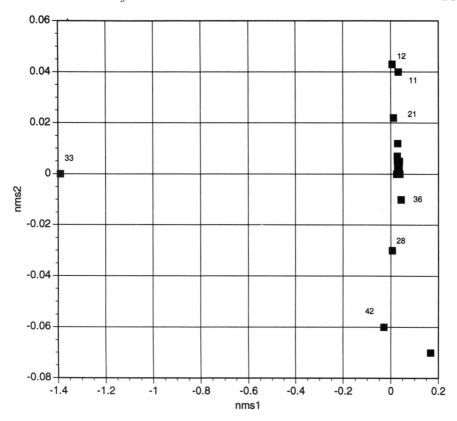

5.26 The distribution of graves at Tianzimao after multidimensional scaling.

Burial 42 included 150 agate beads and eight lacquer bracelets, burial 28 included eight jade tubes and burial 36, 50 agate beads and five jade tubes. It is clear that one large grave, located centrally in the cemetery, contained a male of very high rank, separated from all other individuals represented except burial 33, probably another high status male. This presumed male grave included spindle whorls among the grave goods. There was some distinction between males (with their bronze weapons) and females (with their ceramic spindle whorls), but these register only faintly in the distribution of burials determined by this analysis.

Shibeicun

Shibeicun is located between Shizhaishan and Tianzimao. Excavations over two seasons have uncovered 182 graves which have been divided into three phases on the basis of superpositions and artefact typology (Wang Dadao and Qiu Xuanchong 1980, Hu Shaojin 1984). These span the period from the fifth century BC to the early first millennium AD. The plan of the cemetery uncovered during the second campaign in 1979 reveals four rows of burials, interred on an east to west axis. None stands out on the basis of size, nor wealth. Grave goods include swords, spears and halberds, the last decorated with the same head-hunting scenes as have been identified at Tianzimao. Graves from the third phase, dating to the first century BC, have yielded iron swords, spears and axes with bronze hafts and Chinese coins.

Taijishan

Taijishan is located to the west of Lake Dian. Excavations have uncovered seventeen graves, of which thirteen have been assigned to an early phase dating to the second millennium BC (von Dewall 1967). Most of the artefacts comprise pottery vessels and spindle whorls with little bronze, but the four later ones, which belong to the first century BC, include some bronzes typical of other Dian sites, including two pieces of armour and weapons. Two iron swords with bronze hilts were also found.

Lijiashan

Lakes Fuxianhu and Xingyunhu lie to the south of Lake Dian, and belong to a different drainage system. Archaeological inquiries have revealed evidence for occupation by people closely related to those who lived on the Dian lacustrine plain. The principal site is another cemetery, Lijiashan, 40 km south of Shizhaishan on the western edge of Lake Xingyunhu (Zhang Zengqi and Wang Dadao 1975). Excavations on this hilltop in 1972 revealed 27 graves of which seven, set out in a row, are outstandingly wealthy (Fig. 5.27). A further fifteen are smaller and more modestly furnished, and a third group of five have been ascribed to a late phase of use. Wood from several axe hafts has been combined and radiocarbon dated to (830–400 BC), but this date does not accord with the material culture, which, for the majority of graves and all the rich ones, corresponds to the early Western Han period and therefore, are contemporary with many of the royal graves from Shizhaishan (Pirazzoli-t'Serstevens 1988).

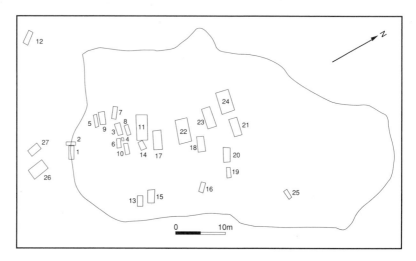

5.27   Plan of the cemetery of Lijiashan.

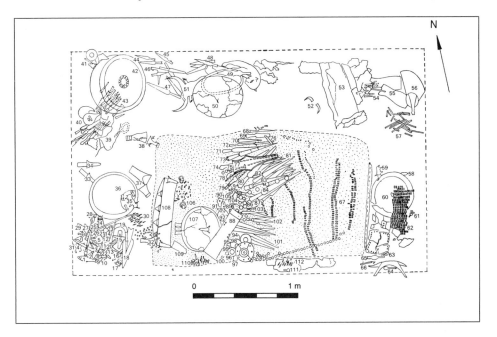

0   1 m

5.28 Burial 24 from Lijiashan
1. Staff head in the form of a fish. **2, 76, 105.** Whetstone. **3–4, 12–13.** Shaft-hole axe (*zhuo*). **5, 7–9.** Round axe (*qi*). **10, 14–15, 33–4.** Halberd (*ge*). **11** Hollow staff attachment. **16–17.** Spear-headed mace (*bang*) **18–19, 21–3, 29, 31, 44–9.** Spearhead. **20.** Battle axe (*yue*). **24.** Wine flask (*hu*). **25, 41.** Trumpet-shaped attachment. **26.** Bronze piece of armour. **27–8, 32.** Axe. **30, 110, 112.** Arrowhead. **35.** Sewing box. **36, 60.** Drum. **37–38.** Footed vessel (*bei*). **39.** Bronze fragment. **40.** Mouth organ (*sheng*) in the form of a gourd decorated with a bull. **42.** Cowrie container in the form of two drums. **43.** Razor, sword, spear, awl, hafting iron, and whetstone. **50.** Oval plate. **51.** Sacrificial altar. **52.** Bronze cattle horns. **53, 62–3.** Back armour. **54.** Hafting iron. **55.** Leg armour. **56.** Helmet fragment. **57.** Small plate. **58.** Yarn or thread holder. **59.** Cattle figurine. **61, 66.** Human-form staff attachment. **64.** Ladle (*shao*). **65.** Carder. **67.** Beads of jade and agate. **68, 70, 78, 103.** Razor. **69, 71–4, 77, 79–87, 101.** Sword. **88** Quiver fittings. **89–91, 97, 99–100.** Decorated plaque. **92–6, 98.** Belt ornament. **104.** Jade armring. **106.** Jade ear pendant. **107.** 'Umbrella'. **108.** Head rest. **109.** Arm armour. **111.** Armour fragment.
Permission: Yunnan Provincial Museum.

The graves reveal a similar ritual and degree of opulence as the elite graves from Shizhaishan. Burial 24, which is located at the northern end of the row of rich graves, measures just over 4 m in length and 2.5 m wide and on an east to southeast orientation (Fig. 5.28). The grave goods were laid out in an orderly manner. Although no human remains survived, the body, to judge from the disposition of ornaments, would have lain along the long axis of the grave. Rows of jade and agate beads cross laterally along the assumed position of the corpse. Beyond the head and the feet, there are two drums, the former being associated with a lidded bronze box embellished with five oxen. Two further drums with cowries are found in the northwestern corner of the grave. A superb bronze headrest was found in the assumed area of the skull. On the northern side of the grave, the excavators encountered possibly the single most impressive bronze from the Yunnan Plateau. It has the form of a sacrificial table, represented by a bull with a tiger attacking its hindquarters (Fig. 5.29). A second, smaller bull is seen under it. The quantity and variety of bronze armaments suggest that this was the grave of an aristocratic warrior. A helmet and bronze armour were found beyond and to the left of the foot of the grave. This has been partially reconstructed. Each shoulder is ornamented with a face, and clouds and lizards embellish the projections to protect the neck. Equally elaborate decoration is seen on armour for the forearm from burial 13 (Fig. 5.30)

A cluster of arrowheads lay in the region of the right hand, next to a bronze quiver. A further set of arrowheads had been placed beside a large, ceremonial spearhead and a halberd beyond the headrest and a cluster of swords covered the area beside the left arm. Some of the decorated axes with bronze hafts must have been more for ceremonial than for use in combat. The area beyond the headrest had been chosen for placing bronze wine containers. One flask, which stands 35.5 cm high and weighs 2.72 kg, was embellished with a bull figurine on the stopper. There are also numerous bronzes fit for the burial of such an aristocrat: a bronze

5.29   Sacrificial table from burial 24 at Lijiashan, in the form of two cattle and a leaping tiger. Length, 76 cm.
Permission: Yunnan Provincial Museum.

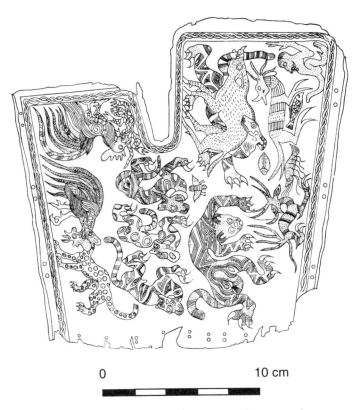

0   10 cm

5.30   Decorated armour from burial 13 at Lijiashan. Length, 21.7 cm.
Permission: Yunnan Provincial Museum.

sheng flute lies beside one of the drums. There are bull figurines and a bronze fish which would have acted as a finial on top of a wooden staff. Jade earrings and bracelets hint at the location of the head and hands. A group of circular belt ornaments cluster to the right of where the right hand would have rested. All the symbols of high status identified at Shizhaishan recur: the weapons, ornaments, banqueting wares, drums, cowrie containers, armour and cattle figurines to symbolise wealth (von Dewall 1988).

If this was a warrior, what of the high status women we encountered overseeing agricultural rituals and presiding over weavers at Shizhaishan? Burial 17 also has a bronze headrest, drums beyond the feet and head, jade earrings and bracelets, cattle figurines and wine containers. But there are no weapons, armour or belt discs. In their place, we find implements used in weaving: a spindle whorl, bobbin and decorated needle case (Fig. 5.31). Burials 11 and 22 also contain weaving tools, suggesting that this group of three graves contain the remains of aristocratic females.

Yun Kuen Lee (1994) has considered this possibility in a detailed statistical analysis of the grave contents from the 22 burials located on top of the hill at

Lijiashan. He has found that an analysis of the many metal, jade, agate and marine shell grave goods highlights bronze weapons, drums, staff handles, weaving implements and headrests as principal components contributing to variability within the assemblage. A subsequent cluster analysis identifies three groups, which he calls A1, A2 and B (Fig. 5.32). Group A graves are significantly richer than those in group B, and some artefacts are restricted to them. Yun Kuen Lee has identified the cowrie shell containers, drums, headrests, quivers, curved axes, wolf fang sticks and sceptres among these, and has suggested that their ownership was restricted to the highest social echelon. The distinction between the graves in groups A1 and A2 also highlights the high status of some women in Dian society, for the former group contains weapons and belt buckles, while the latter includes bronze weaving implements. To judge from a scene from Shizhaishan, weaving was a female preserve. Some particular weapons which combine an iron cutting edge with a bronze haft are found in the A2 group, suggesting that iron had a restricted distribution.

5.31   Decorated needle case from burial 11 at Lijiashan. Height, 27.5 cm. *Permission:* Yunnan Provincial Museum.

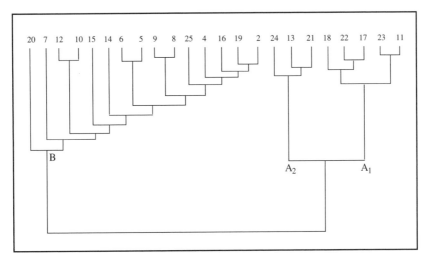

5.32   The results of a cluster analysis on the grave goods from Lijiashan. Reproduced by permission of Dr Yun Kuen Lee.

Indeed, these graves probably predate the period when iron weapons became generally available, but an iron sword with bronze handle of a type with parallels in Sichuan to the north was recovered from burial 26, at the western edge of this group of graves.

While the cemeteries investigated round the shore of Lake Dian are all poorer than the elite graves at Shizhaishan, the row of opulent interments at Lijiashan stand comparison with those of Shizhaishan and in some respects, contained a set of distinct prestige goods. It is conceivable that there were two competing centres. Alternatively, Lijiashan may have occupied a vassal status. Intensive fieldwork and analysis of the mortuary data might help choose between these alternatives, to which we will return.

Dian bronze technology

No casting facilities have been excavated, and metal working scenes have not been found on any of the cowrie containers, nor any other medium from Dian sites. Consequently, the source of our information on the techniques of the Dian bronze workers comes from their products. The Southeast Asian bronze working tradition from the mid second millennium BC involved casting in stone or clay bivalve moulds. Some of the bracelets were cast using the lost wax technique, which was in use in the Mekong Valley sites at least by the period 1000–500 BC. No early bronze age sites corresponding to those in Bac Bo have been identified, as yet, in Yunnan, and the Dian sites therefore present the image of an already highly-developed tradition. Despite the wide range and complexity of the bronzes produced, however, the technology used can be viewed as a development of methods established in Southeast Asia, including Yunnan, over the previous millennium.

These are based on bivalve mould casting and the lost wax technique. The former involved clay, but not to the exclusion of stone moulds. The animal finials found at Lijiashan and Shizhaishan, for example, were cast within bivalve clay moulds. The halberd, although an artefact with origins in the Huanghe Valley, was also cast in bivalve clay moulds. This involved the use of a clay core over which the two mould pieces fitted, separated by chaplets to leave room for the inflow of metal. Even the blades of the halberds were hollow due to the use of a core in this manner. More complex artefacts, such as the wine vessels and cowrie containers, saw an extension of the clay bivalve method to the use of multiple pieces, involving the 'piece mould' technique. A clay core in the shape of the object to be cast was manufactured, including the intended decoration. Clay was then pressed onto the outside, dried, and cut off in sections. At this stage, further decoration could be incised onto the interior of these sections. After scraping back the original mould, the outer pieces were fitted and the metal poured into the intervening space. The number of sections was a function of the complexity of the artefact. In the case of a simple wine vessel, there might be only two, the number rising with cowrie containers. The large, complex head rests were likewise cast in three pieces using this method, and subsequently brazed together (Murowchick 1989). Animal embellishments could be pre-cast and placed onto the mould assembly, or their clay mould incorporated with the section so that one pour cast the whole object. Even the thin armour was cast in piece moulds, although some items were modified by hammering. Other armour sections, however, were hammered into shape from ingots. Weapons, being of relatively simple form, were cast in bivalve clay moulds, but for complex shapes and highly-decorated pieces, the bronze worker turned to wax.

The principle of the lost wax technique is that the intended bronze form is first moulded in wax, usually over a clay core. Wax can be formed into a complex shape, and then invested with a layer of fine clay before being covered with an outer mould of coarser clay. The wax can then be melted out, and replaced with molten bronze. The technique was used to cast the scenes on the cowrie containers, the figures being later riveted or soldered in place. Barnard (1986, 1987) has also described how the use of wax was employed in the casting of drums (Wu *et al.* 1986). Lost wax casting drew upon ceramic as well as bronze casting skills, for a core in the shape of the drum was first manufactured in clay, and clay blocks were prepared, bearing the preferred decoration which was impressed using pattern stamps often later embellished with scenes incised onto the clay with a stylus. These blocks were flat and rectangular, and sheets of wax were impressed onto them, then lifted and bound around the original clay core, so that the decoration faced outwards. Further decoration could then be applied to the wax, which incorporated metal spacers of the same width as the drum wall. Wax was also used to provide for air vents through the exterior clay mould, or to fashion handles. The assemblage was then covered in the outer clay mould before the wax was replaced by bronze. If this sounds relatively straightforward, it misrepresents the technical expertise and artistic ability necessary to reach a successful conclusion.

Dian specialists employed a number of innovations in order to enhance their products. Gold was used to fashion scabbards, which were decorated by the repoussé technique. Decoration was incised onto the surface of thin items, such as armour, after casting and hammering were complete. Gold and silver were used to inlay decoration onto the surface of vessels and halberds, while semi-precious stones were inlaid into recesses on the circular belt ornaments. The Dian gold worker also probably practised gold amalgam gilding (Murowchick 1989). This involved mixing gold with mercury, painting the resulting alloy onto the cleaned surface of the bronze, and then heating the artefact to allow the mercury to evaporate. By this means, gold was applied to the figures of high-status individuals on the Shizhaishan cowrie containers, and on shield ornaments. Although the actual method has yet to be identified, some Dian cowrie containers, weapons and figurines appear to have had a thin layer of tin applied to the surface of the bronze.

There have been few detailed analyses of the alloys used in casting the wide range of bronzes found in the Dian sites. Varying proportions of copper, tin and lead radically change the properties of the alloy, not least the hardness, colour and casting properties. The admixture of tin, for example, increases hardness, lowers the melting point of the alloy and leads to a more silvery colour. Murowchick (1989) has analysed, by atomic absorption spectroscopy, an assemblage of Dian bronzes purchased in a Kunming antique shop in 1947 and later acquired by the British Museum. These, in addition to the analyses which are available from Chinese reports, show that arsenic was only ever present in trace quantities, with tin the preferred metal to alloy with copper. The armour pieces, for example, included 12–13% tin, which would have provided more protection against spear or sword thrusts than would have been provided by copper alone. Lead, which improves the fluidity of the alloy, was identified in quantities of up to 16.5% in some drum fragments, but is little represented in others. Murowchick has suggested that lead was used to modify tonal qualities of the drums rather than the castability of the alloy.

The Erhai region

Tong Enzheng (1977) has explored, through the distribution of different forms of dagger, the relationship between bronze styles and the distribution of the tribes mentioned in historic Chinese sources. He noted in particular, a distinction between his type B daggers, which corresponds to the location of the Dian and Yelang peoples, and the type C, which concentrates in the region of Lake Erhai. The latter, he suggested, was the preferred dagger among the Kunming. This regionality of bronze styles is further confirmed by Song Zhimin (1987), on the basis of different varieties of hoe and spear. Murowchick (1989) has proposed several regional groups of Iron Age sites in Yunnan, of which those in the Erhai

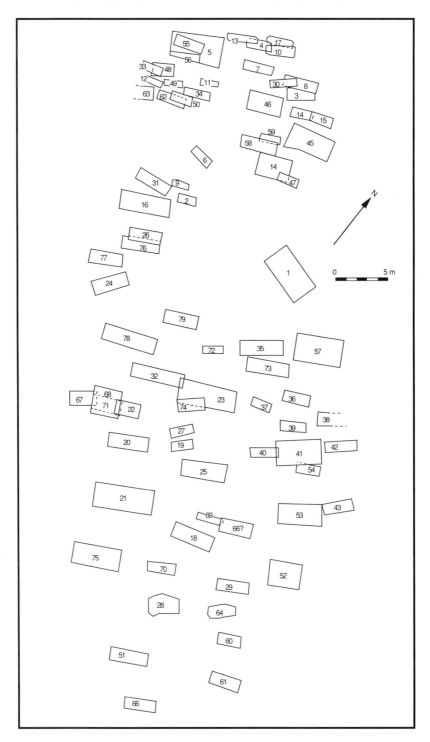

5.33   Plan of the cemetery of Wanjiaba.

region lie close to the Lancang River (Fig. 5.1). All our information is derived from cemeteries, of which Wanjiaba and Dabona are best documented (Qiu Xuanchong *et al.* 1983). Excavations at the former in 1975–6 uncovered 79 graves in an area of 70 × 30 m (Fig. 5.33). There are some superpositions, but most graves were widely spaced. Initially, the excavators divided them into two phases, but Wang Dadao (1985) has more recently suggested that three phases can be identified on the basis of the typology of the artefacts found as grave goods. Both schemes, however, have in common the location of early graves in the northwestern part of the cemetery and later interments to the southeast. Since some graves include wooden coffins and planking, it has been possible to obtain well-provenanced radiocarbon dates. Burial 23 (phase 2 of Wang Dadao) has supplied three dates which when pooled provide a determination of 791–467 BC. Burial 1, which belongs to the third phase, has furnished two dates, which average 523–192 BC. If we allow a century or two to account for the use of mature trees in coffin construction, this cemetery would have overlapped with the Dian cemeteries to the east.

The mortuary offerings include bronze weapons, vessels, bracelets, tubes, chisels, hoes or ploughshares, axes, drums and bells. Among the weapons, we encounter daggers, axes, halberds, spearheads, shield bosses and arrowheads. It is unusual to find so many tin artefacts, for this metal does not survive as well as bronze or iron. There are tin plaques and tubes. There is also a variety of wooden spoons, ladles and platters as well as pottery vessels and exotic ornaments which include amber, coral, agate and turquoise beads and jade bracelets. No iron was encountered.

Wang Dadao (1985) has based his sub-division of the sequence and interpretation of the cemetery on the form of the grave goods, particularly the bronzes. Twelve graves have been ascribed to period 1. They are small, lack wooden coffins, and contain few grave goods. Among them, we encounter a variety of daggers with three prongs on the guard and an oval hilt with spiral ornamentation. The characteristic socketed spearheads have a large blade, and the bracelets were of simple form with narrow bands. No grave included more than two daggers or five spearheads and the graves which included weapons at all usually only had one dagger and a spearhead. Exotic stone jewellery and the sumptuary and utilitarian bronzes such as drums, bowls and hoes, were absent.

The graves of period 2 saw several major changes. Some were now larger, the largest of all measuring almost 6 × 2.85 m and attaining a depth of 6.25 m. Seven of the twelve burials in question incorporated wooden coffins set on a raised wooden platform, and there was a much wider variety, as well as quantity, of grave goods. This was particularly marked in the case of burial 23, which was located in the centre of the cemetery, and measured 5.6 × 2 m, with a depth of 6.7 m (Fig. 5.34). The coffin was raised on a platform under which a set of four drums were placed upside down. The person had been interred with remarkable opulence, the full extent being unknown due to looting. Even so, 352 socketed spearheads were recovered, divided by Wang Dadao into six different forms. There were also seven halberds, 27 arrowheads and three battle axes. The four drums were accompanied by an equal number of bells, and the fourteen hoes reflect the application of metallurgy to agriculture. This individual was also well-endowed with jewellery: 79 bronze bracelets, five roundels of tin and beads of agate and turquoise.

No other burial approached such wealth, but some others still have an impressive inventory of goods. Burials 65, 25 and 57, for example, had well over twenty spearheads each despite some looting, and were found in large graves with the remains of wooden coffins.

Period 3 is represented by only five graves. None rivals those just described in terms of the quantity of armaments found, but there was a typological distinction between the two periods in the hoes. Indeed, burial 1 revealed 53 hoes of two different forms as well as a drum, six bells and 28 socketed axes.

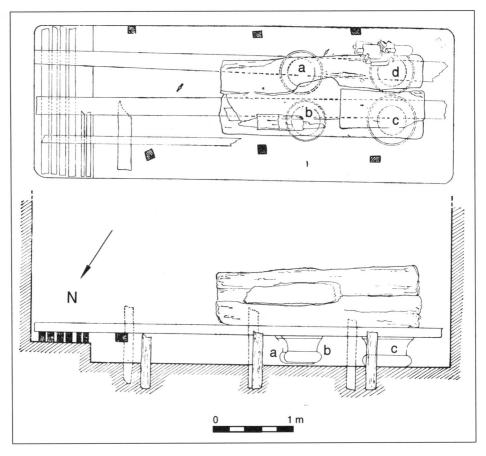

5.34 Burial 23 at Wanjiaba, showing the location of the drums under the coffin (a–d).
Permission: Publications Department, Kexue Chubanshe.

Wang Dadao has considered the typology of the various bronze artefacts, noting that the phase 1 items, particularly the daggers, find their parallels to the west in the sites ascribed to the Bronze Age of the Erhai region. During the second and third phases, however, while similarities to the west remained, the hoes, daggers and armour reveal imports or at least strong influence from the Lake Dian area. Wang Dadao (1985) has combined early textual evidence with a socialist approach to his interpretation of the Wanjiaba cemetery. He has suggested that the first phase graves belong to the Kunming people, who appear in the *Shi Ji* as 'people who braid their hair, and move about with their cattle. They have no fixed settlements and no chieftains'. He has dated this phase to the early Spring and Autumn period (770–600 BC). Phases 2 and 3, in his interpretation, show the continuing use of this cemetery by a new people, the Mifei, who defeated the Kunming in battle and used the cemetery during the middle and late Spring and Autumn period (600–475 BC). He sees the sharp distinctions in mortuary wealth as a result of a slave holding society, the number of weapons in the rich graves indicating their use in controlling forced labour. Given the similarities between the bronzes of these two periods and those of the Western Han in the area of the Dian lakes, these dates seem rather early.

In terms of the social organisation at Wanjiaba, the mortuary assemblages for each grave have been subjected to cluster analysis and multidimensional scaling. The latter reveals, as might be expected, a marked clustering of the majority of graves, with the two most opulent being set apart (Fig. 5.35). When these two were removed from a second computation, four further rich graves were set apart. They show a concentration of goods, but also the presence of most of the wooden coffins and graves with a particularly large volume. As an alternative to the notion of a cemetery reflecting a dislocation in terms of the community which used it and the presence of a coercive, slave society, it is suggested that the group vested authority and prestige in a ruling elite. Their elevated status finds expression in high energy expenditure in their grave construction and the range and quantity of offerings. In this view, the differences in the typology of the bronzes could just as well be the result of changing exchange patterns as the arrival of intrusive belligerents.

The alloys employed at Wanjiaba also show a number of local and exotic features. Murowchick (1989) has assembled the results of 20 analyses, but unfortunately none comes from the first period. Almost half the items from period 2 were cast, for all intents and purposes, from unalloyed copper. This even includes two spearheads, a ploughshare or hoe and an axe, all of which would have been strengthened with an admixture of tin. Two drums contained lead, but only up to 3.5%. Even during the third period, copper was often cast unalloyed. An axe, two ploughshares or socketed hoes and a basin, all from burial 1, were cast from copper despite the clear knowledge of tin indicated by the many tin artefacts recovered. In contrast, armour from burial 23 revealed a tin content of just over 10%, and has all the characteristics of a Dian import. This unsophisticated

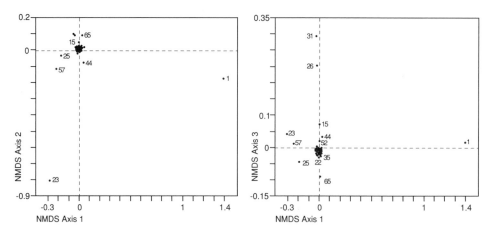

5.35 The distribution of graves at Wanjiaba after multidimensional scaling.

local approach to alloying is matched by the casting techniques. The vessels, cast in clay piece moulds, reveal seams where the moulds were misplaced, and there are numerous other casting flaws.

Dabona

The Dabona site lies approximately 90 km northwest of Wanjiaba. Two graves were discovered there in 1961, one being destroyed but the other surviving intact (Xiong Ying and Sun Taichu 1964, Zhang Zengqi 1964, Li Chaozhen and He Chaoxiong 1986). This is a remarkable burial, for within an outer wooden coffin, the excavators encountered a second, bronze coffin weighing 257.1 kg. It was cast in seven sections which join together, and takes the form of a house raised on stilts (Fig. 5.36). The long sides bear decoration in the form of raised spirals, while the two ends reveal a range of animals, including boars, tigers and birds. A further grave found in 1977 but 1.5 km distant, and therefore belonging to a distinct cemetery, has added to the range of bronzes found. The list includes panpipes, ploughshares or hoes and a weaving implement paralleled, according to Murowchick (1989), in the Dian sites to the east. But other forms, such as the drum, cauldron and cups are more closely matched in the assemblage from Wanjiaba. There is also a house model, not as detailed as those from Shizhaishan, and lacking human figures. But it still shows the same gabled roof with extending finials. Some further items of tin were also recovered, but no iron. The bronze specialists were more favourably inclined to alloying than were their counterparts at Wanjiaba. The great bronze sarcophagus included just over 5% tin and 2.25% lead, and the ladle, bell and cup analysed have a tin content varying between 13.69 and 16.34%.

A radiocarbon determination from coffin wood has produced a date of 566–334 BC, which Murowchick interprets as belonging towards the end of the Spring and Autumn Period but, again, coffin wood might have an inbuilt age of some centuries.

As we proceed in a northwesterly direction and up the course of the Lancang (upper Mekong) River, so we encounter a new configuration. Burial practices changed, the subsistence base was modified and the range of bronzes reflects different tastes and needs. The cemeteries in northwestern Yunnan, for this is the only type of site known, show a preference for a rectangular, stone-lined grave. The most extensively excavated cemetery at Aofengshan reveals 217 inhumation burials, laid out in rows on a north-south axis, with twelve large graves dominating the central area (Fig. 5.37, YPM 1986). The excavators have suggested that there are three phases to the cemetery, the burials including single inhumations, males interred extended with two flexed female skeletons, sometimes an extended male and female, or female and infant together. The earliest phase has a single radiocarbon date of 570–332 BC, taken from human bone. Bronze grave goods include short swords, axes, decorated bracelets of a variety of forms and hair bands and hair clasps. The second phase has a radiocarbon date of 401–91 BC, again taken from human bone. Swords, spearheads and halberds were interred, probably in the main with males, but we also find that bronze bracelets, now of a more simple form, continued. The recovery of typically Southeast Asian stone axe moulds indicates a local tradition of casting (Fig. 5.38). Cremation was favoured during the third phase.

5.36   The bronze coffin from Dabona. It is 2m long and weighs 257.1 kg. *Permission:* Yunnan Provincial Museum.

5.37 The cemetery plan of Aofengshan.

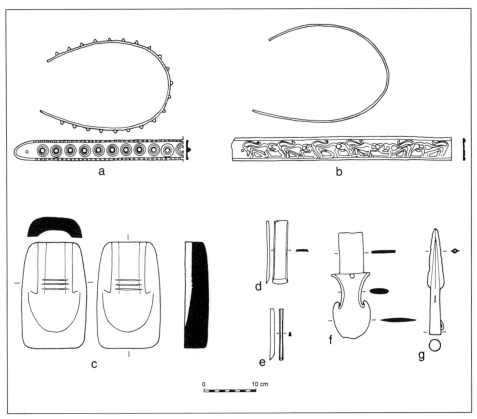

5.38 Grave goods from Aofengshan.
a, b. Hair bands in bronze from burials 156 and 27. **c.** Sandstone mould for casting an axe from burial 74. **d, e.** Chisels. **f.** Socketed axe from burial 75. **g.** Spearhead from burial 2.

It is intriguing to note that Aofengshan and other sites in this northwestern corner of Yunnan Province lack the agricultural implements so prevalent in the Dian cemeteries, but gain a range of hair bands (YPM 1986). This suggests that the early historic records of the Kunming as favouring a more mobile, pastoral existence and of wearing the hair in long plaits is reflected in the archaeological record. Indeed, we are entering an area where goods and the spread of ideas followed a north-south axis down the major river valleys which follow the eastern margins of the Tibetan Plateau in eastern Sichuan, and recent research has disclosed a series of cemetery sites which reflect just such a passage of ideas south to the Yunnan lakes from Mongolia and Gansu.

These incorporate collective dolmen burials in the valley of the Anninghe River of southern Sichuan, and cist graves which concentrate in the upper reaches of the Min River of Central Sichuan, 450 km to the northeast. The former comprise cemeteries in which some of the collective burials contain up to 100 individuals.

Grave goods include bronze daggers, knives and arrowheads, while bimetallic iron and bronze swords and Han coins provide evidence for exchange and the chronological context in the last couple of centuries BC. The former could well have reached southern Sichuan from the Dian area. Exchange also brought exotic stone beads made of agate, jade and turquoise. Rice remains and impressions suggest some settled agriculture, but the hill slopes above the valley bottoms would have been suited to stock raising.

The cemeteries comprise graves lined with stone slabs up to 3.5 m long and a metre wide. The body was inhumed in an extended position over a layer of sand and gravel or, on one occasion, of millet grains. Men were interred with a bronze sword, women with a spindle whorl. Bronze ornaments, mainly in the form of decorated buttons stitched to clothing and belts, were relatively common. In some rich graves, we also encounter iron bracelets, bimetallic swords and Han coins. Food offerings in the mortuary vessels included the remains of sheep and millet. Pirazzoli-t'Serstevens (1988) has stressed typological parallels between this material culture and remains from Gansu, Qinghai and Mongolia to the north, as well as some exchange contact with the Han Empire and Dian to the south.

Summary

Neolithic sites in Yunnan reveal similar decorative techniques on pottery, the same mortuary ritual and chronology as do those in the Mekong, Chao Phraya and Red River valleys. In the concluding chapter, we will return to review the evidence for the Bronze Age of the Yunnan Plateau, Guizhou and Sichuan. For conformity, the term Iron Age will be used to describe the chiefdoms of Dian and Yelang, although it is noted that iron itself was rare. At present, it is noted that, while there is no evidence for a developmental stage of smelting to match that from Central Thailand and the Middle Mekong Valley, the iron age groups identified on the basis of both documentary and archaeological evidence leave no doubt as to their individuality, material richness and complex, centralised social structure. These developed in conjunction with exposure to an expanding empire within which they were ultimately to be enveloped. The grave goods include bronzes dedicated to war, ritual, display and agriculture. Much attention was given to the casting of large drums, and the knowledge of iron working, surely originating in Chinese sources to the north, saw the manufacture of bimetallic weapons, the iron blade being joined with a bronze haft. The societies represented by Dian and Yelang are the most complex and sophisticated in Southeast Asia during the prehistoric period.

CHAPTER 6

BEYOND THE FORTRESS OF THE SKY

The Mekong Valley

The Mekong River runs as a great artery through Southeast Asia. Its upper course takes it through the precipitous uplands of western Yunnan and Laos, but from Vientiane it enters a gentler landscape as it crosses the eastern margins of the Khorat Plateau, where it receives the outflow from the Mun-Chi river system. On the opposite bank, however, the land rises up to the Truong Son Cordillera, known to the Chinese as the Fortress of the Sky. South of Pakse near the modern border between Laos and Cambodia it cascades over the Khone Falls before flowing across the flat lands of Central Cambodia. The Tonle Sap River joins the Mekong at Phnom Penh. When in spate, the waters of this tributary back up to fill the Great Lake, and flooding is widespread as the Mekong branches into its main and Bassac arms before reaching the delta (Fig. 6.1).

The importance of the Mekong River for communication is well illustrated in an account of the first exploration upstream by Europeans in 1641 (Casteleyn 1669, Garnier 1871). Under the direction of Gérard van Wustoff, an employee of the Dutch East Indies Company, a group of merchants travelled by boat from Phnom Penh to Vientiane. Their account has survived, and provides much information on the land and its people. The area was densely forested, and game abounded. On 8 September near Bassac, on the upstream journey, their Lao assistants killed and salted forty deer as provisions, and there was much river traffic concerned with trade. Van Wuystoff noted how much easier it was to travel by boat than on land. The journey from Laos to Siam by land took up to five months if travelling in a train of laden buffalo carts, and three months for the return trip with a lighter load. By foot along established tracks, and with provisions carried by·buffalo, it took a month. But many Siamese merchants travelled to Laos, exchanging bright and attractive cloth for gold. By contrast, a leisurely return trip with many unnecessary stops from Vientiane to Phnom Penh began on Christmas Eve 1641 and finished on 11 April in the following year. By boat, it was also possible to carry a considerable load of goods.

The middle and lower reaches of the Mekong lie east of the junction between the Shan Thai and IndoChina plates, and igneous intrusions at this contact zone through the sedimentary rocks have led to the formation of copper ore (Fig. 3.5). There is a concentration of ore bodies in Loei Province of Thailand, some lying within sight of the Mekong itself. Other deposits are found in Uttaradit and Chiang

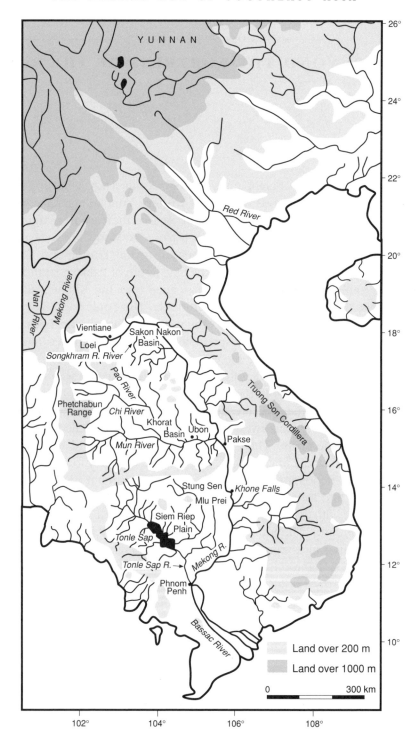

6.1 Map showing the geographic locations mentioned in the text.

Rai provinces. The left bank of the river in Laos is dotted with copper sources with a further concentration just above the Khone Falls. North of the Tonle Sap, copper deposits are known in the valley of the Stung Sen near Samrong Sen and to the southeast in Kratie Province.

The Mekong catchment comprises Coote's (1990) Eastern Province, with deposits of cassiterite being most abundant in Khammoune Province of Laos on the left bank, and upstream from Vientiane in Nan Province of Thailand. Lead ores are known in the same copper-rich area of Loei. Most mineral resources are found in upland margins, but prehistoric settlements cluster in the lowlands. The same situation applied to high quality stone sources, not only for adze manufacture, but also for jewellery. Marine shell, also valued in prehistory for personal ornaments, is unavailable other than through exchange, and here the value of the Mekong River as a conduit to trade is stressed.

One of two recently-excavated copper mining complexes in Southeast Asia is located at Phu Lon on the southern bank of the Mekong River (Figs. 6.2, 6.3). It has been examined as part of the Thailand Archaeometallurgy Project, under the direction of V. Pigott and S. Natapintu (1988). Veins of weathered copper sulphide ore run deep into the limestone of Phu Lon, or Bald Hill. This outcrop is honey-combed with mine shafts, and field investigations, which began in 1983, led to the recognition of mining rubble 50 cm deep on the western slope of the hill. This was associated with river cobbles which had been used in mining the ore (Natapintu 1988a). The adjacent area, known as the pottery flat, was also excavated. The deposits comprised, apart from the rejected and crushed rock matrix, the stone cobbles which had been used to process the mined rock. These were disposed in clusters, suggesting work stations. There were also some crucible fragments lagged with a thin layer of clay. This would have protected their interior surface by reducing the penetration of molten metal into the body of the crucible (Vernon 1995). Part of a sandstone and a ceramic mould were also recovered, indicating local casting as well as ore-processing.

Charcoal from the basal level of the pottery flat has been dated to 1750–1425 BC, but one determination is insufficient to conclude when mining began. Samples from higher in the sequence reveal the continuation of ore processing during the first millennium BC. This is also indicated by a second ore crushing locality at the nearby village of Ban Noi, where a radiocarbon date of 1100–615 BC has been obtained, in association with a socketed bronze axe. A third ore-crushing locality at 'Bunker Hill' also dates to the first millennium BC.

The importance of this copper mine and the associated processing complexes is considerable, not only for the evidence of second millennium BC metal working, but also because of its location. Access to the Mekong River would have facilitated the spread of the knowledge of copper and its properties over a considerable area.

The recognition of the Southeast Asian Bronze Age occurred in the Mekong catchment at Samrong Sen and in Laos over a century ago. But unlike the situation

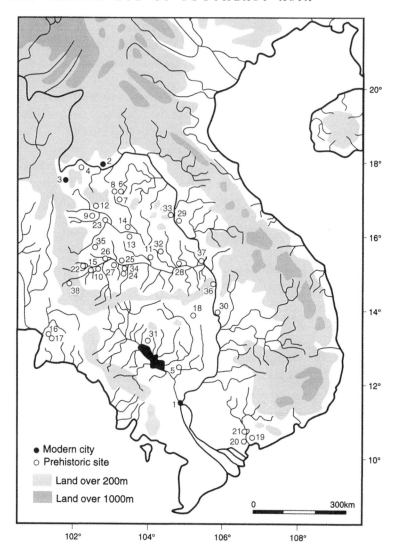

6.2 Map of modern cities and archaeological sites in the Mekong Valley.
1. Phnom Penh. **2.** Vientiane. **3.** Loei. **4.** Phu Lon. **5.** Samrong Sen. **6.** Ban
Chiang. **7.** Ban Na Di. Non Kao Noi. **8.** Ban Phak Top. **9.** Non Nok Tha. Non
Pa Kluay. **10.** Phimai. Ban Tamyae. **11.** Non Dua. **12.** Non Praw, Don Klang.
13. Ban Chiang Hian. **14.** Muang Fa Daet. **15.** Ban Prasat. **16.** Khok Phanom
Di. **17.** Nong Nor. **18.** O Pie Can. Mlu Prei. O Yak. **19.** Cau Sat. Hang Gon.
20. Ben Do. **21.** Doc Chua. Long Giao. Cu Lao Rua. **22.** Noen U-Loke. **23.**
Non Chai. **24.** Ban Takhong. **25.** Non Yang. Ban Yawuk. **26.** Non Krabuang
Nok. Ban Non Udom. **27.** Ban Don Phlong. **28.** Ban Kan Luang. **29.**
Savannaket. **30.** Sane Island. **31.** Lovea. Phum Reul. **32.** Ban Tad Thong. **33.**
Don Tan. **34.** Ban Thung Wang. **35.** Non Tung Pie Pone. **36.** Ban Chi
Thowang. **37.** Ban Na Pho Tai. **38.** Pak Thong Chai.

in the Red River and Chao Phraya valleys, few neolithic sites are known. Moreover, when turning to Non Nok Tha and Ban Chiang, the two principal sources of information, we face a major problem. Both were excavated in the early days of prehistoric inquiry in Northeast Thailand, and neither has been fully published. Their radiocarbon dates fail to provide an internally consistent chronological framework. It is possible, by stressing early rather than late dates, to argue in favour of bronze working in the region even by the fourth millennium BC, and this has indeed been done (Solheim 1968, Gorman and Charoenwongsa 1976). Both sites were used as cemeteries, but neither has a particularly deep sequence, and they have in common a badly disturbed and at times unclear

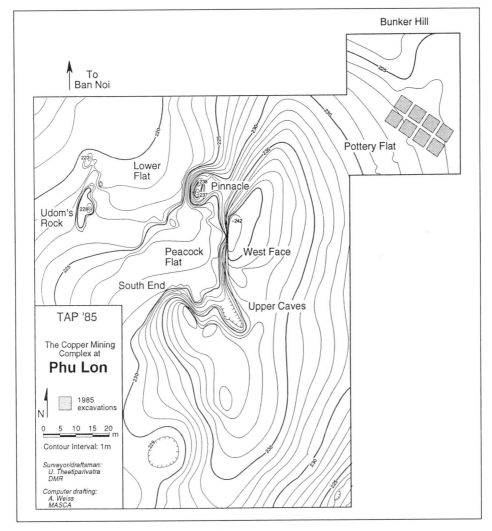

6.3   The mining complex at Phu Lon
Permission: Dr. V. Pigott.

stratigraphy. At Ban Chiang, for example, no grave cuts were detected other than for those cut into the natural substrate.

Excavations undertaken in Central and Northeast Thailand since the research at Non Nok Tha (1966 and 1968) and Ban Chiang (1974 and 1975) have stressed the need to evaluate the social dimension of these cemeteries, particularly on the basis of the spatial distribution of the graves, and the association of men, women, children and infants. Bayard (1984) has offered a social interpretation of the Non Nok Tha cemetery, but none exists for Ban Chiang.

The Khorat Plateau

The Khorat Plateau comprises two major drainage basins, the Songkhram to the north and the much larger Khorat Basin to the south (Fig. 6.1). The latter is drained by the Mun and Chi river systems, which join at Ubon and proceed east to the Mekong. These two rivers link the Mekong and Chao Phraya valleys. The plateau, which slopes gradually from west to east, offers a variety of habitats. The alluvial floodplains are generally narrow, particularly as one proceeds in an easterly direction. They have, historically, been subjected to extensive wet season inundation. Three heavily-eroded earlier terraces flank the floodplain. The lowest is suited to the cultivation of rice, particularly where flooding is not severe or sudden. The middle and upper terraces do not attract rice farming because the soils are too porous for water retention. This problem is accentuated as one moves from the northeast to the southwest, due to decreasing annual rainfall. The western margins provide sources of copper ore and high quality stone, and the plateau itself is rich in deposits of iron ore and salt.

Parts of the plateau have been surveyed for archaeological sites, beginning with the early explorations of Lunet de Lajonquière (1902) and Seidenfaden (1922). More recently, Solheim directed surveys in the vicinity of Phimai, a large late prehistoric and Khmer site in the upper Mun Valley (Solheim and Gorman 1966), which resulted in excavations at several sites. In 1970, a further survey was undertaken by Higham (1977) in the vicinity of the moated site of Non Dua, and the associated salt deposit of Bo Phan Khan, but no Neolithic or Bronze Age sites were found. This rarity or even lack of early sites is evident in all other surveys in the southern basin. In 1981, Higham and Kijngam surveyed the southern margins of the Chi River in Mahasarakham Province (Fig. 6.1). Excavations in three sites revealed an early phase of red painted pottery, but the radiocarbon dates fall within the period 1000–500 BC. The same situation is found in Welch and McNeill's (1991) survey in the Phimai district. Even sites belonging to the earlier first millennium BC were very rare. The Fine Arts Department survey of the lower Mun River valley has likewise failed to reveal any Neolithic sites or Bronze Age settlements within the second millennium BC (FAD 1992).

This situation contrasts with that in the smaller, better-watered Sakon Nakhon Basin, which is drained by the Songkhram River. The first survey undertaken in this region in the early 1960s, under the direction of Solheim, discovered a series of small settlement sites of which Non Nok Tha is best known. A second survey in the adjacent area of Phu Wiang in 1970 confirmed this, the principal site recovered being Non Nong Chik (Buchan 1973). In 1980, Higham and Kijngam surveyed south of Ban Chiang in the watershed of the Songkhram and Pao rivers, finding that early, possibly Neolithic, sites with black incised pottery were few, small, and located in the valleys of tributary streams. There was a substantial increase in number of bronze age sites, although their dates are unknown save for the few which have been excavated (Wichakana 1984). Wilen (1989) has surveyed in the Huai Sai Khao Basin, west of Non Nok Tha, and identified a series of sites of which Non Pa Kluay represents the Bronze Age. He has suggested that such sites were cemeteries used by a small, dispersed population as social foci. This hypothesis could be tested by excavating a site extensively to seek the remains of non-mortuary activities, and to find the small, dispersed settlements.

Bannanurag and Bamrungwongse (1991) have published the results of their major site survey north of Ban Chiang which identified 127 prehistoric sites. These they have assigned to seven regional groups (Fig. 6.4), nearly all being located near stream confluences giving access to low-lying, regularly flooded land suited to rice cultivation. They noted that early sites, corresponding to the Early Period of Ban Chiang, concentrate west of the Songkhram River, while later sites with red painted pottery dating to the late first millennium BC concentrate in Huai Yam and Huai Pla Hang valleys to the east.

Non Kao Noi

During Higham and Kijngam's 1980 fieldwork, the site of Non Kao Noi was discovered. Although it was hard to estimate its size, it is thought not to exceed 75 × 50 m (0.37 ha). A test square encountered a stratigraphic sequence only 70 cm deep, in which there were five inhumation burials. The first, which was not complete, was accompanied by three pottery vessels. A group of green stone beads were found near the feet of one burial, and three pots were found with burial 4. One is black, and decorated with incised motifs, and there is a small bowl with red painted patterns. The burials were orientated with the head to the northwest or the southwest. No radiocarbon dates have been obtained, but the pottery relates to that from early contexts at Ban Chiang.

Non Nok Tha

Non Nok Tha is located in the upper catchment of the Chi River system, and nestles on the eastern side of a hill known as Phu Wiang, an outlier of the Phetchabun Range. Excavation in 1966 and 1968 was a landmark in our appreciation of prehistory in the Mekong Valley, because of the recovery of evidence for bronze working in mortuary contexts. The enduring importance of this site lies in the extent of the excavated area, which allows an appreciation of the spatial layout of a bronze age cemetery (Fig. 6.5, Solheim 1970).

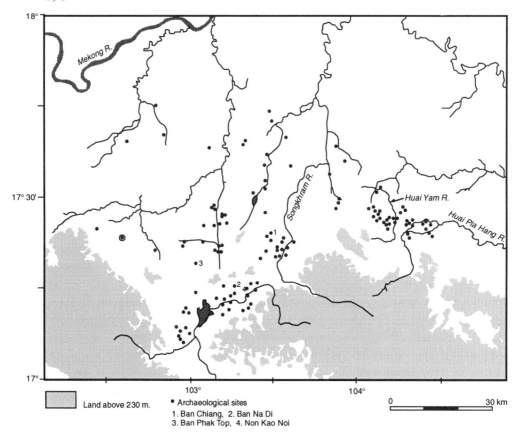

6.4   Map showing the archaeological sites in the survey undertaken by Bannanurag and Bamrungwongse in the Sakon Nakhon basin.

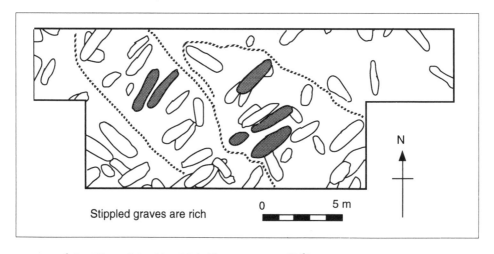

6.5   Plan of the Non Nok Tha cemetery, 1968 season.

The prehistoric stratigraphy, which at just over a metre is not deep, incorporates many graves which intercut or overlie earlier interments. This has allowed Bayard to subdivide the sequence into Early and Middle Periods (EP and MP). The former is divided into three phases of which the first two lacked bronze. Bronze artefacts were found in burials ascribed to EP 3 and the MP, which comprises eight phases.

The interpretation of this site, both chronologically and culturally, has been difficult because of a lack of well-provenanced charcoal for radiocarbon dating. Until recently, the absence of a clear pattern has made several alternative chronologies tenable. With the development of AMS dating of very small samples, however, this problem has been lessened by the dating of rice chaff used in the fabric of pottery vessels. Three of the eleven AMS dates are far too late, but the balance provides some important new information on the chronological framework, provided one accepts the fact that the sherds submitted relate to the phase ascribed them (Table 1). Two dates submitted as representing EP 1 are 2307–1858 and 1770–1310 BC. The dates as a whole indicate that the cemetery at Non Nok Tha belongs within the second millennium BC. The earliest graves might be as early as 2000–1500 BC, but the majority, and this includes those containing bronze artefacts, are more likely to fall within the period 1500–1000 BC. With the exception of OxA-2390, the dates from EP2/3 to MP5 set out in Table 1 are close enough to permit their combination statistically, and the result is 1320–1121 BC. This span supports the short alternative chronology and is favoured in this study. But it has not been accepted by all authorities, because all but two of the sherds submitted for dating came from the archaeological layers rather than burial vessels.

Lab. No.	Level	Conventional radiocarbon age BP	Calibrated date 2 sigma, BC
OxA-2383	EP 1	3650±90	2307–1858
OxA-2384	EP 1	3250±100	1770–1310
OxA-2387	EP 2–3	2950±80	1415–880
OxA-2388	MP 1	2880±80	1312–894
OxA-2389	MP 1	2920±80	1321–921
OxA-2390	MP 4	3285±80	1754–1413
OxA-2392	MP 4	3065±70	1468–1152
OxA-2393	MP 5	3065±70	1468–1152

Table 1   The AMS radiocarbon dates from Non Nok Tha. Three dates have been omitted (OxA-2386, 2389 and 2391) because they fall in the first millennium AD and are too late.

There are seventeen secure burials from EP 1–2, two adult females, two adult males and eleven children aged between 1 and 6 years. Little can be said of the social organisation on the basis of so small a sample, particularly when, as Bayard (1984) suggests, it may come in part from an area reserved for child burials. However, the mortuary ritual followed a widespread pattern. The dead were inhumed in a supine position, accompanied by grave goods. Pottery vessels predominated, other items included three individuals with strings of shell disc beads, and others with stone adze heads, grinding stones, offerings of domestic cattle or pig bones and bivalve shells. One person was found with some red pigment. There is no evidence to suggest that any of these goods were of remote and exotic origin, and insufficient information to draw any conclusions on the presence of different status groups.

The earliest bronze, a socketed axe, was found with burial 90, an adult male

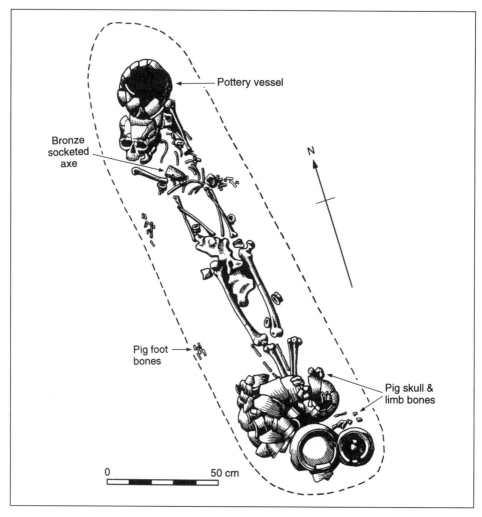

Pottery vessel

Bronze socketed axe

N

Pig foot bones

Pig skull & limb bones

0   50 cm

6.6   Non Nok Tha, burial 90, showing a bronze socketed axe.
Permission: Dr D.T. Bayard.

interred with pig bones and seven complete pottery vessels (Fig. 6.6). Subsequent Middle Period graves provide an unparalleled portrait for the Mekong Valley, of a community which included bronze casting among its activities. In this context, it is important to recall that Non Nok Tha lies only 140 km to the southeast of the Phu Lon copper mines. Burials were laid out with the head in most cases pointing to the southwest although there were cases where the northwest was preferred. The interments recovered during 1968 suggest a series of rows, which contain the remains of men, women and children.

Although the site lies close to the Loei copper sources, of 217 graves or mortuary features, only nine contained bronze items. The sample is dominated by bracelets, 28 being found in five graves, two males, two females and a child. There were also five socketed axeheads, restricted to males. One man was also associated with a crucible and the sandstone mould for such an axe, and other moulds and crucibles were identified in three other graves. A woman was found with two crucibles and moulds had been interred with another man and a woman.

The spatial distribution of these bronzes in the cemetery fails to reveal any evidence for their restriction to a particular group of individuals. Nor do the graves containing bronze stand out on the basis of wealth expressed as other items of jewellery or pottery vessels. Indeed, the range of grave goods in the period following the introduction of bronze hardly increased when compared with that for EP 1–2. We continue to find grinding stones, stone adze heads, shell disc beads, cattle and pig limbs and crania and the use of red pigment. Bayard (1984) has chosen fifteen items of grave furniture as the benchmark dividing rich from poor in a secure sample of 61 graves. Of the fourteen with bronzes, eight fall in the ordinary group and only six among the thirteen graves are designated as rich.

The relative wealth of individuals at Non Nok Tha is, in fact, expressed more in the number of pottery vessels than any other other form of offering. A rich grave, from MP 1, included 32 items. Twenty-one of these were pots, and in addition there was a bone tool, two cow's legs, a cow's skull, three grinding stones and two other human bones which might not be grave goods at all. Twenty-seven of the forty items with burial 33 (1968 MP 4) were pottery vessels, the balance being two grinding stones, a pig's leg and a bone tool.

It is on the basis of the distribution of two forms of pottery vessel within the graves, that Bayard has proposed that the individuals interred at Non Nok Tha may have come from two different affiliated groups, perhaps separated on the basis of their home village linked with the ownership of land. This distinction rests on the nearly complementary distribution of 2L and 2C pots, small footed jars with an out-turned lip. The burials which have the latter tend to be the richer in terms of other grave goods, which has encouraged Bayard to suggest that one affiliative group was itself more successful than its contemporary. This intriguing hypothesis must, however, be viewed as but one alternative, for as I have argued, there are grounds for seeing the 2C vessels as being slightly later, and a chronological distinction, in which later graves tend to have more grave goods, seems the more plausible interpretation (Higham 1996, Bayard 1996). Whichever may be the case, there is no doubting the significance of this site in documenting the organisation and the scale of bronze casting.

As Bayard (1996) has noted, the evidence includes the sandstone moulds, crucibles, casting spillage and finished artefacts. Some bivalve moulds bore cracks and signs of scorching, and had clearly been used. Others were rejected before shaping was complete. Stone sources have been traced to the nearby uplands. Crucibles of clay tempered with rice chaff ranged considerably in size. The smallest would have contained only about 200 g of metal, the largest 2.2 kg. Despite the size of the latter, the 79 artefacts found, together with the fragments and nodules of bronze, weighed just over 2 kg. Bracelets predominate, but there were also axes and arrowheads. The bracelets may well have been cast by the lost wax technique, although no clay moulds similar to those recovered from Ban Na Di have been recovered. It is intriguing to note that all artefacts were alloyed, tin bronzes being the commonest, with the former accounting for up to 15% of the metal. But towards the end of the Middle Period, we also encounter an increasing interest in adding lead to copper. This may have been undertaken in the melting process, for lead is notably rare in the fragments of casting spillage which have been analysed (Bayard 1996).

Non Pa Kluay

This low mound lies in the Huai Sai Khao basin on the western side of the Phu Wiang monadnock, about 25 km southwest of Non Nok Tha (Wilen 1989). Its initial mortuary phase corresponds to part of the Non Nok Tha sequence, and thus contributes new data to the problem of dating the latter site. It is not deep, the cultural stratigraphy incorporating about 2 m of deposition. Nine inhumation graves were found in the early mortuary phase, although the small excavated area meant that most were only partially recovered. The forms of some of the pottery vessels placed with the dead match those from Non Nok Tha, and the number and location of the pots in the grave are also similar. Although not yet identified to species, animal limbs accompanied the dead, and to judge from the available illustrations, these were from cattle and pigs. Males, females, children and infants were present, and as is usually the case in similar sites, the infants were interred with a range of offerings.

No burial was found with bronze grave goods, but local villagers described finding a socketed bronze spearhead and bracelets with some skeletons. Unfortunately, a later mortuary phase was present, so it is not possible to be sure which yielded the spearhead. Villagers had also encountered sandstone bivalve moulds for casting axeheads, and one was also found by Wilen, but not in a firm relationship with a burial. Bronze was found outside burial contexts, mainly in the form of fragments but also as bracelets and fishhooks. There is no room for doubt that the earlier mortuary phase belongs to a period when bronze was available, and that the opening of a bigger area would recover early graves with bronze grave goods. It is recalled that very few of the graves from Non Nok Tha were found with bronzes.

Pottery forms from Non Pa Kluay reveal parallels with the Early and Middle Periods at Non Nok Tha. Burial 13 was associated with two vessels of Bayard's type 1G. This form is found at Non Nok Tha throughout the sequence, 32 being found in EP 1–2, 29 in MP 1–3 and 9 in MP 4–8. A Non Nok Tha type 1A vessel was found broken over the body of burial 13. Bayard has noted that this variety is restricted to the EP and early MP. Burial 8 contained four pottery vessels, including a 1A form which was found early at Non Nok Tha, a 1D, 1F and a 4B. Now, 1D forms are found throughout the sequence at Non Nok Tha, while 1F forms are found throughout the middle period. A probable burial feature at Non Pa Kluay also yielded a 1A form.

I have proposed that the Non Nok Tha cemetery had a brief timespan within the latter half of the second millennium BC. It is, therefore, important to note that pottery forms which predominate in EP graves at Non Nok Tha are found in direct association with vessels which belong to the early and the late phases of the MP there. This, it is argued, supports the compression of the Non Nok Tha sequence. But what of the Non Pa Kluay radiocarbon dates? Four are relevant, all coming from mortuary contexts. The first was found just above the skeleton of burial 13, and therefore in the grave fill. It dates to 1687 BC, the standard error being too large to calculate probabilities. Burial 8 included a 1A vessel which is most abundant at Non Nok Tha during the Early Period. A fragment of charcoal weighing 1.3 g was found beside the elbow of this individual, and was dated to 1460–980 BC. Two dates were obtained for burial 5. One fragment of charcoal weighing 0.6 g was taken from the upper layer of fill within a mortuary vessel. It dates to 1320–830 BC. The second comes from a piece of charcoal weighing 2.9 g found beside the right elbow. It is, encouragingly, virtually identical at 1312–831 BC. With one exception, the dates come from sources which I have questioned as being unreliable (Higham 1983). Wilen (1989), however, has argued that the charcoal belongs to the period of interment. Let us accept this, for the moment at least. He proposed that the two earlier dates indicate that there were two phases to the Non Pa Kluay phase 1 cemetery. But the four available dates can legitimately be combined for one pooled date, 1311–977 BC. On the basis of these four dates, it would be very hard, given the parallels for some of the pots from Non Pa Kluay with early Non Nok Tha, to avoid the conclusion that both cemeteries belong within the period 1500–1000 BC. If the three dates from samples of doubtful provenance are excluded, the survivor sustains the same conclusion.

Non Praw

Recent excavations at Non Praw, located 30 km northeast of Non Nok Tha, have encountered a bronze age inhumation cemetery. It is a small, circular mound covering about 2 ha, and excavations in two 4×4 m squares in 1993 revealed four cultural layers incorporating 25 burials (Buranrak 1994a). Consideration of the depth below the datum for each burial, in the absence of clear grave cuts, indicates two mortuary phases. During the earlier, only males were found with the head pointing to the north or west, while all females and four males were orientated to the east. No bronzes were found with early burials, grave goods being dominated by pottery vessels, shell bracelets and shell disc beads. Burials of the later phase were found orientated to the northwest or the southwest. All but one female fall into the latter group. Five burials were now found with bronzes, which included bracelets and socketed axes. The axes are very similar in form to those from Non Nok Tha, including a specimen with a distinctive, crescentic form (Fig. 6.7). These later burials were apparently cut from layer 2, which included iron slag, but no iron artefacts were found in mortuary contexts. Bronze axes, however, were found in association with two females and an adult, while the bracelets were found with three females and one male. Later grave goods also included shell bracelets and disc beads, and marble T-shaped bracelets virtually identical with those from Nong Nor and Ban Na Di. No radiocarbon dates have been obtained from Non Praw, so we do not know if the early graves predate the availability of bronze. This seems very unlikely on the basis of the form and the decoration on the pots, and it is considered likely that both mortuary phases fall within the period 1000–500 BC.

Ban Chiang Hian

Ban Chiang Hian is located 110 km east of Non Nok Tha, in the upper valley of the Songkhram River (Fig. 6.1). It has been excavated on many occasions, the most extensive being undertaken under the direction of Gorman and Charoenwongsa (1976) in 1974–5. Their preliminary report described impressions gained from two seasons of excavations, the first involving 75.05 m^2 and the second, 55.75 m^2. Their first report noted that bronze was present 'during the initial phase I/II occupation of the mound' (Gorman and Charoenwongsa 1976:17). This they dated to about 3500 BC. Phase IV, characterised by a distinctive incised and painted pottery, yielded many burials associated with bronze and two bimetallic iron spearheads with cast-on bronze socketed hafts. They dated these to 1600–1200 BC.

Gorman's analysis of the material was cut short by his untimely death in 1981. Joyce White, who was given responsibility for the analysis of this site, has provided a revised cultural sequence (White 1982, 1986). The 1974 excavation involved a cultural stratigraphy of up to 2.8 m and the second season reached the natural substrate at a depth of 3.2 m. White's analysis centres on the definition of 'provisional pottery types'. Pottery vessels, principally but not exclusively from graves, were assigned to these provisional types on the basis of form and surface decoration. The graves in question were then placed in sequence, on the basis of the intercutting of one by another, or by superpositions, for a grave overlying another must be later. In instances where provisional types were found associated

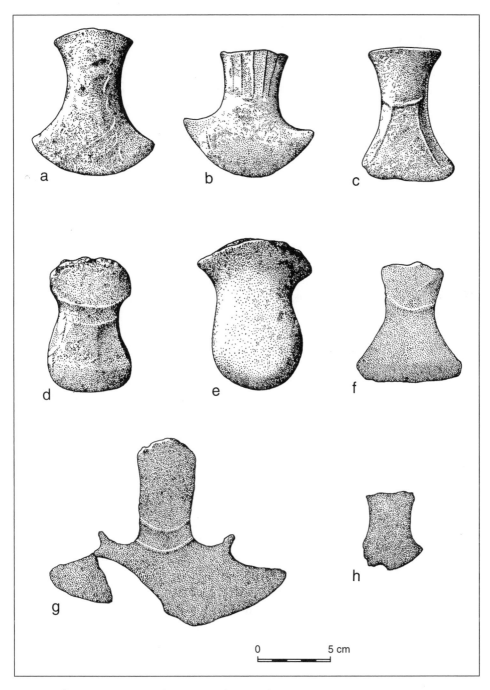

6.7 Bronze axes from Don Klang and Non Praw.
a–d. Four axes from Don Klang burial 7, found in a grave which included an iron bangle. **e.** Non Praw layer 3. **f.** Non Praw burial 2. **g.** Non Praw burial 12. **h.** Non Praw burial 3.

in the same grave or in contemporary contexts, they were ascribed to a group. White proposed 18 provisional types in 11 groups. She then divided the sequence into three periods. The Early Period (EP) has five phases (I–V), the Middle Period (MP) has three (VI–VIII) and the Late Period (LP), two (IX–X). Graves in each excavated area were then assigned to a phase, or, where they did not contain any chronologically diagnostic provisional types, they were given a range of possible phases. No grave assigned to either EPI–II was found with bronze grave goods. One EPIII grave included a bronze spearhead, and a child ascribed to EPIV was found with three bronze anklets. During the Middle Period, bronzes became more abundant, and iron was encountered in mortuary contexts.

The next stage was to define the chronological framework based on a series of 33 radiocarbon determinations. Some came from hearths or charcoal concentrations within the stratigraphic sequence, while the majority derive from charcoal present in grave fill or near the skeleton. The procedure was beset by inconsistencies between the dates and the stratigraphic sequence because there is no assurance that the charcoal providing the latter set of dates was not relocated during the digging of the grave. The two dates from *in situ* hearths in contexts where bronze was also present are 1118–891 and 1620–1409 BC. Unfortunately, the latter comes from the later context. White's (1986) review has resulted in a proposed chronological framework for the early period of occupation with a wide margin being ascribed to each successive phase as follows: (all dates BC). EPI 3600–2500, EPII 3000–1900, EPIII 2100–1700, EPIV 1900–1400 and EPV 1600–900. This framework is now being reconsidered through a programme of AMS dating of mortuary pottery from the successive contexts and further comment will be deferred until the results are available.

During this period, the dead were inhumed to the west of due north, although some were interred in a flexed position. Infants were buried in large jars, a widespread technique at this period in Southeast Asia. Pottery vessels predominated as grave goods, but never in profusion. Burial 52 contained four, but most complete graves contained between one and three and some had none. Most pots were placed over or beyond the ankles, and a few were located beyond the head. There were also a few items of personal jewellery, burial 55 having an ivory bangle on each arm. Compared with the wealth of grave goods at Neolithic sites in Central Thailand, such as Khok Phanom Di and Phu Noi, however, this cemetery is decidedly poor. There are no records of stone or shell bracelets, or shell beads. No EPI–IV graves recovered during the 1974 season contained bronze items.

In one part of the 1975 excavated area, EP graves underlie a concentration of clay, bronze flecks and crucibles resulting from local bronze casting. There are then two clusters of Middle Period graves, separated by 13 m. This Middle Period saw an increase in the quantity of grave goods, and a change in the disposal of mortuary vessels and the first evidence for the use of iron.

Ban Na Di

Until the Ban Chiang sequence is properly dated and the excavation report published, most information on the bronze age of this area will come from Ban Na Di, 20 km to the south. This site was identified during a programme of research in the upper catchments of the Songkhram and Pao rivers. Fieldwork began in 1980 with a site survey, which resulted in the recognition of many mounded sites and the trial excavation of three. Ban Na Di was selected for a major excavation which took place in 1980–1. An area of 65 m² was uncovered to a maximum depth of 4.2 m in two areas separated by 28 m (Fig. 6.8, Higham and Kijngam 1984). The site revealed a clear stratigraphic sequence, partly due to the deposition of sand lenses by flood water. But there are also features which result from human activity. Many pits were found, some sealed by a thick layer of charcoal. There were clay furnaces for heating copper and tin before casting, and lenses of shellfish. Hearths were abundant and the presence of charcoal in undisturbed contexts underwrites a reasonably consistent chronological framework.

Layers 6–8 comprised the lower 2 m of deposit. Layer 8 included thin shell middens, charcoal spreads, sand lenses and pits filled with shellfish and potsherds. Layer 7 above also contained sand lenses, which varied in thickness from 1 to 20 cm. Shell lenses were no longer encountered, but we find clusters of burials, interred beside each other and over previous interments. In one case a bronze casting facility, including a clay-lined furnace, crucibles and mould fragments, was found in the mortuary area. Burials were rare in squares A2 and A3, but there is evidence for a further cluster in A1. The intervening area contained evidence for occupation in the form of hearths, pits and postholes. Layer 6 had no sand lenses, and saw the end of the burial activity during this, the first and major mortuary phase at the site.

This cemetery has yielded sixty burials. Their characteristics, and relationships with the two major mortuary phases described above for Ban Chiang, may be expected to illuminate the nature of these bronze age communities in the Mekong Valley. The spatial distribution of graves recalls that for the Middle Period at Ban Chiang. Both sites have in common a north-south grave orientation, marked clustering of burials and a space between the clusters. Men, women, children and infants are found, infants nearly always being interred near adults without being placed in jars. All males save one were interred with the head pointing to the south, the one exception being orientated to the west. Females had the head pointing to the north. Iron artefacts appeared in a few late burials.

This mortuary phase at Ban Na Di has been divided into sub-phases: 1a–c on the basis of the superpositions of graves, and it was found that, with time, there were several minor modifications in the form of pottery vessels found with the dead. Retention of the same basic mortuary ritual, the clustering of burials into groups and the continuity in the ceramic tradition suggest that the cemetery covers a relatively brief period and contains successive members of the same

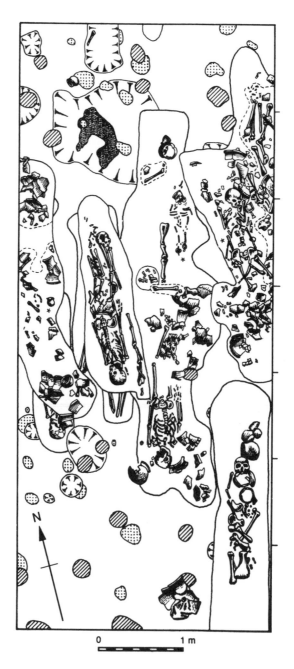

6.8   Squares A3–4 of the excavated area of Ban Na Di showing the mortuary plan.
The burials are tightly clustered, and only three, all belonging to the latest
sub-phase, have bronzes: from east to west, burial 48, a female, has two
bangles, burial 29, an infant, has two anklets and burial 18, a female, was
interred with a single bangle.
* indicates a bronze artefact.

community. But the excavation of two separate areas also permits comparison between the style and relative wealth of two contemporary groups. We can, therefore, consider the characteristics, expressed in the rituals of death, of a community which existed when bronze was an accepted part of the technical repertoire.

Bronze was very rare in the fifteen phase 1a graves. No artefacts were encountered, although scraps of metal and crucible fragments were found even in layer 8. Bronze was found in two graves, where it was used to repair broken stone bracelets. Holes were bored through the bracelet next to the fracture, and bronze was cast through them in the form of a tie-wire (Maddin and Weng 1984). Males in this phase were interred with the head pointing to the south, females to the north. Three main forms of pottery vessel were placed with the dead, a round based bowl, large jar and a pedestalled bowl. Apart from the two exotic stone bracelets, jewellery comprised shell beads and a single bead of stone. A particular feature of these early interments was the inclusion of clay figurines of cattle, deer, humans and an elephant. These are considerably larger than any found at other sites in the area, and some reveal an elegant simplicity of style. One woman was found with the forelimb of a domestic cow.

There are 21 burials in phase 1b, associated with many more grave offerings. Three people wore bronze jewellery. A woman (burial 36) had 19 bronze bracelets as well as a shell bracelet and over 100 shell beads. A seven-year-old, probably a boy to judge from the orientation of the body, wore one bronze bracelet. The child was found beside burial 36. He, or she, was also accompanied by two shell bracelets, over 200 shell beads, two cattle figurines and two pottery vessels. Three further bronze bracelets were encountered with a young woman. This phase also saw a wider range of pottery forms, and vessels were more abundant in some graves. Burial 19, for example, contained eight pots of six different forms. Exchange originating in coastal communities is also demonstrated by the presence of two cowrie shells with burial 15, a two-year-old child.

Phase 1c burials reveal a further increment in the range and quantity of grave goods. Exchange with coastal groups is further shown by the presence of thirteen trochus shell bracelets with a man, but only four of the 24 graves included bronzes (Fig. 6.9). A child was found with two solid bronze anklets, and the adjacent woman had one bronze bracelet. Two bracelets were encountered with another woman, and a man had been interred with a bronze coil. As with all mortuary phases, cattle limbs were placed with the dead. These were in most cases the fore left limb, and may well result from animal sacrifice as part of mortuary ritual. Some phase 1b–c graves also have pig limbs, but these are more rare. Two pots which match vessels from MPVII Ban Chiang were found with 1c graves, and two men were found with iron artefacts: one spearhead, four bracelets, one coil, an iron ring and a knife. Indeed, iron was more abundant than bronze in phase 1c.

The range and quantity of goods increased with time, but we also find that the burials in one cluster (area A) were markedly richer, in terms of exotic goods, than

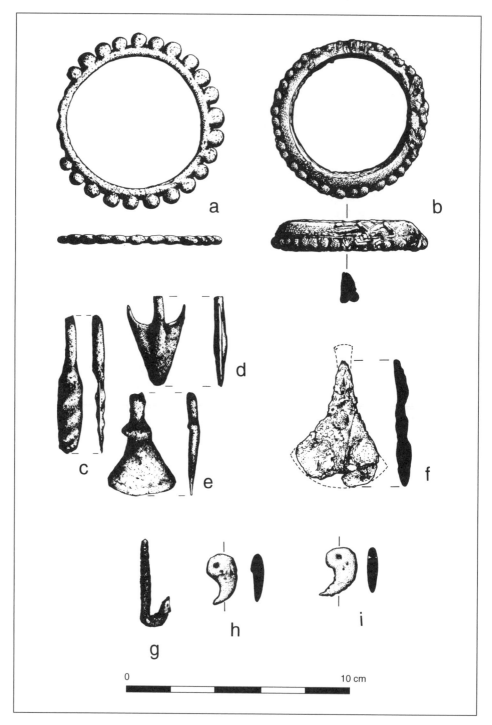

6.9   The bronze artefacts from Ban Na Di.
a, b. Bracelets. **c–f.** Arrowheads. **g.** Fishhook. **h, i.** Beads.

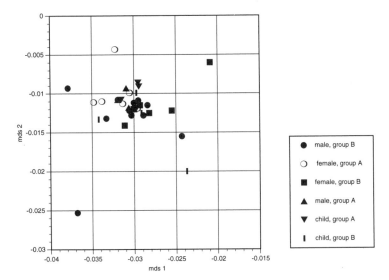

6.10   Distribution of the graves at Ban Na Di following multidimensional scaling.

members of another (area B). Yet, according to the stratigraphy and ceramic styles, the graves accumulated over the same period of time. Group A graves contained all the stone and trochus bracelets, all the clay animal and human figurines, the majority of shell disc beads and the iron artefacts. Twenty-seven of the 32 bronze items were found in Group A graves.

The application of multivariate statistical analyses to the graves has confirmed a marked distinction between the relative wealth of area A and B graves (Fig. 6.10). A cluster analysis has separated out the richer graves, nearly all of which fall into the former. The same situation is found with the results of multidimensional scaling, there being many graves in a concentrated group with a limited range of goods, while those from group A, on account of more and a greater variety of offerings, are more widely distributed.

This has encouraged the excavators to suggest that the members of group A were consistently richer due to their higher status. Perhaps it was a household or family group which had first or a preferential call on the distribution of the exotic prestige goods which entered the community, and used these in mortuary rituals to signal their higher rank. Two group A burials were also associated with crocodile bone. A man was buried with a bored ornament fashioned from a crocodile skull, and a child was interred under a crocodile skin shroud. Could this group have adopted a crocodile totem? These animals are said still to survive in nearby Lake Kumphawapi.

The dating of this mortuary phase is based on ten radiocarbon determinations, all taken from charcoal in firm contexts relating to the burials in group B. No charcoal from *in situ* features was found in area A, but the related ceramic styles between the two areas encourages the application of the dates to both. The burials were all cut after the two determinations from layer 8 at the base of the cultural deposits. They average 1313–903 BC. There are three dates from lower contexts in layer 7, and these when pooled give a date of 2406±36 BP. The calibration curve at this date is complex, and the resulting calibrated range at 2 sigma is 761–680 (23%), 659–635 (3%), 594–581 (1%) and 554–397 BC (73%). There are also four dates from a pit belonging to the same part of the sequence as these three dates. The first determination obtained seemed too late, so three further samples were submitted, and these, too, came out late. The average is 95 BC–AD 252 (95%). The one date from layer 6 is 544–176 BC. In the site report, the excavators suggested that the mortuary phase 1 cemetery dated soon after the initial occupation and lasted for about 800 years (c. 900–100 BC, Higham and Kijngam 1984:435). This remains a tenable interpretation, but subsequent experience at Khok Phanom Di, and a consequent accentuation of the social aspect of such cemeteries, has encouraged me to compress this range considerably. I now feel that a date for the cemetery of 600–400 BC is rather more likely.

The Middle Chi Valley

The upper Songkhram Valley is linked to the Khorat Basin by the Pao River, which includes Lake Kumphawapi in the region of its headwaters. The Pao joins the Chi River northeast of Mahasarakham, and it was in this area that Higham and Kijngam (1984) undertook a site survey and limited excavations as part of the same research programme which saw the excavation of Ban Na Di. Ban Chiang Hian is a moated site on the southern edge of the Chi flood plain. The moats enclose an area of about 38 ha, and a recent study of satellite images has revealed a complex system of water control. The moats were fed by a diverted stream, and incorporated a reservoir. Small canals then issued to the north from the moats, presumably to supplement the natural availability of water in ricefields bordering the Chi flood plain (Parry 1992). We do not know the date of these earthworks, but the excavation of a small test square in 1981 has allowed some insight into the chronology of this site (Chantaratiyakarn 1984).

Cultural deposits in the central part of the mound attained a depth of 5 m, divided into eleven layers. Stratigraphy was very clear, and there were numerous charcoal lenses, hearths and, towards the base, sand lenses. The earliest pottery included much red-on-buff painted ware, with a wide range of geometric and some curvilinear motifs. This style continued into layers 10 and 9, and a cluster diagram for the body decoration shows marked similarities for these three layers which include the basal 1.5 m of the deposit. These layers incorporate part of a cemetery, although the small area excavated rules out the recovery of complete graves and no pottery vessels were recovered. Grave goods included a heavy marble bracelet and shell disc beads. The deepest burial, that of a male, was buried with the head pointing to the west, while a female, interred directly above him, had the head directed to the east. Although most bronze and crucible fragments were found in layers 6 to 8, two pieces of crucible were identified in this mortuary phase, one in layer 11 and a second in layer 9. There are three radiocarbon dates for this basal context. One was obtained from charcoal scattered through layer 11, and the result is clearly too late and fails to conform to a pattern. The other two determinations come from hearths about 80 cm above the substrate, and they average 944–797 BC, suggesting a date in the first century or two of the first millennium BC.

Burials were cut from layer 6, on the same orientation as burials 4 and 6. Most bronze fragments were found in layer 6, and iron, which first appeared in layer 7, became abundant in layer 6. There is no radiocarbon date for it, but the dated contexts above and below suggest a date in the second half of the first millennium BC. What Ban Chiang Hian tells us is that the Chi Valley was occupied by people locally casting bronze at the beginning of the first millennium BC. The pottery used at this site has little in common with that from Ban Chiang or Ban Na Di at the same period.

Muang Fa Daet lies 30 km north of Ban Chiang Hian, on the opposite side of the Chi River. It is among the largest of moated sites on the Khorat Plateau, covering an area of 171 ha, but the plan of the moats strongly suggests that they were excavated over a considerable timespan. The innermost and presumably earliest moated enclosure surrounds a discrete occupation mound known as Ban Muang Kao and excavations there in 1991 revealed three inhumation graves associated with an iron harpoon and socketed axe and glass, agate and carnelian beads (Indrawooth *et al.* 1991). These were stratified over a layer of red-on-buff pottery which might well relate to the early ceramics from Ban Chiang Hian.

The Upper Mun Valley

This important region which links the Central Plain and the Khorat Plateau has been surveyed for prehistoric sites by Welch and McNeill (Welch 1984, Welch and McNeill 1988-9, 1991). They found that prehistoric settlement, represented by the Tamyae phase at five sites, began within the period 1000–600 BC. Only three partial burials were found during excavations at Ban Tamyae itself, so little is known of the material culture of mortuary traditions involved. A bronze bracelet fragment was, however, found in layer 7. This phase was succeeded by the Prasat Phase (600–200 BC), during which iron made its appearance, and four times as many sites were recognised. If not accounted for by the invisibility of deeply stratified layers, there appears to have been a considerable growth in population.

Ban Prasat is a large site, covering 750 × 450 m, which lies adjacent to the Tarn Prasat stream, a tributary of the Mun River (Fig. 6.1). It was excavated by Suphot Phommanodch in 1991, and three widely-separated areas on the site were opened (Monkhonkamnuanket 1992, Phommanodch 1991). Each revealed a deep stratigraphic sequence which included inhumation graves, and in two squares, two mortuary phases were represented. Two radiocarbon dates from a context equated with the later part of the first mortuary phase fall within the mid first millennium BC, and suggest that the initial settlement took place between 800–500 BC. The second mortuary phase belongs within the period 500 BC to AD 500 and will be considered below.

The early phase graves in square 1, which lies at the approximate centre of the mound, were found from 4.6 to 5.2 m below datum. Six burials are involved, although a further eight have been ascribed to a transitional period. These were found at depths of 3.3 to 4.6 m. A particular feature of these interments is the quantity and quality of the pottery vessels. The dominant form is a carinated vessel with a ring foot and broad trumpet rim. These were burnished and red slipped, and some bear spiral and running curvilinear designs. There are many other forms, including round-based globular pots, flat-based open bowls and trumpet-rimmed vessels lacking a pedestal or ring foot. One of the problems faced in reviewing this cemetery is that all skeletons were left in the ground to form an open museum. Consequently, whenever a burial overlay an earlier one, the latter was only partially uncovered. This, unfortunately, was the case with burial 5, which underlay burials 7 and 14. Only the upper right hand third of the skeleton and lower left leg was revealed, the entire middle part of the burial remains sealed. Nevertheless, it is possible to appreciate the wealth of the man in question. He was interred with at least 49 complete pots, placed in a straight line down his right hand side, beyond the head, over the body and beyond the feet. He wore five marine shell bracelets on his right wrist. One female, burial 13, was interred with fifteen similar shell bracelets on the left and a further eight on the right arm. Burial 3 contains the remains of a male with a socketed bronze axe on the chest, many shell disc beads and at least five pottery vessels. Pots and pig bones were also found with children as well as with adults. Burial 7 had a marble bracelet just like that found at Ban Na Di, and similar marble and shell bracelets, shell disc beads and trumpet-rimmed pots were found with the transitional burials above. Whereas the earlier graves were orientated with the heads pointing to the southeast, the later ones were much more variable in terms of orientation.

Square 3 also revealed a group of burials at a depth of 3.7 to 4.1 m below datum, and although the excavators equate them to phase 1 in the main square on the basis of the similar pottery tradition, there are some differences. The layout of the graves follows a pattern seen earlier in Central Thailand at Khok Phanom Di, the two female and seven childs' graves being laid out in rows with the head pointing to the east (Fig. 6.11). More burials contained pig bones, and pottery vessels were often broken and distributed over the bodies. The pots in question have the same trumpet rims and red slipped finish seen in the early graves in square 1. Some burials included clay spindle whorls, but only burial 6 included any items of bronze. This child wore four bronze bracelets on the left arm and three, along with a shell example, on the other.

Square 2 contained two late graves, but there was also an area with much burnt material, charcoal fragments and both a clay mould for casting a socketed axe and a crucible virtually identical to those from Ban Na Di and Ban Chiang. The

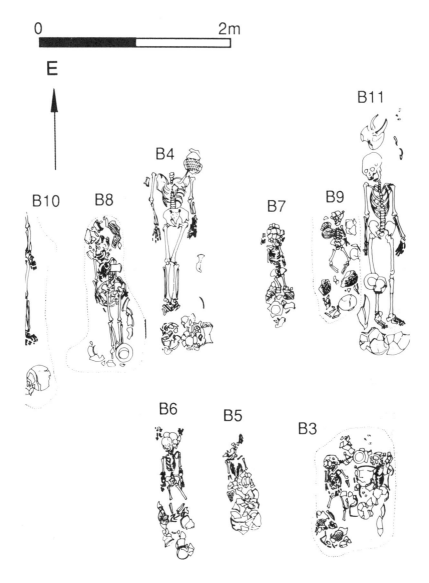

6.11 The distribution of graves at Ban Prasat excavation square 2.
Permission: Fine Arts Department, Thailand.

excavators have suggested that this area on the edge of the settlement was reserved for bronze casting.

Ban Prasat has also yielded many other artefacts. Clay anvils attest local pottery making, and there is a clay figurine of a pregnant woman. The shell jewellery, including bracelets and disc beads, provide parallels with both Khok Phanom Di and Ban Na Di, while the marble and bronze bracelets recall both Ban Na Di and Nong Nor assemblages. The mortuary ritual involved rows of interments, matching that seen at Ban Chiang, Nong Nor, Khok Phanom Di, Ban Na Di and Non Nok Tha. A date within the first half of the first millennium BC equates this mortuary phase with early Ban Na Di, Nong Nor, Middle Period Ban Chiang and Nil Kham Haeng.

The Tonle Sap plains

Archaeology in Cambodia has ground to a halt. All we can do in examining its role in the bronze age of the Mekong Valley is to refer to the early work at Samrong Sen and in the Mlu Prei area (Fig. 6.1). Samrong Sen was a site of considerable extent with an economy which benefited from proximity to rich riverine resources. It has furnished a number of bronzes, almost all found by villagers while digging for shells. These include socketed spearheads and axes, bracelets, a bell and a crucible containing metallic scoria. Mansuy (1923) also recovered a sandstone mould for casting an axe. The only hint as to the site's date comes from a single radiocarbon determination based on shell (1749–1253 BC), which is compatible with the dates obtained in Northeast Thailand, although its relationship to the stratigraphic sequence, let alone bronze in the site, is not known. Mansuy (1923) has also published a number of ornaments with parallels at Khok Phanom Di. These include shell discs, pendants, disc beads and stone and shell bracelets. One of the bracelets was fashioned from tridacna shell.

Sandstone moulds for casting an axe and a sickle as well as crucible fragments have also been found at the site of O Pie Can (Lévy 1943). Bronze bracelets have been reported with inhumation graves at the nearby site of O Yak.

The Lower Mekong

The cultural sequence in the lower reaches of the Mekong River incorporates a Late Neolithic Period, represented by the sites of Cau Sat and Ben Do. Both demonstrate a skilled stone industry which includes large polished shouldered adzes and stone bracelets (Pham Van Kinh 1977). Cu Lao Rua is probably the earliest site with evidence for bronze in this region, although no radiocarbon dates are available. A villager is said to have recovered a socketed bronze axe from the site, but the material culture, with its many stone adzes and items of jewellery, show parallels with Cau Sat. Doc Chua 10 km to the northeast has, however, provided important evidence for metal working in this region following excavations there between 1976 and 1979 (Le Xuan Diem 1977, Dao Linh Con and Nguyen Duy Ty 1993). Thirty-two burials were found, as well as a sample of over fifty sandstone and clay moulds, some complete and others unfinished. Many items of material culture precisely match artefacts from the Khorat Plateau, including pellet bow pellets and potsherds cut into a circle. The bronze axes could also come from Khorat sites, although they are more abundant in the graves at Doc Chua. Of the 32 graves, seventeen include bronzes. These included the

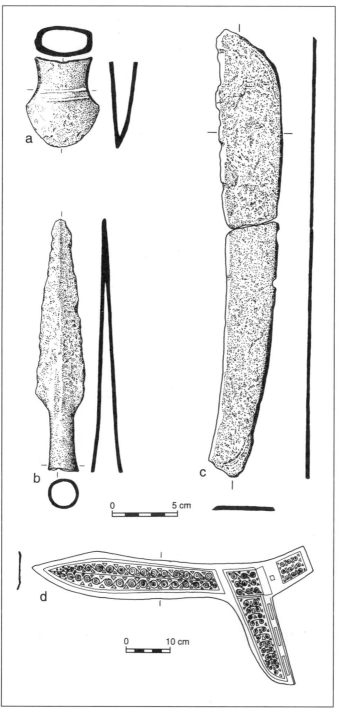

6.12 Bronze artefacts from Doc Chua (a-c) and Long Giao.
a. Socketed axe. **b.** Socketed spearhead. **c.** Knife. **d.** Halberd.

socketed axes with a splayed blade, eight spearheads and halberds of clear Chinese form (Fig. 6.12). A total of thirteen such halberds have been reported from Doc Chua, and Murowchick (1989) has found their closest parallels in the Warring States sites to the north. There were also some bracelets, one of which was ornamented with two bells and animal figures – a dog and a lizard – cast in bronze. Seven graves include spindle whorls, and there is some evidence for a complementary distribution between these and weapons, because five graves with spindle whorls lack bronzes. One further grave without bronzes also contains a clay potter's anvil. This distinction might well reflect different assemblages for males and females.

Sandstone moulds are also abundant (Fig. 6.13), and disclose the casting of axes (35), spears (8), harpoons, a chisel, fishhook and a bell. The analysis of the bronzes reveals that most were cast of a 10–15% tin bronze, but the halberds contained very high levels of lead (up to 42.7%, Nguyen Duy Ty and Dao Linh Con 1985). Murowchick (1989), noting the absence of moulds for casting halberds locally, has suggested that these implements might have been used for display rather than conflict, for the high admixture of lead would have softened the alloy. The wealth of the local bronze industry, however, is an indication of the amount of copper and tin being exchanged, trade which must have been facilitated by the Mekong River route.

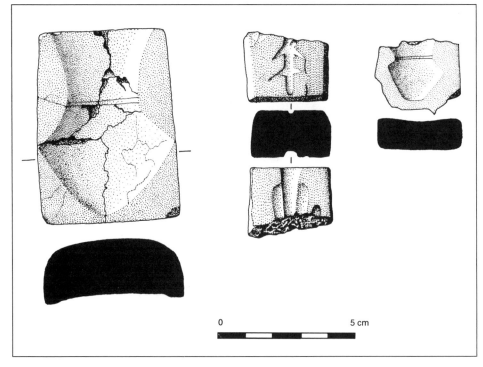

0   5 cm

6.13   Sandstone moulds from Doc Chua.

Two radiocarbon dates have been obtained, 1700–1050 BC and 796–472 BC. The former probably dates the lower occupation deposits, while the latter is more likely to indicate the date of the burials and the bronze industry. This is sustained by the parallels between the halberds and those from the period of Warring States (475–221 BC). A further nineteen of these implements were discovered nearby at Long Giao in 1982. In his analysis, Pham Duc Manh (1985) has stressed their similarities to those of Doc Chua while also finding parallels, in terms of the decoration, with motifs found on Dong Son drums. He dates them to the second half of the first millennium BC.

In 1960 Saurin (1963) examined a site disturbed by a bulldozer at Hang Gon in southern Vietnam. He found concentrations of pottery which he felt might be house locations, as well as sandstone moulds for pins and axes. This site has achieved an element of notoriety because a radiocarbon date from the organic crust adhering to a piece of pottery has been used to support the very early dates for metal working proposed for Non Nok Tha. The actual determination, 3044–1745 BC, has no stratigraphic relationship to the moulds.

The Iron Age

The Iron Age in the Mekong Valley is best documented on the Khorat Plateau. Virtually nothing is known of this period in Cambodia. The earlier bronze age settlements concentrated in the well-watered Sakon Nakhon Basin. No site in the Khorat Basin has been found which dates within the second millennium BC. Yet first millennium BC sites are abundant, particularly where isolated pockets or ridges of the middle terrace provide safety from flooding, but give easy access to low terrace land which encourages rice cultivation. It was in this area that Williams-Hunt (1950) identified numerous moated settlements from air photographs (Fig. 2.8). Further fieldwork has added considerably to the corpus of sites (Fig. 6.14). Hitherto, the archaeology of this area has virtually been restricted to cemeteries at the expense of domestic or industrial sites. This situation is reversed for the Iron Age: we know of many settlements, but no cemeteries have been extensively excavated.

The moated sites have proved enigmatic. No acceptable dating evidence has been obtained, and even the configuration of the moats remains unknown. Were they shallow or deep? Gradually, however, field research is casting some light on this group of settlements. They concentrate in the valley of the Mun River, though their distribution extends into the Chi Valley, the Siem Reap plains and Central Thailand. The Mun Valley is particularly dry, and most agree that the moats represent a form of water conservation and control. This receives support from the common association of reservoirs and canals with systems of moats. Dating is inferential. Many sites were abandoned after a period of Iron Age occupation. At Noen U-Loke, for example, Iron Age burials are found less than a metre from the present surface of the mound within the moats. This suggests that the moats were

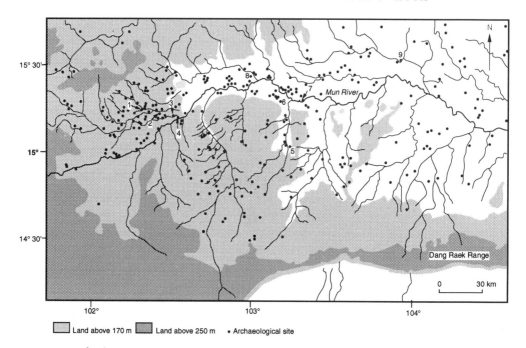

6.14   The distribution of moated sites in the Mun Valley.
1. Noen U-Loke. **2.** Ban Prasat. **3.** Ban Tamyae. **4.** Phimai. **5.** Ban Takhong.
6. Ban Don Phlong. **7.** Muang Yang. **8.** Non Krabuang Nok. **9.** Non Dua.

in place by the end of the prehistoric period. A site survey in the upper Mun Valley by Higham and Thosarat has shown that the moated sites are found regularly placed along the margins of the Mun Valley and at tributary stream confluences (Fig. 6.15). Welch and McNeill (1991) have also pointed out that some sites are located close to or bordering the Mun River itself.

It has been suggested that the moats might also have had a defensive function. This could be investigated through the excavation of the banks which lie between moats to see if there they were fortified in any way. But the lack of evidence for any form of rampart at the junction of the settlement with the innermost moat makes a defensive function unlikely.

Non Chai

Non Chai illustrates many of the variables which typify the Ion Age in this region. It was much larger than the earlier bronze age sites. We cannot ascertain the actual extent because it has been removed to serve as road fill. But estimates vary between at least 18 to 38.5 ha. The former figure was based on the surviving area in 1978. Bayard *et al.* (1986) report that it formerly covered an oval measuring 1000 × 500 m and rose 15 m above the surrounding area. Van Liere (1979) has described the vestiges of a moat or canal round it. This might well be so, and could be confirmed by the analysis of early air photographs. The settlement commands

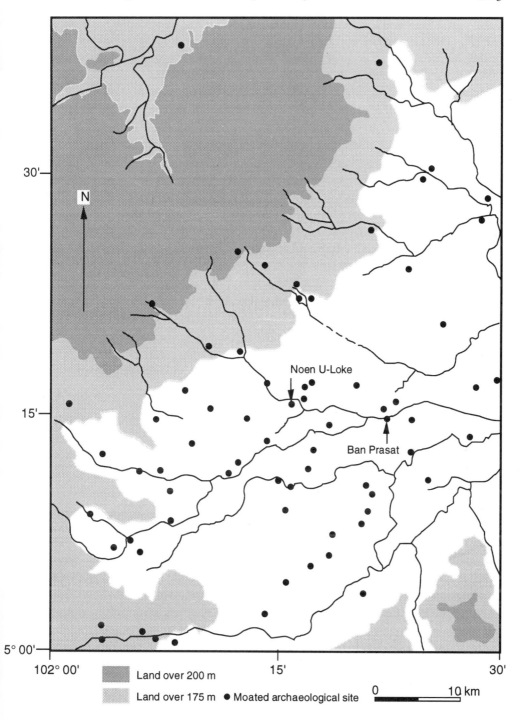

6.15 The distribution of moated sites in the upper Mun Valley.

a strategic location at the junction of the Chi and Phong rivers, an area which still contains extensive lakes and marshland, although Non Chai itself sits on a relict middle terrace safely above the flood zone. Excavations under the direction of Pisit Charoenwongsa began in 1977, and 14 months later, they reached the substrate at a depth varying between 4.7 m and 5.5 m in an area of 76 m².

The site provided a large sample of pottery, faunal remains, and evidence for bronze casting and iron smelting. On the basis of the ceramics and the archaeological layers, the excavators have proposed five cultural phases which exclude traces of a possible early and separate bronze age occupation at the very base (Bayard *et al.* 1986). The radiocarbon dates form a consistent series, which suggest that phase I belongs from 400 BC, or even a century earlier, phase II–III to 300–200 BC, phase IV to 200–1 BC and phase V to AD 1–200.

Pottery styles and forms are in sharp contrast with those representing the bronze age at Non Nok Tha, Ban Na Di and Ban Chiang. Most pots were decorated with red slip or painted geometric designs, yielding in the final phase to a preference for plain and cord-marked wares. The majority of the material was tempered with rice chaff, including 'blebs'. This term has been applied by Vincent (1988) to the use of clay mixed with rice chaff and then roasted before being pounded and included in the potting clay.

Both bronze and iron were found in the phase 1 layers. The iron was represented by fragments and pieces of slag, indicating local smelting activity. The bronzes include bracelet fragments and small bells, the latter being highly characteristic of this late phase of bronze working in the Mekong Valley sites. From phase 2, the ceramic sample includes fragments of crucible used in bronze casting, and broken pieces of clay moulds were recovered from phase III onward. These were used for casting bells and axes, the former through the lost wax process. The blue glass beads were found from phase II onwards. These might have been made in Southeast Asia, although the initial impetus resulted from exchange with Indian traders.

Up to and including phase III, freshwater shellfish were numerous, and the remains of crocodiles and rhinoceroses confirm a low, swampy habitat. Domestic pig, cattle and water buffalo were present from the earliest phase, and there is much evidence for hunting, particularly deer, and fishing. The abundance of rice as a ceramic temper suggests a diet based on rice and fish.

Non Chai is in many respects a pivotal site when considering the Iron Age of the Chi Valley and the Sakon Nakhon Basin. Its occupation was of relatively brief duration, so we can conclude that sites of considerable extent, possibly ringed by moats, were present between 400 BC and AD 200. The well-dated and intensively studied pottery enables parallels to be made between its sequence and that in other sites (Rutnin 1979). In terms of metal technology, Non Chai was a base for smelting iron and casting bronzes, which involved bivalve and lost wax methods. Similar sites are distributed within and along the margins of the Chi and Mun valleys.

Ban Chiang Hian

The 1980 site survey programme in the middle Chi Valley was centred on the moated site of Ban Chiang Hian (Fig. 6.16). While the distribution of the moated settlements can be recognised on the basis of air photographs, ground surveys are necessary in order to identify smaller sites. The results of the survey showed that Ban Chiang Hian is located on the edge of the Chi flood plain, a position shared by several smaller settlements. Prehistoric occupation also penetrated the tributary stream valleys, and concentrated on slightly elevated middle terrace margins giving access to the good rice soils of the low terrace.

Ban Chiang Hian is set within a broad moat with an exterior bank. The aerial photograph taken by Williams-Hunt in 1945 has recently been re-analysed by Parry (1992), who identified a cross-valley dam which would have retained water flowing past the site and diverted it into the moats and a reservoir (Fig. 6.17a). Four canals then took water out onto the floodplain. There is no clearer example of the water management system represented by the moated sites of the Khorat Plateau. The second occupation phase, incorporating layers 8–6, has been dated between 600–1 BC (Chantaratiyakarn 1984). The pottery in question shows a preference for impressing the surface with a carved paddle, in contrast to the earlier red-on-buff painted styles. But the later phase 2 assemblage also includes

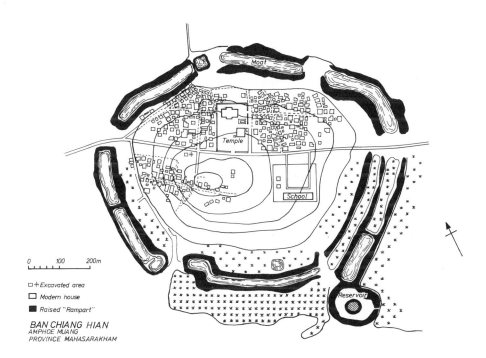

6.16   Plan of the moated site of Ban Chiang Hian.

Raised bank   Modern temple   Irrigation canal

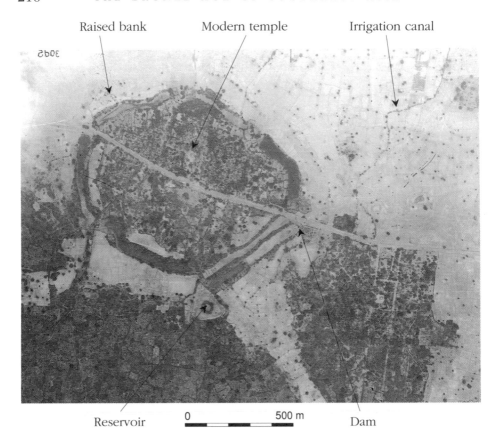

Reservoir   0   500 m   Dam

6.17a   Air photograph of Ban Chiang Hian taken in April 1945.
Permission: Williams-Hunt collection, School of Oriental and African
Studies, University of London.

some exotic sherds: there are examples of Non Chai rim forms, and others show close affinities with pottery found respectively at Non Dua in the lower Chi and in the Phimai area in the upper Mun Valley.

The same layers at Ban Chiang Hian also contained material which parallels finds from Non Chai. Bones of the water buffalo appeared for the first time in layer 8, and layer 7 saw the first iron. The main concentration of clay moulds used in the casting of bells and bracelets, as well as crucibles, came in layers 8–6. A bronze fishhook was also recovered. The third ceramic phase is represented in layers 4 and 5. The assemblage was distinct from phase 2, and includes thin white wares paralleled at Non Dua in the second half of the first millennium AD.

Dating the period of dam and moat construction and relating it to the cultural sequence is a clear priority. At present, one could present reasonable arguments in favour of phases 2 or 3. In the case of the former, we know that Non Chai covered a similarly large area during the period 400 BC–AD 200, and might have been associated with a moat. Iron was available, and Welch and McNeill (1991) have suggested that moat construction was under way in the Mun Valley by this period. The much larger moated site of Co Loa in Bac Bo also belongs to this period, and there was exchange contact between the two areas over the Truong Son Range. But there is no substitute for reliable archaeological dating. In the case of the latter, we know that similar water control systems were widespread in the lower Mekong Valley with the development there of powerful centralised polities at such sites as Īśānapura (van Liere 1980). There is also the possibility that the water distribution system at Ban Chiang Hian began in phase 2 and was continuously improved. Parry (1992), for example, has suggested that the reservoir might be a late addition.

Non Dua

The Lam Siao Yai is a small river which bisects the area between the lower Chi and Mun rivers before flowing into the latter. It was the focus of a site survey undertaken in 1970, which centred on the large, moated site of Non Dua (Higham 1977). Non Dua lies on a surviving pocket of the middle terrace, overlooking extensive low terrace soil to the north, and the narrow band of river alluvium which borders the Lam Siao Yai to the south. It covers an oval area about 2 km long and 1 km wide. The river itself meanders round the site and Parry (1992) has identified a canal which links it with the moats (Fig. 6.17b). Substantial deposits of rock salt lie nearby, and the present inhabitants boil the brine to produce salt

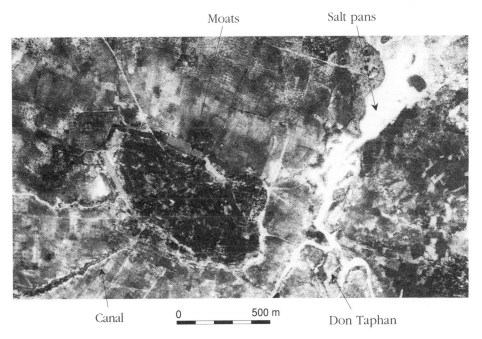

6.17b   Air photograph of Non Dua, taken from 25,000 feet in October 1967.

during the dry season. This activity has led to the accumulation of mounds around the salt flat.

Trial excavations were opened within the moated enceinte at Non Dua, at Bo Phan Khan, a mound adjacent to the salt flat, and at a third mound, known as Don Taphan, which is located on the opposite side of the river to Non Dua. The longest sequence was found at Non Dua, where deposits reached a depth of 4.5 m. The eighteen layers have provided much pottery, and this sample has been divided into three successive phases (Higham 1977). The earliest was dominated by polished and red slipped pottery with painted rims. This was followed by a middle phase characterised by 'Roi-et' ware, called after the province of the same name. This was cordmarked, smoothed and painted with red bands. It in turn was succeeded by a third phase in which plain white pottery dominated. These three phases are so clear that it is possible to integrate the sequence with those of Bo Phan Khan and Don Taphan. The former was excavated to a depth of 5.3 m, and the phase 2 Roi-et ware was found in the basal layer, and lasted through almost to the surface, when the first phase 3 white ware made an appearance. Pottery in this site, however, was dominated by a coarse and thick ceramic which was probably used to boil brine in preparing salt. The site has yielded charcoal-rich areas with pits and disintegrated plaster surfaces which have been interpreted as the remains of industrial salt extraction. It is apparent, therefore, that the salt working was vigorously pursued during phase 2 at Non Dua. Don Taphan, which covers at least 15 ha, is more enigmatic, because excavations took place near the edge of the site and some of the 61 layers were probably redeposited by wet season flooding. The excavation reached the water table at 5.85 m, at which point the pottery assemblage contained much Roi-et ware, and a radiocarbon date of 250 BC–AD 341.

Layer 49 has provided a date of 111 BC–AD 259, layer 9 AD 111–452 and layer 7, AD 751–1044. By layer 7, phase 2 ceramics were giving way to phase 3, the thin white ware. The phase 2 ceramics in basal Bo Phan Khan have been dated to AD 228–597. At Non Dua, the radiocarbon chronology is internally contradictory. Layer 12, the lowest with Roi-et ware, has provided a date of 49 BC–AD 341, but layer 13 below has been dated to AD 34–1010. Taking the dates as a whole, Higham (1977) has suggested that phase 1 should be dated to c. 500–1 BC, phase 2 to AD 1–700 and phase 3 from AD 700–1000. This is reasonably close to the sequence proposed for Ban Chiang Hian, 50 km to the north, although the beginning of phase 2 at Non Dua might be a couple of centuries earlier than 1 BC.

The limited excavations at these sites means that we have no information on bronze casting, but iron was found from the base of Non Dua. On the other hand, the evidence in favour of salt extraction from at least 1 BC suggests that the phase 2 occupation at Non Dua witnessed the exploitation, and surely the exchange of this critical resource. There is no dating evidence for the moats or canal, but a phase 2 context is a strong possibility.

The Upper Mun Valley

This area has one of the best documented sequences on the Khorat Plateau. Research began with excavations within the Khmer sanctuary of Phimai in 1966 (Solheim and Ayres 1979). These revealed a ceramic assemblage containing black pattern-burnished pottery now widely known as 'Phimai Black'. One of the three radiocarbon dates – two were effectively of modern age – was 164 BC–AD 267. Subsequent research in this area has been undertaken by Welch and McNeill, and by a number of officials of the Fine Arts Department. The former have concentrated on the distribution of sites, their size, relationship to the different environmental zones and changes in all three variables with time. The latter have concentrated on the excavation of Ban Prasat and Noen U-Loke.

Welch and McNeill have undertaken extensive site surveys in three environmental zones. These are the alluvial plain of the Mun River, the surrounding low terrace and the uplands (Welch and McNeill 1991). In categorizing the sites identified, they have developed a cultural sequence on the basis of the excavated sites and the available radiocarbon dates. The first, or Tamyae phase, is named after Ban Tamyae, and has been dated to 1000–600 BC. The former figure has not been confirmed by any radiocarbon dates and relies on reasoned guesswork. The latter date, which saw the transition to the Prasat phase, is based on a radiocarbon date of 735–529 BC from Ban Tamyae. The Prasat phase lasted until about 200 BC, and is best known from the earlier of the two mortuary contexts at the site of Ban Prasat. Welch and McNeill note that iron appeared at Ban Tamyae at or near the beginning of the Prasat phase, but no iron artefact was found in the earlier cemetery at Ban Prasat itself. The following phase is called after Phimai, and has two divisions: the Classic (200 BC–AD 300), and the Late Phimai (AD 300–600).

The Tamyae phase is represented by only five sites, all on the alluvial flats with four being adjacent to a stream. As was noted in the Middle Chi survey area, early phases are always likely to be under represented because their material is so deeply stratified that it may well not appear during surface surveys. Nevertheless, sites with known Tamyae occupation were found in the most desirable natural locations for rice cultivation. Four times as many sites were found in the survey areas with Prasat phase ceramics, and these, while concentrating still in the alluvial plain, are also found in the low terrace and upland zones. Fifty-three sites were ascribed to the Phimai phase, and again there was an expansion in the settled area: fourteen of these sites were found in the low terrace and six in the uplands.

Welch and McNeill (1991) have cited the low and unpredictable rainfall as a factor which encourages water storage and its distribution to rice fields in this region. They have suggested that the first steps in this process were undertaken during the Prasat phase, no doubt facilitated by the availability of iron implements. Ban Prasat itself, as well as Ban Tamyae, were partially ringed by moats. By Phimai times, over half the sites exceeded 10 ha in area, and the same

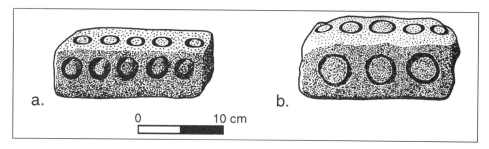

6.18   Clay open moulds for casting bronze rings.
a. Ban Non Udom. **b.** Ban Prasat.

proportion were moated. The extension of the Phimai phase pottery across the area confined by moats in many of these settlements suggests that such extensive and labour demanding works belong to this phase if not earlier. Moreover, the expansion of settlements onto higher elevations, where natural flooding could not be counted on, is hard to envisage without artificial methods of water management. Once the techniques were in place, however, control over salt and timber resources could be contemplated.

The burials of the Phimai phase at Ban Prasat differ in a number of respects from those which belong to the Prasat phase cemetery. We find that shell beads and bangles were no longer interred with the dead, their place being taken by a new range of bronze jewellery and exotic items of stone and glass. Apart from a number of pottery vessels in the Phimai Black tradition, we encounter with burial 1 from the main excavated area, an adult interred with agate and blue glass beads near the skull. Bronze bangles, anklets and finger and toe rings were abundant. Burial 2 had three bronze bangles on each wrist and two bronze finger rings. A male in burial 3 was interred with five bronze finger rings and a complex bronze headdress with spiral ends over each ear. Fourteen anklets were encountered on the legs of a child, who also had blue glass beads over the face. A child in burial 6 had four bronze bangles on the right arm and ten anklets. Rings were found on the toes and across the skull, perhaps components of another headdress, with burial 1 in square 2. Many bronze coils and rings, one covered in iron, accompanied a burial in the third excavation square. Apart from these grave goods, bronze was also found in the form of earrings and bells. An open ceramic mould for manufacturing such rings in numbers indicates local casting activity (Fig. 6.18; Phommanodch 1991). The rarity of any bronze or iron weapons in this cemetery contrasts with the contemporary situation in Bac Bo, Yunnan and the Chao Phraya Valley.

Noen U-Loke

Noen U-Loke is a large settlement surrounded by five moats, the most found in any prehistoric site in Southeast Asia (Fig. 6.19a, b). It is located between two streams, the Huai Don Man Kasak and the Huai Yai, about 12 km west of Ban

Prasat. A canal links the moats with the former, and a second, straight canal joins the moats with the latter. A third canal, parallel with the second, joins the two streams about 300 m to the east of the site. There is no assurance that the moats and the canals are contemporary, but the fact that one follows a straight line from the outermost moat is strong circumstantial evidence that they were. Each moat is flanked on the outside by a bank which may reach a breadth of 25 m. It seems likely that the surface soil was removed and mounded to create the moats.

In 1986, Wichakana (1991) excavated two squares, one in the approximate centre of the mound, the other on the southeastern edge. The former, which measured 3 by 6 m, revealed a sequence of layers about 4 m deep, which included three phases of inhumation graves. The lowest included graves orientated on a north-south axis and cut into the natural substrate. The grave goods included pottery of the Prasat phase, shell disc beads and bracelets of both bronze and marine shell. During the second phase, burials were orientated from east to west. Again, we find bronze bracelets some of which had a cross-section like those from

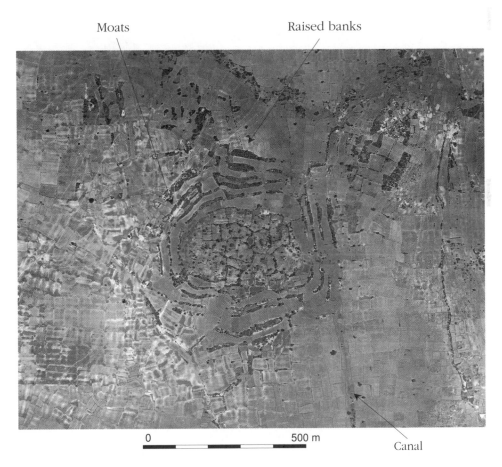

6.19a   Air photo of Noen U-Loke.

6.19b   The moats of Noen U-Loke.

Nong Nor in Central Thailand. But there were also a small number of agate
ornaments and two fragments of glass bead. No iron artefacts were found, but by
the same token, no burial was found complete. The third phase saw a reversion
to a north-south axis, and the pottery vessels belong to the classic Phimai phase.
The grave goods were richer and much more varied. Burial 2, for example, which
was found at a depth of just over a metre, was associated with a bronze headband,
bronze earrings and a bronze belt with a central buckle or plaque (Fig. 6.20). Iron
rings had been placed at the shoulder and in the groin area, the latter position also
being found in the case of burial 1. A tanged iron knife was found at the left
shoulder and a socketed axe or tip for a digging stick had been placed at the left
elbow.

Similar iron tools were also found with burial 1: a tanged sickle and a knife
were found near the left hand. Both were of a form still in use locally. This
individual also wore bronze bracelets on each wrist, a double bronze earring on
each ear and a glass bead. Numerous such orange glass beads were found with
burial 5, as well as an agate stud, an iron ring and nine bronze bracelets.

The abundance of iron during this late phase is easily accounted for. The
southeastern edge of the site includes many iron smelting furnaces, eroding from
the present surface of the mound. Nor should we overlook the industrial
importance of salt. Just over a kilometre to the west, there are two high but small
mounds which probably result from salt processing and again, salt working
continues as a local industry to this day.

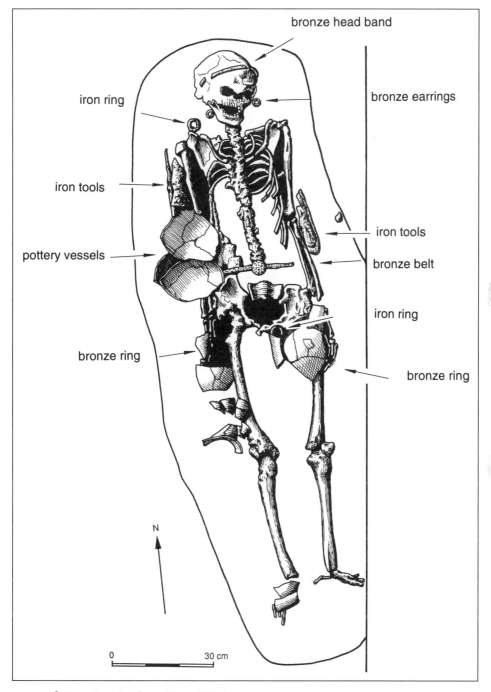

6.20 Burial 2 from Noen U-Loke.

Until firm dating evidence has been obtained for the moats and canals, it seems most likely that sites like Noen U-Loke were settled during the first few centuries of the first millennium BC, and that the advent of iron smelting, linked perhaps with a growing population in the established villages, was a catalyst for the construction of moats. It would be difficult to have moved so much soil without iron tools.

McNeill and Welch (1991) have considered the distribution of the Phimai Black pottery in the context of intra-regional and long distance exchange. Their excavations have made it possible to compare assemblages from domestic and mortuary contexts, and they have found that the former yield little evidence for exotic goods. The distribution of the Phimai Black pottery suggests that it was restricted to the upper Mun Valley with little circulating beyond a 50 km radius of Phimai itself. It was found in large and small, moated and unmoated sites, and the variety of forms hint at a wide range of uses. Only at Ban Prasat and Noen U-Loke do we encounter any evidence for mortuary goods, and this reveals a continuity and change in the acquisition of exotic items. Bronze was more abundant and was cast into new forms, particularly body ornaments. Weapons and vessels are absent. In place of shell and marble, we find carnelian, agate and glass jewellery. These cemeteries developed during a period of growing population, intense interest in the provision of moats around many settlements, and, as Welch and McNeill have convincingly suggested, agricultural intensification linked with efforts to counter the exigencies of an inhospitable climate.

As one moves down the Mun River valley from Phimai, the distribution of the pattern-burnished Phimai Black pottery peters out. None was found at Ban Takhong (Moore 1992), nor at Non Yang or Non Krabuang Nok near the confluence of the Mun and Sathaet rivers (McNeill and Welch 1991). This conforms to a pattern of regionality in ceramic styles already noted for the Chi Valley sites. But the same problems of water retention were present, and many moated sites have been identified in the middle reaches of the Mun River and its tributaries. Moore (1988) has undertaken a detailed study of the structure and distribution of the moated sites in the Mun Valley, and has suggested that three phases are represented. The first saw the provision of moats, nearly always of a circular or oval shape, around settlements located either on the flood plain or on pockets or the margins of the low terrace. These, she suggests, might have originated as copies of a natural phenomenon, where a site located in the bend of a stream was ringed by flooded margins during the wet season, thus providing a circle of water around the settlement. Ban Prasat is a site which could fit this formula. The second phase, which she dates to the later first millennium AD, saw a major expansion of the area within the moats, which now paid less attention to local topography. She has related these to the large, irregularly-shaped moated sites of the Central Plain. They nearly always contain structures matching those of the Dvaravati civilisation and fall, as does the Khmer phase 3, beyond the scope of this study.

Vallibhotama (1984, 1991) has undertaken extensive site surveys in the Mun and Chi valleys, and has stressed a number of important characteristics of the moated sites. They often provide surface evidence for iron smelting, and the further downstream, the more often one encounters a novel burial rite, involving interment in lidded burial jars. We have already seen that salt extraction took place at Non Dua by at least two millennia ago. In the Mun Valley, Nitta (1992) has excavated a site of similar antiquity at Non Tung Pie Pone. This mound is 5.5 m high, and excavations have revealed water storage tanks and furnaces for filtering and boiling brine. The pottery, as at Non Dua, was dominated by coarse industrial wares, but some sherds of Phimai Black show that the earliest of the nine phases of salt extraction belong to the late prehistoric period. Now we can also add intensive iron smelting to the industrial repertoire, for at Ban Don Phlong, Nitta (1991) has excavated a moated site which incorporated 17 iron-smelting furnaces in an excavated area of 16 × 5 m, overlying an inhumation cemetery. The twelve radiocarbon dates indicate that these phases belong from the fourth to the second centuries BC.

The best-preserved furnace comprised a clay-walled structure 32 cm long and 25 cm wide, in front of a pit for raking out the slag. It had been used at least three times for separate smelting operations. The remains of tuyères and much slag, taken in conjunction with the number and succession of furnaces on top of earlier ones, suggests that this area was set aside for iron smelting over a considerable time. An analysis of the slag suggests that the abundant local laterite ores were used.

Graves in the inhumation cemetery followed the convention of being interred in a group, usually with a similar orientation. At this site, most were buried on a north-south axis. The burial which stands out, number 6, was an adult male found within a grave lined with clay walls. His face had been covered by a block of clay. Three bronze bangles were found on each arm. Earlier bangles from the Khorat sites were narrow, but these were particularly deep and therefore involved more metal and skill in casting. Three bronze rings were also present, one on the chest, another on the right hand. The man's necklace included 10 agate and 31 glass beads. Traces of a split tree trunk coffin were found, and fabric near the skeleton might have come from clothing or a shroud.

Burial 3, another male, was also interred with several bronze ornaments: there were 15 rings on one hand and five on the other, a bronze ring on the chest, three further loose bronze rings, and a green glass ornament in the neck area. Burial 4 was only partially excavated, but ten bronze rings were found near the hand bones. Burial 7 incorporated a further clay-lined grave containing a child with a bronze bracelet on each arm and a third on the chest.

When surveying the corpus of bronzes from the seven graves, we find that there were ten bracelets, some up to 12 cm long, and 42 rings. The latter were popular during this late prehistoric period. An open mould for casting them in batches has already been recovered from Ban Prasat, and a complete example is known from Ban Non Udom, just north of Amphoe Chumphuang, with provision for casting five rings on each of the four sides (Fig. 6.18; FAD 1990). While increased planning and energy went into burial ritual when compared with earlier prehistoric sites on the Khorat Plateau, it is stressed that neither bronze weapons nor objects of iron were found.

Non Yang lies on the left bank of the Mun River, about 50 km northeast of Ban Don Phlong. Much has been eroded by the river in spate and only the northern third remains. Suchitta (1983) cleared a profile through the site during a 1981 site survey, noting that the mound then stood about 10 m above the surrounding rice fields. Nitta (1991) conducted excavations in 1989–90 and identified aspects of the domestic architecture and probably defensive structures for the first time in mainland Southeast Asia. His consideration of the complete sequence at this site is based on the exposed, eroded edge of the site adjacent to the river. He recognised eight cultural layers of which only the last three correlate with the section excavated. Clearly, little is known of the first five layers, except for the typology of the potsherds and the fact that many instances of burning were noted. The pottery parallels that described as Roi-et ware by Higham (1977), and very similar rim sherds to those from lower Non Dua, dated between 500–1 BC, were identified. The third cultural layer in the exposed edge of the site corresponds to Nitta's period G within the excavation.

This period revealed four structures, all built at ground level. They were constructed first by excavating a rectangular area for a foundation which comprised a row of circular timbers running across the short axis. The walls were built of clay over a timber frame, the interior surfaces being smoothed, the exterior being rougher. In the case of the best-preserved structure, S9, the north wall still stood to a height of 30 cm, and the room had maximum dimensions of 2.6 × 1.7 m. The foundation timbers, which were probably placed to prevent subsidence, were in turn coated with a layer of clay. Three similar, although badly disturbed, buildings were also uncovered, one having two pottery vessels placed under the foundations and another being associated with a cache of over 100 carbonised rice grains and husks under a jar. The carbonised support timbers for these structures provide excellent material for radiocarbon dating, and a consistent series of six determinations has been obtained which indicate that they belong to the period 300–1 BC. This conforms well with the date for the underlying Roi-et ware. Nitta has ruled out any possibility of these structures being used as pottery kilns, and concludes that they are probably the remains of domestic buildings which were destroyed in a conflagration. The only other known structure in this part of Southeast Asia is the mortuary chamber from Khok Phanom Di, where the building materials were again clay and timber. The rooms appear too small for dwellings, and Bayard (pers. comm.) has suggested most plausibly that they were rice stores.

The destruction of the buildings was followed by the excavation of two ditches 0.5–1.0 m wide and 0.7 m deep. One contains a curving row of large postholes.

Since the ditch was filled as one event, it seems likely that it was dug to facilitate the erection of a palisade. An iron spade was found within the fill. The second ditch, which runs parallel, was never finished. The next two phases saw the interment of lidded jar burials and digging of some small pits. A socketed iron axe was also found. With period C, a very large ditch up to 4.4 m wide and 2.05 m deep crossed the excavated area. When in use, the height from the base to the top of the wall within would have been 3–4 m. Its orientation suggests that it might have ringed the settlement. A charcoal sample from the base has been dated to 263 BC–AD 79, but Nitta has pointed out that the dated material might have been relocated during construction. However, the two latest phases saw a continuation of interment in lidded jars in groups, one of which followed a linear plan. This continuity of burial ritual and pottery typology suggests that the upper layers do not date markedly later than the four buildings below. Unfortunately, very few human remains survived in the urns, and no bronze or other artefacts have been reported as grave goods. The excavations nevertheless have provided unique evidence for possible defensive structures and secular buildings firmly placed within the Iron Age.

Ban Takhong is a small moated site adjacent to and overlooking the Lam Takhong Stream, a tributary of the Mun. It occupies the end of a tongue of middle terrace land, and is ringed by a two moats and a further moated extension on the southern side (Fig. 6.21). The river flows past the eastern side. Moore (1992) has excavated in the interior, and encountered a cultural stratigraphy almost 6 m deep. Two charcoal samples from depths of 1.7 and 2.5 m in one of the squares have been dated to AD 117–1001 and 778 BC–AD 146, and a sample almost a metre deep in a second test square has been dated to 101 BC–AD 381. But the fourth available sample is enigmatic in that it places a layer 3.2 m deep at 2049–1670 BC. It came from a layer containing fragments of bronze. Further dates are necessary from this and lower contexts, because if correct, it would require a complete revision of the prehistory of the Mekong Valley. The excavation also yielded clay derived from walls or floor features, which might match the structures from Non Yang, while a socketed iron tool, and iron bracelet and a ribbed bronze bracelet place at least part of the sequence firmly within the Iron Age.

Ban Krabuang Nok is another moated site which has been examined recently through excavation (Indrawooth *et al.* 1990). It lies between the confluence of the Mun River and one of its tributaries, the Lam Sa Thaet. A series of squares within the moat reached the natural substrate at a depth of 8.5 m, and the basal layer included much red slipped and red-on-buff painted pottery in association with evidence for both bronze and iron working. Much iron slag reveals local smelting, while bronzes included rings, bracelets and bells. This context has been dated between 300 BC–AD 200 and later phases included evidence for burial in lidded urns.

Vallibhotama (1991) has described a further cemetery within a moated enceinte at Ban Tad Thong, Yasothon Province, where inhumation graves associated with

6.21   Oblique air photograph of the moated site of Ban Takhong.
Permission: Dr Elizabeth Moore.

red slipped pottery underlay a second mortuary phase where the dead were interred in lidded jars. Similar burial jars, again associated with evidence for iron working, have been reported from Ban Yawuk (Surin Province) and at Ban Thung Wang (Buriram Province). Unfortunately, reports on these sites are not available, but some information on the jar burial tradition has been obtained from Ban Kan Luang, just north of Ubon at the confluence of the Mun and Chi rivers. This cemetery was encountered during the levelling of the ground for a housing development. It comprised a series of lidded burial jars containing human remains and grave goods. Woods and Parry (1993) briefly examined the site and reported on an important range of grave goods. There has not been a systematic excavation, but they noted that the owner of the site had a collection of 52 bronze artefacts and 16 of iron. Once again, the former was dominated by profusely ornamented armlets, bracelets and rings, although on this occasion, two spear-heads were present. These differ from the earlier example from Ban Chiang, because it has a solid tang and very long and narrow points one each side of the blade. Iron, on the other hand, was represented by axes or adze heads and knives, an arrowhead and a sword blade. A bronze figurine of a man standing 45 mm high was found in one of the urns, the decoration on the body, which Woods and Parry describe as discoid motifs, being matched on the bracelets.

Excavations and further investigations at Ban Kan Luang undertaken by the Fine Arts Department (FAD 1992) have added to our understanding of this site. In

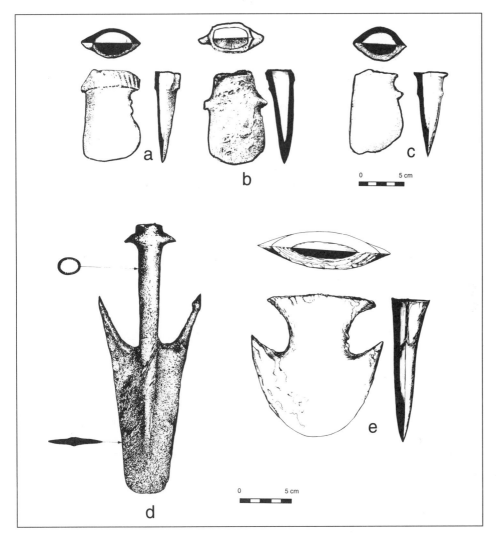

6.22a Bronze weapons and tools from Ban Kan Luang.
a–c, e. Socketed axes. **d.** Spearhead.
Permission: Fine Arts Department, Thailand.

addition to iron slag, a series of burial jars were identified which included eight varieties of decorated bronze bracelets, two types of axe, a spearhead, arrowheads and a knife (Fig. 6.22a and b).

Representations of human figures in bronze are virtually unkown in Khorat Plateau sites, but they are common in Yunnan and are also present in Bac Bo at the same juncture. Ban Kan Luang is within easy access of the Mekong River, beyond which there are passes across to the coast of Vietnam. For a number of years, reports of a major but seriously looted site at Don Tan on the right bank of the Mekong River have circulated. These include the presence of Chinese coins and burials which include bronze drums. Vallibhotama (1991) has also noted the recovery of a large bronze drum, now housed in the local temple. Such drums are commonly found in Dong Son contexts in Bac Bo, and across southern China with a particular concentration in Yunnan, where they belong to the second half of the first millennium BC.

It is, therefore, of particular interest to find that the lowlands where the Mun joins the Mekong have yielded several such drums (Sørensen 1992). Rarely is the provenance known in detail. The so-called Laos drum, for example, cames from 'a rice field in southern Laos (on the road to Ubon, Thailand)' (Bernet Kempers 1988:420). The Nelson drum was formerly owned by a man of this name living in Pakse, on the left bank of the Mekong opposite Ubon. Two further examples come from the Savannaket area, 170 km north of the Mun's junction with the Mekong. More recently, Sørensen (*ibid*) has described a more precise find spot. In 1990, a fisherman discovered a drum on the bank of Sane Island in the Mekong, 130 km south of Pakse. This is a large example, reaching a metre in width and formerly standing nearly 60 cm high. It was decorated on the mantle with at least six boats, and there are numerous feathered warriors. In his preliminary analysis, Sørensen has noted parallels with the other drums of the southern Laotian area, particularly their size and ornamentation. The latter includes a saw tooth motif which is particularly common in Yunnan, and which Sørensen cites as a characteristic of the Yunnan school of decoration. Further Heger 1 drums have

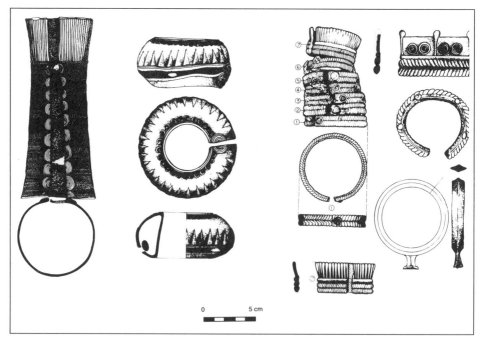

6.22b   Bronze bangles from Ban Kan Luang.
Permission: Fine Arts Department, Thailand.

been found at Ban Na Pho Tai at the confluence of the Mun and Mekong rivers, upstream at Ban Chi Thowang and at Pak Thong Chai. The last site lies on the arterial route between the Khorat Plateau and Central Thailand (Nitta 1994).

It is certainly likely, given the arterial nature of the Mekong River, that exchange contact with Yunnan provided the means whereby these highly prestigious drums reached the lower Mun area, while the Mun River would have facilitated exchange into the hinterland. Their concentration in this region supports the proposal that the control of traffic up and down the Mekong gave the local leaders the opportunity to enhance their standing.

The Siem Reap Plain

The Mun drainage system is served by many rivers which originate in the Dang Raek Range (Fig. 6.1). These narrow uplands rise little more than 300 m, and are crossed by numerous routes. To the south lies the extensive plain of Central Cambodia, interrupted by the Kulen Hills. The Siem Reap Plain lies between these hills and the Tonle Sap, the Great Lake. Several streams rise in the Kulen Hills and flow south to the lake, and these were diverted to serve the massive hydraulic works of historic Angkor. Moore (1989, 1992) has recently undertaken a site survey in this region, associated with a consideration of aerial photographs. She identified 69 mounded sites in the valleys of the Puok, Siem Reap and Roluos rivers some of which are ringed by moats and ramparts. Lovea, for example, has a diameter of 350 m within the moated area and Phum Reul covers 30 ha. It is clear that these sites, which parallel in location, size and shape those from the Mun Valley, fall within the same tradition. This reflects the dry climate and unpredict-able rainfall. Excavations are needed to identify the chronology and cultural relationships between moated sites north and south of the Dang Raek Range.

The Sakon Nakhon Basin

The Sakon Nakhon Basin receives considerably more rain than the Siem Reap Plain and the Mun and Chi valleys, and it lacks broad flood plains. There is a notable rarity of moated sites, although one small example, Non Pa Kluay, was noted during the 1980 site survey centred on Lake Kumphawapi (Higham and Kijngam 1984). This period is best documented at Ban Na Di. The bronze age cemetery there incorporated two late male graves containing iron weapons and ornaments. These saw the end of the cemetery in the areas excavated. There was then a major cultural change, seen in the establishment of a bronze casting facility in layer 5, and a second mortuary phase in layer 4. The former incorporated a series of small clay-lined furnaces, ringed by bronze fragments, broken crucibles and pieces of clay moulds used for casting decorated bracelets and bells by the lost wax procedure. The crucibles, according to Vincent (1988), were made of local clay. They were also, in contrast to the earlier examples, lagged with a thin layer of clay and contained far less bronze scoria than hitherto. Moulds were made of two layers of clay, the inner one of very fine material to take the shape of the bell or bracelet, enclosed in a second layer of much coarser clay. This layer also provided iron slag.

This change in the use of the site was accompanied by a new range of material items. The pottery, for example, now included novel forms, a preference for painted decoration and the inclusion of bleb temper. It results in a distinctive change in fabric which Vincent (1988:184) has described as 'dramatic and comprehensive'. He has also shown that the pottery tradition of Non Chai included identical temper and a similar preference for painted pottery.

Among the associated changes, we also find distinctive clay seals and rollers. Layer five does not include a mortuary component, but several bronze artefacts were found. We have seen that later burials at Ban Prasat and Ban Don Phlong included bronze rings. Similar bronzes appeared at Ba Na Di for the first time during layer 5. Bracelets were also present, but no weapons or tools were encountered. Rings and bracelets dominate the layer 4 assemblage, but there was also a piece of a bowl. Rajpitak and Seeley (1984) have subjected most items to quantitative elemental analyses, and their results were then analysed using multivariate factor analyses. The choice of alloys was much more variable than in earlier bronzes. Lead, in particular, was now favoured. There were also four items with very high admixtures of tin. A ring from layer 5 included 27% tin, a bracelet from layer 4 had 21% and a fragment from layer 4 almost 30% tin. Although Rajpitak and Seeley did not analyse more than a handful of bronze which might have resulted from casting spillage, they suggest that these high tin bronzes were probably imported. All iron artefacts from layers 4 and 5, excluding the burials, take the form of small knives with hooked ends. These have been interpreted as rice-harvesting knives.

Layer 4 includes five infant burials, each contained in a lidded burial jar. They were grouped in one part of the excavated area, and it is hard not to see this distribution as representing an area exclusively for the newborn. This itself is a significant departure from earlier preferences. Burial 4 contained the remains of an infant which died about 8 months after conception. The only associated offering was an iron knife encrusted with rice remains. The infant might have been covered in rice at burial, but only that in contact with the iron has survived. Burial 5 contained a 1–2 year old, associated with three miniature bronze bracelets. The jar for burial 7 contained the remains of a six-month-old fetus, while burial 8 included an infant aged about 7 months, with a tiny bronze bracelet, five blue glass beads and six pieces of corroded iron.

Higham and Kijngam (1984) have suggested that the marked changes in material culture and mortuary behaviour can best be explained as the result of a movement of people who originated in the Chi Valley, with the Non Chai area as the most likely point of departure. The ceramics at Ban Na Di are most closely related to those found in the upper rather than the middle or lower Chi Valley. There are also parallels in the casting technology, the glass beads, familiarity with iron working and the clay cylinders or seals. This, it is stressed, was unlikely to have been a major and pervasive expansion, rather the infiltration of a leader or two and their followers. The possibility is supported by the recognition at Ban Muang Phruk, a settlement 10 km southwest of Ban Na Di, of very similar pottery in the basal level (Wichakana 1984), while Vincent (1988) has identified the bleb tempered pottery at a high proportion of the sites recognised during the 1980 site survey in this region.

There were also major changes at Ban Chiang, 20 km to the northeast. Here, the Late Period burials were also associated with a new pottery style, many vessels being painted in red designs on a buff background. Few burials were encountered during the earlier excavations of 1974–5, but more recent investigations have covered an extensive area, and revealed a series of rows of interments (Fig. 6.23;

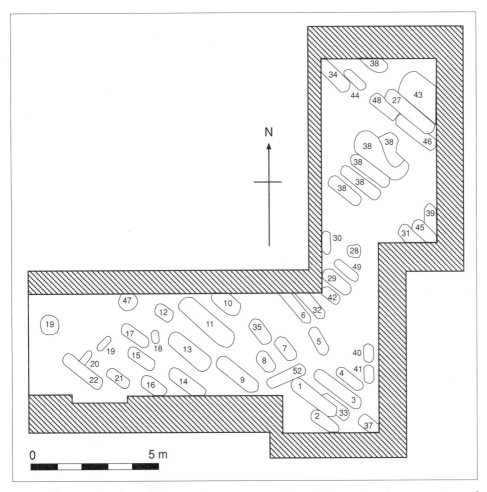

6.23   The plan of the Iron Age cemetery at Ban Chiang, after the excavations of
          Thosarat and Bamrungwongse.
          Permission: Dr Rachanie Thosarat.

Bannanurag and Khemnark 1992). Some were associated with a profusion of the red-on-buff painted pottery vessels, but the mortuary wealth in terms of bronzes pales before that seen on the contemporary Yunnan Plateau sites (Fig. 6.24). What we find is that iron was used for some weapons and implements, and bronzes were converted into ornaments in which the bangles became increasingly ornate in terms of their decoration and embellishments. Vincent (1988) has noted that the presence of hornblende in the clay used to make some of the red-on-buff painted pots recovered from surface surveys in this area rules out local

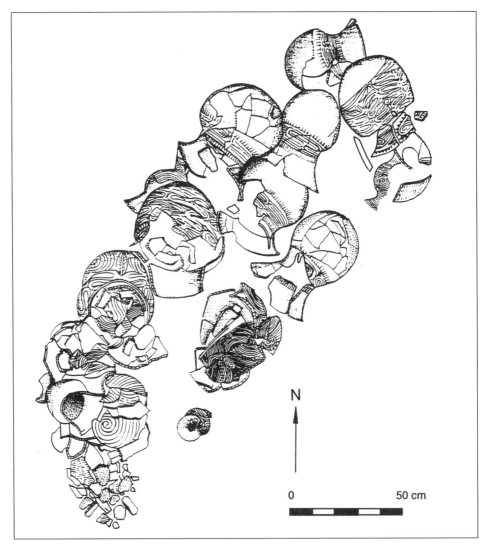

6.24   The plan of an Iron Age burial at Ban Chiang after the excavations of Thosarat and Bamrungwongse.
Permission: Dr Rachanie Thosarat.

manufacture. He has proposed that such ornamented vessels were made in a number of specialist centres and then exchanged. Other parallels with Ban Na Di include the presence of clay rollers or seals, glass beads and high tin bronze jewellery.

Don Klang

We have seen that Non Nok Tha, Non Praw and Non Pa Kluay represent small, bronze age cemeteries located in the western piedmont margins of the Khorat Plateau. Although the Sakon Nakhon Basin during the Iron Age saw a major dislocation in the material culture, the more remote piedmont zone, removed from the major river valleys, appears to have seen less change. This is best illustrated at the site of Don Klang, which is located 10 km west of Non Praw. First examined by Schauffler (1976), the site belongs to the Iron Age. There was much iron slag on the surface, and some of the dead were interred with iron artefacts and glass beads. The six radiocarbon dates he obtained suggest occupation in the last few centuries BC.

Recent excavations in two squares just off the centre of this 2 ha mound, separated by about 30 m, have revealed a further sample of 17 burials (Buranrak 1994b). In one square, the burials were placed with the head to the southeast, and in the other, to the north. The lowest burial included an iron bracelet and the latest, an iron axe. Both were males. It is, however, intriguing that the interment of complete pig or cattle limbs, and the form of the pottery vessels and bronze axes are strikingly similar to those from Non Nok Tha (Fig. 6.25). A bronze axe from burial 3 is paralleled at Middle Period Non Nok Tha, and burial 7 included a group of four socketed bronze axes which also recall those from Non Nok Tha. It is evident that both the metallurgical and ceramic traditions of the local Bonze Age continued unchanged into the period when iron had been established.

The Mekong Valley: bronze technology

The information gained from Phu Lon makes it possible to chart virtually the entire bronze working procedure in the Mekong Valley. The complex includes mine shafts running tens of metres into the host rock and at least three ore-processing areas. Malachite was mined with stone mauls, but there is some evidence for the use of metal mining tools later in the sequence. The area known as the lower flat is covered by at least 50 cm of mining debris interspersed with mauls used to crush and concentrate ore. The pottery flat lies about 50 m to the northeast of the ore body and, according to Pigott (1992), it represents a single stratigraphic unit up to 50 cm thick. A basal date, said to represent the initial use of this area, indicates commencement in the mid second millennium BC, and two further dates show the ores were crushed here in the first millennium BC (1000–420 and 790–275 BC). Finds from Pottery Flat include crucible fragments and two pieces of mould, one of sandstone and the other of clay.

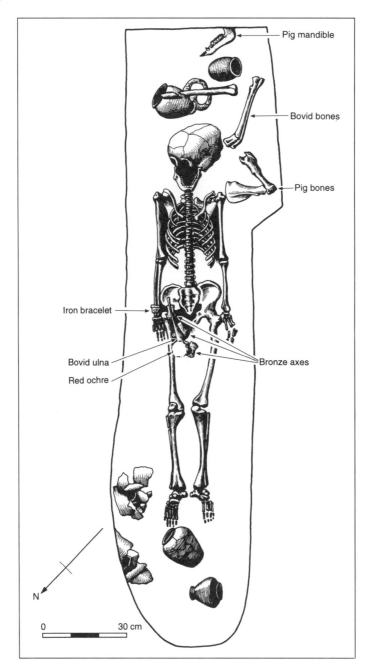

6.25 Burial 7 from Don Klang.

Vernon's analysis of 91 crucible fragments indicates a similar size to the complete specimens from Ban Na Di and Ban Chiang (Fig. 6.26, Vernon 1996, White *et al.* 1991). Most were tempered with rice chaff and retained the remains of slag which incorporated small fragments of copper, tin bronze and tin itself. It would seem that they had been used in melting bronze prior to casting, although the possibility that they were also used for smelting cannot be ruled out. Thirty-one were lagged with a quartz-rich silty layer, to improve the thermal qualities of the crucible and lengthen its life. This feature has also been found at Ban Na Di, but only in crucibles post-dating the first mortuary phase, and probably belonging to the late first millennium BC. This suggested date is matched by a radiocarbon determination at the end of the first millennium BC for the ore source at Bunker Hill, a second ore deposit at Phu Lon.

Local casting of artefacts took place at Phu Lon, but it is likely that ingots were also produced. There are reports that copper and tin ingots have been found by looters at two sites near Ban Chiang. To judge from the widespread recovery of sandstone moulds at sites in the Mekong catchment, ingots and/or bronze artefacts were melted and cast away from the copper mines. Sandstone moulds have been found in excavations at Non Nok Tha, Ban Chiang, Ban Prasat, Non Pa Kluay, Ban Na Di, Samrong Sen, O Pie Can, Hang Gon and Doc Chua. These came

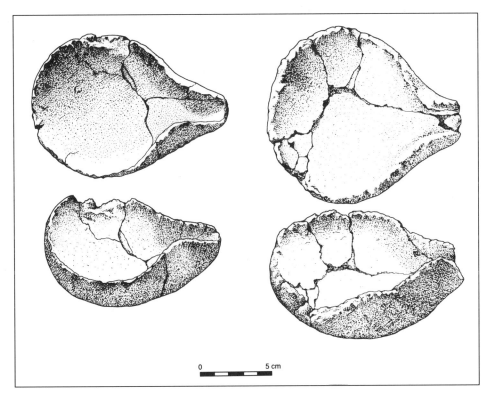

6.26 The crucibles for bronze casting from Ban Na Di.

in matching pairs, or a bivalve configuration and were nearly always made from sandstone. At Doc Chua, we can follow the course of their manufacture from initial rough outs to the preparation of planed surfaces, the mapping of the intended artefact and chiselling and smoothing of the area designated to receive the metal. Not all were successful, some were rejects. A debate has followed the recovery of a lead-tin casting sprue from Iron Age contexts at Ban Na Di. This is the solidified metal left in the adit to the mould. Its recovery poses the possibility that these stone moulds were initially used to receive lead, which melts at a much lower temperature than bronze, the lead product then being invested in clay for a 'lost lead' casting technique. In this procedure, the lead would be melted out and replaced in the clay mould with bronze, for it is probable that clay can withstand the thermal shock better than stone. No fragmentary clay moulds have been recovered in contexts which would support the practice of lost lead casting. By pre-heating a stone mould, successful bronze casting may well have been possible, though experiments to test these alternatives are desirable.

At Ban Na Di and Ban Chiang, clay-lined bronze-casting furnaces have been found, dating probably to the early first millennium BC (Fig 6.27). The former took the form of a shallow bowl-furnace, ringed with bronze detritus and crucible fragments. Stone moulds for casting a socketed axehead and arrowheads have been found. Pilditch (1984) has also examined the bracelets from this site, and has concluded that some, at least, were cast by the lost wax technique. At Ban Na Di, this involved placing wax around a clay core, then investing the wax with a very fine skin of clay to match the surface decoration on the proposed bangle, followed by a thicker layer of chaff-tempered clay. The wax was then melted out and replaced by bronze. No clay moulds have been found in the layers corresponding to the early cemetery phase at Ban Na Di, but many were found in layer 5 above. It is also likely that clay moulds were used by the metal workers who repaired fractured stone bracelets with a wire-like casting through prepared holes.

Rajpitak and Seeley's (1984) analysis of artefacts from bronze age Ban Na Di has shown that the preferred alloy was bronze with tin varying between 2.5 and 13%. One comma-shaped bead was cast from a leaded copper, which makes casting easier. Its presence indicates that the caster had access to relatively pure copper when preparing the alloy. While the bracelets reveal no working or modification after casting, the arrowheads were annealed and cold worked to increase sharpness. Maddin and Weng (1984), in a preliminary consideration of the wire-like casting used to repair the stone bracelets, have noted the use of a ternary tin-copper-arsenic alloy. Although the EDAX technique (energy dispersive X-ray analysis) only provides for general conclusions on the alloy composition, they have suggested preference for this ternary alloy, which would have reduced the melting point. In their analysis of a layer 8 crucible fragment, Maddin and Weng have also concluded that these small vessels were used for melting rather than

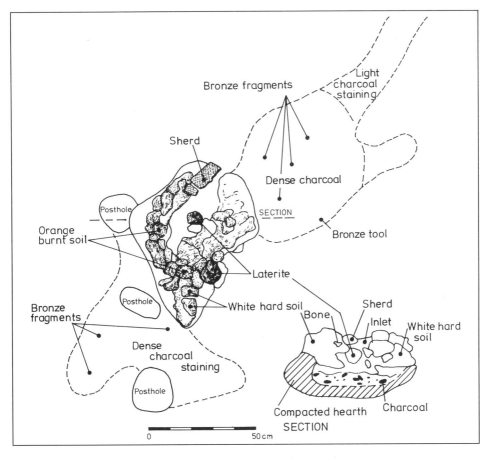

6.27   Plan and section of a bronze-casting furnace from Ban Na Di.

smelting. A small bead of metal found adhering to the interior of the crucible comprised 95.55% copper and 2.94% arsenic, with only trace amounts of tin.

The particular advantage of Ban Na Di is the recovery of the remains of occupation and industrial activity. It is from these that we have recovered pits, hearths and a bronze-casting furnace. There are also many bronze and crucible fragments, 33 of the latter being found across the main excavation square in layer 8. It is also possible to compare bronze artefacts from mortuary and non-funerary contexts. In the former, bracelets and anklets predominate almost to the exclusion of anything else. But in the latter, we find not only bracelets (8) but also arrowheads of three or four types (4), beads (2), fishhooks (2) and an axe, to judge from a stone mould.

The Early Period bronzes from Ban Chiang reveal a number of parallels with those from Ban Na Di. PIXE analysis of the spearhead from burial 76 showed that it was made of 9.17% tin bronze, and that it had been annealed and cold worked after casting as a single unit in a bivalve mould (Stech and Maddin 1988). None of the five items subjected to PIXE elemental analysis from the Early Period showed any deliberate admixture of lead, and arsenic levels were all below 0.1%. Lead was added to five of the ten Middle Period bronzes analysed, in quantities varying between 1.27 and 13%. Tin values were also high, and, as at the phase 1 cemetery at Ban Na Di, there was an appreciation of the value of lead but it was not widely employed. Eight of the objects in question were bracelets or anklets, and none reveals any post-casting modification. Bayard's (1996) summary of the bronze technology at Non Nok Tha indicates that tin and copper were the preferred constituents of the bronzes, but that, towards the end of the Middle Period, lead was also employed. Some of the bracelets were probably cast by the lost wax technique, but bivalve moulds made from local sandstone were used for casting axes.

The Iron Age saw a series of changes in bronze technology. Ornaments remained the most abundant type of bronze. Bracelets became much larger and the enlarged surfaces were used as vehicles for ornament. Finger and toe rings were introduced, cast in multiple open clay moulds. At some sites, clay moulds for the casting of bells and bracelets by the lost wax technique have been recovered. A barbed spearhead has been recovered from Ban Kan Luang, but weapons as a group are rare, a sharp contrast with the developments on the Yunnan Plateau and in Bac Bo. There is also a consistent thread of evidence that the techniques of the bronze workers during this period became more complex. Apart from the sophisticated lost wax castings of figures and jewellery, there are some ornaments which employed the very high tin bronzes which demands considerable expertise. At Ban Na Di, lead was often turned to in alloying, a marked contrast to the earlier bronzes at the site. The form and decoration of the drums from the lower Mun Valley suggests that there was exchange via the Mekong River with Yunnan.

The Mekong Valley: summary and conclusions

There are hopeful signs that the vexed issue of chronology is close to resolution. Few issues in Southeast Asia have generated so much heat and little light as the chronology of bronze at Non Nok Tha and Ban Chiang. This resulted in the advocacy of early dating frameworks from sites where the issue was unclear. When submitted, the sherd samples from Non Nok Tha were described as being securely provenanced, and the results suggest an initial date for bronze casting between 1500 and 1000 BC. After these dates became available, some doubt was cast on the stratigraphical security of the samples. There is one date available which is associated with early copper mining at Phu Lon and more are needed. Most other sites, such as Ban Na Di, Ban Chiang Hian and Non Pa Kluay, while not necessarily dating the earliest bronze horizon known, reveal the establishment of bronze casting by the second half of the second or within the first millennium BC (Fig. 6.28). AMS dating of mortuary ceramics from Ban Chiang, no

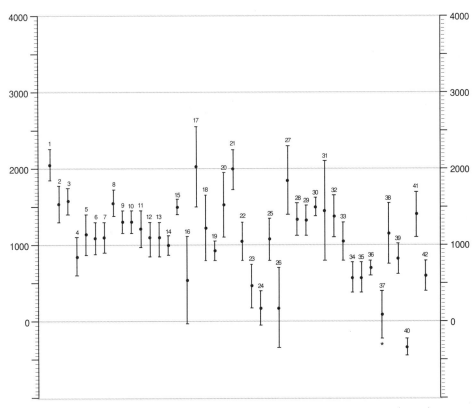

6.28 Radiocarbon dates for the Neolithic and Bronze Age of the Mekong Valley (2 sigma corrected range BC).
1, 2. Non Nok Tha early period (OxA 2383-4). **3–4.** Phu Lon (Beta 17053, 17051). **5–10.** Non Nok Tha early period 3-middle period (OxA 2387-2390, 2392-3). **11–13.** Non Pa Kluay (Beta 2071, 13984, 13981). **14–20.** Ban Chiang (P-2455, 2457, 2398, 2456, 2404, 2668, 2454). **21–26.** Non Nong Chik (R-2931/3, 2809/4, 2931/4, 2809/3, 2809/9, 2931/5). **27–31.** Ban Phak Top (P-2726, 2686, 2446, 2732, 2731). **32–37.** Ban Na Di (NZ-5242, 5241, 5240, 5378, 5473-6). **38–40.** Ban Chiang Hian (NZ-25373, 5547, 5472). **41–42.** Doc Chua (Zk-422, Bln-1973).
* indicates a pooled range for four determinations from the same pit.

less than the excavation and dating of further sites, will contribute to this issue and it remains possible that dates earlier than 1500 BC will be obtained.

At present, the chronological evidence places the initial settlement of the middle and lower Mekong Basin within the same chronological and cultural context as has already been seen in the Late Neolithic of Bac Bo and Lingnan. We do not yet have a good corpus of dates for initial settlement, but it would not be surprising if the earliest contexts belong to the later third millennium. This would place the initial settlement of Ban Chiang and Non Kao Noi in the same period as the Phung Nguyen sites. It is possible that they represent an expansionary phase of agricultural settlement involving permanent settlements, cemeteries in which related people were inhumed and, it is suggested, Austroasiatic languages. The immediate origins, however, are pure speculation.

Despite lingering uncertainty, we are now far better able to discuss the Bronze Age in this area than a decade ago, due to excavations in the copper mines themselves, and the availability of final reports (Higham and Kijngam 1984, Wilen 1988, Monkhonkamnuanket 1992). Copper ore was mined at Phu Lon and locally prepared, smelted and cast. There was intensive activity there during the first millennium BC, which may have been undertaken seasonally. No evidence has been identified for casting ingots, but their presence in the Khao Wong Prachan Valley sites and from looted contexts on the Khorat Plateau, shows that copper and tin were exchanged in this form. Many sites have furnished the remains of moulds, crucibles and at least at Ban Chiang and Ban Na Di, heating furnaces. Bronzes were cast within these settlements into a range of artefacts. Bracelets cast by the lost wax technique from a tin bronze predominated in cemeteries, but bivalve stone moulds were also employed for producing fishhooks, socketed axes, spearheads and arrowheads. These were also made from a tin bronze, and were hardened by annealing and cold working. The properties of lead were appreciated towards the end of this period.

Most of our information derives from cemeteries. These reveal a common pattern of mortuary ritual with local preferences. Bodies were interred supine and in groups which often take the form of rows. Superpositions of graves are not uncommon. Men, women, infants and children were found next to each other. Their grave goods included pottery vessels. Clay anvils are nearly always present in these sites and, while the majority of pots found in graves were probably locally made, some were exchanged, as has been shown for Ban Na Di (Vincent 1988). Where there is a sequence, grave goods tended to become more numerous and diverse with time. The dead were interred wearing jewellery, of which bracelets and shell beads in the form of waistbands and necklaces were most common. Bracelets of exotic marine shell at Ban Na Di make it clear that exchange networks involved coastal communities. Stone bracelets were also obtained from exotic sources. Among bronze offerings, bracelets dominate the sample, but anklets and socketed axes and spearheads were also used and bronze was used to repair fractured stone bracelets. Bronzes were never abundant either within a given grave, or across a cemetery as a whole. There is no evidence at Non Nok Tha for an enclave within the cemetery of particularly wealthy individuals. But at Ban Na Di, one area included most graves with exotic offerings. Where it is possible to estimate site size, they covered a far smaller area than the later moated settlements such as Ban Chiang Hian. It is unlikely that any covered more than 1 to 5 ha.

These small communities, for which there is no evidence for regional centres or ranked hierarchies, chose to live in lowland areas near water sources where flooding would have encouraged the cultivation of rice. Biological remains include rice chaff as a temper in potting clay, rice grains from Ban Na Di, fish bones and shellfish, wild animals and domestic cattle and pig. Where site surveys have been undertaken, it seems that settlements were well spaced, and no evidence has been presented in favour of crowding or population pressure. This might well be due, in part, to the late occupation of these extensive lowlands by communities practising agriculture.

Pervasive cultural changes occurred on the Khorat Plateau between 500 and 1 BC, but the timing and the details are often obscure. Iron was adopted widely. Laterite ore is widespread, and of sufficient quality for local smelting. At some sites which were to reach a considerable size, such as Non Dua and Non Chai, iron was present from the earliest identified contexts. At Ban Prasat, Ban Chiang Hian, Noen U-Loke and Ban Tamyae, iron was introduced later in the sequence. The widespread occurrence of iron slag and the presence of furnaces indicates that smelting of local ores rather than exchange took place. There is an assemblage of iron knives, possibly for rice harvesting, from Ban Na Di, and weapons and tools have been reported from Ban Chiang.

We have no large mortuary samples from this period. Where burials have been recovered, bronze was preferred to iron in providing mortuary offerings, but not to the exclusion of the latter. There is also a consistent body of evidence that salt extraction was intensified during the Iron Age. Three sites examined comprise thick mounds which accumulated over a lengthy period as a result of salt working, and initial activity in each commenced during the period under review. Salt is an essential dietary item and is used to preserve food intended for dry season consumption.

Both settlement and mortuary contexts also indicate new sources of jewellery. Shell and stone bracelets and shell beads gave way to blue and red glass beads, and exotic agate and carnelian ornaments have been found with some regularity.

These changes took place in much larger settlements. Non Chai is critical in this respect, because it was only occupied during this period. There is no firm archaeological evidence for moat and defence construction, but most workers, on the basis of the cultural sequence within the perimeter, agree that at least the earlier moats date from the later first millennium BC. The social milieu associated with these settlements cannot be defined until we have information on the internal organisation and chronology. Domestic architecture might have involved large residences. Much of the interior could have been unoccupied. The cemeteries might include enclaves containing the graves of an elite. The moats could belong to the later first millennium AD, but the interiors of some sites saw iron smelting and the use of cemeteries during late first millennium BC. It is not unreasonable, therefore, to assume that moats and defences belong to this same period. A consideration of the possible social organisation in question could then be approached through the location of the sites, their size, likely population, and the agricultural potential of the immediately surrounding terrain.

We will begin with the Middle Chi survey, because it has been one of the two areas where these variables have been considered in some detail (Chantaratiyakarn

1984). The survey was designed to locate the pattern of prehistoric sites relative to the large moated settlement of Ban Chiang Hian. It was found that small settlements were located along the margin of the Chi flood plain, and on the fringes of elevated middle terraces which gave access to low terrace land suited, at least today, for rice cultivation. We cannot be sure how many were occupied contemporaneously with Ban Chiang Hian, which covers a far bigger area than the second largest settlement. On the basis of modern population densities, Chantaratiyakarn has suggested that Ban Chiang Hian could have had a population in the region of 2000 people. The other prehistoric sites range in size from 0.7 to 5.4 with an average of 2.3 ha. Her estimated population for these varies from 35 to 270 people.

Average daily rice consumption in Thailand is 0.49 kg. Rice is the staple, being consumed as part of three meals a day. During prehistory, with a much more varied habitat, a lower figure is likely. But we will follow Chantaratiyakarn's figures and their implications. Under plough cultivation and a broadcasting regime, the average rice yield per hectare is 1338 kg, although there is considerable variation (Hanks 1972). These figures suggest that the smallest settlement in the Chi survey area would have needed to produce 6370 kg of rice per year, which could be obtained from 8 cultivated hectares. The largest village would have needed 62 ha. The sites are located near streams. A belt 200 m deep running along 1.5–2 km of stream margin would have produced enough rice to cover the estimated requirements of the average community. In the case of Ban Chiang Hian, the figures rise sharply to 355,000 kg of rice from 449 ha. This would have involved a belt 400 m deep running along the edge of the Chi floodplain for 11 km. The aerial photograph shows three canals issuing onto the floodplain from the moats (Parry 1992:9). They cross an area of 400 ha, and they penetrate at least 1.7 km beyond the site.

The figures employed are the most general of estimates, but they suggest that the population estimated for Ban Chiang Hian could have been sustained from the area served by canals. This does not imply that rice relied upon the delivery of stored water, for the monsoon usually brings sufficient rainfall. But if there was a brief dry period within the rainy season, then moat water could have been a supplement.

Chantaratiyakarn (1984) has also reviewed the energy which would have been involved in the excavation of the moats at Ban Chiang Hian. She adopted a conservative estimate of an average depth of only one metre, and suggested that one man could move 2 m^3 of fill a day, with two others being required to move it to the edge. Under these circumstances, excavation would have required 400,000 man hours. The moats were probably much deeper but, again, excavation is needed to verify this. Even using the minimum estimate of depth, a hundred men would have worked for over 4.5 years. This does not include any effort needed to construct the dams, reservoirs, canals, or the walls. Moreover, it is hard to imagine moat digging even being possible during the rainy season. Sites such as Ban Chiang Hian stand out not only for their size, but also the energy expended in the provision of water control and, probably, defensive structures.

Welch (1985) has undertaken a similar analysis of the pattern of settlement in the Phimai area of the upper Mun Valley. His basic data match those for the Middle Chi Valley closely. He used an identical figure, 50 people per hectare, and an average daily consumption of 550 g against the 490 g used by Chantaratiyakarn. There is one major site, Phimai, with an estimated area of 40 ha. Other sites range in size from 2 to 31 ha. He then calculated the amount of rice which could be grown within a radius of 2 km of the site under three different methods: transplanting, broadcasting and non-intensive flood farming. Naturally, the smaller the site the easier it was to supply the necessary amount of rice. Only with non-intensive farming in the radius of the two largest sites was there a deficiency. Welch has suggested that this could have been alleviated by importing rice from other communities, intensifying production through transplanting, or extending the 2 km radius to cultivate more land. If the latter were followed, then each community would have been self-sufficient in terms of rice, even when they reached a population measured in thousands.

This finding, it is stressed, applies to the most arid part of the lowlands of Southeast Asia. Moore (1988) has particularly emphasised the importance of the moats as instruments of water control needed where the dry season was so intense. She has referred to the sites as centres of water harvesting. It is not as if all moated sites are large and apparently dominant. Ban Takhong only covers 6.4 ha and Ban Mai Si Llan, only 5 ha within the moats. The middle Chi survey area has the one centrally placed, moated site, but there are several, of varying sizes, in the Phimai survey area. It may well be that we are dealing with several variables. Some of the larger sites might have been regional centres in a settlement hierarchy with at least two tiers. But this did not exclude the adding of moats to smaller sites in their orbit.

Moore has also suggested that this technique for water control encouraged settlement in the low and middle terraces where lack of extensive rice land was compensated for by the presence of salt, iron ore and timber.

When reviewing this pattern of settlement, and the associated evidence for technological change and new items of exchange, possible explanations will be considered and the situation compared to developments in other regions.

Note 1: chronology

The confusion over dating bronze age contexts at Non Nok Tha and Ban Chiang has spawned an extensive literature (White 1982, 1986, Bayard and Charoenwongsa 1983, Higham 1983, 1996, Loofs-Wissowa 1983, Solheim 1983, Bayard 1996). The problem stems from the relationship between the charcoal which has been dated and the context within the site. In my view, the dating of charcoal found in the grave fill does not necessarily relate to the interment, because charcoal can be lifted and redeposited during the digging of the grave. It is, therefore, to be expected that determinations from such sources are contradictory.

The recent development of AMS dating of very small organic samples has made it possible to avoid this dilemma by analysing rice chaff found as a ceramic temper in provenanced mortuary pots. In the case of Non Nok Tha, however, most samples submitted did not come from such vessels, but from sherds found in the general cultural layers. This has provided further grounds for confusion. While I accept Solheim's statement that the samples were from secure provenances, Bayard (pers. comm.) expresses reservation on account of, in his view, the insecurity of their origins in the site.

The present redating of the Ban Chiang by using this new technique will, it is hoped, resolve the problem there. A word of caution, however, must be made: as Bellwood *et al.* (1992) have noted, this method might have its own inbuilt problems of which we remain unaware, for some of his results were rather earlier than anticipated. The same situation obtains at Pengtoushan, where the AMS dates are highly variable, and at Nong Nor, where two of the five determinations are rather earlier than the other three, and the one securely provenanced conventional date.

The corpus of AMS dates from Non Nok Tha conforms well with the dates for a virtually identical bronze industry stretching from Central Thailand to coastal Lingnan. These fall within the period 1500–1000 BC. It will be surprising if the same range is not ultimately established for this same bronze tradition at Ban Chiang Hian. The implication of this, and the alternative possibility that bronze at Ban Chiang Hian is significantly earlier, are considered further in chapter 9.

CHAPTER 7

CENTRAL THAILAND

Central Thailand is dominated by the broad flood plain of the Chao Phraya River (Fig. 7.1), but also includes the drainage systems of the Bang Pakong to the east and the Mae Klong to the west. During much of the period under review, the sea level was significantly higher than at present, and the Gulf of Siam considerably larger. Many sites now far from the coast would have been much closer, and others would have been located on the shore (Fig. 7.1). It is possible to subdivide Central Thailand into subregions on the basis of landforms and climate. While the whole area has a tropical monsoon climate, the western margins are relatively dry, due to the rain shadow effect of the Tenasserim Range. Drought is also a regular phenomenon, particularly during the critical first few months of the monsoon (April–June). The upper plain is crossed by the main channel of the Chao Phraya and several tributaries. The pervious soils do not encourage rice cultivation. Nor is rice extensively grown in the foothills which flank the eastern and western edges of the plain, although the importance of tributary streams and their flooded margins should not be underestimated in attracting early settlement by rice farmers. The upper and lower deltas are prone to severe flooding and only recent drainage canals and dam construction have opened them to agriculture.

To the east of the lower delta, one encounters the valley of the Bang Pakong River, which has been the subject of an intensive research programme designed to illuminate the pattern of coastal settlement in prehistory (Higham and Thosarat 1994). This area, in microcosm, illustrates the sharp contrast between occupation of the flat alluvial plains, with their potential for rice cultivation and exploitation of marine resources, and the surrounding uplands. In the former, many raw materials were lacking, especially stone. In the latter, there was little scope for agriculture but an abundance and wide variety of stone.

Copper ore is found in the Bang Pakong Valley and at various locations around the Central Plain, but the best known and most significant source is found just north of Lopburi on the eastern edge of the upper delta region. There are two granite provinces in Central Thailand which incorporate tin ore (Coote 1990). The Western Province covers Burma and the Tenasserim Range, and the Main Range Province is located in the middle and lower Chao Phraya catchment. Both yield cassiterite and wolframite.

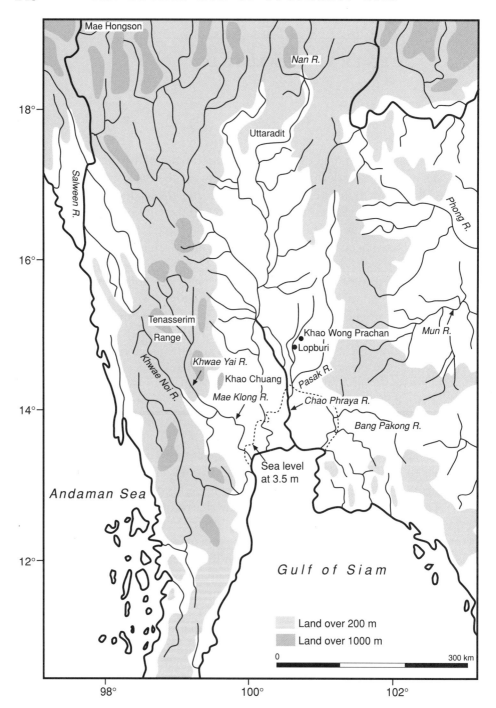

7.1a   Central Thailand, showing geographic locations of places mentioned in the text.

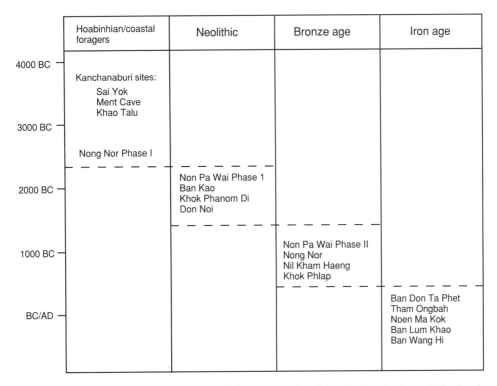

	Hoabinhian/coastal foragers	Neolithic	Bronze age	Iron age

7.1b The cultural sequence and the principal prehistoric sites in Central Thailand.

The Neolithic settlement

Although archaeological research in this area is a recent development, it is one of the most important in any consideration of early metal working, not only because of the abundance of ores and the evidence for their exploitation, but also due to the intimate knowledge we have of Neolithic societies within which metallurgy was adopted (Fig. 7.1a).

There are several upland sites which evidence broad-scale foraging during the Holocene. These rock shelters have provided material culture and radiocarbon determinations which place them alongside the groups described in Lingnan and Bac Bo as Hoabinhian (Pookajorn 1984, Shoocondej 1994). Recent research on a former raised coastline has also revealed a number of shell midden sites of which Nong Nor has been excavated and dated to about 2450 BC (Fig. 7.2; Higham *et al.* 1994). This does not mean that there was no earlier lowland settlement. Kealhofer (1992) has reported rice phytoliths in cores from the Lopburi area as early as 4000 BC and Maloney (1991) has published a series of sediment cores from the vicinity of Khok Phanom Di which were taken to illuminate the Holocene environment prior to the occupation of that site, and assess the human impact following its establishment. Two episodes saw a rise in grass pollen,

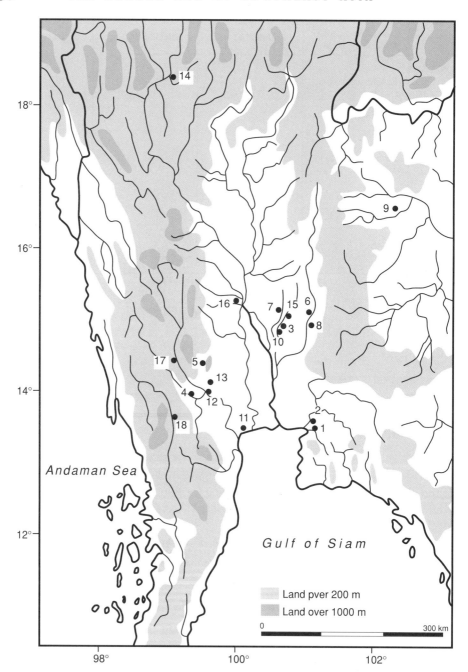

7.2   The location of the prehistoric sites mentioned in the text.
1. Nong Nor. **2.** Khok Phanom Di. **3.** Non Pa Wai, Nil Kham Haeng, Non
Mak Klua. **4.** Ban Kao. **5.** Don Noi. **6.** Khok Charoen. **7.** Phu Noi. **8.** Sab
Champa. **9.** Non Nok Tha. **10.** Ban Tha Kae. **11.** Khok Phlap. **12.**
Kanchanaburi. **13.** Ban Don Ta Phet. **14.** Ban Wang Hi. **15.** Noen Ma Kok.
16. Ban Lum Khao. **17.** Ongbah. **18.** Khao Jamook.

accompanied by increased charcoal and pollen from plants which today grow as rice field weeds. These have been dated to 4400 and 3560 BC. They may result from clearance to create favourable conditions for rice cultivation. On the other hand, they might reflect natural conflagrations, or the burning of vegetation to attract game animals by hunter-gatherers. It is not possible to be sure, but current research on the rice phytoliths in these and other cores taken from the Central Plain may well inform us on whether rice cultivation significantly antedates the earliest known archaeological context, which is at present about 2000 BC at Khok Phanom Di, and perhaps a few centuries earlier at Non Pa Wai.

Early coastal settlement

In Lingnan and Bac Bo, we encountered much evidence for affluent foragers who took advantage of the richly supportive coastal environment. The slower pace of research in coastal Thailand has deferred the recognition of equivalent sites, and only in the last three years has this void been partially filled by the excavation of Nong Nor. Although the material is still under analysis, it is possible to present some conclusions. It was a small settlement comprising shell middens interspersed with ash lenses, hearths and lenses of soil reddened through burning. It was located on low-lying terrain overlooking an extensive marine embayment (Boyd 1994). The species of shellfish collected indicate proximity to mangroves and an open, sandy shore, and the remains of fish and marine mammals evidence coastal subsistence. There were discrete activity areas, indicated by concentrations of different artefacts: in some areas, the clay anvils and burnishing stones used in forming and decorating pots. In others, bone was worked into awls, fishhooks and, possibly, weaving shuttles. Polished stone adzes were found, and the sandstone abraders on which they were honed. Yet, despite the wealth of biological remains, and the abundance of pottery, no evidence has been found for the presence of rice either surviving in the midden itself or as a ceramic temper. Nor is there any evidence for the domestic dog. In effect, Nong Nor may be cited as further evidence for the presence of at least semi-sedentary coastal groups during the third millennium BC which correspond to those so thickly distributed on the raised shorelines of Lingnan and Bac Bo. Even the single burial which might belong to this phase of settlement was found, as at the Bac Bo sites, interred in a seated, flexed posture.

Khok Phanom Di

This is a far larger site than Nong Nor, and is located 14 km to the north. It was located on an estuary which represents a rather later shoreline, confirmed by the radiocarbon dates which place settlement between 2000–1500 BC. There have been three major excavations, the last in 1984–5, when an area of 100 m² was exposed to a depth of nearly 7 m. Excavations uncovered a neolithic cemetery in conjunction with many artifacts and much biological material (Higham and Bannanurag 1990, 1991, Higham and Thosarat 1993, 1994). It provides an opportunity to examine the social, economic and technological characteristics of a community which just precedes the earliest settlements which evidence copper smelting. As has been shown by O'Reilly (1994), there are many parallels between the material culture of this site and Nong Nor. This includes pottery forms and decorative techniques, adze types and the bone industry.

When first settled, Khok Phanom Di was located on or near a major river estuary. This is evident from an examination of the natural deposit on which the lowest cultural remains accumulated (Aitken 1993), and the biological remains found in these deep layers. Mason's (1994) analysis of the shellfish reveals a predominance of species from a muddy estuarine habitat, although species also adapted to the sea front mangrove forest were also abundant. The initial settlers left caches of stone adzeheads, clay anvils and pebbles used to burnish pottery. They were skilled in pottery making and the marine clays in the vicinity of their settlement provided the necessary raw material. But stone resources were at a premium. Neither the shore, nor the thick mantle of clay deposited while the sea covered this flat terrain, provided stone, and stone artefacts are often exotic. The many ash spreads and postholes, some with wood surviving in them, show that woodworking for houses, and doubtless boats, was undertaken. The ash spreads probably accumulated as a result of firing pottery vessels.

The lowest 60 cm of cultural remains at Khok Phanom Di were probably deposited rapidly, even over a decade or two, because shell middens and ash spreads take little time to accumulate. Six burials, ascribed to the first of seven mortuary phases (MP), might well represent early, if not the earliest, settlers. They exhibit burial practices which were to develop over about twenty generations. The fact that burials were clustered into groups on a chequerboard pattern which retained their spatial identity over four or five centuries makes possible the examination of issues rarely documented by prehistoric data (Fig. 7.3). Tayles (1992), for example, has considered individual health, age at death, fecundity, stature and diet and physical condition. Choosiri (1992) has identified genetically determined skeletal conditions which suggest that some of those interred in close proximity were probably related by blood. Individuals were usually buried with grave goods, which allows insight into the material culture of the group, the presence of exotic goods obtained through exchange, personal status exhibited by the wealth of mortuary offerings, and how all these variables changed with time. Since these took place within the context of a developing environment, it has been possible to consider the two in conjunction (Higham *et al.* 1992).

We find that there were seven distinct mortuary phases, incorporating several clusters of burials. These were probably interred within wooden structures and as time proceeded, so the dead were interred over their ancestors. The mortuary ritual included the placement of grave goods with the dead: pottery vessels, shell and stone jewellery, anvils and burnishing stones used in pottery manufacture, and large, shaped turtle carapaces. Since these varied in numbers and form through time in their association with men, women, children and infants, we can

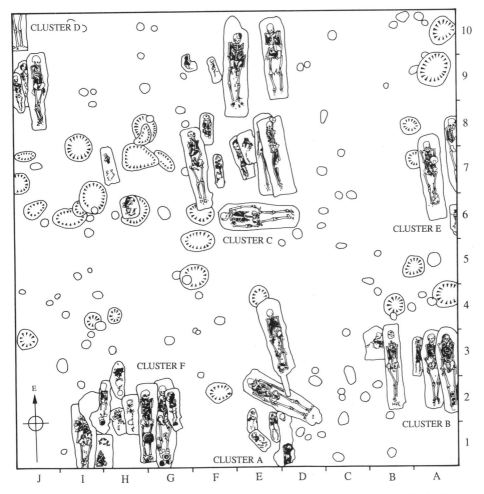

7.3 The distribution of graves belonging to mortuary phase 2 at Khok Phanom Di. Scale in metres.

trace changes in behaviour which reflect social as well as technological and environmental variables.

The continuity in the basic ritual within clusters and regular associations between adults, infants and children pose the possibility that they represent social groups. There are numerous cemeteries in China, many of which have been more extensively excavated than Khok Phanom Di, in which family, lineage or clan divisions have been reconstructed (GPM 1978a, Zhang Zhong-Pei 1985). In some cases, clustering is clear, but in none are burials superimposed during such a long sequence. The lowest grave at Khok Phanom Di is about five metres below the uppermost. This situation is the result of the rapid accumulation of shell middens and ash lenses; it seems as if the pace with which the mound formed matched that with which successive generations lived and died.

This situation encouraged the excavators to examine the minutiae of the burial sequences in each cluster and reconstruct family trees (Fig. 7.4). Some bones are currently under analysis to try and extract mitochondrial DNA. If successful, it will permit the relationships between individuals and clusters at the site to be more closely defined. Clusters C and F were durable, with approximately sixteen 'generations' in each. Others were less successful. They might be represented outside the excavated area, or some families, given the poor health of the community, might have failed to produce the next generation. Again, one or more families could have split away and moved elsewhere. Whatever the case, we will now consider the burial record with particular reference to the two clusters which lasted throughout the sequence. This involves acceptance that the treatment of a person in death is, at least in part, a statement concerning that person's status, activities, special skills or achievement when living. Infant burial might reflect the parents' perception of themselves. In a situation as at Khok Phanom Di, where there was a considerable variation in the grave goods with different people, consideration of such offerings in relation to a person's age, sex or group affiliation is a way of isolating social issues.

The results of the statistical analyses have been reported elsewhere (Higham and Thosarat 1994). It has been found that there was an early peak in wealth in mortuary phase (MP) 2, a decline in MP 3–4, then a sharp spurt in MP 5 followed by another trough. During MP 1–3, there was no perceptible difference in the treatment of men and women. During MP 4, however, they were distinguished on the basis of the turtle carapace ornaments, restricted to the former, and clay anvils which were exclusive to female burials. There was then a sharp rise in wealth, and continued restriction of anvils to women and some children. We also find that infants who survived for more than a few months were accorded similar treatment to adults, being interred with a range of grave goods. Richer adults were usually associated with richer infants. At no stage was age identified as a factor in determining mortuary wealth, nor was a given cluster consistently richer than any other. Despite some elements of continuity, however, there was a sharp disloc-ation with MP 5, for the few graves were outstandingly rich. Increased elaboration in mortuary ritual continued into MP 6, when a raised structure covered three wealthy graves, and a wooden building to its west contained individuals who were poorer, at least in terms of grave goods. It is also noted for cluster C that the last seven generations are represented only by women and the young.

The environment changed between MP 3 and 4. A loop of the river may have been severed from the main stream, or the river channel might have moved to the west, while a prograding shore and sedimentation would have distanced the site from the estuary and the open sea. Before these changes, the men were robust, with strong upper body development, and there were no obvious differences between the treatment of men and women in the cemetery. During MP 2, the men and women had different tooth pathology, due to a different diet. There was also a change in overall dental wear and health. Before the change in environment,

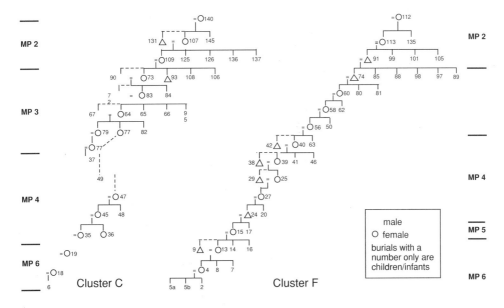

7.4 The sequence of clustered burials at Khok Phanom Di has made it possible to reconstruct possible family trees through seventeen 'generations'.

teeth were subjected to an abrasive diet and caries were prevalent. After it, the diet was less abrasive, but caries persisted. Tayles (1992) has suggested that this is compatible with a diet of rice and shellfish in the early phase, with less emphasis on shellfish later. There was very high mortality among infants before the change, in contrast to a low figure afterwards which was associated with more child deaths.

Again, Tayles (1992) has identified a possible environmental factor, for changes in the water regime in the vicinity of the site could have modified the number or even the species of mosquitoes, thus reducing exposure to malaria. The reduction in the stature, longevity and the declining upper body strength of men from MP 4 could also have an environmental link. If the site was no longer on the river, the sea was further away and the habitat for the shellfish best suited to shell jewellery reduced, then the men would not have been accustomed to habitual canoeing. Such an activity matches well the muscle development of men up to MP 3, also phases in which shell jewellery was abundant.

After the environment changed, there was an increasing distinction between the sexes in terms of burial goods, a new range of shell artefacts fashioned from exotic species, particularly the tridacna, and the development of much larger, intricately-decorated pottery vessels. The new forms of shell jewellery included large discs and bracelets (Fig. 7.5). It suggested that all these separate changes are compatible with a society going through a rapid adjustment in its exchange organisation (Higham *et al.* 1992). Until and including MP 3, men obtained shell

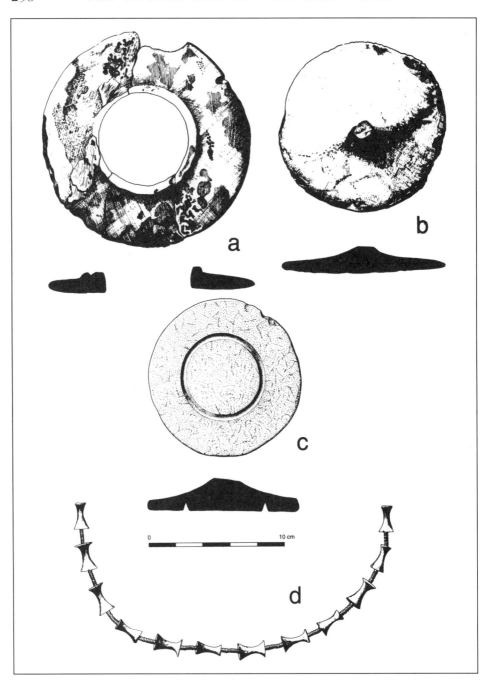

7.5   Novel grave goods of exotic shell found in later contexts at Khok Phanom Di.
a. Bangle from burial 43. **b.** Horned disc from burial 43. **c.** Partially completed bangle from burial 43. **d.** Necklace from burial 33.

locally from clean sandy and offshore coralline habitats. This involved much vigorous canoeing. It is necessary to appreciate the importance, in recent Melanesian contexts, of the capacity to control sources of shell, its distribution and ownership (Battaglia 1983, Lepowsky 1983). Cowrie, tridacna, trochus and conus shells require clear water. A coastal community with such advantageous access would be able to manufacture and inject shell ornaments into a network of exchange involving prestige valuables and necessary items such as, in the case of Khok Phanom Di, stone tools. The end of the availability would seriously impair participation. That shell jewellery ceased to be so readily available during MP 4 is evident in the mortuary record.

Thereafter, however, clay anvils were found in graves, and some individuals interred with them were buried with much finery, including novel, heavy shell items made from tridacna shell. There is no evidence that the preferred habitat for this species, clean coral reefs, existed near Khok Phanom Di. It is, therefore, suggested that women, who made pottery vessels described by Vincent (1987) as masterpieces, were now responsible for the principal objects which were exchanged from Khok Phanom Di: high quality pottery vessels. This was a route to status, indicated by the ownership of the new range of shell ornaments obtained in return for their pots. Men would have lost social prominence, they certainly became smaller and physically weaker, and took to wearing ornate turtle carapace ornaments. Yet a rich male in MP 5 should not be forgotten: at least one man was interred with considerable finery (Pilditch 1993). If this proposed new social role of women is correct, then it would help us understand the wealth and nature of some of the later infant burials. This turns on the assumption that young girls represented the future of the group within its exchange network, and their loss was a grievous blow to their family. In one case, such an infant was buried with a miniature anvil under a pile of clay cylinders. It would also suggest that women were too valuable to lose to the community through marriage. Stressing the matri-pole, the females in the group, is perhaps seen in the long sequence of female graves in later generations of cluster C. Did these women have no brothers? Did some men die on long-distance trading missions to be buried elsewhere? Prehistory provides many cases where answers are not forthcoming, but the data from Khok Phanom Di, a society living just prior to our first evidence for copper smelting, still provides us with much valuable information.

During the centuries leading up to the earliest copper smelting, Khok Phanom Di was, it is suggested, occupied by a community which recognised no hereditary rank, but within which individuals could gain status through their ability and ambition. While successful people endowed their offspring with fine grave goods, the next generation had to begin from scratch. One route to such status appears to have been pottery making. The achievements of individual potters at the site were considerable, some of their products being of the highest quality. The manufacture of pottery in this part of the world is a dry season activity, for the wet season militates against drying and firing, and the calls of rice agriculture are also high. The pottery industry does not suggest mass production, rather the work of individuals, probably working singly or in small family groups.

They also worked within the framework of a wide-ranging exchange network. The stone adzeheads, sandstone abraders, leucogranite for hoes, shale for bracelets and quartzite for burnishing stones came from a wide arc around the site (Pisnupong 1993), while H-shaped beads have been found in graves in the Khao Wong Prachan Valley. The importance attached to marine shell is seen by its presence in many inland sites. Such exchange routes carry not only goods, but ideas. The initial use of copper belongs in the context of communities keenly interested in exotic artefacts, and who traded them within networks in which river-ine and coastal transport were particularly effective. Before turning to the early sites which have yielded copper, however we will examine other communities in Central Thailand which were broadly contemporary with Khok Phanom Di.

The Bang site, Ban Kao

This was the first prehistoric cemetery in Thailand examined scientifically (Sørensen and Hatting 1967). It covers only 0.8 ha, and is located on an inland river terrace in the valley of the Kwae Noi River, Kanchanaburi Province (Fig. 7.2). The excavated area, 400 m^2, was four times that of Khok Phanom Di, but it was also a much shallower site, with only 90 cm lying between the uppermost and the lowest grave (Fig. 7.6). They were found in a cultural deposit containing a rich sample of cultural and biological remains. Iron, glass and bronze artefacts were restricted to the upper part of the site (Sørensen 1973). Forty-four graves have been excavated, two of which contained iron artefacts, and are intrusive within a cemetery which, to judge from the radiocarbon dates (Fig. 7.7), was active within the span of Khok Phanom Di.

Ban Kao lacked clear stratigraphy, making it difficult to seriate the graves. This is exacerbated by the lack of superpositions. Sørensen set the graves out in order of depth below datum, on the assumption that earlier graves were the lower. He then divided the pottery vessels, which are very variable, into different forms and sought a correspondence between the forms, form groups, and the depth of the graves. He concluded that the graves belong either to the Early or Late Neolithic. There are, however, graves which are intermediate, indicating that the two groups were not separated by a long time interval.

The early availability of Sørensen's report has attracted several attempts to re-work his data and modify his conclusions. Parker (1968), for example, has paid particular attention to burial 12, one of the two graves with an iron artefact. This grave included three pottery vessels which are distinct from those ascribed by Sørensen to the Neolithic phases. Several other vessels were found beyond the feet of burial 12, which may well have belonged to burial 3, which is Neolithic. Parker seems to have misunderstood this qualification, for he regards them as part of the grave furniture for burial 12 itself. Having noted parallel forms in the neolithic graves for these vessels, Parker suggested that the entire cemetery

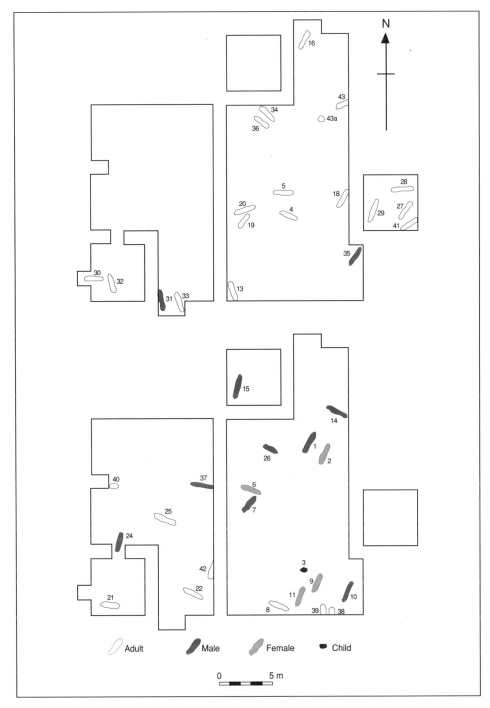

7.6 The distribution of graves from early (upper plan) and late phases at Ban Kao.

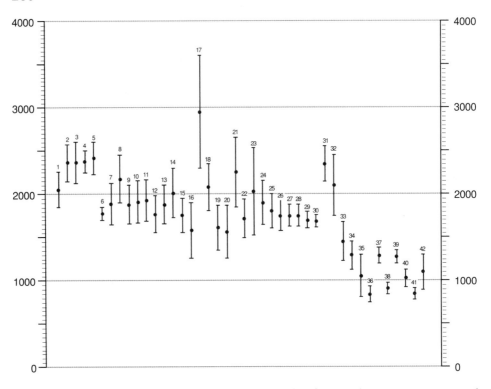

7.7 The principal radiocarbon dates available from prehistoric sites in Central Thailand (2 sigma corrected range BC).
1–6. Nong Nor phase 1 (Wk-2025-9, 2847). **7–22.** Khok Phanom Di (ANU-5493, 5490, 5492, 5491, 5488-9, 5487, 5486, 5485, 5484, NZ-7063, 7070, 7033, 6973, 7021, ANU-5483). **23–30.** Ban Kao (K-838, 1088-9, 842, 1090, 1087, 1091-2). **31–2.** Non Pa Wai phase 1 (Beta-24455, 27367). **33–5.** Non Pa Wai phase 2 (Beta-27364, 24453, 27365). **36–41.** Nong Nor phase 2 (Wk-2461, OxA-3846-50). **42.** Nil Kham Haeng phase 1 (Beta-24459).

belongs to the Iron Age, and that graves were cut into a Neolithic settlement. Subsequent research on sites which are similar to Ban Kao, and a greater understanding of the nature of Iron Age pottery in this area, rule out Parker's reinterpretation.

Solheim (1969), on the basis of the chronological changes in the orientation of graves at Non Nok Tha, then considered this variable as a key to understanding the sequence. His results bore little relationship to changes in pottery forms and MacDonald (1978) has rejected them during a statistical analysis of the distribution and contents of the graves. MacDonald then applied statistical tests to the contents, distribution, orientation and wealth of the graves. He set aside Sørensen's use of the depth of the human remains as an index of relative chronology because he claimed that the depth of a grave could indicate energy expenditure rather than the part of a sequence during which it was cut. He then applied the value known as Robinson's index of agreement to the pottery forms in each grave, on the assumption that changes in pottery related to the passage of time. Having placed the graves in a sequence on this basis, he noted that a majority of supposed late graves are located in the eastern part of the excavated area, on an east-west orientation. He then subdivided the burials into eastern and western groups, but his dividing line follows a curious course with no obvious rationale other than to sustain the integrity of his eastern group.

The basic problem with MacDonald's interpretation is his assumption that two graves with different sets of pots are distinct chronologically. At Khok Phanom Di, where relative chronology is intimately known, there are contemporary burials with different assemblages of vessels. Some pots might be locally made, others obtained by exchange and used as symbols of status. A pot might also have been provided as part of the mortuary offerings by a person related to the deceased, but from another settlement. While pottery preferences change with time, this is not sufficient in itself to permit the seriation of a group of graves. It has also led, in this case, to a sequence in which graves in close proximity and on the same orientation are set apart from each other on the chronological list. MacDonald also suggested that the east-west alignment of most members of his eastern group is explained if two social groups within the community had their own burial area. This is an interesting possibility, but relies on a decidedly strange dividing line between them.

We will now look at the Ban Kao sample in the light of the evidence from Khok Phanom Di that the location of burials might reveal social information. During the early phase, the dead were placed on their back, and there was no preference for an easterly orientation. Only one infant was reported. Perhaps they were interred separately, since it is hard to envisage a community with such low infant mortality, particularly given the skeletal evidence for the condition of thalassaemia. The graves were not clustered in the manner of Khok Phanom Di, but there was an orderly pattern. Burials 34 and 36 lie alongside each other on the same orientation. The former is an adult, buried with one pot, the latter is a ten-year-old child with two pots. Burials 31 and 33 are also found adjacent and on the same orientation. One was probably a male aged about 30 at death. He was accompanied by a pot. The other was a 35-year-old adult with two pottery vessels. At the eastern edge of the excavated area, there are five early phase burials. The three intact graves are orientated in a southwesterly direction. From west to east, burial 18 was an adult, lying on the broken remains of three pottery vessels with the sherds from a further five being found over the lower limbs. Burial 29, which lay alongside, was also an adult. A stone adzehead was found under the skull, and six broken pots were present in the region of the head and shoulders and below the knees. Burial 28 was associated with at least three pots, while with burial 27, we have another adult on a southwesterly orientation with an adze under the skull. Twelve deliberately broken pots were associated with the human remains, three over the chest, the balance over the lower limbs. The last of the five comprises a row of eight pots in a straight configuration, but with no human remains.

The wealth of these graves, in terms of pottery vessels, contrasts with that for two other early graves found alongside each other with the heads orientated to the southeast. Burial 34 involved an adult, buried with a single broken pot in the ankle area. Burial 36 was a ten-year-old, found lying on a sherd sheet representing two broken vessels. Graves for burials 19 and 20 also lie alongside each other. The former, which contained the remains of a person who died when about seventeen years old, included three complete pots, one beside the face and two beyond the feet. The latter involved an adult, interred with four complete pots and a stone adzehead under the skull. The graves are orientated in opposite directions, one to the northeast, the other to the southwest. The last pair of early graves, burials 4 and 5, contain a woman aged about 35 years and an eighteen-year-old. They were both interred with the head to the northwest. Six pots and two stone adzeheads were placed beside the woman's head and beyond the feet. The same disposition of five pots was found with the other burial, and a stone adzehead was present under the skull.

The early phase at the Ban Kao cemetery will now be considered to see if the location might be patterned. There are five pairs in which the individuals were buried in close proximity. Most of the remainder are located towards the edge of the excavated area, and could, therefore, have been paired. Although there is no regular orientation, the paired burials lie parallel with each other. In four cases, the head was pointing in the same direction but burials 19 and 20 are found in opposite directions. Unfortunately, the preservation of the bone has ruled out sexing more than a handful of the skeletons, so the possibility that the pairs were male and female cannot be determined. When the paired burials are examined more closely, it is found that they also lie at virtually the same depth below datum. In the case of burials 31 and 33, both were relatively poor: one had two pots, the other one. The same situation obtains for burials 34 and 36. Burials 19 and 20 contained three pots, and four pots and an adze. Burials 4 and 5 were much richer, the former having six pots and two adzes, and the latter five pots and one adze. The pots were also placed in the same locations relative to the body. Again, the pair interred in graves 18 and 29 were accompanied by many pots: eight in one case, six, together with an adze, in the other.

Ban Kao: the late phase

The grouping of graves noted above continued into the late phase. Burials 9–11 lie parallel with each other on a northeast-southwest orientation, the two females have the head to the southwest, the male in the opposite direction. In each case, grave goods were markedly richer and more varied than hitherto. Burial 9, a 35-year-old woman, was accompanied by eleven pottery vessels, eight of which were disposed in a line beyond the feet, such that the grave would have been at least 5 m long. One further vessel was found between the knees, and two beyond the head. Burial 10 lay almost 2 m to the east. The male was over fifty years at death, and his grave goods included four pottery vessels beyond the head. In this same area, there was also a large stone ring with a hole in the centre, traces of polishing hinting that it is unfinished. There were also two stone adzes between the ankles, and a remarkable deer antler, the tines of which were cut at right angles to the shaft and shaped into tubular ends. The remains of two young pigs were also found beyond the head. Burial 11, a woman who died when about thirty years old, was particularly rich. There were nine complete pottery vessels, six beyond the feet, two at the left knee and one by the right shin. Six adzes were distributed around the body, which to judge from the location of a pig's foot bones, had been partially covered by a pigskin shroud. There was also a necklace made up of two strands of 642 shell disc beads and two tubular stone beads.

The next group also includes three burials. Burial 6 is a female aged about 45 years at death, interred in a grave orientated with the head to the northwest. Ten pots were associated, two beyond the head and eight beyond the feet. There were also six stone adzes, pig's bones disposed round the body as if there had been a pigskin shroud, and four pebbles. Two were placed beside the left ankle and two in the vicinity of the abdomen. Though not described as such in the text, it is possible that these were burnishing stones. Three modified shells from a freshwater bivalve were also present. Burial 7 was poorer. The male, interred with the head pointing east, was found with two crushed pots in the ankle area. He was about 30 at death. Burial 37 was another male, found with the head orientated in the opposite direction to burial 6. He, too, had been buried with a freshwater bivalve under the head. Three pots covered his lower body, and a cut bone and carved stone in the form of a phallus were also found.

Burials 1 and 2 lie parallel. The former, a male, was laid out with the head to the northeast, the latter, a female, in the opposite direction. The man, who died when about forty years old, was interred with seven pots, two adzes, two barbed bone harpoons and two small shell disc beads. The woman was five to ten years older, and was accompanied by five pots located beside the head and beyond the feet, and four stone adzes. Burials 38 and 39 were also found in close proximity to each other, but only just impinged into the excavated area.

There is much evidence in favour of continuity between early and late phases. When superimposed, burials from the latter do not disturb the former. Presumably the location of graves was known. The mortuary ritual, despite some modifications, remained similar. Graves in close proximity were found on a similar orientation, with males and females being placed in opposite directions. People were still interred with pottery vessels and stone adzeheads, although offerings were more varied and abundant. New items include shell disc and stone beads, worked shell, bone harpoons, a carved sandstone phallus, a modified antler and pig's foot bones. A heavy, perforated stone disc was found in the same grave as the worked antler.

There are also intriguing similarities and differences between the mortuary ritual at Ban Kao and Khok Phanom Di. The former is a much smaller sample, but it is argued that grave layout was structured: orientation may not have been so regular, but people were still interred in clustered groups, and there was a regular contrast between the orientation of males and females. Pottery forms display changing preferences within the same ceramic tradition which, to judge from the number of burnishing stones recovered, involved local industry. Finds from non-burial contexts also show that Ban Kao was a base for the manufacture of stone bracelets. Grave goods also became richer with time, and there is some evidence to suggest that burials clustered together had similar wealth. Pottery and stone adzeheads predominated, while shell jewellery was extremely rare. This contrasts with Khok Phanom Di, where adzeheads were hardly ever encountered, but shell ornaments abounded. Ban Kao was also a much smaller site, covering only 16% of the area of Khok Phanom Di. The pottery forms in each site differ, those from Ban Kao having their parallels in peninsular Thailand and Malaysia. It documents a small inland settlement, located on a river flood plain where aquatic resources, and presumably marshland suited to rice cultivation, were available. Its inhabitants never displayed the same high level of wealth in mortuary ritual which characterised MP 5 and 6 at Khok Phanom Di, yet they participated in an exchange network, and some individuals, particularly in the later phase, were interred with an impressive collection of grave goods. Graves were few and far between. In the richest part of the site of equivalent area to Khok Phanom Di, there were 15 graves, one-tenth of the number from Khok Phanom Di. If this is representative, it is unlikely that Ban Kao was occupied for long.

Recent research in peninsular Thailand and Malaysia has led to the recognition of many sites with a pottery tradition which involved cord-marked vessels raised on tripods. Leong (1990, 1991) has discussed their distribution and chronology and proposed that they represent related communities which introduced agriculture to the coastal plains of the peninsula. The most significant site, Jenderam Hilir in Selangor, was located near the confluence of two streams. It is now 43 km from the coast, but during its occupation, it would have been considerably closer. The material there has been redeposited by river action, which has ruled out the assessment of *in situ* cultural contexts, but the pottery, heavy stone adzes, grinding stones and bark beaters reflect a sedentary community. The location near the best available agricultural soil also suggests that rice cultivation was undertaken. Leong has discussed four radiocarbon dates from this site, one derived from a sample of charcoal and the other three from organic material associated with pottery. The former (2147–1876 BC) is very similar to one of the Oxford AMS dates (2207–1866 BC). Two other AMS dates suggest a second phase or a long single occupation (1456–1191 and 1406–1031 BC). These dates are encouragingly close to those from Ban Kao, and confirm that a group of Neolithic settlements was established towards the end of the third millennium BC from west central Thailand down to the equator. The other peninsula sites are confined to burials in caves, which are commonly stratified over the preceding Hoabinhian occupation.

At Gua Cha, extended inhumation burials were associated with marble and nephrite bracelets which recall those found in Central Thailand (Sieveking 1954).

The pattern of settlement in the Ban Kao area is not straightforward, and much research is necessary before a fuller picture is available. This is well illustrated by the site of Don Noi, which lies 65 km north of Ban Kao, and comprises a 5 ha area covered with pottery and flaked stones (Bronson and Natapintu 1988). Described by them as 'maybe the largest and most nucleated Southeast Asian settlement thus far discovered anywhere in Southeast Asia beyond Northern Vietnam and Southern China' *(ibid.*:95), the stone industry differs from that of the Hoabinhian and the local neolithic. There are no ground stone implements, most of the artefacts being utilised flakes, flaked adzes and utilised cores. Many have a glossy sheen on the working surfaces thought to result from use in cutting silica-rich grasses, including bamboo. The pottery is largely cord marked or red slipped and burnished, and no parallels with the ceramics from Ban Kao are evident. The status of this site has recently been clarified by excavation (FAD 1991). It was evidently a stone workshop for the production of polished bracelets. The actual quarries and associated working areas have been identified in the foothills of the Khao Chuang Insi nearby, jasper and white chert being the source material (Shoocondej 1991). It is now necessary to trace the products of this workshop to other neolithic and doubtless later sites, for the upper layers also yield iron slag. Nor is Don Noi alone; other similar sites are known in the neighbourhood which also took advantage of the locally available chalcedony, chert and jasper, and Prishanchit (1988) has identified related quarry sites, but with few if any pottery remains, in Mae Hongson, Nan and Uttaradit provinces to the north.

Khok Charoen

Khok Charoen was extensively excavated between 1966–70 (Watson 1979, Ho 1984). It is located in the Pasak Valley, which lies to the east of the Central Plain. None of the 44 burials from the first two seasons has been sexed or aged, and virtually nothing is known of the last two seasons pending the availability of a final report. The chronology has not been established, there being two thermoluminescence dates: 1480–800 BC for burial 1, and 1380–780 BC for burial 10. These dates, if an accurate indication of the date of the cemetery, would place it well within the period when copper ores were being smelted at Non Pa Wai, 60 km to the southwest. On the other hand, no metal has been found with any of the graves, despite the considerable area uncovered (500 m^2 in 1967 alone). It may be that the dates are inaccurate, and the burials at Khok Charoen belong to the first half of the second millennium BC. This receives a measure of support from the way some of the burial vessels were ornamented. About one in ten were decorated with incised bands infilled with impressions, a style characteristic of early Non Pa Wai and the assemblage from Khok Phanom Di. Burnishing was also applied to the surface of some vessels. The inhabitants of Khok Charoen made some of their own pots, tempering the clay with crushed sherds or rice chaff.

The mortuary goods recall those found at Khok Phanom Di. There are limestone, marble, ivory and marine shell bracelets, shell disc beads, stone adzes and pottery vessels. Some graves stand out for the wealth of the grave goods, the richest (burial 24), being associated with 19 pots, 10 shell and 9 stone bracelets on one arm, 843 shell disc beads and some beads of stone. Either Khok Charoen represents a pre-metal cemetery which confirms the widespread nature of exchange during that period, or it was a site which, due perhaps to its peripheral position relative to the Central Plain, did not receive any copper-based items even after they were in circulation.

Phu Noi

Phu Noi is a site of considerable importance, located 40 km north of Lopburi (Fig. 7.2). Natapintu (1992) has excavated a square measuring 3 × 5 m there, and despite the small area, encountered 26 burials which he has subdivided into three mortuary phases. Their density matches that found for some of the Khok Phanom Di clusters, and they surely represent a social unit of some sort. The earliest three ascribed to mortuary phase (MP) 1 contained adults with a much wider range of grave goods than was found at Ban Kao. Burial 26, for example, included six pottery vessels, a polished stone adze, stone bead, a bone fishhook, bracelets of shell, turtle carapace and ivory, and a string of shell beads. Ten pottery vessels accompanied burial 25, and there were also shell disc beads around the waist and a stone bracelet which had been broken in antiquity. At some other sites in Thailand, such breakages were repaired by boring holes on either side and linking the pieces with a cast bronze 'wire' (Maddin and Weng 1984). In this case, the holes contained the remains of a fibrous substance.

Ten burials belong to MP 2. The distinctive pottery vessels include bowls on very high pedestals and tubular beakers, the manufacture of which required high expertise. Further examples of stone and shell bracelets were found, as well as beads of marine shell and turtle carapace ornaments with a central perforation in the form of a star. Pig's limb bones were also included as grave goods. The MP 3 burials were on the same northeasterly orientation and directly over earlier graves. Between two and ten pots were found in each grave, and Natapintu has divided them into twelve general forms. These include pots in the form of a pig or a cow, with a small bowl over the back (Charoenwongsa 1987). Similar vessels have been found at Non Nok Tha in Northeast Thailand.

No radiocarbon dates have been obtained for this site, nor has any metal been recovered during excavations. However, Natapintu has reported that villagers found a mould for casting a socketed axe and a copper-based bracelet on the surface. Further excavations are planned and metal artefacts might be found when a larger area is opened. At present, Natapintu's suggestion that the site dates to the mid second millennium BC is probably correct. It would thus just antedate the earliest evidence for copper smelting in the area.

Non Pa Wai

This site has received intensive study from the Thailand Archaeometallurgical Project, under the direction of V. Pigott and S. Natapintu. It covers about 5 ha, and was the location for intensive copper smelting and casting. Recent reports, however, have also described an early phase cemetery both under and beside the mound, dated by two radiocarbon determinations (2565–2146 and 2456–1750 BC; Natapintu 1991). The latter area yielded 25 interments during excavations in 1992 (Pigott 1994). None contained any copper-based artefacts. Grave goods include stone adzes, anvils for shaping pottery vessels, a limestone disc with a central projection recalling the examples in shell from Khok Phanom Di, and H-shaped shell beads again showing resemblances to those from Khok Phanom Di mortuary phases 6–7. Early indications also reveal that the terrain included both forest and swamps, and though not yet clear, it is anticipated that rice was cultivated during this initial occupation phase.

The Bronze Age

Now that we have a clearer idea of the sequence of pottery styles in Central Thailand, it is possible to undertake site surveys with the objective of identifying changing patterns of settlement and demography, on the premise that the area of a site has a relationship with its population. Mudar (1993) has recently undertaken a series of such surveys in the Lam Maleng Valley, an area which incorporates a series of distinct environments (Fig. 7.8). The Yang Tong stream, a tributary of the Maleng, runs through an area of porous soils unsuited today for rice cultivation. The Khao Chak Chan ridge is also poor in rice soils but features a series of springs. The Chon Khut stream includes some land near springs where rice is grown today, while the Lam Maleng Valley proper includes much low-lying land where bunded rice fields today provide one crop of rice a year. The last area, known as the Huai Pong stream, begins with the Khao Wong Prachan Valley with its abundant stone and copper resources and includes access to both river transport and rice land.

Mudar has divided the prehistoric sequence in this area into three phases. The early phase from 2500–1500 BC is essentially the Neolithic. The Middle Phase (1500–1000 BC) saw the development of copper smelting. The late prehistoric (from 1000 BC) covers the period when iron was worked, and it would seem more logical to choose 500 BC as the dividing line between the middle and late phases. On the basis of the dentate stamped pottery which is such a diagnostic feature of the ceramics from Non Pa Wai and Khok Phanom Di, Mudar has assigned twenty sites to the early period. They concentrate in the Yang Tong stream valley, the Khao Chak Chan ridge and in the vicinity of the Chon Khut stream. Only three sites were located in the better agricultural land of the Lam Maleng Valley. Sites range in size from 0.33 to 6.3 ha, and Mudar has suggested, on the basis of the site distribution and size, that they represent autonomous village communities which occupied their settlements for some long time on the basis of agriculture.

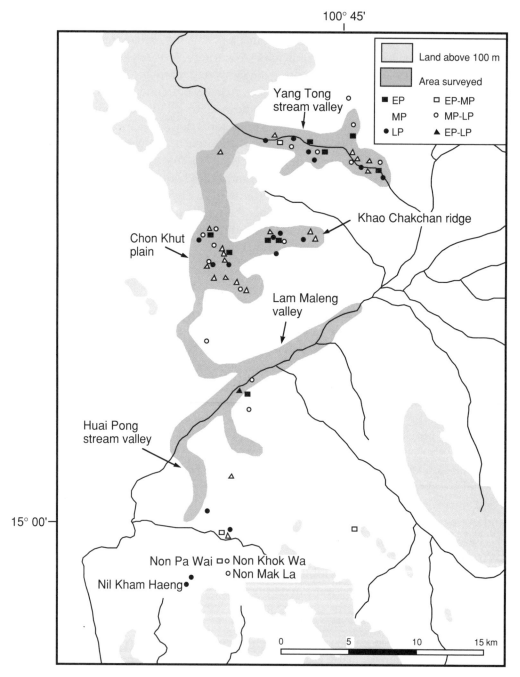

7.8   The distribution of sites identified by Mudar in her surveys north of the Khao Wong Prachan Valley.

The middle period, defined on the basis of pottery from Phu Noi and Non Pa Wai phase 2, saw continuity in the area settled and the probable subsistence base. Five sites were rather larger, four with areas of between 10 and 18.2 ha, and one, Non Mak La, covering 20 ha. Mudar has suggested that these larger sites indicate an increase in socio-political complexity. She proceeds to speculate that the difference in the site sizes – the area of the largest exceeds that of the early period by a factor of three – might be due to the development of a tributary economy. If this were to be demonstrated through excavation, it would be a finding of first class importance, because it would provide some evidence for political central-isation during the Bronze Age. But a word of caution is necessary. The largest middle period site, Non Mak La, was occupied during the Iron Age: excavations uncovered much copper and iron slag (Natapintu 1988a). Its extent during the middle period or Bronze Age is not known.

Ho (1992) has undertaken a series of site surveys in Central Thailand and its eastern margins. Her first area, the Khao Heng Talat complex, lies to the east of the Khao Wong Prachan copper mines. This is a particularly dry area with few river bottomlands suited to rice cultivation, yet it contains good sources of stone for adze making. Khao Mogurt also has deposits of carnelian and agate. Khok Charoen is located in this region. The Khao Samphot complex included a number of sites ascribed to the Bronze Age, and one source of copper. At Ban Sab Champa, large numbers of cores and other waste material from the manufacture of marble bracelets have been noted (Ho 1984). In contrast, the Khao Phu Ka complex is low-lying, well watered and includes a number of copper ore sources in the Khao Wong Prachan Valley, which runs through a series of hills thrusting up from the alluvial soils.

Khao Wong Prachan Valley

Copper mineralisation here has occurred at the junction between the tertiary rocks and limestone and several sources of copper ore have been identified, including Khao Phra Bat Noi, Khao Phu Kha, Khao Tap Khwai and Khao Sai On (Fig. 7.9, Bennett 1989, Ciarla 1992, Cremaschi *et al.* 1992). Ores include malachite, azurite and chrysocolla with up to 10% copper. These hills are flanked by prehistoric sites which evidence, in one form or another, the exploitation of copper. One of these, the Lopburi Artillery site, has been well known for 25 years as a rich later prehistoric cemetery in which about fifty burials have been recovered, associated with bronze and iron artefacts (You-di 1976). According to the excavator, some individuals even had a bronze ring in place on each toe. Two TL dates suggest occupation from the second well into the first millennium BC. In 1984, Natapintu (1988a) collected fragments of copper ore and smelting slag there, indicating that it was also a processing site.

Huai Yai is a particularly interesting site, because it has furnished burials associated with discs of marine shell and H-shaped beads which are paralleled at Khok Phanom Di. These beads at Khok Phanom Di come late in the sequence,

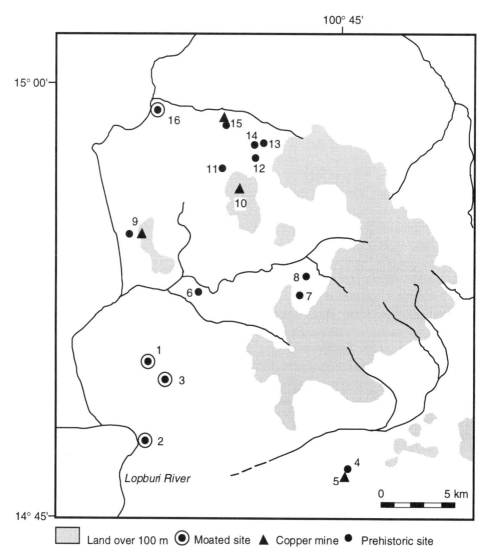

7.9   The location of sites and ore sources in the Khao Wong Prachan Valley.
1. Ban Tha Kae. **2.** Lopburi. **3.** Thanon Yai. **4, 5.** Khao Sai On. **6.** Lopburi
Artillery Camp. **7.** Sung Nam. **8.** Huai Yai. **9.** Wat Tung Singto. **10.** Khao Phu
Kha. **11.** Nil Kham Haeng. **12.** Non Mak La. **13.** Non Pa Wai. **14.** Non Khok
Wa. **15.** Khao Tap Khwai. **16.** Phrom Thin Tae

and are dated there to about 1500 BC. Huai Yai has also provided evidence for the
manufacture of polished stone adzeheads, shell and stone bracelets. It was also
a copper working site, for excavations have produced crucible fragments and
casting slag, but the relationship between the H-section beads and the copper slag
is not known with precision. Non Mak La was excavated by Natapintu in 1985, and
copper and iron working had been undertaken there, again during the first

millennium BC. Non Khok Wa, the object of limited excavations, is another ore-crushing site, while at Nil Kham Haeng, the remains of crushed ore and slag fragments have accumulated to a depth of five or six metres. The successive layers are very clear, and have also yielded ceramic moulds, including some for the casting of circular ingots, and a burial interred with a bracelet which combines bronze and iron segments. Of all these sites, however, Non Pa Wai stands out as being the largest and most significant.

Non Pa Wai

The remains of copper smelting and casting at Non Pa Wai cover about 5 ha (Pigott 1992, 1995). The early occupation layer and cemetery was followed by a period of abandonment which probably lasted for about five centuries. When the site was reoccupied, graves were cut into it. One contained the remains of a 25-year-old man with two halves of a clay mould for casting a socketed copper axe. A second grave contained such an axe. The layer from which the grave was cut included copper slag and crucible fragments, heralding a phase of copper processing which was to last for eight centuries and accumulate to a depth of 2–3 m. There are three radiocarbon dates from the lower part of this phase, which come from, in effect, the earliest context we have for copper smelting in Central Thailand. They are 1690–1225, 1450–1136 and 1270–800 BC. A fourth date from later in the sequence is 834–530 BC (Natapintu 1991). It would seem that copper smelting began at this site within the period 1500–1000 BC.

This dense concentration of metal-working debris, taken in conjunction with the other sites which cluster around the copper deposit, is one of the largest prehistoric extracting complexes in Asia. Ore was smelted in crucibles set in the ground, linked with chimney furnaces. The procedure, as described by Pigott and Natapintu, involved

deep, large-volume vessels (crucibles) which are thick-walled and tempered with chaff. We believe that they served as reaction vessels for the smelting process. There are strong indications that the crucibles were used in conjunction with portable ceramic furnace chimneys ... These cylindrical chimneys, *c.* 20 cm in diameter and 15 cm tall, apparently were placed atop the crucibles to contain the charge and to promote updraught of hot smelting gases. This whole smelting apparatus may have been placed in a shallow pit dug into the site's surface. The chimneys have holes in their walls, presumably to admit the bellows' blast, though strong prevailing winds sweep the Khao Wong Prachan Valley during the dry season and may have been sufficient to drive the smelting operation. (Pigott and Natapintu 1996)

Perhaps the most important aspect of this material is the quantity of clay moulds shaped to produce circular metal ingots. Few artefacts were encountered, but these included barbed points and socketed axes. The moulds were made from clay, and bear incised markings which might well indicate ownership. No alloying with tin took place.

In a series of experiments, successful smelting following the techniques documented at Non Pa Pai has been achieved (Rostoker and Dvorak 1989). It took ninety minutes to reach smelting temperature in bowl furnaces set in the ground. The problem faced by the discharge of poisonous arsenic vapour was obviated by sealing the crucible with clay, a technique which might have been used in prehistory.

Nil Kham Haeng

Nil Kham Haeng is a second copper-working site. It has been damaged, but still covers 3 ha, and has a cultural stratigraphy at least 6 m deep. There are two principal phases. The earliest already contains evidence for copper production and pottery similar to that for period 2 at Non Pa Wai. It has been dated by a single radiocarbon determination to 1301–900 BC. The cultural stratigraphy for the second phase comprises many thin horizontal lenses which Weiss (1992) has interpreted as the remains of dry season metal working redeposited by intense rainstorms. The deposits included crushed slag, while there were also many ash lenses rich in charcoal. Enough material has survived *in situ,* however, to reveal the presence of activity areas which involved ore preparation, smelting and casting. There was, it seems, no permanent work force repeatedly using fixed copper working facilities. Rather, metal working continued as a small-scale, probably seasonal, occupation in which the principal activities began with mining, then ore preparation and sorting, smelting and casting. The physical remains comprise mauls, clay-lined bowl furnaces or smelting crucibles, clay furnace chimneys for concentrating heat, crucibles and ceramic moulds (Fig. 7.10). Weiss has suggested that the workers at Nil Kham Haeng used lower grade ores than at Non Pa Wai, perhaps due to the early exhaustion of the highest quality sources, and therefore had to break them down more finely to concentrate the copper-rich material. The radiocarbon dates from this phase are 900–400 and 800–380 BC.

From about 700 BC, there are signs of change at Nil Kham Haeng. Fourteen inhumation burials have been excavated, the north-south orientation being preferred. The head of burial 1 in operation 1 lay on a cache of copper ore, and there were three pots beyond the head. A series of bracelets were present, made from copper and iron. The first use of iron was for decorative purposes. Burial 5 in the same area included a sea turtle over the head, a copper bracelet, copper ring, three pots beyond the head and a mass of copper ore. The presence of copper ore recalls the placement of clay cylinders, the raw material for pottery working, in graves at Khok Phanom Di. Burial 1 in operation 4 contained five pots, iron bracelets and a complete furnace chimney. There were also five carnelian beads.

At this same juncture, during the period from 700–300 BC, there appears to have been a surge in production at Nil Kham Haeng, with particular emphasis on casting small socketed implements which Weiss has described as projectile points. They continued to be made from the high arsenic copper, but one or two

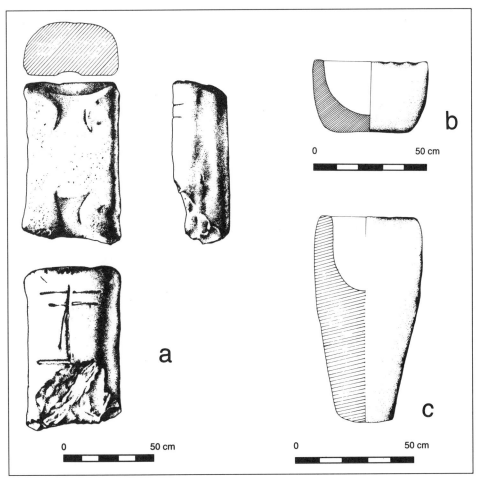

7.10   Non Pa Wai clay moulds.
   a. For casting small socketed implements. **b, c.** For casting ingots. Compare
   the form of the artefact cast in **a** with the copper-based socketed implements
   found at Nong Nor (Fig. 7.12).
   Permission: Dr. V. Pigott.

items, in particular a socketed spear, comprised of 10% tin. These are alien to the
local metal tradition, and are best interpreted as imports.

   The site of Wat Tung Singto has not been excavated, but surface finds include
ingots, ingot moulds, stone crushers, traces of copper ore and crushed slag.
Natapintu (1988a) has suggested that the material belongs to the first millennium
BC. Two mounds at Huai Yai have also revealed much relevant material. The site
known as Huai Yai has furnished burials with a series of shell ornaments,
including marine shell discs and H-shaped beads. There is also evidence for the
local production of stone adzes and bracelets, shell bracelets and casting copper-
based artefacts. A later phase at the site has also produced slag from iron working.

The latter context probably equates with occupation at Huai Yai Reservoir site, where iron, bronze, carnelian and agate items have been recovered (Natapintu 1988a).

Copper technology in Central Thailand

Much light has been thrown on the techniques of these prehistoric metal workers by Bennett's analysis of the slags (Bennett 1989). She has described at Khao Phu Kha, one of what may have been many mines, the ore being malachite and chrysocolla with up to 10% copper. Non Pa Wai, Non Mak La and Nil Kham Haeng are located nearby. She has suggested that most ore crushing and sorting occurred near the mines, where some final processing took place at the slag sites, for large ore-dressing stones have been found. Slag accumulated in the archaeological build-up, but also adhered to the walls of what Bennett has termed clay reaction vessels. There are numerous fragments of these and possible reconstructions reveal a vessel about 12 cm in height and up to 20 cm in external diameter. The organic temper would have increased resistance to thermal shock. Analysis of the associated slag shows that smelting was facilitated by employing a haematite flux. Little metal remains in the slags, which shows that smelting successfully liquified most of the copper, at temperatures of between 1150–1250°C. The recovery of complete, circular cakes of slag suggests that the contents of the crucible were poured onto the ground, leaving at the base a pool of copper. This was then poured into ingot moulds, some of which had a long base, which may have facilitated securing them before the pouring procedure. Nil Kham Haeng has also produced a copper axehead and ingots. This industry is most significant, because it provides the evidence for copper working without alloying, a procedure often cited as a necessary condition for the presence of an independent centre of metallurgy.

One of the most important aspects of the research undertaken in the Khao Wong Prachan Valley is the fact that there are so many sites which vary in their size, chronology and contents. It is, therefore, possible to evaluate social organisation in communities which combined rice cultivation with copper production and exchange. Ban Tha Kae was a large mound located about 15 km south of the copper source. Most has been removed by contractors to be used as land fill, but a small remaining area has been examined by archaeologists. The lowest of three cultural contexts there has furnished a number of burials, grave goods including shell disc beads and bracelets of stone, shell and bronze. Rispoli's (1990) analysis of the pottery from the earliest cultural horizon stressed the occurrence of the technique of applying a thick polished red slip to the rim. There are also pots with curvilinear incised lines infilled with impressed decoration on vessels with black, burnished surfaces. The former are paralleled in the early cemetery at Non Pa Wai, while the latter is widespread during the second millennium BC, at Khok Charoen, Khok Phanom Di, Non Nok Tha, Samrong Sen

Nong Nor
Central Thailand
1991-3 excavation.
Cemetery plan

Male

Female

Infant

Child

Adult

E

0   5 m

7.11   The distribution of graves in the cemetery of Nong Nor.

and Ban Chiang. Even further afield, it was used at Phung Nguyen in the Red River Valley. The radiocarbon dates from Ban Tha Kae indicate that this phase predates 1500 BC, and probably began in the vicinity of 2300 BC.

The second cultural phase at Ban Tha Kae has revealed much evidence for the local manufacture of marine shell and limestone bracelets, and is equivalent to Non Pa Wai phase 2. The radiocarbon dates lie between 1500–1000 BC. There followed a period of abandonment before reoccupation towards the end of the first millennium BC saw the excavation of moats round the settlement (Ciarla 1992, Cremaschi *et al.* 1992, Rispoli 1992).

Nong Nor

Nong Nor is one of the few sites in Central Thailand which belong to the period just before the major changes which involved the adoption of iron working from about 500 BC and exposure to Indian mercantile expansion a century or two later. Excavations have revealed 170 burials cut into or overlying the earlier occupation deposits (Fig. 7.11). As is often the case with cemeteries, very little securely provenanced charcoal has been found. Indeed, the only available sample comprises charcoal found within a lidded burial jar, and it has been dated to 940–760 BC. The excavators, therefore turned to the AMS technique, whereby minute samples of organic matter can be radiocarbon dated. Five dates have been obtained on the basis of rice chaff temper in burials pots. These confirm use of the site as a cemetery between 1200–800 BC. This chronological context provides the opportunity to contrast mortuary behaviour not only with the earlier remains from Khok Phanom Di, but also to assess the use to which copper-based artefacts were put at a time just before the major burst in smelting activity at Nil Kham Haeng, 150 km to the northwest.

Some characteristics of the Khok Phanom Di mortuary ritual recur. The orientation was usually in an easterly direction. Most individuals were interred supine, and with a range of grave goods. Yet there were also some differences. Infants, for example, were found only in lidded jars, often at the feet or the shoulder of an adult female. A woman was found in a prone position. There was also considerable variation in the orientation of the graves, even in the same part of the cemetery.

The layout of the graves reveals some intriguing patterns. In the western half of the site, there appear to be three rows, with a marked preference for an easterly orientation of the head. The northwestern part of the excavated area has no interments, which may well indicate the edge of the cemetery. To the east, there is a concentration of graves, many of which have intercut or overlie earlier burials. The orientation is variable, with several people being found interred on a north-south axis. We do not yet know whether this contrast is a result of chronological change, or the presence of two groups perhaps differing on the basis of social affiliation. There is no stratigraphic evidence to distinguish between the two, but there are hints in the material culture that the eastern group of graves is slightly the later.

For the moment, the burials comprising the westerly rows and those in the eastern concentration will be treated as two groups. Tayles (1994) has ascribed tentative ages and sexes to the sample as a whole, and it is apparent that each group contains the remains of males, females, infants and children. The western (Group A) has approximately sixty graves, but only five infant jar burials. Group B to the east has a much higher proportion of infants.

There is a wide range of grave goods. Some are found often, some rarely, while others are unique within the site. The first group comprises pottery vessels, bracelets made of stone, shell and bronze, dogs' skulls placed beyond the human head and shell disc beads. Less common are sandstone abraders, bracelets and earrings of tin, long shell pendants bored longitudinally, serpentine ear ornaments, the remains of pig, cattle and deer, fish bone and small, socketed

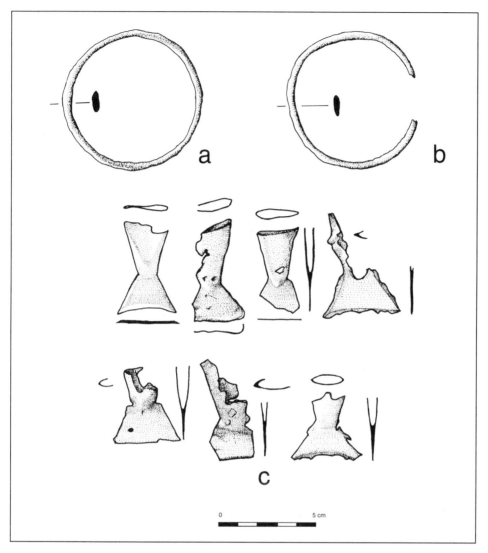

7.12 Bronzes from Nong Nor.
a, b. Bangles. **c.** Socketed implements.

implements cast from copper or bronze (Fig. 7.12). Some objects were specific to a single burial. One man had a large pair of cattle horns placed around his skull. Another was interred with four carnelian beads. There was a single jade ear ornament, a set of bone points, a boar's tusk, a group of conus shells, a bronze pendant and a particularly large bronze bracelet. The stone bracelets and ear ornaments include exotic items. Apart from the jade, there is talc, marble, carnelian and serpentine.

The row of graves forming the western edge of the cemetery comprises nine females, six males, three children and thirteen disturbed graves for which it is not possible to determine the sex. From north to south, we begin with burial 132, an adult female found with a single pot. Burial 36, an old adult male, was found with eight pottery vessels, which were located beyond the head, by the shoulders, beside the waist, and by the ankles. Shell disc beads in the pelvic area may represent a belt of some sort, or an embroidered garment. Stone, shell and bronze bracelets were worn. Burial 39 lay alongside, but its grave had cut through a previous one, and the human remains from this, burial 67, were probably those stacked neatly east of the new grave and at the level of the grave cut. This young adult male had been interred with eleven pottery vessels which had been positioned round the body. Two stone bracelets were present on the left wrist, and another on the right, together with two copper-based examples. Again, there were disc beads in the pelvic area, under which a shark's vertebra had been placed. There was also a disc bead necklace, and a dog's skull was in position beyond the head. Burial 60 contained the remains of an adult buried with four pottery vessels, and it preceded burial 35. This adult female was also richly endowed with pots, ten being found mainly in the region of the head. Two dogs' skulls were also present there. This individual also wore six bronze bracelets, all but one on the left wrist, alongside a shell bracelet on the left and a stone one on the right wrist. Two long shell pendants were present around the neck, and the shell disc beads at the left wrist might represent yet another bracelet. The next grave is one of the longest identified in Central Thailand, measuring four metres. The adult male, as might be expected in such a large grave, was well endowed with grave goods. Most prominent was a large T-sectioned bronze bracelet on the right wrist, while a stone example was found on the right. The former was the only such bracelet found at Nong Nor. Six pots were disposed around the body, one concealing a fish jaw. This man also wore a circular tin earring.

Burial 93, the next in line, suffered looting and the central part of the body is missing. There remained a dog's skull beyond the head and three pots. Further graves in this row have also been disturbed, but burial 33 contained the remains of a child, associated with at least five pottery vessels, two shell pendants at the neck, a shell bracelet and a dog's skull. Burial 23, an adult male, was only partially found within the excavation area, but it was associated with a very large shell bracelet, a whetstone, a dog's skull, shell pendant, whole pot and a fragment of bronze, possibly representing a bracelet, at the left wrist.

Although this group contained many shell, stone and bronze bracelets as well as an impressive assemblage of pottery vessels and other grave goods, it does not stand apart, on the basis of mortuary wealth, from some individuals found with group B. Burial 109 in the latter, for example, involved a 3.25 m long grave. The adult male was buried with at least ten pots. There was a sandstone grinding stone under each hand and a third at the left shoulder. Jewellery included a serpentine bracelet, which had been burnt and broken in antiquity, but repaired with bronze cast in the form of tie-wire. A shell pendant was worn around the neck, and there were numerous shell disc beads in the body area. A shark's vertebra was identified in the region of the right hand, and a line of four conus shells extended beyond the head.

Burial 112 to the south, a young adult male, was poorer in terms of pots, with only the one, but there were also two bronze bracelets, a shell disc necklace and shark's tooth. The old adult male in burial 106 was associated with seven pots and pig remains. Shell disc beads were present around the body, and there was a stone bracelet over the chest. Burial 87, an adult male, had been rather disturbed, and some pots may be missing. But it still contained unusual artefacts. A shell bracelet was in place on the left wrist, but 11 tridacna shell discs over the chest also indicate that bracelets were made locally, for these discs are the central blank which had been removed in forming the bracelet. There were, in addition, two shark's teeth and a cache of bone points. The adjacent burial 83, an old adult male, included some unusual items. Three serpentine bracelets or bracelet fragments were found, one on each wrist and a serpentine belt ornament was found under the pelvis. A large boar's tusk had been placed under the right leg and three pots were also present. A clay anvil for shaping pots was found near the right shoulder.

Burial 145 lies towards the northern edge of this group, and contains the remains of a mid-age adult male. A set of bull's horns circled his skull, eight miniature pots had been placed in the grave fill, and five further vessels were present around the head and over the ankles. A further male lay on the same alignment and at the extreme western edge of the cemetery. He was accompanied by ten complete pots and three small socketed, probably copper, implements of unknown purpose. A dog's skull had been placed among the pots beyond the head. Fifteen metres to the southeast, a further mid-adult male (burial 47) had been interred in a deep grave, together with many offerings: eight pots, a dog's skull, stone bracelet and shell disc beads.

There are few female graves in this group. Burial 118 included four complete pots and a shell bracelet. Two infants were interred in jars nearby, one by the ankles and the other beyond the head. Burial 114 was unusual in being buried prone. Seven pottery vessels were found in association, together with the foot bones of a dog. The adult woman in burial 148 was found with a single pottery vessel and burial 37 had a shell bead, but burial 8 was richer, being found with three pots and barrel and disc shell beads in the ankle area. Many fragments of bronze bracelet were found in the general area, but none actually on the wrists. Some of the infants found in lidded jars were associated with grave goods, which include shell bracelets and, in the case of burial 49, a miniature bronze bracelet.

In order to assess the relationships between the sexes, people of different ages, and those assigned to the two major spatial groups, the complete interments have been subjected to various statistical analyses. Fifty intact graves have been ordered by a cluster analysis, and it has identified a distinct group, distinguished by a relatively large number of pots, as well as bracelets. Of the twelve graves in question, two are females, there is one child and nine males. Four of the row of deep burials in group A are included, but bronze or tin artefacts are not by any

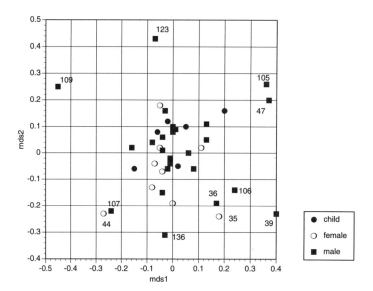

7.13   The relationship between Nong Nor graves on the basis of multidimensional scaling.

means dominant or restricted to these burials. Rather, we find that males were interred with more grave goods than most, but not all, women. Burial 35, for example, a rich female in group A, is found alongside males. This greater variation among males is also seen in the distribution which results from multidimensional scaling (Fig. 7.13). Here, we find a central group of men, women and children and rich outliers, most of which are males.

Copper or bronze artefacts are dominated by bracelets with a simple oval section. Only one, found with burial 105, had a more complex, T-shaped profile. Two burials contained socketed implements, and bronze or copper was also used to repair broken shell pendants or bracelets. There was one example of a bronze pendant. The distribution of bronzes fails to reveal spatial patterning. It is present in the graves of both groups, with males, females, children and infants. It may be that the relatively wealthy graves from 36 to 105 form a cluster with an unusual quantity of bronze bracelets, but graves with bronze items in group B are scattered within the area as a whole with no clear nucleation. Bronzes are found in the same proportion in men's as in women's graves.

If the range and quantity of grave offerings with adults is accepted as a rough index of personal achievement, then it is apparent that older men were to the fore in the Nong Nor community. We find deep, long and well-furnished graves containing males in each group. Burials 146, 145, 109, 47 and 109 particularly stand out in this respect, and they are well spaced within the cemetery. The inhabitants of this site cultivated rice, consumed fish, and made pottery vessels and shell bracelets. Goods obtained by exchange were more varied and came from a much larger catchment than those found at Khok Phanom Di. We find that copper, tin, carnelian, marble, talc, jade and serpentine were used in jewellery. None of these was found at Khok Phanom Di. There are also numerous shell ornaments and pottery vessels, some of which could well have been made locally. Nong Nor may be proposed as one of doubtless many communities which added value to local raw materials in order to participate in an exchange network. Exotic ornaments were used in death, and doubtless displayed in life, to reflect a degree of attainment and social standing. But no individual or group stands out above others, and we must acknowledge that, on the basis of this evidence, metal ornaments took their place with those of stone and shell without serious modification to the social order within autonomous communities which had already existed in the area for over a millennium.

The western margins of the Bangkok Plain

Glover (1991) has stressed the lack of bronze age sites on the western margins of the Central Plain and has suggested that this area, while receiving bronzes by exchange from the mining and casting sites to the east, proceeded directly from the Late Neolithic into the Iron Age. If this is the case, it might be due in part to the plentiful supplies of high quality stone found there. On the other hand, as Glover reports, Wilaikaeo (1988) has published evidence for the casting of bronze arrowheads and socketed axes from Ban Karn Sian near Kanchanaburi. It would be surprising if similar sites are not ultimately found, particularly given the abundant deposits of tin.

Although there are no radiocarbon dates available, the site of Khok Phlap provides the closest parallels with Nong Nor. It is located about the same distance from the present coast, and equidistant between the Chao Phraya and Mae Klong rivers. Mortuary vessels containing shellfish suggest a marine habitat (Daeng-iet 1978). The interment of one individual with four pots and three potters' anvils recalls the situation at Khok Phanom Di, while jewellery included bracelets of turtle carapace, shell, stone and bone. One turtle carapace example with projecting points was reproduced in bronze, and a socketed bronze spearhead was also present. The form of the stone jewellery and absence of any indication of iron both place the site at about the same date as Nong Nor, during the centuries preceding the major changes in the social and technological order which will now be considered.

The Iron Age

The transformation of our understanding of this period over the last two decades is illustrated in comments made by Bronson in 1973 with particular reference to his excavations at Chansen (Bronson 1979). This moated site revealed for the first time, a cultural sequence linking the later prehistoric period with the development of the Dvaravati state in the mid to later first millennium AD. His comments on the Iron Age noted that:

Central Thailand presents a picture of sub-regional isolation and sociocultural stasis ... By comparison with the intensive economic and political activity of other regions after they came into possession of metals and intensive agriculture, late prehistoric Central Thailand is distinctly backward. (Bronson 1979:319, 321)

These statements were made when few sites had been examined, and all contained pottery with few or no parallels elsewhere. Our understanding of the Iron Age has now been transformed by new site surveys and excavations, particularly that of Ban Don Ta Phet. Site surveys undertaken by Ho (1992) in three regions emphasise the regional diversity of Central Thailand and the variation in the cultural sequences even in areas close to each other. She has, however, identified a common factor in each of her regional complexes. All contain a moated centre, and smaller sites with Iron Age material clusters within 10 km of them. Again, each moated site, Ban Tha Kae, Khok Plord, Sab Champa I and Lopburi, has earlier prehistoric material at the beginning of the settlement phase. She has concluded that the Iron Age settlement pattern developed from local origins. The dating of moat construction is, as in the Mekong Valley, a major issue for future research and only at Ban Tha Kae have the profile and fill of the moats been recovered through archaeological research. Ciarla (1992) and Cremaschi *et al.* (1992) have shown that the earlier of the two moats there was filled by layers of gravel containing potsherds, laid down by running water, interleaved with clay lenses which accumulated under still conditions. Ciarla has ascribed the moats to the Iron Age, a finding which receives support from the proposed dating of some of the many moated sites found on the adjacent Khorat Plateau to the east.

Ban Don Ta Phet

There have been three seasons of excavations at this site (You-di 1976, Glover *et al.* 1984, Glover 1989, 1990). It comprises a cemetery within a circular enclosure marked by a bank and ditch with a diameter of about 40 m. The graves were laid out in rows on an east-west orientation, a familiar pattern for Central Thailand (Fig. 7.14a). It is unfortunate that the soil conditions do not preserve bone well and little has survived. It is possible that some of the graves contain secondary burials, where individuals were relocated from elsewhere. Some of the grave goods are only partially present, which could be the result of such a procedure. Yet enough survives from a few burials to indicate the presence of a complete, articulating skeleton. None of the burials intercut or damage earlier ones, and Glover has concluded that the cemetery represents a brief period of use. According to the AMS radiocarbon dates, obtained from organic material in the pottery vessels, the site belongs to the early fourth century BC (the pooled average date is 390–360 BC).

No domestic remains have been found: the excavators appear to have identified a specified cemetery enclosure. There might well be an occupation area nearby, perhaps under the present village, because the site is located on the end of a tongue of elevated terrace commanding low-lying land suited to rice

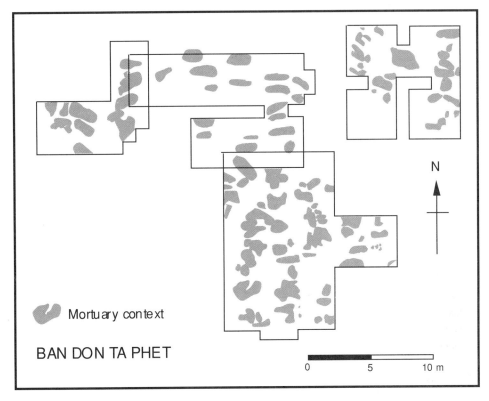

7.14a The distribution of graves in the cemetery of Ban Don Ta Phet.

cultivation. This was a widely preferred settlement location in prehistory. The 1980–1 excavation season involved an excavated area of 168 m² and 19 burials were recovered. A further 31 were encountered in 1985. These were associated with a range of grave goods which indicate a marked departure from those seen at Khok Phlap and Nong Nor. Burial context (BC) 55, for example, included 26 pottery vessels, some of which took the form of concentrations of sherds, eleven bronzes, four objects of iron, nine spindle whorls and 185 glass beads. BC 46 included several pottery vessels, the bronze figurine of a fighting cock, bronze bowls and many bracelets (Fig. 7.14b). Bronzes from this site reveal many innovations when compared with such sites as Nong Nor: there were four small rings and a handful of small bronze bowls. Iron took the form of three socketed hoes or digging stick ends and a socketed billhook (Fig. 7.15). This early context for glass is most easily explained as the result of exchange with an area where glass already had a long history, and the most obvious candidate is India.

An unusual aspect of this cemetery enclave is the uniformity of most graves, in terms of the range and quantity of offerings. BC 56 included further glass beads, two bronze vessels, one of which took the form of a situla or bucket, thirteen iron tools and weapons, including blades, digging tools and spearheads, while beads

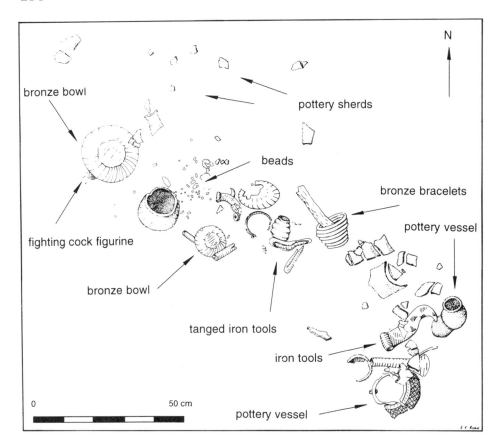

7.14b   Burial context 46 at Ban Don Ta Phet.
Permission: Centre for Southeast Asian Studies, University of Hull and Dr I.C.
Glover.

were made of carnelian and agate. Twenty pottery vessels or sherd groups were
also present. BC 73, in addition to a bronze bowl and an anklet, included twelve
iron tools and a remarkable find, a carnelian pendant in the form of a leaping lion.
This item reveals beyond any doubt, exchange links with India.

The assemblage of bronzes from the second and third seasons presents a most
informative pattern. Not one of the 288 artefacts was designed for conflict or even
for industrial purposes. There are no weapons and no axes. Numerically,
ornaments dominate. Sets of plain bracelets are most frequently represented, but
some bracelets and anklets are more complex, having U or O sections. Finger
rings and bells were found, neither being part of the earlier, Bronze Age
repertoire. The second category of bronzes incorporates containers. Two forms
dominate: a knob-based bowl standing 6–7 cm high and with a diameter of 12–
14 cm. Looking into the interior, a knob is visible in the centre at the base.
Hemispherical bowls are also found, some being decorated. There are also seven
of what Glover (1990) has termed canisters, vessels with a cylindrical body

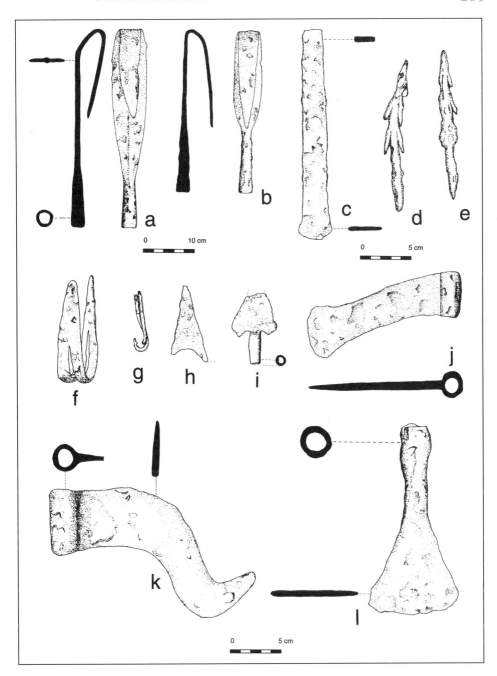

7.15 Iron artefacts from Ban Don Ta Phet.
a, b. Tanged spearheads. **c.** Long adze. **d, e.** Harpoons. **f.** Split implement.
g. Fishhook. **h, i.** Arrowheads. **j.** Shaft-hole axe. **k.** Billhook. **l.** Digging
implements.
Permission: Centre for Southeast Asian Studies, University of Hull and Dr
I.C. Glover.

standing 6–7 cm high and 5 cm wide. There is one unique decorative bronze, a cockerel standing on top of its cage.

The bronzes from the first season of excavation are also dominated by these vessels, 163 being represented (Rajpitak and Seeley 1979). There were also 38 bracelets, seven anklets, sixteen rings, a ladle, bells and bird finials.

The vessels have attracted much interest because they were made from an alloy of copper and about 23% tin. According to Rajpitak and Seeley, this alloy is so brittle as to be virtually unworkable, but imparts a golden colour. They have suggested that they were first cast in a rough form by the lost wax method. Subsequent working is facilitated by heating to between 600 and 750°C and working on a lathe or wheel to produce the finished form, which bears parallel

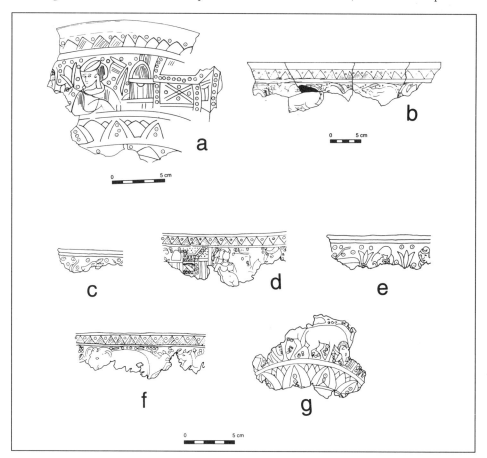

7.16   Scenes from bronze bowls.
a, b. Ban Don Ta Phet bowls, showing human, animal, floral and geometric motifs. **c–g.** Khao Jamook bowls, showing women, elephants and other animals possibly including a horse and sheep.
Permission: Centre for Southeast Asian Studies, University of Hull and Dr I.C. Glover.

working striations. The degree of expertise is evident from a wall thickness of only 0.3 to 0.5 mm in some cases. Some were then incised with decorative scenes or geometric designs. As part of the manufacturing process, the bowls were raised to a temperature of over 520°C and then quenched, a procedure which has the effect of reducing the degree of brittleness.

Decoration includes human and animal figures, the former being the first dated representations of the people in Central Thailand. The central person in Fig. 7.16, probably a woman, has a sophisticated coiffure, possibly a hat and a large ear ornament. The background includes floral designs, a possible circular structure and a pattern of hatched triangles and circles. Another vessel reveals a procession of animals. Although broken, water buffalo and horses seem to be represented, the latter being the earliest evidence for the horse in this area. Similar scenes and decorative techniques have been found on bowls from Khao Jamook. These include naked women with elaborate coiffures, animals, buildings and both floral and geometric designs (Bennett and Glover 1992). The vessels provide a sharp contrast to a situla from Ban Don Ta Phet BC 56 not only in form, but in alloy, for it includes a high admixture of lead. Glover (1989) has stressed the parallels between this item and the bronzes from the Red River Valley in northern Vietnam.

The graves contained many iron artefacts, forged, according to Bennett (1989), without lengthy tempering and quenching. Nevertheless, they were of sufficient strength and durability to perform their various functions. It is clear that iron was now preferred to bronze for industry, agriculture and conflict. While the old tradition of hafting by means of a socket continued, some iron artefacts were provided with a tang. The commonest item was a socketed implement with a splayed working surface which, following Glover, was probably used in agriculture as a digging implement. The billhooks, a new and distinctive form, could also have been used in agriculture. The shaft-hole axes and adzes are probably related to carpentry. We find that tanged and socketed spear and arrowheads were manufactured, but there is no evidence of an interest in swords or daggers. Fishhooks and harpoons were also found. The form of the arrowheads and fishhooks recall those found in bronze at Ban Na Di, while bone harpoons are known from Neolithic contexts in Central Thailand. The clarity of the division between a preference of bronze for ornaments and vessels, and iron for cutting implements and weapons, is remarkable.

Ban Don Ta Phet has provided the largest and best provenanced sample of Iron Age beads in Southeast Asia. The majority of the sample of approximately 3000 are made of glass, but 600 were fashioned from stone: carnelian, agate, rock crystal and jade. Although there are sources of carnelian and agate in Central Thailand, some fifty of the stone beads were etched, that is given a patterned decoration by the application of caustic soda to parts of the surface before heating (Glover 1989). This technique was developed in India, which is surely the origin for the majority of the Ban Don Ta Phet beads. Williams (1984) has suggested that the holes for stringing were cut with a diamond drill bit.

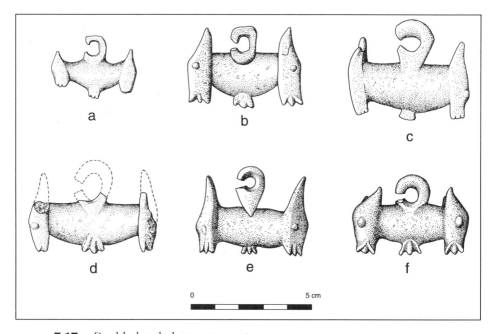

7.17   Double-headed ear ornaments.
a, b. Phu Hoa **c.** Hang Gon **d.** Sa Huynh (all Vietnam) **e.** Ban Don Ta Phet
(Central Thailand) **f.** Duyong Cave, Philippines.

The Indian origin of the glass and stone beads reinforces the evidence from the leaping carnelian lion, that the inhabitants of this site were, directly or indirectly, being exposed to a new range of exotic goods through a greatly expanded exchange network. Communities, far from being hermetically sealed, were being opened to new ideas and opportunities. Rajpitak and Seeley (1979), for example, have traced the occurrence of bowls similar to those from Ban Don Ta Phet in some Indian sites. A specimen from Coimbatore in southern India, for example, contained 23.58% tin and was made using the same techniques as at Ban Don Ta Phet. The Bhir mound at Taxila has furnished two such bowls in layers dated to the second or third century BC. They have also drawn attention to a passage in Strabo's *Geography,* derived from a fourth century BC report by Nearchus, that Indians used bronze bowls so brittle that they fractured, like pottery, when dropped.

We have already seen some evidence for contact with Bac Bo, northern Vietnam. This has been confirmed by the discovery of an animal pendant featuring two heads (Fig. 7.17). This is a singular form, which is paralleled at Phu Hoa, Hang Gon and Sa Huynh on the coast of southern Vietnam, at Xuan An near Vinh in a Dong Son context, and at Duyong Cave in the Philippines (Loofs-Wissowa 1980–1). These items are usually described as being manufactured from jade.

Ban Don Ta Phet illustrates both continuity and change. The layout of the graves in rows and the preferred orientation recall the cemeteries of Nong Nor and Khok Phanom Di, respectively 500 and 1500 years earlier. But the likelihood that some individuals were reinterred, and the wide range of exotic and novel grave goods, are new. It is particularly stressed that the bronze industry involved major technical advances and a concentration on receptacles and ornaments to the exclusion of tools or weapons. Iron was preferred for these purposes, and was present in abundance. The old preference for beads and bracelets of shell or stone gave way to exotic carnelian, agate and glass, and a new range of large bronze bracelets.

This site is located strategically near the eastern end of the Khwae Yai and Khwae Noi river valleys. These give access ultimately to the Andaman Sea and India. Glover (1989, 1990) has emphasised the growing evidence for exchange between Central Thailand and India which, on the basis of the new evidence from Ban Don Ta Phet, was underway by the fourth century BC. This brought new goods and also novel ideas. The lion, for example, is one of a number of ways in which the Buddha was represented before it became acceptable, from the first century AD, to portray him in human form. But contact was also established with communities to the east, and as will be seen, the evidence is not confined to Ban Don Ta Phet.

Recent excavations at several sites in the Central Plain illustrate the widespread nature of the new Iron Age complex. Mankong (1989) has reported on a limited excavation at Noen Ma Kok, a low mound which covers about 5 ha 20 km northeast of the Khao Wong Prachan Valley. No burials were found in the two small squares excavated, but the range of artefacts is matched at Ban Don Ta Phet. There are clay spindle whorls and beads of agate, carnelian and glass. Fragmentary bronze bracelets were encountered, and a stone bracelet had been repaired with bronze ties. Iron socketed digging sticks and hoe-like blades also fall within the range of iron tools from Ban Don Ta Phet, but there was also a clay mould for casting a bronze item, the actual form being hard to identify.

To the north, in Uthai Thani Province, Natapintu (1988b) has encountered a similar pattern at Ban Lum Khao. Again, there are spindle whorls, beads of carnelian, agate and glass and fragments of bronze bells and bracelets. Slag indicates a local iron industry. Three burials were uncovered, each on a north-south axis. One was associated with 239 glass beads and four pottery vessels. Another had green stone earrings in addition to two glass beads.

Chiawanwongsa (1987) has excavated two small squares at Ban Wang Hi, just south of Lamphun and on the left bank of the Kwong River. Each contained inhumation burials with the head orientated to the east. Glass and agate beads were present in the area of the graves, and socketed iron tools were found regularly placed beside the head and legs. Burial 2 in the second square was found with four large bronze bracelets.

Tham Ongbah

This pattern of graves with bronze ornaments and iron implements might well have been found at Tham Ongbah, a site of profound potential significance which was ravaged by looting only shortly before being examined by Sørensen (1973, 1988). Ongbah is a cavern located in the upper reaches of the Khwae Yai River. Its location and the wealth of the graves within may be due to the local lead deposits. The cave had a long sequence of prehistoric occupation, the third and final phase being dated to the last few centuries BC, and therefore well within the Iron Age. According to the excavations, and reports from those who had worked for the looters, the site had once contained over ninety wooden coffins. The few surviving pieces, and three which remain intact, reveal that they were fashioned from a local hardwood with birds' heads at each end. Some lids were rendered in a similar form and fitted by mortice and tenon joints into the coffin proper. The body was laid out within, associated with grave goods which, apparently, included glass and stone beads, bronze ornaments and iron weapons and tools. Descriptions of the contents by eye witnesses included reference to long strings of beads and bead necklaces and belts, bronze ornaments and vessels. One vessel closely similar to those from Ban Don Ta Phet has been illustrated by Sørensen. A radiocarbon date from a coffin fragment has provided a date of 403 BC–AD 25.

Six bronze drums of Heger type 1 were included among the grave offerings, probably in pairs. They have been described in detail by Sørensen (1988) who has stressed their broad affinities with the group known as Heger 1. The distribution of these drums concentrates in southern China and northern Vietnam, where dating evidence, while sparse, places them within the period 500 BC–AD 100. The striking surface, or tympanum, and the upper part of the side, or mantle, are usually covered in zones of decoration and their style has formed the basis for chronological subdivisions. It is usually assumed that the more stylised scenes are later. OB 87, which was probably located between two boat coffins, has eight zones on the reconstructed tympanum, including a row of birds and ten human figures which represent feathered warriors. There are also two houses, raised on piles and equipped with a ladder for access. Carved birds on the gable ends recall those found on the coffins. OB 89 is slightly larger and has ten zones of decoration, including flying birds and feathered men. The mantle includes boats manned by feathered warriors, a common feature in the genre, but in this case unusual because the boat was steered, it seems, by a fixed rudder rather than a helmsman and a paddle (Fig. 7.18). Sørensen has stressed the high status attached to the ownership of such drums, and the stylised decoration suggests a late date within the life of such drums in agreement with the radiocarbon dating of the coffins. The origin of these drums is more difficult to identify, but it is likely that they were obtained by exchange from an exotic source.

The excavations at Ongbah identified a small group of inhumation graves which escaped the attentions of the looters. A cluster of five were interred with

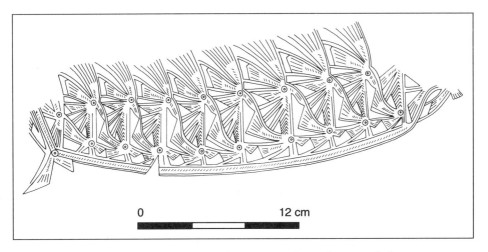

7.18   The boat represented on drum OB 89 from Tham Ongbah.
Permission: Dr Per Sørensen.

the head pointing to the east, and three others were found on a northeast-southwest orientation. These burials were associated with a range of iron artefacts. A tanged hoe 24.5 cm long was found on the chest of burial 5, while burial 6 had been interred with two iron knives and a possible spear blade. Other iron objects, which dominated the grave goods numerically, include arrowheads and chisels, although corrosion ruled out identifying the use of some items. The similarity between the iron artefacts from these graves and those from the coffins has encouraged Sørensen to suggest that the two groups were contemporary, and distinguished from each other by social status.

Two graves from Ban Kao contained iron artefacts, and an assemblage from the upper occupation deposits from this site match those from Ongbah. Again, we find knives, chisels for woodworking, arrowheads, a harpoon, a fishhook, a tanged axe or adze and reaping knives. The assemblage recalls that from Ban Don Ta Phet, with the exception of the billhook which is so common at the latter site.

Summary

On the basis of available evidence, the Central Plain of Thailand sustained Neolithic communities dated between 2400–1500 BC. It is possible that groups which cultivated rice were present considerably earlier than this, but only indirect evidence drawn from pollen, phytolith and charcoal frequencies is available. A sedentary coastal community reliant on fishing, shellfish collecting and the hunting of marine mammals is known at Nong Nor dated to 2450 BC, and no evidence for rice consumption has been found. The earliest evidence for cultivated rice comes from Khok Phanom Di (Thompson 1992), and this site, taken with those in the Khao Wong Prachan Valley, indicate a Neolithic exchange network linking coastal and inland groups with stone and marine shell being traded. Khok Phanom Di, Non Pa Wai, Ban Kao and Khok Charoen have yielded dentate-stamped pottery with widespread parallels at this juncture in Southeast Asia. These sites could represent the arrival of agriculturalists who brought Austroasiatic languages and a long-established tradition of interment in inhumation cemeteries. The contribution of local sedentary groups of affluent foragers, however should not be set aside.

The mortuary data from Khok Phanom Di suggest that craft skill was a route to status. The ceramic industry there and at Non Pa Wai indicates a high level of expertise in manufacture and firing. Copper smelting and casting began at Non Pa Wai within the period 1500–1000 BC. Local ores contained arsenic, and tin was not used in alloying. Clay bivalve moulds were used to cast axes and projectile points, and many cup moulds indicate the casting of ingots. Slightly later, we find that the Nong Nor cemetery contained tin and bronze jewellery, but not in abundance. This site is located some distance from the copper mines, and two graves contained socketed implements matching those from Nil Kham Haeng. These comprise unalloyed copper. Bronzes include three varieties of bronze bracelet and a coil. A local villager also reported finding a socketed axe.

Nong Nor is located 14 km from Khok Phanom Di, and it is possible to compare a Neolithic with a Bronze Age cemetery. While the latter has a greater range of exotic stone jewellery and ornaments of tin and bronze, there is no major dislocation in mortuary ritual nor the wealth of individuals. Bronze and tin were employed as further exotic items for personal adornment. Later contexts at Nil Kham Haeng included a growing number of projectile points and evidence for iron working, both variables which contributed to the development of more complex, centralised communities of the Iron Age.

These are best represented at Ban Don Ta Phet and Tham Ongbah. The former, which has been dated to the early fourth century BC, is a cemetery within an enceinte, thought to represent a brief interlude and, in the main, contain secondary burials laid out in rows. Technological change was dramatic: there were many tools and weapons of iron, and bronze was reserved for ornaments and decorated bronze bowls. The latter have a very high tin content and the casting procedure would have entailed specialist skills. The range of beads in exotic stone and glass, as well as a carnelian lion and double-headed animal pendant provide compelling evidence for involvement in exchange which encompassed India, Vietnam and the Philippines. That this was a two-way relationship is suggested by the presence of bowls in India alien to the local tradition but matching that of Ban Don Ta Phet. There is no evidence within the cemetery for a rich enclave, but the fact that so many graves contained numerous exotic goods, iron and bronzes within a restricted area might reflect the high status of all those buried there.

Tham Ongbah, although severely looted, contained graves in wooden coffins with an equally rich set of grave goods, including bronze drums most closely matched in northern Vietnam and Yunnan. Here, however, we also find poorer graves without coffins, which might be due to the presence of two, unequal, social groups. Tham Ongbah is located near a source of lead ore, and Ban Don Ta Phet was strategically placed at the eastern end of the Three Pagodas Pass. According to Ho (1992), this period on the western edge of the Central Plain also saw the development of unusually large sites the moats of which may belong to the Iron Age. Far from being a period of isolation and cultural stasis, as was suggested two decades ago by Bronson (1979), the Iron Age in Central Thailand was one of dynamic change and involvement in a trading network which was soon to link the Roman and Chinese empires.

CHAPTER 8

EASTERN INDIA, THE ISLANDS OF SOUTHEAST ASIA AND COASTAL VIETNAM

A full appreciation of the Bronze Age in Southeast Asia cannot be gained without reference to the cultural developments in adjacent regions. It would be illogical to review the mainland material in conjunction with that of the *zhongyuan* and the Yangzi Valley while simultaneously ignoring the bronze tradition of India. In the case of island Southeast Asia, it is important to note that its own Bronze Age was stimulated by exchange with the mainland. This occurred at a time when the emerging chiefdoms in the latter area were stretching their sinews and increasingly participating in an exchange network which was soon to incorporate the Roman and Han empires.

Eastern India

One of the most intriguing issues raised by the distribution of Austroasiatic languages is the presence of a sub-family in eastern India. The Munda languages, according to Diffloth (1991), are distributed in southern Bihar, west Bengal, Madhya Pradesh and Orissa, and there is sufficient internal differentiation to recognise northern and southern groups (Fig. 8.1). Zide and Zide (1976) have reconstructed a proto-Munda language, and then sought cognates which throw some light on early cultural practices. These include a series of similar roots for words concerned with rice cultivation, including words for uncooked and husked rice, all shared between Lawa, Rumai, Khmu and Mon-Khmer, Southeast Asian languages in the Austroasiatic family. They suggested that at least 3500 years ago, proto-Munda languages had words for rice, millet, legumes, husking and pestle and mortar. Another cognate shared between old Mon, Khmer and Munda languages is the word for copper-bronze. Blust (pers. comm.) has suggested that proto-Munda and proto-Mon-Khmer languages diverged at least six millennia ago.

The evidence for the introduction of rice cultivation into India is subject to controversy due to unfounded claims for very early contexts. Glover, however, has critically reviewed such evidence, in particular the proposed date in the seventh millennium BC for rice at Koldihwa, and found it wanting (Glover and Higham 1993). He has substituted a date in the mid to late third millennium BC as being more realistic. This finds agreement in the date of 2544±100 BC for period 1 at Khairadih on the Ghaghra River in Uttar Pradesh, a settlement mound which has yielded rice remains (Bellwood *et al.* 1992). Thereafter, a considerable

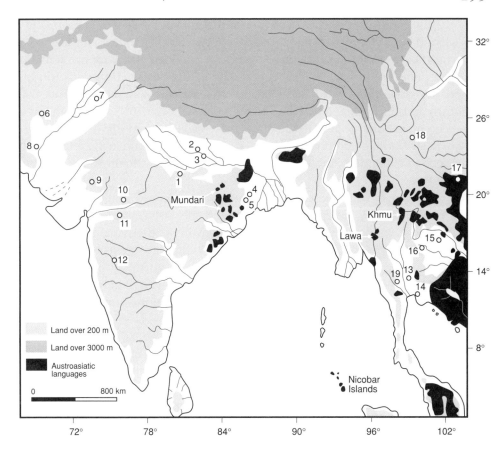

8.1 Map of the Indian subcontinent and part of Southeast Asia, showing the location of sites mentioned in the text.
1. Koldihwa. **2.** Khairadih. **3.** Chirand. **4.** Mahisadal. **5.** Pandu Rajar Dhibi. **6.** Mehgarh. **7.** Harappa. **8.** Mohenjo-daro. **9.** Ahar. **10.** Kayatha. **11.** Navdatoli. **12.** Inamgaon. **13.** Non Pa Wai. **14.** Nong Nor. **15.** Ban Na Di and Ban Chiang. **16.** Non Nok Tha. **17.** Thanh Den. **18.** Shizhaishan. **19.** Ban Don Ta Phet.

number of sites with rice remains fall into the second millennium BC, and the first evidence for this plant in the Indus Valley falls after 2000 BC.

The centre of rice cultivation is firmly located from the Yangzi Valley south into Southeast Asia, and Munda languages occupy the extreme western edge of the distribution of Austroasiatic languages. The simplest hypothesis to account for the presence of Munda in eastern India is that expansive agricultural communities reached the area ultimately from the Yangzi Valley. It is, however, not at present possible to point to any convincing similarities in material culture. Some settlement sites in Bihar and Bengal, however, include the remains of rice and copper implements. Chirand in Bihar, for example, has a sequence divided into three periods. The first has been called Neolithic, but towards the transition to period 2, the earliest copper has been reported (Agrawal 1982). Pandu Rajar Dhibi is a second site, where rice remains and copper rings, bangles and a tanged arrowhead have been found. Mahisadal has also provided abundant rice remains as well as a flat copper axe and extended inhumation burials. Unusually for this period in India, they were laid out on an east-west orientation. The five radiocarbon dates from period 2 at Chirand range between 1650 and 715 BC, and three determinations from Mahisadal fall between 1380 and 855 BC. This East Indian metal working tradition, therefore, seems to have begun in the second half of the second millennium BC, and lasted until overtaken by the Iron Age in about 800–700 BC.

Alloying copper with tin, lead and arsenic was practised in the much earlier urban centres of the Indus civilisation during the last centuries of the third millennium BC, and as excavations at Mehrgarh in southern Baluchistan have demonstrated, copper beads were present by 6000 BC, in contexts which suggest very early contacts with Near Eastern metallurgical knowledge (Muhly 1988). Harappan bronze workers between 2300 and 2000 BC were highly skilled. They were familiar with lost wax casting to produce human figurines, and were familiar with annealing and riveting. Their output included vessels in a wide range of forms, as well as arrowheads, spearheads, knives and axes. The casting of sickles suggests that bronze was also used in improving agriculture. An urban focus for smelting is also revealed by the discovery at Mohenjo-daro of a pit containing a large supply of copper ore.

As might be expected, the knowledge of copper and its alloys was not confined to the Harappan civilisation, and many regional cultures in India included metal in their technical repertoire from the end of the third millennium BC. Agrawal (1982) has succinctly summarised their distribution and main features. The Banas culture of Rajasthan, for example, is best known on the basis of excavations at Ahar, a mound covering 13.5 ha and rising to a height of 13 m. Based on farming millet and rice, and clearly sustaining a reasonable population, this site has yielded five axes, a knife, a bracelet and two rings. The presence of copper slag and proximity to the copper deposits of the Aravalli hills also reveal local mining and smelting activity (Allchin and Allchin 1982). The castings, however, were poorly executed and there is no evidence for annealing. The Kayatha culture occupies part of Madhya Pradesh and the copper industry from the eponymous site includes bangles, axes and a chisel. The Malwa culture of Madhya Pradesh and Maharashtra is best known on the basis of excavations at Navdatoli and Inamgaon. Once again, we encounter copper working in the context of agricultural villages. Wheat, barley and rice were all represented at Navdatoli. The metal working tradition is quite different from that of Southeast Asia. The range of artefacts, which included bronze with only up to 3% of tin, includes bangles, rings, flat axes, arrowheads and chisels and a spearhead. But they were heated and hammered to shape, rather than cast into their final form.

Copper and bronze were widely employed in Pakistan and Central India by

2000 BC. During the second half of the second millennium BC, a bronze industry was established in eastern India, in areas now occupied by the speakers of Munda languages. The metallurgical techniques and artefacts are distinct from those of Southeast Asia. Were it not for the presence of Austroasiatic languages of some considerable time depth, it could easily be concluded that the Indian and Southeast Asian bronze traditions were separate. A shared cognate for copper-bronze between Munda, Khmer and Old Mon leaves the nagging feeling that there was some link between metallurgical traditions in the two areas.

The Bronze Age of island Southeast Asia

The arc of islands from Sumatra in the west to Luzon in the east, presents radical differences, in terms of the environment and the cultural sequence, to the mainland (Fig. 8.2) As one approaches the equatorial regions, the distinction between wet and dry seasons fades and the regular rainfall encourages a tropical, evergreen rainforest. The triple canopy of vegetation screens the sun and rain from the ground, and without a potent technology, forest clearance for agriculture is highly demanding. Luxuriant regrowth without a dry season pause also presents difficulties for rice cultivation, but more important still, rice is not adapted to the forested tropical habitat. In nature, it depends on a predictable period of sunshine and length of daylight. This may well account for the fact that the expansion of cultivators speaking Austroasiatic languages did not penetrate into the islands of Southeast Asia. As one moves into eastern Java and Bali, southern Sulawesi and Timor, however, the seasons become more marked. This is also a volcanic region and soils are richer than the heavy acidic soils under the rainforest.

From Taiwan south through the Philippines and so into the islands of Indonesia, the majority of the population today speak an Austronesian (AN) language. Blust (1976, 1985, 1993b) and Reid (1993) have recently argued in favour of an original link between Austronesian and Austroasiatic languages spoken on the mainland. In considering the settlement of the Southeast Asian islands, the linguistic evidence speaks more clearly than the archaeological record. The greatest time depth in any AN language is found on Taiwan, and as Blust (1976, 1985) has convincingly demonstrated, differentiation between regional languages indicates a north to south expansion. Bellwood (1985, 1989, 1992) has proposed that Austronesian languages reached island Southeast Asia ultimately from Taiwan and beyond to the Chinese mainland, in a process of human expansion which originated in the Neolithic rice-growing communities of the lower Yangzi. He has suggested that this expansion reached Taiwan from about 4500 BC, and the Philippines 1500 years later. As they encountered less favourable conditions for rice cultivation, so they substituted, if one accepts the linguistic evidence, plants better adapted to the tropics, such as bananas, yams and taro. To this day, a mixture of bananas and coconuts forms a nutritious basis

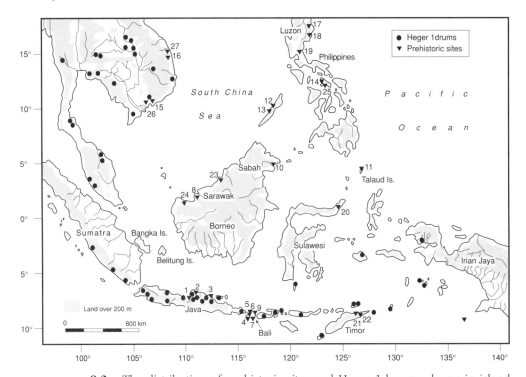

8.2   The distribution of prehistoric sites and Heger 1 bronze drums in island
Southeast Asia.
1. Gunung Pati. **2.** Plawangan. **3.** Kradenanrejo. **4.** Pejeng. **5.** Gilimanuk. **6.**
Sembiran. **7.** Manuaba. **8.** Selindung. **9.** Pangkungliplip. **10.** Tapadong. **11.**
Leang Buidane. Leang Tuwo Mane'e. **12.** Tabon, Manunggul. **13.** Duyong.
14. Kalanay. **15.** Phu Hoa. **16.** Sa Huynh. **17.** Rabel, Andarayan, Arku. **18.**
Dimolit. **19.** Pintu. **20.** Ulu Leang. **21.** Uai Bobo. **22.** Lie Siri. **23.** Niah Cave.
24. Gua Sireh. **25.** Batungan. **26.** Hang Gon. **27.** Hau Xa.

to the diet of coastal fishing groups in peninsular Thailand. Bellwood has
suggested that Austronesian speakers reached Borneo and Timor by the mid third
millennium BC.

Archaeological documentation of this proposed expansion is not straightforward, although there is enough evidence, in the form of pottery technology,
adze forms, shell jewellery and spindle whorls to mention some of many artefacts,
to identify a common pattern stretching from Taiwan through the Philippines to
Sulawesi. I have stressed that on the mainland opposite, the archaeological
record, while replete with so-called Early and Middle Neolithic sites containing
pottery and polished stone tools, has failed to provide any evidence for rice until
about 2800 BC at Shixia. On the western coast of Taiwan, a group of sites ascribed
to the Dapenkeng culture likewise provide much evidence for a ceramic industry
but no vestiges of rice. The earliest radiocarbon date, from Bajiacun, has entered
the literature as evidence of agriculture by 4300 BC, but this determination is
highly suspect (Meacham 1991, Spriggs 1991). That this culture flourished during

the third millennium BC is not in doubt: recent excavations by Tsang (1992) at Guoye has confirmed similarities with the mainland Middle Neolithic and provided a new and important corpus of dates. These suggest that the terminal stages of this phase fall in the period 2500–2000 BC. While Chang (1986) has suggested that the people were concerned principally with coastal gathering and fishing, with perhaps some horticulture, Bellwood (1985) prefers to see them as representing the initial intrusion into the island of early Austronesian speakers who brought agriculture with them and, in effect, provided the wellspring for further maritime expansion to the south. My own preference is to equate the Dapenkeng culture with the Middle Neolithic groups on the mainland opposite, because there is no evidence which supports agriculture.

This contrasts with the later culture of Fengbitou, where the assemblages include tripod pottery vessels, a feature of mainland forms, slate reaping knives, stone hoes and the actual remains of rice which at Kending, have been dated in the vicinity of 2000 BC (Fig. 8.3). This provides a problem, for the earliest presence of pottery vessels, thought to equate with the intrusive Neolithic in the Philippines, has been dated at basal layers of Rabel Cave from about 2800 BC (Spriggs 1989). To conform with the linguistic evidence, either Rabel Cave is dated too early, or there are earlier Fengbitou sites to be found on Taiwan. Third, Dapenkeng sites might in due course provide the missing evidence for rice.

These issues should not cloud the likelihood that the expansion of agricultural communities south from the Yangzi into mainland Southeast Asia, a third millennium BC phenomenon, is matched by the available evidence from Taiwan and the Philippines. In the latter area, ceramics associated with a range of new artefact forms have been found at a number of sites. Dimolit in northern Luzon has furnished plain and red slipped pottery in association with the plans of rectangular houses (Peterson 1974). The radiocarbon dates of 2703–1953 and 1782–1302 BC provide a broad chronological spread. Dates in association with rice remains have been obtained at Andarayan (1762–1256 and 1980–1415 BC), and the same ceramic assemblage has been recovered at Musang, Pintu (2140–984 BC) and Arku Cave (1527–910 BC) (Bellwood 1985, Spriggs 1989). Intrusive settlement thereafter reached Sulawesi, for at Ulu Leang, Glover (1976) has identified a sharp change in the archaeological record which saw the introduction of rice and pottery. The dating of this change has not been finalised (Glover and Higham 1993), but pottery appeared at Uai Bobo 2 by 2410–1887 BC. Further to the west, a rice grain has been found in a prehistoric pottery sherd from the site of Gua Sireh in Sarawak. This has been AMS dated to 2923–1603 BC, a result close to a second determination reported by Spriggs (1994). This broad span is compatible with the spread of agriculturalists into the tropical island habitat of Southeast Asia, perhaps towards the end of the third millennium BC (Bellwood *et al.* 1992).

This expansionary movement has the merit of integrating the available archaeological and linguistic evidence. It is not universally accepted, but this is

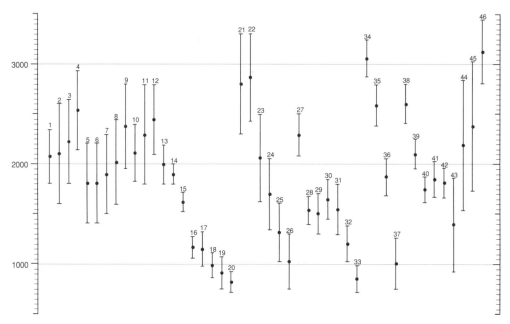

8.3   Radiocarbon dates for the spread of agriculture into island Southeast Asia
(2 sigma corrected range BC).
1-3. Kuo Yeh (Gx-10594-5, 13597). **4.** Pei-Liao (GX-11273). **5.** Chi-Pei (GX-
10224). **6.** Lian-wen-kang (GX-10597). **7, 8.** Suo-kang (GX-10221-2). **9, 10.**
Nan-kang (GX-10222, 11275). **11.** Li-yü-shan (GX-10226). **12.** Tsao-hsieh-
tun (NTU-224. **13.** Kending (GX-6997). **14.** Niu Chou Tzu (NTU-304). **15–
20.** Fengbitou (Y-1580-1, 1649, 1578, 1584, 1648). **21-6.** Rabel (GaK-9932,
9929, 9933, 9892-3, 9896). **27, 8.** Dimolit (GaK-2937, 2939). **29, 30.**
Andarayan (SFU-86, RIDDL). **31.** Pintu (GaK-2942). **32, 3.** Arku (GaK-7041,
7040). **34–6.** Ulu Leang (PRL-231, Har-1734, PRL-230). **37.** Leang Burung
(ANU-391). **38.** Leang Tuwo Mane'e (ANU-1515). **39, 40.** Uai Bobo (ANU-
239, 414). **41, 2.** Lie Siri (ANU-172, 235). **43–6.** Gua Sireh (ANU-7047, CAMS-
725, ANU-7049, 283).

not necessary for the issues under review. The basic point is that expansionary
trends, which probably originated in Taiwan and the adjacent mainland, saw the
settlement of the coastal tracts of island Southeast Asia. Remarkably, there is no
linguistic or archaeological evidence for landfall and settlement on the Southeast
Asian mainland at this juncture, although the Cham speakers settled coastal
Vietnam considerably later. This may be due to the presence there of hostile and
well organised coastal communities.

Bellwood (1985) has defined a Late Neolithic phase in island Southeast Asia,
although again, it is not well documented and we have insufficient data upon
which to base a realistic assessment of social organisation and subsistence. In
some areas, such as Sabah, Talaud and Luzon, the earlier red-slipped pottery
tradition appears to have continued unchanged to the beginning of the Bronze
Age. At Batungan on Masbate, on the other hand, the pottery dated in the vicinity

of 900 BC was intricately decorated with stamped designs. Much more on this important phase could have been determined at the great cave of Niah, but as Spriggs (1989) has shown, the chronological framework there is unacceptable. The most that can be inferred from the early excavations is that there was probably a Neolithic cemetery there incorporating jar burials, a tradition which became widespread during the Bronze Age, and which might date back into the second millennium BC.

The first metal in island Southeast Asia

Copper is relatively abundant in parts of island Southeast Asia, but absent in others (Fig. 8.4). Some of the largest deposits in East Asia are to be found on Luzon and there are smaller sources of ore in southern Java and Sumatra. Tin, however, is virtually absent beyond the rich belt which runs from Bangka and Belitung islands north through Malaysia to Central Thailand. The principal point of relevance to this study, is that the earliest evidence for metal belongs to the last few centuries BC. Bronze and iron are found together from the start. Moreover, the origin of the first bronzes and of the technological repertoire when local casting was established was emphatically on the mainland of Southeast Asia. This is most convincingly seen in the typology and the distribution of bronze drums in

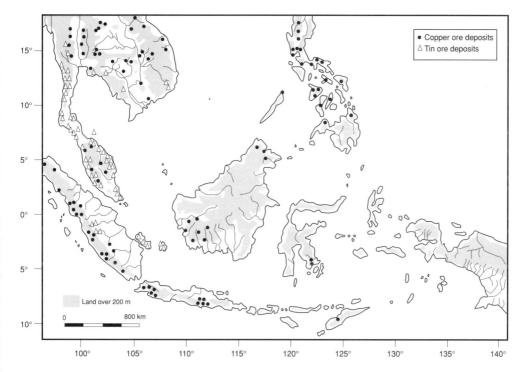

8.4   The distribution of tin and copper ores in island Southeast Asia
Source: Bronson 1992.

Indonesia (Soejono 1993). The Heger 1 form, which has its mainland concentration in the Red River Valley up to Yunnan, is the most widespread in the islands of Indonesia (Fig. 8.2). There can be little doubt that these drums were cast on the mainland and obtained through exchange relationships.

This suggests that the local communities were sufficiently complex to find a role for such large exotic imports, and this receives confirmation in the way in which some of the drums were used. That from the cemetery of Plawangan in Central Java was used as a coffin (Bintarti 1993). This site involved interment in jars, in association with a range of grave goods including bronze ornaments and a spearhead. The drum in question had been placed upside-down over a child, and contained the flexed skeleton of a second child. The cemetery also included inhumation and jar burials associated with iron knives, a bronze fishhook and a ring, and glass beads (Soejono 1993). A second Javan site, Kradenanrejo, included a similar burial within a Heger 1 drum, but associated with a Pejeng style drum. The latter are seen as local copies of the imported form. At Gunung Pati and Selindung, Heger 1 drums have been found containing gold ornaments, glass beads and objects of bronze and iron.

Bellwood (1985) has pointed out that these drums may have arrived in the islands of the Sunda Chain long after their date of manufacture within the period of expanded exchange during the early first millennium AD. Yet there are other bronzes of mainland inspiration: a dagger handle and bracelets. Moreover, the exotic stone jewellery from mainland and Philippine sources discussed above point to the establishment of maritime exchange links over considerable areas by the end of the first millennium BC.

The bronze industry of Bali

The introduction of such imports also stimulated the development of a local casting industry. Ardika (1987, 1991) has described several sites on Bali which have yielded mould fragments. The three stone specimens from Manuaba, which were probably intended to impress patterns onto the wax, include the representation of a human face similar to those found on Pejeng drums. Another stone mould fragment was found in 1989 at Sembiran on the northeastern coastal plain. Since such casting took place on an island with no sources of copper or tin, it follows that metal must have been traded. Given the potential for control over supplies which such exchange provides, it is intriguing to note the range of local bronzes which were preferred. Ardika has described a wide range from the later prehistoric stone sarcophagus burials of Bali, which concentrate on the southern fertile slopes of the island. Many contain bronze offerings: bracelets, finger protectors of wire form set in a spiral, long bronze armlets or 'arm protectors', necklaces, belts and ear and finger rings. Some rings were linked, again for decorative purposes, into chains. The high status assumed to have been associated with those interred in sarcophagi with bronzes receives support from the recovery of gold eye covers at Pangkungliplip and Gilimanuk in western Bali, while some of the graves also contain exotic beads of carnelian and glass. Axes of a wide variety of forms are also found, but weapons are absent.

Ardika has noted that the Balinese axes and bracelets were made of a ternary alloy of copper, tin and lead. This admixture was widespread at the same period on the mainland of Southeast Asia and reinforces the likelihood that the inhabitants of favoured coastal situations on Bali participated in major long distance exchange of valuables. Exotic Indian rouletted ware from Sembiran puts the issue beyond doubt. Indeed, one sherd bore writing in the Kharoshthi script of northwest India, which was current for seven centuries from 300 BC.

The Tabon Caves

Excavations at the remarkably rich and intact cave cemeteries on Lipuun Point, a promontory on western edge of Malumut Bay on the island of Palawan, have done much to allow an integration between the mainland and island traditions of bronze casting. Known collectively as the Tabon Caves, the area is strategically located facing westward towards the mainland. In 1964, the chance discovery of the Manunggul Cave on a sheer rockface opened the opportunity of examining two burial areas within, that in Chamber A belonging to the first millennium BC but, it seems, before the availability of bronze. Chamber B, which has been radiocarbon dated to about 200 BC, provides evidence for the introduction of bronze and iron to the Philippines (Fox 1970).

The earlier jar burials provided a range of grave goods, including jade beads and bracelets and three agate bracelets, but no objects of metal, glass or carnelian. The pottery vessels display a remarkable expertise including arguably the most impressive example from Southeast Asia, a vessel 66.5 cm in height, topped by a soul boat transporting away the dead (Fig. 8.5a). The ceramic tradition continued into the metal age vessels found in chamber B, but now there is a greater variety of grave goods, including fragments of iron, beads of glass and carnelian and bracelets made of glass. This period also included bronze artefacts. The burial cave of Uyaw, just to the east of Manunggul, included a bronze socketed axe, while Batu Pati cave contained a ceramic mould for casting such an implement (Fig. 8.5 b–d). Although the few socketed axes from this region were decorated in a distinctive local style, they clearly fall within the mainland casting tradition. There is also evidence for the use of socketed bronze axes and tanged arrowheads. The presence of moulds for casting bronzes with up to 11% tin, in an area with no known tin source, suggests that the metal was brought from the mainland.

In considering the form and decoration of the burial jars from Tabon, Fox (1970) has unequivocally assigned them to the Kalanay tradition first proposed by Solheim (1964) following his excavations at Kalanay on Masbate Island, 600 km to the northeast. The Kalanay tradition is also closely paralleled in the Sa Huynh sites of the mainland, a link confirmed by the numerous slit earrings and the double-headed animal pendants found on Palawan and mainland sites from Hong Kong to central Thailand. The conclusions are clear: the last century or two of the first millennium BC saw a major development in seaborne exchange which linked Palawan with adjacent islands and the mainland. This brought the first bronzes to the islands, where they were received by societies which already showed high technical skill as potters and an interest in exotic personal ornaments.

Jar burial cemeteries akin to those from the Tabon caves are found in many other parts of island Southeast Asia, from the Philippines to eastern Malaysia and Indonesia. Bellwood (1985), for example, has excavated such a site at Leang Buidane in the Talaud Islands, finding copper or bronze bracelets, a socketed axe and clay moulds in association with glass, agate and carnelian beads. The style and etching applied to the agate beads indicates an Indian origin. Stone moulds for bronze casting and jar burials, again showing typological affinities with the Sa Huynh ceramics, recur on the Tapadong Massif in Sabah.

The central and southern coastal plain of Vietnam

The broad plain of Bac Bo gives way to the south first to the Ma and Ca rivers, and then to a narrow coastal tract pierced by a series of rivers which originate in the Truong Son Cordillera. That this area attracted Bronze Age settlement is seen at Binh Chau, a settlement with inhumation graves located in the Thu Bon Valley. This river provides access over the mountains to the Mekong catchment. The site has yielded crucibles, moulds, a bronze socketed axe and a ribbed arrowhead. Ngo Si Hong (1980) maintains that the site belongs to the late second or early first millennium BC.

The subsequent settlement of this area represents a significant departure from all other Iron Age communities on the mainland of Southeast Asia. Appreciating the distinctiveness of this area is best understood by the sequel, the historic civilisation of coastal Vietnam. The early inscriptions, associated with the Hindu religion and associated temple architecture, include passages in Cham, an Austronesian language with its closest parallels in Acehnese and Malayic languages spoken in Southwest Borneo, and it is hard to find an alternative to the settlement of coastal Vietnam from this area (Blust 1993b).

Solheim (1959) has summarised the discovery of the Sa Huynh culture, which represents the late prehistoric precursor to the Cham civilisation. In 1909, M. Vinet, a customs inspector, reported a group of large burial jars containing stone beads and pots in the sand dunes near Sa Huynh. Fourteen years later, the site was further investigated by Mme Labarre, during which Henri Parmentier visited the soundings, excavated himself for a day or two, and subsequently published the material himself (Parmentier 1918b). Further investigations in what must have been an impressively large cemetery took place in 1934 under the direction of Colani, and by Janse five years later. Parmentier described a typical mortuary assemblage as including small pottery vessels, iron implements, glass and

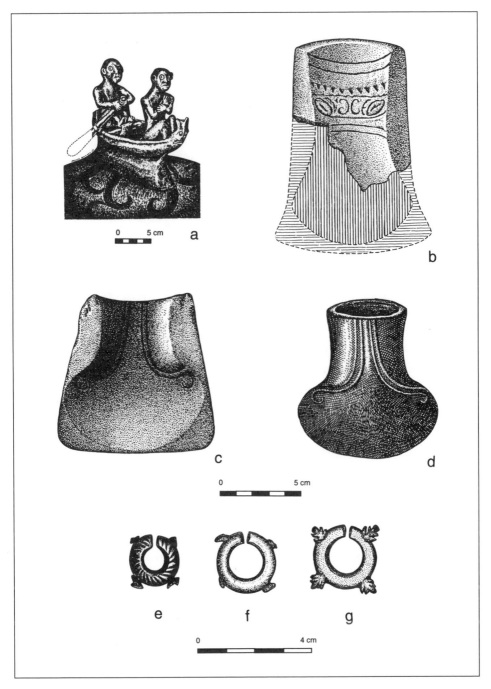

8.5 Artefacts from the Tabon Caves.
a. Part of the soul boat from Manunggul Cave. **b.** Socketed axe mould from Duyong Cave. **c.** Socketed axe mould from Batu Pati Cave. **d.** Socketed axe from Uyaw Cave. **e–g.** Jade *lingling-o* ear ornaments,

carnelian beads and sometimes bronzes, including bells. Solheim (1959) has noted that bronzes are relatively rare in the mortuary jars from Sa Huynh and the similar site at Phu-co, 5 km to the north, where Colani excavated 187 jars in 1937. They include a bracelet, small bells and a vessel. Iron, however, was more abundant and included socketed hoes and daggers or swords, as well as a remarkable range of animal figurines. The large, lidded mortuary vessels, often red-slipped and decorated with shell impressions, fail to strike a chord with any other assemblages on the mainland, but Solheim (1964) has stressed their similarities with the Kalanay assemblages of the Philippines.

Our knowledge of this Sa Huynh culture has expanded considerably since these early inquiries. Sites are located from just south of the Hai Van Pass to the vicinity of Saigon, over 700 km of coastline. Ngo Si Hong and Tran Quy Thinh (1991) have investigated an urnfield cemetery at Hau Xa, for example, and found the burial vessels clustered together in groups. They have ascribed them to the late Sa Huynh culture, and suggested that it developed, in the early centuries AD, into the Cham civilisation. At the southerly end of this range, Fontaine (1972) has investigated forty burial urns, set out in clusters, at Phu Hoa. Two radiocarbon dates have been obtained (1408–38 and 814–164 BC), suggesting occupation in the second half of the first millennium BC. The burial jars contained a similar range of grave goods as in the Sa Huynh area, including glass and carnelian beads and bracelets of stone, iron, glass and bronze. Both socketed and tanged iron implements were also present and slit earrings of jade. Saurin (1973) has described an urnfield cemetery at Hang Gon on the banks of the Suoi Gia Leu River which matches in many respects the discoveries at Sa Huynh itself. As with Phu Hoa, the radiocarbon dates indicate settlement in the last few centuries BC (pooled mean 400–32 BC). He encountered rows of burial urns with lids, containing much charcoal, potsherds and ornaments, but few if any human remains due, perhaps, to the local soil conditions. Many of the pots and other objects, as at Ban Don Ta Phet, had been deliberately broken as part of the burial rite. Even iron axes were found with damaged sockets. Jar 1 included stone polishers, fragments of bronze, an iron axe and beads of olivine and crystal. Jar 4 contained potsherds and an iron axe, while jar 5 included potsherds and eleven zircon beads. Other beads were made of carnelian, agate, glass and on one occasion, of gold. One burial was accompanied by an iron sword, and iron slag found in a concentration towards the southeast of the cemetery might represent the grave of a smith. This site also yielded a pendant with a double-headed animal figure.

Such a singular ornament has provided convincing evidence for contacts, of one form or another, with other parts of mainland as well as island Southeast Asia. The centre of gravity of the distribution is in the Sa Huynh area. Four are known from Sa Huynh itself and two from Phu Hoa as well as the example from Hang Gon (Loofs-Wissowa 1980–1). An example from a Dong Son context is known from Xuan An. A surface find from U-thong in Central Thailand is also known, together with the specimen from Ban Don Ta Phet. The presence of a further find in jade from Duyong Cave on Palawan Island in the Philippines strongly suggests wide-ranging maritime exchange during the second half of the first millennium BC.

This receives confirmation from the distribution of a second ornament usually rendered in a precious stone, such as jade, or glass. It is a slit earring, often known by its Philippine name, *lingling-o* (Fig. 8.5 e–g). These are also found at Sa Huynh and Phu Hoa, but their distribution exceeds that of the double-headed animal pendants, for they are also found at Lamma Island, Hong Kong, Samasama Island off Taiwan, in the Philippines at Tabon, Samrong Sen in Cambodia and in Central Thailand. Loofs-Wissowa (1980–1) has suggested that the similar ear pendants found at Lung Hoa and Dong Dau represent a Bac Bo prototype.

While these small ornaments provide evidence for exchange contacts along the coast of Vietnam and beyond, there remains a sharp contrast between the mortuary assemblages of Dong Son and Sa Huynh. Drums, bronze weapons and vessels so characteristic of the former are rare or absent in the latter. This rarity of bronzes, and their limited repertoire, is most easily understood if the Sa Huynh cemeteries represent intrusive groups from island Southeast Asia who arrived, presumably some time in the early first millennium BC without any knowledge of bronze. Iron tools and weapons, on the other hand, are rare in Bac Bo but relatively common in Sa Huynh cemeteries. Indeed, the most intriguing parallels in the mortuary ritual of Sa Huynh are to be found over the Truong Son Range in the lower Mun Valley at such sites as Ban Kan Luang. Is it possible that the Cham speakers expanded into this inland region and acquired their knowledge of iron smelting on encountering the local inhabitants? This possibility should be considered in conjunction with the most unusual stone jar burials of upland Laos, investigated by Colani (1935). These crematoria and interments probably date to this period, and attest to the expansion of Iron Age communities into the uplands of interior Southeast Asia.

The coastal tracts and eastern uplands of the Truong Son favoured by the Sa Huynh culture are relatively dry. While we know virtually nothing of the subsistence base of the Sa Huynh people, a remarkable series of stone-lined terraces in the Giao Linh uplands of Quang-Tri Province provides some intriguing possibilities (Colani 1940). Water for the rich volcanic soil was reticulated through reservoirs and channels to the terraces in integrated valley systems. These, as Wheatley (1983) has stressed, were linked with large standing stones, seats, and earth mounds of a tradition more closely linked with island than mainland Southeast Asia. By a process of elimination and in the absence of excavation, Wheatley has proposed a late prehistoric origin for these systems, which would equate them with the Sa Huynh culture. Such water control measures, if the dating is correct, would make these systems contemporaneous with the most likely dates for the intensification of agriculture through canals, moats and reservoirs in the Mekong Valley. On the other hand, Lam My Dung (1993) has recently excavated some of the wells and recovered a sample of ceramics which indicate that the system was being used between the seventh-twelfth centuries AD.

Summary

Expansion south by Austroasiatic-speaking rice farmers petered out on the northern shore of the Strait of Melaka. Intrusive agricultural communities reached the islands to the south by a different route, but probably from the same fecund source in the Yangzi Valley. These people spoke Austronesian languages, and they expanded across to Taiwan and thence through the Philippines to a new island world. We lack the archaeological evidence for large village communities so common on the mainland. These may remain to be identified, or alternatively the luxuriant tropical forest habitat might have militated against the easy establishment of rice cultivation. Nor do we have access to a large corpus of mortuary data to document social organisation. But the evidence of the Late Neolithic jar burials in the Philippines does disclose groups interested in exotic grave goods and ceramics of the highest quality.

Copper, tin, lead and iron reached the islands through a trade network which grew swiftly in the second half of the first millennium BC. This also introduced mainland drums, Indian pottery, carnelian and glass. From the Philippines to Java, we find the establishment of local casting, the adaptation of mainland forms to local tastes and the development of new varieties of bronze: finger covers, wire necklace units, arm protectors. This inception of a local bronze industry echoes the suggested origin of the mainland tradition in the context of exchange with the *zhongyuan*. Once again, the idea saw a local technological adoption and adaptation.

The expansion of Austronesian speakers ultimately brought Malay to the mainland, and there was clearly an intrusive settlement along the coast of Central Vietnam witnessed by the present and historic distribution of Cham languages. These people maintained vigorous exchange relationships with their cousins on the islands.

The intrusive movement of Austroasiatic speakers into eastern India brought rice cultivation there, it is suggested, during the third millennium BC, but the development of the local bronze industry owes little, probably nothing, to the Southeast Asian tradition. Contact between the two areas was only re-established from the later first millennium BC.

CHAPTER 9

DISCUSSION AND CONCLUSIONS

Although good documentation on the Bronze Age in Southeast Asia is unevenly distributed, we have enough information to recognise trends which, while variable regionally, contribute to a pattern. It is appreciated that further research in this area may well lead to major modifications in the sequence summarised in this book.

The expansion of rice cultivation

On the basis of the available information, rice agriculture originated in the Yangzi Valley, and through a gradual expansionary process lasting millennia, settled agricultural communities came to be established in Southeast Asia by the middle of the third millennium BC. It is confidently anticipated that similar settlements will one day be identified in the Salween and Irrawaddy valleys, while in eastern India, the same date has been identified for early rice farming communities.

In Southeast Asia, we can recognise two widespread forms of adaptation to the hot, humid tropical habitat which existed at the period of initial agricultural settlement. One involved small and mobile groups of foragers in the canopied evergreen forests. The other saw sedentary settlements on coasts only recently formed following a rise in sea level which involved a rapid and major loss of land. The nature of the societies which withdrew with the rising sea and whose settlements were inundated is unknown.

When the sea reached its maximum height and then started on a downward trend, the rich coastal habitat attracted groups versed in pottery making and the polishing of stone adze heads, but not revealing any biological evidence for agriculture. The analysis of pollen, charcoal and phytoliths from the lower Bang Pakong Valley in Central Thailand has revealed episodes of burning, increased frequencies of grass remains and plants which flourish today as invasive weeds in rice fields. These have been dated as early as the fifth millennium BC, but it is not at present possible to determine whether they result from natural or human agency.

The earliest evidence for cultivated rice in our region comes from Shixia in Lingnan, but this was only a few centuries before the settlement of Phung Nguyen, Baiyancun, Non Pa Wai and Khok Phanom Di. These sites are linked to many others in sharing pottery vessels decorated with incised curvilinear lines infilled with dentate stamping. Several workers have seen this as a universal Southeast

Asian phenomenon which reflects a major expansion of human settlement by rice cultivators who spoke Austroasiatic languages (Zide and Zide 1976, Diffloth 1991). These languages today share cognates for rice and many aspects of rice cultivation which link the Munda speakers in the west to Mon-Khmer in the east.

This interpretation should not overlook the fact that already, sedentary coastal communities long since familiar with pottery making and polished stone implements contributed to the regional establishment of rice agriculture.

Social organisation

Our knowledge of the social organisation of these Neolithic communities in Southeast Asia is slight. A large cemetery has been exposed at Khok Phanom Di, where we can identify a widespread exchange network, the manufacture of pottery vessels by skilled women, and the replacement of communal by single graves which contained the remains of exceptionally rich individuals. The skill of the potters and lapidaries of the Phung Nguyen culture is self-evident from an examination of the variety and sensitivity of their products. In Lingnan, we find equal proficiency in the manufacture of stone and ivory ornaments, while pottery was fired in the controlled atmosphere of sophisticated kilns. Both in Lingnan and Bac Bo, these groups also became familiar with jade *yazhang* blades and *ge* halberds from *zhongyuan* or Yangzi Valley sources, and by the same exchange routes came late Shang bronzes.

It was within such communities, some of which recognised exotic ornaments of shell and stone as status symbols, that the first copper-based artefacts were cast and circulated. As far as can be judged, this first took place some time between 1500–1000 BC, although it remains possible that earlier examples might be identified. We have enough information to reconstruct the extractive techniques, where casting occurred, the artefacts which were in demand and their abundance as grave offerings compared with the traditional symbols of attainment. This bronze age lasted for about a millennium, and was followed by major cultural changes.

From about 500 BC in much of lowland Southeast Asia, the small and probably autonomous bronze age communities were incorporated into hierarchic organisations which involved large, regional centres. This development varies between regions. In Central Thailand, iron was abundant, and used for weapons and tools while bronze was now converted by a technically demanding procedure into bowls turned on a lathe and intricately decorated. The hallmark of this industry was a very high admixture of tin which made casting and working so difficult as to require specialised bronze workers. The arid Khorat Plateau and Siem Reap Plain saw the development of large, moated settlements in which iron was smelted and forged, and from which salt was extracted in considerable quantities. Bac Bo was the base for a warrior aristocracy in which land ownership, bronze weapons, sumptuary vessels and drums played a prominent role in projecting status, but iron was relatively rare. On the Yunnan Plateau, the restricted lacustrine plains of the inland lakes saw intensified agriculture in the context of elaborate court societies ruled by an aristocratic elite but threatened by an expansionary state. These individuals reveal themselves in their decorated bronzes as being involved in warfare, the rituals of the agricultural round, and as recipients of surplus agricultural produce. Again, iron was rare and late.

There is no doubt that, with this wealth of information, it is possible and necessary to follow Hutterer's (1982) demand that Southeast Asia be found its place on a wider stage.

The source and transmission of Bronze Age technology

This study has not given specific consideration to the origins of bronze working and no firm conclusions are offered. It is, however, possible to propose two alternative hypotheses.

The first hypothesis is that the technology arrived from the north in the course of trade. If the chronological framework presented above is proved correct, then the initial smelting of copper in Southeast Asia is comfortably later than in the Huanghe Valley. Moreover, the presence of halberds and *yazhang* ceremonial jades in Bac Bo and Lingnan opens the possibility that goods and ideas were being exchanged between these communities and the early states of the *zhongyuan* and Yangzi Valley before local copper smelting was established. The scale of the metallurgical activity at Sanxingdui between 1700–1100 BC was so great that it would be surprising if the knowledge of the properties of copper ore did not extend into Southeast Asia. Indeed, if we follow the Austric settlement hypothesis of Blust (1993a), the Mekong, Red, Ganjiang and Xiangjiang valleys would have been a conduit for the passage of people, goods and ideas long before the Bronze Age. I have also described how some later Shang and early Western Zhou bronzes have been identified in Lingnan.

The second hypothesis is that there was an earlier and independent development of copper smelting in Southeast Asia. This would be sustained, in my view, if sites were found which beyond reasonable doubt fell within the period 2100– 1800 BC. This is, indeed, most of the date range proposed by White for the first phase incorporating bronze artefacts at the site of Ban Chiang. Her proposal, however, rests on radiocarbon dates from unsatisfactory contexts, and a new dating programme under way will, it is hoped, clarify this issue.

The first alternative would see the initial bronze industry of Southeast Asia developing in Lingnan, among the sophisticated Late Neolithic communities which were receiving goods directly or through intermediaries from the *zhong-yuan* and the Yangzi Valley. It could hardly be expected that these people, confronted with bronzes of such sophistication, would have shown any interest in casting Shang-style bells or wine vessels, since both were quite inappropriate to their needs. But as Pacey (1990) has shown, while there are occasions when there are two genuinely independent inventions in different places, there is also the alternative that, in his words,

the most important factor was that the achievements of one society stimulated people elsewhere to make different but related inventions. (Pacey 1990:vii)

He proceeds to contrast a straight transfer of technology, to 'the stimulus which can arise from the spread of knowledge or even from the mere rumour of an unfamiliar technique' (*ibid.*). Within this framework, it is argued that exposure to actual bronze imports, together with the spread of the idea that by exposing certain coloured rocks to heat, it was possible to obtain this material for alloying and casting, were stimuli to the beginning of a local industry. When the first castings were being essayed, quite naturally they were designed to fulfil local requirements. Stone axes were copied in the new medium, as were stone arrowheads, spears, bone fishhooks and stone and shell bracelets. If this interpretation is proven correct, it remains fascinating that the further dissemination of this technique should have occurred so rapidly across Southeast Asia. Doubtless, this would have been expedited by the existing networks of exchange.

I have set out the cultural and chronological framework within which such a transition could have occurred in Lingnan and Bac Bo, and suggest that to ignore this interpretation would be to set aside a large and relevant corpus of data.

The second hypothesis, involving a local and independent innovation, would place the Southeast Asian tradition alongside a handful of other such centres in the Old and New Worlds. This alternative would need to account for the remarkable coincidence that in Lingnan and Bac Bo, bronzes happened to be locally cast just as Neolithic societies were exposed to one of the most vigorous and dynamic bronze age civilisations known. As has been stressed, the viability of this hypothesis turns upon the establishment of unimpeachable evidence that bronze casting took place in some part of Southeast Asia before there was any possibility of the transfer of knowledge from the *zhongyuan* or indeed, from eastern India. To be on sure ground, this would mean a date in the later third millennium BC. I have been unable to identify such evidence anywhere in Southeast Asia. In the Chao Phraya Valley, there were a number of Neolithic communities by this juncture, as indeed there were in Yunnan and Bac Bo, and possibly in the middle Mekong Valley. Let us, however, assume that a consistent series of AMS dates from EP-III at Ban Chiang reveals evidence of bronze casting in the vicinity of 2000 BC. This would be compatible with a local, indigenous tradition of bronze casting which, presumably, would then have taken hold progressively in the Chao Phraya Valley to the west, into Bac Bo and then along the coast of Lingnan to at least the Zhujiang Estuary. There, by an extraordinary coincidence, the Shang tradition and this southern development would have arrived at about the same time: two different traditions of bronze metallurgy converged from different points of the compass.

I leave it to time and the reader's judgement to determine which of these alternatives is the more likely, but not without first asserting that I am more comfortable with a single source in the *zhongyuan* which contributed in due course to the development of a distinctive Southeast Asian tradition, appropriate to the social and technical demands of the local communities.

The social impact of bronze artefacts

Of considerably more interest is the social matrix within which copper and bronze items were accepted and used. Bronzes may be seen as emblems of status. But their availability as transferable personal property, as Renfrew (1986) has stressed, may also be a contributory factor to the development of ranking behaviour. It is now necessary to explore in more detail Muhly's (1988:16) observation that Southeast Asia in the Bronze Age is anomalous in that it fails to conform to a widespread pattern of increased social complexity.

Neolithic remains are little known, but there is now evidence that some individuals attained high rank through their personal qualities. The clearest expression of this situation comes from Khok Phanom Di, where the first ten or so generations saw burial in communal wooden structures with relatively little variation in the grave goods which accompanied men, women and the young. Following a major environmental change which restricted or ruled out access to local sources of decorative shell, we find rich individual graves. Women interred with anvils for fashioning pottery vessels were now found with considerable mortuary wealth. Some anvils were incised with what might be ownership marks. The burnishing stones found in association have flattened wear facets from long and consistent use. One woman, interred with garments encrusted with over 100,000 shell beads, would have dazzled with reflected sunlight. Another was found under a raised mortuary chamber. Here, within one site, we find a detailed mortuary record which saw the replacement of communal by individual graves and the attainment of personal rank as a legitimate social goal.

This occurred in Southeast Asia during the neolithic period. Khok Phanom Di was located in an exceptionally rich habitat, but is unlikely to have been *sui generis*. Lung Hoa, a Phung Nguyen cemetery, included deep graves needing much energy expenditure, and the quality of the pottery and stone artefacts there match those from Khok Phanom Di. Along the coast of Lingnan, and up the river valleys, there were numerous Late Neolithic sites which reveal an interest in exotic imports. On available evidence, however, Southeast Asia also saw a relatively late neolithic settlement. While there are elusive hints in pollen and phytolith cores for conflagrations which might reflect opening land to agriculture, the earliest sites belong to the early third millennium BC. Given this situation, it is considered unlikely that Neolithic or early Bronze Age sites would have been particularly large or densely distributed. This receives some confirmation in the site surveys undertaken in the Mekong Valley and Central Thailand. Bannanurag and Bamrungwongse (1991) have shown that early sites in the former area, identified on the basis of the black incised pottery, have a restricted distribution. For the Mun Valley, no Neolithic sites have been identified at all.

It is argued that this expansion down the inland river valleys by small groups would not have been a fertile context for the development of a system where rank was inherited, even if bronze were available through exchange. A common thread can be detected at Non Nok Tha, Ban Chiang, Ban Na Di and even at the rich coastal site of Khok Phanom Di. It is that early graves are poor in grave goods, particularly those made of exotic objects. The earliest mortuary phase at Khok Phanom Di could only muster a handful of shell beads between six individuals.

One variable which recurs in all the relevant mortuary assemblages is the rarity of bronze grave goods. The 1975 excavation of Ban Chiang furnished 44 Early Period inhumation graves of which only two contained bronzes. At Non Nok Tha, nine out of over 217 graves or mortuary contexts included bronze artefacts: four people each with a socketed axe, and 28 bracelets distributed between two men, two women and a child. Apart from bronze ties to repair broken stone bracelets, no bronze was found in the earliest phase of graves at Ban Na Di, and even during phases 1b-c, only seven out of 45 graves included bronzes: 27 bracelets, two anklets and a coil shared between four women, a man and two children. At Ban Prasat, a site with an extraordinary abundance of high-quality pottery grave goods and ornaments of exotic stone, only two early period graves contained bronzes: a child with seven bracelets and a man with a socketed axe. In Central Thailand, most of our information comes from Nong Nor. This site is within easy exchange contact with the Khao Wong Prachan Valley copper mines, but again, bronze grave goods were infrequent and dominated by bracelets. Of the fifty intact burials, ten people shared eighteen bracelets, and one man was buried with a few copper socketed implements. There is no evidence at any of these sites that individuals interred with bronzes were rich in terms of other grave goods. Indeed the contrary is often the case. Moreover, Nong Nor is located only 14 km south of Khok Phanom Di and would have had access to coastal resources. But no grave in this Bronze Age cemetery approaches the wealth of the richer Neolithic graves of Khok Phanom Di.

There are no comparable Bronze Age cemeteries from Yunnan or Bac Bo, but the information available shows that bronze was not often used in mortuary rituals. We have far too few occupation layers, but those available confirm that bronze artefacts are equally rare.

This might be considered surprising given the size of Non Pa Wai and the extent of crushed ore at Phu Lon. But it must be viewed in conjunction with the emerging picture of how mining and smelting were managed. Rowlands (1971), for example, has stressed the importance of seasonality in small-scale metal extraction undertaken at a time of subsistence agriculture. Nowhere is seasonality more pervasive than in mainland Southeast Asia, with its acute contrast between the wet and dry seasons, a distinction which emphasises the likely integration during prehistory between wet season rice cultivation and dry season craft activities. This contrast continues to this day. The dry season in Northeast Thailand is the time for salt extraction, pottery making, trading and house construction. The wet season is devoted to farming and preserving seasonally abundant foodstuffs.

This makes Weiss's (1992) observations on the stratigraphy of Nil Kham Haeng all the more relevant. The deep stratigraphy reveals a series of almost horizontally bedded lenses of detritus resulting from ore processing and smelting. These are most easily explained by site abandonment during the wet season and redeposition by water runoff of the residue from working the ore. Pigott and Natapintu (1988) have also suggested that the mining activity at Phu Lon was seasonal, and that people might have come to the copper source from some distance to extract and take away their supplies.

Equally intriguing is the evidence that most of the copper was locally cast into ingots, rather than finished artefacts. This runs counter to the situation in the Bronze Age of northern Europe, where early exchange in bronzes was in prestige goods. Only when bronze became abundant and commonplace, and therefore used more for utilitarian than sumptuary goods, do we encounter ingots in significant numbers (Kristiansen 1987).

Seasonal extraction and exchange in ingots harmonises with what we know of casting. From Doc Chua in the south to the Zhujiang Estuary in the north, numerous sites remote from ore sources have been found to contain bivalve moulds. Ban Na Di has yielded a small furnace, ringed by broken crucible fragments. It is reported that ingots themselves were found in the Ban Chiang region by a looter. The inhabitants of small villages, it seems, obtained their raw materials by exchange or, if suitably located, by seasonal visits to the mines. The mortuary remains from some of these sites include men interred with bivalve moulds. It is suggested that casting occurred in villages on a small scale as ingots were obtained. These would have involved both copper and tin, to judge from the composition of fragments of metal still contained within the crucibles.

Many of the artefacts copied stone or shell antecedents. Some T-sectioned bracelets match the section of those rendered in slate or marble. Fishhooks follow bone prototypes. Socketed axes were cast and used alongside versions in stone. The bronzes themselves can be divided into three categories. Ornaments predominate, including bracelets and, very rarely, beads. Axes are the most abundant of the bronze tools, although sickles are also known. Arrow and spearheads represent weapons. Of this limited range, bracelets and anklets were preferred as grave offerings, although axes and spearheads have also been found.

If the Neolithic expansion into mainland Southeast Asia took place in the third millennium BC, and the Bronze Age commenced between 1500–1000 BC, it is hard to construct a social context within which the inclusion of limited quantities of bronze could stimulate a rapid increase in social ranking. The small, autonomous communities in question settled near low-lying river flats in which rice could be cultivated, given a good monsoon. Once established, the capacity of rice to grow in regularly flooded terrain, even on poor soils, would have underwritten settlement stability, particularly when the ready availability of fish and large game is considered. The remains of these people reveal a good diet and robust strength. The universal presence of inhumation cemeteries in association with the settlements allows us to appreciate how exotic goods, such as ceramics, marine shell, stone jewellery and bronzes were used in mortuary ritual. There is some evidence at, for example, Ban Na Di, that one cluster of burials interred between about 700–500 BC contained more than their share of exotic goods. At Nong Nor and Non Nok Tha, quite large areas have been opened without any compelling evidence for a rich enclave of burials. There are hints of ranking within communities, but it was not marked, nor was it linked in any detectable way with the ownership of bronze.

The Southeast Asian Bronze Age in broader perspective

It is argued that the Bronze Age in Southeast Asia lasted no longer than a millennium before the development of centralised societies which were involved in agricultural intensification, the maintenance of craft specialists and the use of bronze to advertise the status of a social elite. Are ten centuries an unusually, or anomalously long time before such trends manifest themselves? Let us consider events in other areas, beginning with that closest to hand, the Huanghe Valley.

Comparison with the Huanghe valley

In contrast to Southeast Asia, bronze was first used within complex Neolithic communities which had proliferated over many millennia. By the time that bronze became available, status differences in the cemeteries were widespread and recognised in the provision of jades and high quality ceramics which strongly suggest the maintenance of specialist producers. The Machang phase in the Liuwan cemetery, for example, includes some outstandingly rich graves and others with virtually no grave goods within the period 2400–2000 BC. At that juncture, metal was appearing with some regularity in the Huanghe Valley, but not in abundance. Qijia culture sites in Gansu, for example, have been dated between 2300–1800 BC. The excavation of the Qinweijia cemetery has revealed 128 graves, including stone adzeheads, pottery vessels and pigs' mandibles. Associated storage pits contain a few copper and bronze artefacts: an axe, a ring and a disc. Dahezhuang has provided a mortuary sample of 82 graves, none with metal artefacts, but a copper item, possibly a knife, was found in one of the village houses. Huangniangniangtai has furnished a sample of 32 copper-based artefacts, including knives, awls, chisels and a ring. A few were found in graves.

Further down the Huanghe Valley, we encounter large walled settlements which date to the last few centuries of the third millennium BC. Pingliangtai covers over 5 ha with a set of inner walls and a sophisticated drainage system. The only evidence for bronze is a pit containing verdigris-like dust. Wangchenggang, another walled centre, yielded only one item of bronze, possibly a vessel fragment. Taosi covers about 300 ha. Over 1500 graves have been uncovered. Some rich graves contain up to 200 offerings, including jades and even wooden drums and music stones, described as royal symbols in early Chinese texts. One bronze item, a bell, was found.

The proliferation of bronzes in a Huanghe context came at Erlitou, which was initially settled about 1900 BC. Stage I–II bronzes were rare, but by the third stage, we encounter palaces, city walls, a bronze-working atelier and a cemetery including elite burials in painted coffins with bronze vessels, halberds and a battleaxe.

It seems that the properties of copper and bronze were known among socially sophisticated groups in the Huanghe Valley by at least the last few centuries of the third millennium BC, and possibly much earlier still. Yet many centuries were to pass before the social elites represented at Erlitou began to control specialists and demand the production of sumptuary bronzes. If such a time interval is to be found in this densely settled and competitive social milieu, is it surprising to encounter the passage of up to a millennium before corresponding trends were manifested in the small, scattered Bronze Age communities of Southeast Asia?

Comparison with Mesopotamia

The lowlands of Mesopotamia offer interesting parallels with Southeast Asia, in that extensive alluvial lowlands are juxtaposed with highlands rich in ore sources. Tin, however, is very scarce. Smelting technology in Mesopotamia followed a long period during which native copper was converted into small tools or ornaments. The earliest evidence for copper smelting comes from northern Mesopotamia during the sixth millennium BC. Copper rings and bracelets and a lead bracelet have been found at Yarim Tepe in conjunction with malachite ore (Moorey 1988). Merpert and Munchaev (1982) have shown that the artefacts come from smelted, not native, copper. Moorey has also emphasised that this metal industry was contemporaneous with a sophisticated pottery tradition involving kiln firing. He has described the ensuing millennia up to 3500 BC as a period of trinket technology. Copper objects were rare in small agricultural communities and even by the early fourth millennium, no metal items were found at Eridu or Ur despite the excavation of 193 and 50 graves respectively. Turquoise and lapis lazuli, both of distant origin, served to denote high status.

The situation changed dramatically from the mid fourth millennium. As in the Huanghe Valley, the quantity of metal, range of artefacts and alloys and concentration of specialist skills took place in the context of large, defended settlements. These provide convincing evidence for marked social differentiation and rivalry between competing centres. As Moorey (1988:30) has emphasised, these developments in metal working to incorporate craft specialists took place after a major social change involving the development of social elites. The sequel was the casting of complex ornaments, tools and armour, daggers and axeheads some of which were placed with the dead. It was a period of innovation which saw the development of the lost wax casting technique and experimentation with alloys of copper and arsenic, lead and tin.

The properties of metal, particularly copper and lead, were known in Mesopotamia for millennia before competing social elites chose bronze as a means of increasing their power and status. Again, we find similarities in the Southeast Asian sequence.

Comparison with Iberia

Gilman (1987) has examined the cultural sequence in two areas of the Iberian Peninsula: the Tagus Estuary and Almeria. The former is better watered and has more fertile soils, the latter suffers from aridity. Both sustained vigorous communities ascribed to the copper age and dating between 3500–2250 BC. The best known of these, the cemetery and fortified settlement of Los Millares, includes collective tombs some of which were relatively richer and located close to the walls of the settlement. The nature of the collective burial rite rules out consideration of the relationship between burial offerings and individuals, but the former included utilitarian, ritual and prestige goods: ivory, ostrich egg shell, amber, jet and copper (Chapman 1981). The copper artefacts comprise awls, flat axes and daggers. The sites in the Tagus area also include defended sites, collective burials and a common range of copper artefacts. As in Bronze Age Southeast Asia, copper was cast within settlements. There is no evidence for specialisation, and Chapman (1982) has stressed that copper casting was essentially a part-time activity.

In Almeria, this copper age was succeeded towards the end of the third millennium by the El Argar culture. This saw the establishment of new settlements on easily defended hilltops, a preference for individual graves and the inclusion as grave goods of silver and bronze jewellery and bronze weapons. Some graves were markedly richer than others, although bronze was not abundant. At El Argar, bronzes from 1200 graves weighed only 34 kg, half that of a single Dong Son drum. Gilman (1987:23) sees the variation in grave goods as a reflection of increased wealth and class distinctions. Chapman (1982) has noted that this period also saw the opening of new, higher-altitude copper mines and a greater range and abundance of bronzes, although bronze was not abundant (Gilman 1991). Copper, he claims, had become a status indicator. Yet, there is no equivalent to the Argaric bronze age in the well-watered Tagus area.

Gilman has explained this as a reaction, at least in part, to the development of agricultural intensification through the provision of irrigation works in the arid zone of Almeria. The emergent elites were, therefore, able to derive more commodities from the producers and use these to underwrite warfare, maintain specialists and display prestigious goods to indicate their status. Irrigation was unnecessary in the vicinity of the Tagus Estuary, and there, the old traditions were maintained.

Comparison with the Eastern Mediterranean

The Eastern Mediterranean, and particularly the mainland and islands of Greece, provides most important comparative information. Renfrew (1972) has outlined a sequence and identified significant aspects of metal working which are almost precisely mirrored in Southeast Asia. The metallurgical revolution, he noted, took a very long time. At Sitagroi, copper beads were worn in a final Neolithic context during phase II followed by the local casting of pins and awls. These contexts belong to the early fourth millennium BC, and are widely paralleled in other parts of Greece. Copper axes, for example, have been recovered from Sesklo in Thessaly and Knossos on Crete. Emborio on Chios has provided needles, a fishhook, and an awl. The first tin bronze artefacts appeared during phase V at Sitagroi, which represents the Early Bronze Age 1 period (3200–2700 BC), but still bronzes were relatively rare and restricted in form.

The major change in bronze working came with Early Bronze Age 2 (2700–2100 BC), with new casting skills and an expanded range of artefacts. More complex castings in bivalve moulds and by the lost wax technique were produced, riveting was undertaken and bowls were formed from sheets of metal. Daggers and spearheads show how these new skills were turned to the requirements of warfare. A new range of tools was produced, including axes, chisels, knives, gouges and awls. It is perhaps not coincidental that this period also saw a quickening of international trade through the medium of improved boat building. Ornaments and toilet articles, such as tweezers and scrapers, show a concern for personal appearance and a new range of bowls, buckets and drinking vessels indicate that elite feasting was now a necessary part of court life. Renfrew's summary of this situation is that:

In discussing the origins of metallurgy in the Aegean it has now to be conceded that the basic techniques were long known, perhaps for more than a millennium, before the great expansion during the Early Bronze Age 2 period. (Renfrew 1972:311)

This situation is echoed in Southeast Asia. Again, we encounter a Bronze Age which lasted a millennium before a rapid change which saw bronze being used in warfare, for personal ornamentation and in feasting and ritual. The argument that the Bronze Age of Southeast Asia is anomalous is rejected. This is necessary for at least two reasons. The Bronze Age lasted for a far shorter span than has been suggested on the basis of dates from Non Nok Tha and Ban Chiang. The application of a protocol for chronometric hygiene and availability of AMS dates rather indicates that the Bronze Age lasted no more than a millennium before the development of elites within societies whose members employed bronze, among other prestige goods, as a means to indicate and augment their status. In several comparative cases, we have encountered similar, often longer, periods when bronzes were cast in less complex societies before the first signs of hereditary elites and craft specialisation.

Social hierarchies in Bronze Age society

It is now necessary to return to Muhly's (1988:16) concern that:

In all other corners of the Bronze Age world — China, Mesopotamia, Anatolia, the Aegean and Central Europe — we find the introduction of bronze metallurgy associated with the 'rise of the state'. Only in Southeast Asia, especially in Thailand and Vietnam, do these developments seem to be missing ...

The term 'rise of the state' is unfortunate. There is no evidence for this development to my knowledge in Central Europe, nor in Southern Spain. It would be more appropriate to substitute the term 'development of social hierarchies'. If this is accepted, then Thailand and Vietnam should be added to the list for, as has been shown, this development took place in Southeast Asia from the mid first millennium BC.

General theories

In their review of causes for the development of complex societies, Brumfiel and Earle (1987) considered a number of explanatory approaches subsequently weighed in the context of Polynesian, American, African and East Asian societies. Essentially, they and their associates were seeking explanations for the very changes which have been isolated above. To what extent do the transitions to complex societies in Southeast Asia reveal similarities, or differences?

They first considered a commercial development model, the essence of which is that increasing complexity results from the stimulus of growing economic activity without continuous and intentional direction from emerging elites. Under this model, for example, specialised activities, new exchange links and more efficient production interact with each other in favour of a more complex social organisation. One product of such a process of increasing commercial activity, therefore, is the establishment of managerial elites.

In the adaptationist model, the order is reversed and the seminal role of political elites is stressed. Particularly where essential resources are scattered, elite organisation of exchange in order to make, for example, salt, rice or dried fish available where needed, not only ensures the wellbeing of dependent communities, but also serves to augment the status of the elite themselves. The diversion of a proportion of the goods being exchanged could then be used to sustain the central court and its functionaries, among which are numbered a new class of full-time craft specialists. It is from their workshops that the prestige symbols, the new weaponry and sumptuary goods originated. In Southeast Asia, this could involve a lowland area where rice can be cultivated in association with uplands rich in stone or ore. Specialisation in each, and the exchange of products, might again be best undertaken through the medium of non-producing managers, whose reward lies in an elevated position in the hierarchy. The construction of moats around the settlements as a buffer against environmental unpredictability, or the maintenance of specialist bronze workers, could be permitted under this system.

Brumfiel and Earle considered this model in the context of the Inka state and Hawaiian chiefdoms, and found that it was not satisfactory. Regional differences can be offset by a society integrating different environments within their territory, and the leaders, rather than managing transactions in bulky primary products, rather took for themselves a proportion of the subsistence goods and zealously guarded access to critical raw materials, such as feathers and copper, and the specialists able to convert them into status symbols. The control of water reticulation can result from local cooperation without the presence of a managerial class.

The political model turns elites from benefactors of the population at large to a self-serving minority working to maintain and strengthen their position. Its essence lies in the appropriation of goods by political leaders, and the exercise of control over the raw materials which specialists convert into the very goods which confer status, and therefore inequality. Through the control and direction of craft production, it becomes possible to restrict access to certain strategic goods, such as feathers, jade, or bronze and the ornaments or the weapons manufactured from them. Where the population is growing in a restricted area, the development of status rivalry between different polities adds its own dynamic to this procedure. So, too, would pressure from a more powerful and predatory group.

At ground level, this model may be illustrated in the control of the West African slave trade, where chiefs organised a supply of export slaves in exchange for a new range of exotic prestige goods, such as firearms. Restricted ownership of ore or salt deposits, or the best agricultural land, is a second factor. A monopoly over the sacred symbolic objects which confer power is a third.

Choosing the right model

It might well be asked how a prehistorian can consider the respective merits of these models, which include such abstruse variables as motive and intent, on the basis of the available data. In order to clarify this difficult issue, Brumfiel and Earle (1987:4) have considered three areas of activity.

The first concerns the goods subject to production and exchange. While recognising that these comprise a continuum, they also identify two major divisions. The first incorporates subsistence goods necessary for any group to maintain itself. In Southeast Asia, this centres on rice, fish and the salt needed to preserve the latter for dry season consumption. The appropriation of these foodstuffs by the elite are, naturally, essential for them to maintain themselves and their followers. The second class comprises goods which denote wealth and prestige. Many possible examples of these have been identified in the preceding chapters. Exotic bronze, shell and stone jewellery and beautiful pottery vessels appear early in the sequence. But we can also recognise a major change when the range and quality of such items increased, particularly in the assemblage of bronzes. Where the early repertoire was dominated by simple bracelets, the later one included sophisticated weaponry, armour, musical instruments, drinking vessels and highly-ornamented jewellery. These came at about the same time as expanded exchange in objects of remote origin, such as glass, carnelian, cowries and agate from India and Chinese coinage, mirrors, sumptuary vessels and weapons.

The second area of activity involves the circumstances under which artefacts were produced and centres on the contrast between what Brumfiel and Earle describe as independent and attached specialists. How, for example, did the organisation of copper mining, exchange and casting develop over time? Is it possible to identify a pattern in which ore sources came under the central charge of elites, who maintained a tight control over craft specialists and their products?

This variable integrates with the third, and central, area of activity: the manner in which the elites established and maintained themselves. It is self evident that they must divert a proportion of subsistence production to the needs of themselves and their court. In very large and complex polities, the redistribution of bulky foodstuffs presents considerable logistic problems and might be avoided by the payment of valuables to retainers with which individual subsistence goods could be purchased. But the scale of the societies we are dealing with in Southeast Asia was much smaller, and the deployment of subsistence goods, or staple finance, is not seen as a major issue. Wealth finance, that is the extraction and control over status symbols, however, is of critical concern.

Brumfiel and Earle have identified two different ways in which wealth finance might operate. The first involves the distribution of status objects down the social ladder in return for loyalty. This leads to their widespread occurrence within the community. The second, identified in Bronze Age Scandinavia with particular clarity by Kristiansen (1987), took the opposite course of restricting the circulation of prestige goods to the small upper echelon of society, the members of which used them to advertise their high status. He particularly emphasised the importance of bronze weapons in such a competitive social milieu.

Social hierarchies in Southeast Asia

The key variables outlined above must now be weighed within a Southeast Asian context. The area is extensive and there are regional differences. The environment, for example, is greatly influenced by the monsoon. The Khorat Plateau, Tonle Sap Plains and western margins of Central Thailand suffer a particularly long dry season, and rainfall during the wet season is unpredictable. Bac Bo and the Yunnan Plateau, by contrast, are better watered. Coastal settlement is less prone to the impact of the monsoon, because most marine resources are unaffected by it.

Rice: the key to subsistence

Annual wild rice is a marsh plant which responds to the monsoon climate by a period of rapid growth and seeding in the wet season and dormancy during the dry. It also derives nutrients from water rather than the soil. Unlike seed agriculture in the Near East or Europe, therefore, soil exhaustion and field rotation are not issues where rice is grown in naturally marshy habitats. This is exactly the situation preferred by the earliest known agricultural communities in Southeast Asia. Wherever possible, they occupied slightly elevated situations near low-lying land where flooding was predictable and within which rice would flourish. The stability of settlements over several centuries was, it is argued, underwritten by this regime, which was integrated with the maintenance of domestic pigs and cattle, much fishing and collecting, as well as trapping and hunting. It is very difficult to conceive of a situation, even in the dry interior, giving rise to a shortage of food. The condition of the human remains reveals a well fed population. This does not diminish the importance of adapting to the monsoon. Where the dry season is long, the preservation of wet season surpluses is encouraged. Rice is readily stored. Fish can be preserved with salt, or sun dried.

The heavy rains encourage vigorous plant growth and the difficulty of travel overland is a recurrent theme in the reports of early European explorers (Casteleyn 1669, Bock 1883). Communication by river is much quicker, and boats can carry weighty goods as well as many people. This is one reason why the component parts of Southeast Asia considered above are determined by rivers rather than modern political divisions. The strategic significance of rivers for settlement expansion and the spread of new ideas and goods is integral to any review of cultural change.

It has been argued that the occupation of interior Southeast Asia by agriculturalists came late in the prehistoric period. There is no acceptable archaeological evidence for the expansion of agricultural communities much before 2800 BC, and most of the Khorat Plateau seems to have been unoccupied before 1500 BC. A lesson we learn from the available cemeteries is that infant mortality was high. At Khok Phanom Di, over half of early graves belong to infants. This situation, it is argued, diminishes the likely relevance of population pressure as a variable significant to the development of social complexity. This point has been cogently argued by Welch (1985). However, it must also be noted that the terrain suited to rice cultivation in naturally flooded swamplands is circumscribed. When villages grew beyond a certain population threshold, shortages of critical resources could have been felt. Foremost is water during the dry season. Again, a population measured in thousands would almost certainly have difficulty producing sufficient rice in its immediate environs without some form of agricultural innovation. This could take the form of water reticulation from reservoirs, or the conversion of land too dry under normal circumstances to the swampy conditions of the rice field. The latter is achieved today by building low bunds to retain rainwater where it falls (Fig. 9.1). The use of the plough and animal traction is a third means of intensifying rice production. The managed landscape seen today in much of lowland Southeast Asia might be a product of the last century, but it involves many innovations each of which has contributed to the stability of human settlement.

The uplands between the major river valleys ensured distinct patterns of

9.1 The lacustrine plain between Shizhaishan and Lake Dian illustrates the intensive system of rice agriculture, whereby low bunds are raised to retain rainwater where it falls.

exposure to alien expansion into Southeast Asia. Two and a half millennia ago, the vast majority of the population would have spoken an Austroasiatic language, with an enclave of Austronesian speakers in coastal Vietnam. Since then, the region has seen intensive settlement, nowhere more so than in Lingnan, Yunnan and Bac Bo. When reviewing the development of social complexity, it is necessary to stress warfare, particularly in those groups whose independence was threatened by imperial ambitions. The Mekong Valley, coastal Vietnam and Central Thailand, while distanced from immediate threat, were exposed to the more subtle impact of exchange in exotic goods with India and island Southeast Asia. A strategic location in this network would have opened new opportunities.

Social development in Lingnan

This area provides one of the best documented sequences in Southeast Asia. It has been argued that the coastal sites described as Coastal Neolithic represent affluent coastal foraging and fishing communities. The initial settlement by agricultural groups resulted from intrusive expansion from the Yangzi Valley, dating to about 2800 BC. Agriculture was thereafter established widely and many of these Late Neolithic communities developed considerable expertise in the controlled firing of pottery vessels as well as the manufacture of stone ornaments. Some of their products were used as mortuary offerings. The progressive expansion in exchange which incorporated the early states of the *zhongyuan* and Yangzi Valley saw exotic jades and bronzes reaching Lingnan during the middle to late second millennium BC, and by 1300 BC, a local bronze industry was in being. This could have originated in local technological innovation resulting from exposure to the presence, and the knowledge, of exotic bronzes. As the first millennium BC proceeded, the demands of the Chu state in the mid Yangzi Valley for tropical products opened opportunities for the local leaders to control the flow of goods, and we encounter increasingly rich burials in favourable settings for agriculture and exchange. During the fourth century BC, iron was introduced, and at Yinshanling we find that rich graves contain Chu imports, animal-headed staffs thought to symbolise high status, and many bronze weapons. They were larger than poorer contemporary graves. Men and women were provided with different sets of grave goods, but both are found in the larger graves. No evidence has been found for the reservation of a distinct area for these rich interments, however.

Social development in the Yunnan Plateau

During the Neolithic period in Yunnan, mortuary rituals followed a widespread practice of interment in clusters without marked differentiation between individuals in terms of grave goods. The early graves of Tazaijinshan suggest continuity, and few bronzes were present. While there are tantalisingly few sites corresponding to the Bronze Age in Central Thailand or the Mekong Valley, it is evident that major social changes were underway in the lacustrine plains of the Yunnan Plateau from 500 BC. It is important in considering the plateau, to recall that land suited to rice cultivation is restricted by forested uplands, a situation which would emphasise the importance of controlling the lakes and their margins. The Yunnan Plateau, according to Chinese accounts, supported many competing chiefdoms. These have been investigated through the excavation of a series of cemeteries.

The bronze sarcophagus from Dabona illustrates an important development widespread in Lingnan and Yunnan. The dead were now interred in individual graves, some of considerable size and opulence. The elaborately decorated Dabona bronze coffin, for example, weighed 257.1 kg. The cemetery of Shizhaishan also illustrates how the members of the elite were not only provided with individual graves, but were set apart in a royal necropolis located on a prominent hill commanding the surrounding plain. Much energy was devoted to the graves. They were large, insulated against damp and provided with a wooden platform of lacquered timbers. The coffins were also lacquered and painted. Lijiashan is a second hilltop necropolis, but Tianzimao provides a significant contrast. Although there are one or two central graves which rival in opulence those from Shizhaishan, there are also many ordinary ones containing few grave goods.

The contents of the royal graves allow a consideration of staple and wealth finance, specialisation and exchange in the Dian polity. Members of the elite were buried with a remarkable array of goods notable by their absence in the poorer provincial cemeteries. Bronzes predominate, and can be divided into a number of categories. Of particular significance are a number of ceremonial staffs held by bronze figures, which Tong Enzheng (1991) has interpreted as symbols of office. A series of bronze vessels, which were used in feasting, bronze headrests and a bronze altar as well as musical instruments, particularly drums and panpipes, represent the ceremonial paraphernalia of this elite group. The bronze containers filled with cowrie shells provide direct evidence for the accumulation of wealth.

Much attention was given to weaponry, not only for functional purposes, but also for display. Armour was intricately decorated, shields were ornamented, horse harness was elaborated beyond basic needs. A novel range of aristocratic weaponry is encountered: bronze quivers, maces and crossbows. When iron became available during the second century BC, swords with bronze hilts were sheathed in decorated golden scabbards. Battle scenes reveal gilded elite warriors on horseback, while their followers fought on foot. But it is important to note that the latter were also equipped with bronze weaponry, albeit less elaborate. Warfare was also conducted by boat. The size of the craft represented on the drums suggests considerable, quite probably specialised, skill on the part of boat builders.

The elite were interred with agricultural implements, suggesting an interest in agricultural production. Von Dewall (1988) has stressed the ubiquity of cattle remains or figurines in the elite graves, and it is considered highly likely that cattle and cavalry horses were a major means of accumulating wealth. Feasting scenes show joints of beef and pork laid out, and there are ornaments which suggest that cattle raiding was undertaken in association with conflict. Heavy bronze hoes or ploughshares, spades and sickles represent a substantial investment in rice production. This concern finds confirmation in models showing elite participation in agricultural rituals involving spring sowing and the autumn harvest. These were presided over by aristocratic women, who arrived borne high on sedan chairs. One scene shows the accumulation of rice in a central repository. Another includes the offering of food to a gilded woman, and many house scenes show feasting in progress. Feasting also took place during a probable alliance ceremony, while elites also participated in the hunt.

The appropriation of surplus agricultural production sustained the elite, but a review of Dian technology suggests the presence of attached, full-time specialists. This is seen in the quality of the artefacts, and the expertise necessary in their manufacture. We do not have any knowledge of the organisation of copper ore mining, but the contemporary mines of Tongshiling and Tonglüshan to the northeast saw an investment in extractive facilities and a scale of operation far greater than at Phu Lon or Nil Kham Haeng. It is likely too that metal was used in long-distance exchange. The concentration on symbols of status occurred in conjunction with the development of gold amalgam gilding, gold repoussé work and gold and silver inlaying. Specialists were not confined to working in bronze or other metals. Elite ornaments were also made of jade, turquoise and agate.

Much of this specialist production was dedicated to symbols of high status. But the elites also armed their followers, and it is at provincial cemeteries that we find the men interred with ordinary weapons and women with the ceramic spindle whorls which provide such a sharp contrast with the splendid bronze weaving implements from Lijiashan.

The cemeteries of Shizhaishan and Lijiashan are sufficiently extensive to support the conclusion that a line or lines of aristocratic rulers prospered for centuries. When compared with provincial cemeteries, we can judge that the elite were able to monopolise access to a range of high status ornaments, weapons and utensils and musical instruments of bronze, but also including gold, silver, cowrie shells and semi-precious stone. There is no indication that such symbols were transmitted vertically as a means of attracting followers, other than equipping them with a limited set of bronze weapons. Many of the artefacts reflect specialist production. We have no knowledge of where settlements or workshops were located or organised, but it is hard not to visualise attached specialists, especially when we consider the interest shown by the elite in food production. This took at least two forms. Bronze agricultural implements were produced, and elites directed the necessary agricultural rituals. If Tong Enzheng is correct in his interpretations, some of the rice harvest was centrally stored.

Muhly (1988) has identified Southeast Asia as anomalous due to the lack of developing social complexity in societies which exploited the qualities of bronze. The Dian polity illustrates the opposite. Bronze may have contributed to the development of status differences; it was certainly used to reflect them.

Social development in Bac Bo

The rise of complex societies in Bac Bo, which took place contemporaneously with that in Lingnan and on the Yunnan Plateau, occurred in a constrained river plain flanked on three sides by precipitous uplands and by the sea on the other. In many respects, the situation is similar to Dian, but with a distinct local flavour and less concentrated wealth in elite burials. It is possible that graves similar to those from Shizhaishan lie concealed within the ramparts of Co Loa, but on present evidence, the richest assemblages come from Viet Khe and Dong Son. Again, bronzes predominate, and show a social demand for sumptuary vessels. The Viet Khe and Chau Can cemeteries also reveal a trend in favour of individual rather than collective burial ritual. At Lang Ca, we hear of a concentration of bronzes in an enclave of the cemetery, and a considerable rarity in the majority of other graves. Yet several characteristics of the Dian polity are absent. There is no evidence for the use of the horse. Bimetallic items are very rare, and there are fewer Chinese imports.

Nevertheless, Dong Son elites showed an interest in high-status bronzes represented by drums, drinking vessels, body plaques, the range of decorated weapons and heavy bronze hoes or ploughshares. The casting of drums as large and complex as those from Co Loa or Ngoc Lu could only have been achieved by specialists. The scenes portray elite activities: a procession of feathered warriors, a musical group which includes a row of drums and elegant, richly-decorated watercraft. One recurrent scene shows the processing of rice.

Again, therefore, it is possible to detect parallels with Dian, for similar bronze hoes or ploughshares were cast in Bac Bo, and according to surviving texts, the Dong Son elite, following a period of annexation by the Chinese, were confirmed in their ownership of high-grade land. This, it is further noted, took advantage of the tidal flows in the management of water. Is this a further example of the elites' concern for the necessary rice surpluses to sustain themselves and their followers and their tied specialists?

Social development in Central Thailand and the Mekong Valley

In Lingnan, Yunnan and Bac Bo, most weapons and tools were made of bronze. Iron was rare and relatively late, a situation which should be considered in conjunction with a contemporary Chinese edict against its export to southern barbarians. This contrasts with the situation in Central Thailand and the Mekong Valley, where the same period saw an abundance of iron and less enthusiasm for bronze other than for ornaments or vessels. The Khorat Plateau is also particularly dry, and events there during the Iron Age differ markedly from those just described. There is an abundance of settlement data, but there has been no extensive exposure of a single cemetery. The former situation is explained by the visibility of moated sites from the air, the moats being a response to the extent and intensity of the dry season. Once settlements reach a certain population threshold, the provision of dry season resources, particularly water and rice, is accentuated. We are still unsure of the dating of the moats, but the consensus is that some, if not all, belong to the Iron Age, and this will be assumed in the following discussion.

In the middle Chi Valley, the large moated site of Ban Chiang Hian was located in an advantageous position to take advantage of the flat terrain south of the river. The moats were designed to receive water from a feeder stream, and distribute it north to the presumed rice fields. While the moats might well have had defensive properties, they were also built for water control. There are several smaller, unmoated sites near Ban Chiang Hian, and it is possible that this and related sites were regional centres, occupied by a social elite.

As one proceeds to the drier Mun Valley, the contrast between large moated and smaller, presumably dependent villages, loses clarity for there are also many quite small sites ringed by moats. However, these have a number of common features. They are, for example, associated with iron smelting. Some are also located to take advantage of salt deposits, which were consistently exploited from at least the Iron Age. Excavations at Non Yang have encountered possible rice stores and defensive structures. The moated sites also contain cemeteries.

Few cemeteries are known, and none has been extensively examined. Nevertheless, there is no hint of the same level of individual wealth, concern with weaponry and provision of ritual vessels or drums as has been documented in

Yunnan or even Bac Bo. The few graves excavated at Ban Don Phlong indicate aspects of continuity with earlier traditions seen at Ban Prasat and the Sakon Nakhon Basin Bronze Age sites, as well as some changes. Individuals were interred in a group, and there was still a preference for bronze bracelets. These were now much larger, and richly decorated. Finger and toe rings are an innovation. There are also exotic beads of glass and agate, and graves were prepared with clay-lined walls and split tree trunks for coffins. The same is true of the later graves of Ban Prasat, where bangles, anklets and finger rings predominated, and one person was interred with a complex bronze head ornament. Large, decorated bangles, anklets and rings recur at Ban Kan Luang, although two bronze spearheads, an iron arrowhead and part of a sword blade were also present. The Iron Age graves at Ban Chiang include glass beads, a bronze necklace with a very high proportion of tin, but little if any bronze or iron weaponry. The principal grave offering, which might compensate for the poverty of these graves when compared with their contemporaries to the north and northeast, is an elaborately decorated red-on-buff painted pottery.

During the Iron Age, the occupants of the Khorat Plateau showed little interest in the conversion of bronze into objects of high prestige or of a range of weapons comparable to those found in Yunnan or Bac Bo. The few drums found probably came by exchange down the Mekong River route, there are few vessels, and weapons are rare. Yet some moated sites were of considerable extent, and probably harboured populations in four figures. The virtually ubiquitous evidence for iron smelting may, of course, have been directed in part towards forging weapons which were not selected as grave offerings. Even if this was the case, there is still a lack of the high status bronzes we have encountered in Bac Bo and Yunnan.

There may be several reasons for this situation. Dong Son and Shizhaishan are located in physically constrained areas where alluvial land is at a premium. Both were exposed to competition and strife, ultimately manifested in a predatory state. In both areas, rice cultivation was intensified through new metal technology. The environment of the Chi and Mun valleys is more open. If original settlement does belong to the second and early first millennia BC, there would have been little time for marked population growth to place a pressure on resources. Even if it did, there was still the option of moving to the middle terraces, where indeed we encounter the establishment of several moated sites. Welch (1985) has made the important point that the moats may have been a response to environmental unpredictability in this arid zone. Chantaratiyakarn (1984) has concluded that much labour was necessary to complete the earthworks at Ban Chiang Hian, a procedure doubtless expedited with iron tools. Was it necessary for an organisational elite to be in place to direct such engineering works? Cooperative endeavour during the dry season without central direction is an alternative, a situation mirrored in the current organisation of salt extraction at Bo Phan Khan.

There is insufficient archaeological evidence to weigh these alternatives judiciously. Extensive excavations are necessary in order to evaluate the social dimensions associated with the large, moated sites. Our understanding would be greatly improved, for example, if an Iron Age cemetery within a large moated site were found to contain a lobe set apart for an elite group. It would be instructive if we could find that carnelian, glass and agate beads had a restricted distribution which concentrated in the large moated sites at the expense of smaller, dependent settlements. We know that at Non Yang, there were ditches and palisades. What area did they demarcate? Did they, for example, ring a central area of rice stores, or a distinctively large domestic residence? Is it possible that the ubiquity of iron ore lessened competition for sources of metal? Again, the Khorat Plateau was not exposed to early and direct exchange contact with Indians.

The Khorat Plateau was, and remains, isolated from events and trends in the metropolitan delta areas. During the Iron Age, the populations in some settlements grew and the provision of water and, perhaps, defence, led to moat construction. It is likely that this occurred in conjunction with the development of social elites, the members of which sought restricted ownership of vital resources: iron ore, salt, timber, exotic new exchange goods. But this possibility is posed with the proviso that it exists to be tested.

The dating of the few possibly early moated sites in Central Thailand is also unclear, but two cemetery sites provide marked contrasts to their contemporaries on the Khorat Plateau. The lower plains of the Chao Phraya Valley are strategically placed to participate in coastal exchange activity and we know already from Khok Phanom Di that social inequalities were manifested here even during the Neolithic period. Later evidence from Nil Kham Haeng confirms this, in the presence of tree coffins and manufacture of projectile points.

Ban Don Ta Phet is a critically important site in considering the Iron Age in this area, because it incorporates rows of rich individual graves. The ditched enclosure might well have been intended to demarcate an elite cemetery, but excavation to identify the corresponding poorer graves would be necessary to confirm this. In any event, those buried were associated with a new range of exotic goods, access to which would have been facilitated by the site's proximity to the eastern gates of the Three Pagodas Pass. Some of the carnelian and agate jewellery, found in such profusion, originated in India. The inhabitants clearly separated the roles of iron and bronze. The former was forged into tools and weapons. The hoes and billhooks would have assisted in agriculture. Spears and arrowheads were the preferred weapons. Bronze, on the other hand, was converted into ornaments and vessels. Bracelets, anklets and rings predominate, but there was also an interest in vessels which required considerable, surely specialised, skill to shape and decorate. These high tin bronze receptacles represent a local workshop tradition, some products of which seem to have interested Indian traders, for examples have been found in India itself.

Ban Don Ta Phet has also yielded a bronze situla and an animal-head pendant with close parallels in Dong Son and Sa Huynh contexts. In this, the site is similar to Tham Ongbah, where six exotic bronze drums were associated with a cemetery of wooden coffins. These, as far as has been possible to reconstruct the situation before looting, contained bronze ornaments and vessels, strings of glass and stone beads and iron weapons and tools. Sørensen (1988) has also suggested that a contemporary group of graves without wooden coffins represents the non-elite segment of society. They were found with iron tools and weapons which belong to the same tradition as that of Ban Don Ta Phet.

At least on the western margins of Central Thailand, therefore, it is possible to identify trends which recall those seen in Bac Bo and Dian. Metal, in this case iron, was used to improve the efficiency of agriculture, though we meet no evidence for ploughing. Iron weapons were also used, while bronze was preferred for ornaments and vessels which represent a far greater level of expertise than has been documented for the preceding millennium. This took place at a time when a new range of exotic goods became available and exchange opened with remote sources. The presence of a rudder on one of the boats represented on a drum from Ongbah hints at maritime transport, and this is convincingly confirmed by the distribution of ornaments in exotic stone, and high status bronzes of mainland inspiration, in island Southeast Asia. Indeed, it was at this period that the communities in the islands were first acquainted with bronze.

Central Thailand has now provided us with evidence with counters Bronson's early suggestion that the societies there lived in 'almost hermetic isolation from one another' (Bronson 1979:320). On the contrary, it was a period of burgeoning international exchange and innovation in bronze and iron technology, one in which we can again recognise the presence of social elites.

There is also compelling evidence for the settlement of the coastal plains of Vietnam from an island source. The Sa Huynh sites, with their novel method of jar burial, represent an alien tradition, and when the area entered the historic period, we encounter an enclave of Austronesian speakers at the eastern extremity of an area in which Austroasiatic languages were spoken from Bac Bo to eastern India.

The sequel

Southeast Asia passed from prehistory into the historic period during the first few centuries of the first millennium AD. Historic sources incorporate contemporary accounts and a corpus of inscriptions, the analysis of which has tended to impose a watershed between historic societies and their predecessors. This is particularly to be found in the syntheses of Coedès (1968), whose principal thesis was that Indian mercantile contact brought civilisation within reach of simple Neolithic villagers.

This view has long been superseded, and it is now possible to appreciate how local elites took advantage of the opportunities provided by long distance trade in order to increase their social standing and control. In the context of this trend, we can further examine how the early and recent Southeast Asian states find their roots in the prehistoric past.

This subject is related to but not part of the purpose of this study, and has been treated in detail elsewhere (Wheatley 1983, Hall 1985, Higham 1989, Taylor 1991). A summary of the principal points, however, clarifies and places into their proper perspective the social changes which occurred during the Bronze Age of Southeast Asia.

There is a major divide between the societies which had to confront the expanding Chinese Empire, and those which entered into relationships with Indians and island Southeast Asians. The Yelang, Dian, Dong Son and numerous other chiefdoms on the southern marches of the Han Empire grew in complexity, at least in part, in reacting to the powerful and expansionary state to the north, which offered opportunities for defining exchange transactions, accepting new military technology and required organised means of defence. The surviving Chinese documents provide fragments of this process, which ultimately saw these 'Southern Barbarians' subjugated. The *Shi Ji,* referring to the year 109 BC, noted that the King of Dian had an army numbering tens of thousands. Even discounting hyperbole, the force available must have been significant. After the conflict which followed, the King submitted and Dian was converted into the Commandery (Province) of Yizhou. The population was given as 580,463 people.

There followed many allusions to insurrection and conflict between Yizhou and the Han administration. Only four years passed before the *Han Shu* refers to a rebellion, and another took place in 86 BC. In 83 BC, the governor of the commandery was killed. A second governor is recorded as being killed in AD 14 according to the *Zizhi Tongjian.* Tranquillity appears to have been established by AD 67, when the local Han commandant was described in the *Shu Han* as being the object of gratitude for his civilising influence, but this was shortlived. In AD 119 there was a major rebellion and many Chinese officials were killed. It was during this period of instability that the great royal necropolis of Shizhaishan was abandoned.

The same pattern of rebellion against Han dominion took place in Bac Bo, although in this instance, Chinese rule was to last for only eight centuries. Documentary sources refer to the imposition of Chinese laws, the creation of commanderies and extinction of the power and authority of chiefs, although this did not pass without many instances of insurrection, most notably under Trung Trac and her sister in AD 40. Archaeologically, the Dong Son tradition of interment ceased, and was replaced at the higher social level by the construction of brick vaulted Han tombs. Despite almost a millennium of sinicisation, the Vietnamese were able to reassert themselves after gaining independence, and today trace their origins through the Dong Son chiefdoms to a remoter prehistoric past.

In many ways, the course of events beyond the 'Fortress of the Sky', as the Chinese named the Truong Son Cordillera, was more interesting and varied. As we have seen, the second half of the first millennium BC saw the widespread distribution of exotic beads of glass, carnelian and agate some of which are of Indian origin. Buddhist thinking is seen in the carnelian lion from Ban Don Ta Phet. Both are harbingers of the rich strands of Indian ideas, political philosophy, writing systems and religious beliefs and their architectural expression which run through the fabric of Southeast Asian states (de la Loubère 1693). It has been argued that the rising elites of the first millennium BC sought control over the casting of high-status bronzes and imported exotica. To this extensive list, we can now add a new area of potential control, that of esoteric knowledge.

The Hindu religion, and in particular Śaivism, the worship of Śiva, provide a means whereby a mortal can assume the qualities of divinity (Wolters 1979). This is achieved through ascetic devotion which is rewarded by the god's *śakti,* or physical and spiritual power. In about AD 250, two Chinese representatives of the Wu emperor visited Southeast Asia, and returned with descriptions of palaces, walled settlements, taxation in silver, gold and pearls, a legal system and intensive rice cultivation. They encountered an ambassador from the Murunda King of India, and described a writing system. Their description of the local rulers and their recent history discloses a dynastic succession concerned with enlarging the area under central control through force. It is unclear precisely where they made landfall and encountered this society, but it may well have been in the Transbassac region of southern Vietnam, a flat and swampy plain to this day (Pelliot 1903). Archaeologically, we now have verification of their description in the many settlement sites linked by an extensive system of canals, of which the best documented is Oc Eo (Malleret 1959–63). Excavations have revealed a rectangular site of which 450 ha lie behind five ramparts and four moats. Exotic Iranian, Roman, Indian and Chinese artefacts reveal participation in an extensive exchange network, while the presence of rings and seals engraved in characters of the *brāhmī* script confirm knowledge of an Indian writing system.

Oc Eo lies at or near the development of state-like polities in the lower and middle reaches of the Mekong Valley which ultimately gave rise to the great complex at Angkor during the early ninth century AD. These polities were focused on a central court, seat of the overlord. Whereas the rulers described in the third century Chinese account had indigenous personal names, the inscriptions on carved stone stelae of the fifth century incorporated the rulers' names in Sanskrit, and a notable example from the Dong Thap Muoi refers to the overlord's promotion of marsh drainage, presumably to expand the agricultural base. Some inscriptions, however, include text in both Sanskrit and the vernacular language. In the case of the middle and lower Mekong area, the latter is the Austroasiatic archaic Khmer.

The many polities which rose and fell in this area up to the establishment of Angkor are known both from archaeological and epigraphic evidence, and several common features can be identified which suggest continuity from the late prehistoric period. The most widespread is a concern for water conservation.

Īśānapura, for example, included a reservoir outside a walled elite centre covering 400 ha and dated to the early seventh century. This name derives from the overlord, Īśānavarman, a Sanskrit name meaning 'protégé of Śiva'. We have seen how important water control was in this arid region, which saw initial moated settlements a millennium earlier. From the advent of Indian religous ideas, water reservoirs took on a religious as well as economic purpose, for the home of the Hindu gods, the mythical Mount Meru, is surrounded by the oceans. It suited the purpose of the overlord, therefore, to depict his court centre as a representation of heaven on earth. To this purpose, they also built stone temples for the worship of the *liṅga*, or phallic representation of the polity which like the city itself, was named after the ruler.

Vickery (1986) has traced the importance of the relationship between titled individuals and reservoirs on the basis of the corpus of inscriptions. During the early seventh century, a *poñ* was a highly ranked official who owned or administered a *travāṅ,* or reservoir. By AD 650, the *pon* were found lower in the hierarchy, below a new class of the elite known as *mratāñ,* who in turn was subservient to the *rāja,* or king. It is also evident from the inscriptions that this period saw intense competition and warfare between competing overlords. The ruler Jayavarman campaigned, it is recorded in a notable inscription from Baset dated AD 658, in autumn, when his enemies' moats were dry.

By the early ninth century AD, these trends towards greater centralisation and complexity reached a new and more durable form in the establishment of a ruling dynasty at Angkor, which lies between the Tonle Sap, or Great Lake, and the Kulen Hills. Again, the provision of water for symbolic and economic reasons was expected of the overlord, who now increasingly assumed divine status. But we can also identify further aspects of behaviour which are echoed in recent history and may well have much earlier origins in Southeast Asia. The first is the importance of staple finance. The Khmer civilisation had no form of currency, and the court centre was also a focus for the receipt and distribution of a huge array of subsistence goods, including rice, fish, honey and salt. Second is the notion of merit making. Temples dedicated to the present or past deified rulers required supplies, and this was achieved by assigning to new foundations, a series of village communities as sources of the necessary goods and labour. The villagers were not repaid with tangible rewards, but rather with merit, the satisfaction and glow that issues from pleasing the gods. The maintenance of this system, therefore, required the control of people's minds within a state system of belief. In this context, we can appreciate the signal importance of the symbolism expressed in the mysterious enclosed precincts, the temples, iconography and reservoirs. Angkor was, literally, heaven expressed in stone.

These polities were occupied by people who spoke Khmer, and whose ancestors occupied such Bronze Age settlements as Samrong Sen. On the Vietnamese coastal plain, we encounter a similar phenomenon, of large court centres, the worship of Śiva and related Hindu deities and the adoption of Sanskrit names. But in this context, the vernacular language was Cham. Their ancestors during the first millennium BC were, beyond reasonable doubt, responsible for the urnfield cemeteries named after the site of Sa Huynh.

The Khorat Plateau, as we have seen, was the focus for the construction of many moated sites during the Iron Age. This continued into the historic periods, some sites seeing the expansion of the enclosed area in association with the construction of Buddhist monuments. Muang Fa Daet is one of the most intriguing of these sites, for it is possible to trace the extension of the moats from an initial circular site to one incorporating 171 ha, with the addition of a rectangular reservoir which alone covered 15 ha. The site is best known for the considerable number of Buddhist *sema* stones which were used to demarcate sacred space. One of the decorated examples shows a defended city wall. Excavations in 1991 within the presumed early enceinte revealed Iron Age burials, but the greater part of the site belongs to the second half of the first millennium AD.

Muang Sima is a second large moated centre on the Khorat Plateau, situated strategically in the upper Mun Valley. A seventh century inscription in Sanskrit and Khmer records a meritorious donation to the temple by the overlord of Śri Cānása. A century later and 50 km to the south, another overlord with the Sanskrit name Nṛipendradhipativarman erected four *sema* stones and gifted rice land, cattle, an elephant, silver utensils and a plantation of betel nut trees to the local temple to gain merit. The impression gained from such evidence, is that there was a strong element of continuity from the Iron Age, which saw a further strengthening of the trend to social elites in the context of the new, esoteric Buddhist and Hindu religion.

In Central Thailand, there are variations on the same theme. Excavations at Chansen have revealed an almost continuous settlement which began during the late prehistoric period and continued into the later first millennium AD, the period of the Dvāravatī polities. We are unsure if there was one unified state, or a series of competing centres, or indeed a combination of both. At Chansen, periods 3-4, which belong to the third–seventh centuries AD, have yielded a similar range of artefacts as Oc Eo, including tin amulets, bronze bells and the stone moulds for casting small items of jewellery. It was during phase 5 that the large moat and associated reservoir were excavated, and the increase of pottery within the enceinte suggests increased activity and populace (Bronson 1979). Such moats are a distinctive feature of other Dvāravatī sites, and while Chansen may be considered small and provincial, the larger sites, such as Nakhon Pathom and U-Thong incorporate substantial Buddhist monuments and associated artefacts which indicate the presence of a sharply stratified society.

Nakhon Pathom is the largest such centre, the moats enclosing an area measuring about 3700 by 2000 m. The name Nakhon is derived from the Sanskrit *nāgara*, or holy city. This is cognate with the Khmer word Angkor, and the Cham *nāgar*. Two silver coins found under a central sanctuary bear the inscription 'the meritorious work of the King of Dvāravatī' in a seventh century script. Bronze continued to be used for high status objects, for a bronze chandelier, bells, cymbals and a statue of the Buddha were found under the central tower. Two terracotta toilet trays, for mixing cosmetics, also contain symbols of royalty including the parasols which feature prominently in the graded list of accoutrements allowed the Khmer hierarchy at Angkor, and which are held over the King of Thailand to this day on appropriate occasions. The moated centre of Ku Bua has yielded stucco figures of elite members of society, prisoners, guards and visiting Semitic merchants. There are fewer inscriptions in Central Thailand than in the middle and lower Mekong area, but they reveal familiarity with the exotic Pali script. It was this language which attracted the interest of Simon de la Loubère (1693) when visiting the court of King Narai at Ayutthaya in 1687. His conclusions, which anticipated those of Sir William Jones a century later, linked Pali with the Indo-European languages of Europe and encouraged him to speculate on Thai origins. We can now appreciate more clearly how they were rooted firmly within Southeast Asia, and see, in the court rituals of the Chakri Dynasty, a pattern which has been developing over two millennia and, indeed, beyond even that span and into the prehistoric past.

CHAPTER 10

SUMMARY

This study has involved a rigorous comparative review of the Bronze Age in Southeast Asia. Rigour has been applied to two complementary variables: the chronological framework and the social contexts in which metals were deployed. It is inevitable, in the initial and exploratory stages of research into the prehistory of such a large and complex area as Southeast Asia, that there will be elements of confusion and contradiction. This only emphasises the need to review the accumulating evidence periodically, and in as judicious a manner as possible. Ultimately, the energy involved in writing this book has been fuelled by the conviction that Southeast Asia should take its place alongside other major regions and cultures, such as the Chinese civilisation of the Huanghe Valley, South Asia and the Near East, rather than be consigned to the footnotes of world prehistory. After all, Southeast Asia today sustains a significant proportion of humanity, and its past played a part in the beginnings and spread of rice cultivation, the origins of the world's greatest diaspora of peoples, some of the most potent and extensive early civilisations and, last but not least, the adoption of bronze and iron working.

Fortunately, the writing of this book has coincided with the first conjunction of disciplines which has already showed the capacity for broad syntheses and deeper understanding of prehistory. I refer to the consideration of archaeological evidence together with that of linguistics and molecular biology. We are in the early stages of this new avenue, but it promises much (Renfrew 1994). Even while the final chapters were being written, Blust (1993a) and Reid (1993) announced that it was possible to join Austroasiatic and Austronesian languages into the Austric phylum. Formerly, separation of the two encouraged a search for at least two origins of rice cultivation: in the tropics and in the Yangzi Valley. But the validity of Austric, the progenitor of the myriad of languages which now stretch from Malagasy to Easter Island, and from New Zealand to India, has allowed us to recognise in the archaeological evidence for Southeast Asia a broad pattern compatible with the intrusive expansion of rice cultivators down the lines of least resistance, the rivers which radiate out from the region of the upper and middle Yangzi Valley.

Bellwood (1993) has identified this movement with the establishment of Southern Mongoloid peoples across an area hitherto lightly populated by inland foragers, and with sedentary groups in favoured coastal enclaves. These intrusive agriculturalists, who seem to have reached the river valleys and shore of Southeast Asia during the third millennium BC, established a number of cultural practices with a long ancestry in the Yangzi Valley: sedentary villages, rice cultivation, the domestication of cattle, pigs and the dog, and the maintenance of ancestral, inhumation cemeteries. They also entered an area which presented new challenges, not least the sharp seasonality of the monsoon climate, and new potential, seen in the rich deposits of copper, tin, iron and lead ores.

The development of a distinctive Southeast Asian cultural tradition must necessarily be reviewed against a backdrop of the development of a potent, expansive and innovative civilisation in the valley of the Huanghe River to the north. The Neolithic sites of Southeast Asia had been established for little over a millennium before exchange originating in the Huanghe and Yangzi valleys brought exotic jades to Lingnan and Bac Bo. Lingnan also received a number of late Shang bronzes. By this juncture, the mid second millennium BC, the civilisations represented at Sanxingdui in Sichuan, and Zhengzhou in Henan, were already displaying a mastery of bronze casting which was unsurpassed in the ancient world. There must, therefore, always be the possibility that the Southeast Asian tradition of copper-based metallurgy was initially stimulated by the spread of ideas and goods down the very rivers which introduced the rice farming groups a millennium or so earlier.

This possibility, which necessarily involves scepticism over the validity of the dates which have led to claims for bronze in Southeast Asia before the mid second millennium BC, should not underestimate the individuality of the local bronze tradition. The Chinese and Southeast Asian bronzes cannot be confused. The former involved a huge scale of specialist production, the use of piece moulds and the production of large sumptuary vessels of remarkable virtuosity. The latter at the same juncture could hardly have been more different. Examination of the copper mines and associated ore processing and smelting sites, as well as the villages where ingots were cast and the dead buried with metal artefacts, reveals a distinctive local tradition. But this distinctiveness does not exclude its origins in the recognition of the nature of copper and tin ore through the spread of knowledge, and I have indicated how contact between the Shang Dynasty and later Neolithic communities in Lingnan could have facilitated this. I am not, however prepared to reject an alternative hypothesis, that there were quite independent, local origins to this southern bronze tradition, because it is still possible that acceptable assemblages of dates before 1800 to 2000 BC for bronze casting will one day be obtained. My preference for the former alternative is based solely on the information which is currently available.

The still sparse evidence for the social principles on which Neolithic communities were structured shows that individuals could obtain social standing through personal skill and industry. At Khok Phanom Di, we find that female potters were transforming the abundant local clay into vessels of high quality. On occasion, their tools were interred with them at death. Ceramics, shell and stone were converted into personal ornaments and widely exchanged. When we encounter the early Bronze Age cemeteries, this habit persisted. At Non Pa Wai, Non Nok

Tha and Yuanlongpo, some individuals were interred with moulds for casting bronzes. Both the ceramic anvils for shaping pots at Khok Phanom Di and the later clay casting moulds bore distinctive marks which might indicate personal ownership.

The two copper mining and processing complexes which have been examined reveal a long-term exploitation, with changing procedures as the high quality ores were exhausted. Pigott and Weiss have been at pains to stress, for the Khao Wong Prachan sites, the probable seasonal nature of extraction, the predominance of ingot moulds and the lack of interest in alloying with tin. No bronze age site in the vicinity of these mines indicates the presence of a hereditary elite which might have controlled the supply and distribution of ingots or artefacts. The ingots, rather, entered established exchange networks. At Ban Na Di, over 100 km from an ore source, copper and tin were alloyed and locally cast into bracelets, arrowheads and axes, a pattern seen at nearby Ban Chiang as at Doc Chua, almost 1000 km to the southeast. The furnaces for melting the copper were small, and the crucibles held little metal. At the same period, similar stone moulds were in use at the mouth of the Zhujiang River, 1500 km to the northeast of Ban Na Di. It is argued that the knowledge of alloying and casting, and the exchange of ingots, were rapidly disseminated between 1500–1000 BC.

We can learn much from the artefacts which were preferred, and it is particularly important to note that most bronze was cast into forms which copied earlier shell and stone bracelets. Polished stone adzes are ubiquitous in Neolithic and Bronze Age Southeast Asian sites, and small, socketed bronze axes came to serve alongside them. We have little evidence for Neolithic arrowheads – perhaps bamboo was used – but bronze was cast into these projectile points in a variety of forms. In mortuary contexts, bronze joined other exotic items – marble, slate, serpentine, trochus and conus shell – as items of personal finery. It was never abundant and only a small percentage of individuals were buried with bronzes. They included men, women, children and infants, but there is no evidence that those associated with bronze were distinguished from others through their location, mortuary wealth or energy expended in their interment. This is seen at its clearest when contrasting the cemeteries at Khok Phanom Di and Nong Nor, the former Neolithic, the latter Bronze Age. They are separated by 14 km and perhaps nine centuries. Individuals were buried along similar lines, on the same orientation, with a similar placement of grave goods. The presence of a limited number of bronze bracelets is the principal distinguishing characteristic between the two.

The latter half of the first millennium BC saw a number of major changes, and the development of a marked regionality. The Yunnan Plateau, Zhujiang and Red River valleys were exposed to Chinese expansion, and there was a brief interlude of luminous aristocratic leadership before the areas entered the dull uniformity and provincialism of remote Han commanderies. The Dian leaders, among whom are numbered men and women, chose bronze as a means of arming their followers and advertising their status. Iron was rare, and used principally for weapons which were on occasion sheathed in gold. The bronze drums, cowrie containers, ornamented armour and weaving implements, no less than the scenes rendered in bronze and the hilltop cemeteries of the aristocratic lineages, provide a clear picture of a society which incorporated specialist bronze workers and a new plane in the quantity and range of castings, development of new alloys and interest in novel decorative techniques. The bronzes were employed in ritual, war and the improvement of agricultural productivity. If Dian workshops represent the apogee of the Southeast Asian bronze tradition, those of Dong Son and Lingnan were not far behind.

Beyond the Truong Son Cordillera, changes with the coming of iron were quite different. Spared from the threat of conquest, the inhabitants of the middle reaches of the Mekong and its tributaries encountered a new environmental problem. As rice-growing communities expanded into the dry valley of the Mun River, and across the plains which flank the Tonle Sap, and as their populations grew, so they had to confront seasonal flooding and then the long dry season. Iron was used to forge digging tools, heavy knives and sickles. Settlements were ringed by a succession of broad moats which conserved water for the dry season and, through a system of associated canals, helped to distribute surplus water during the rains. Here, we find little evidence for conflict. The moated sites were not ringed by high ramparts and the cemeteries within have not, as yet, produced much weaponry. Bronze, however, was used for a new range of display items: headdresses, belts, finger, toe and earrings and deep, richly decorated bracelets.

In contrast to these Middle Mekong sites, Central Thailand was exposed early to direct contact with Indian traders bringing with them a range of new trade goods, and a novel religion. At Ban Don Ta Phet as at many other sites in this region, we can identify the rise of social elites, manifested by a range of novel and demanding bronzes. Very high-tin bronze bowls were cast and intricately decorated using specialist techniques. Exotic glass, carnelian and agate beads were sought and used in mortuary rituals. A carnelian lion, and a bronze cockerel cast with its cage, and quantities of iron spearheads and billhooks, along with the ornate wooden coffins of Ongbah, reflect a society which appreciated the new exotica, the control over which would have been a means for securing status.

All these innovations were linked to a structural change in the organisation of society. In place of men and women of ability, whose manual skills were recompensed by social standing, we find hierarchies which, through the maintenance of specialists, could provide the implements needed for agricultural innovation, the weapons to arm their followers, and the sumptuary goods to complement their elevated status. The socially driven organisation of bronze casting was universally involved in this change, in the production of weapons, vessels for feasting, armour, ornaments and agricultural implements.

This sequence of events, fitted into a briefer span than has been suggested on the basis of unacceptable dating contexts at Non Nok Tha and Ban Chiang, finds a number of parallels in the Bronze Ages of India, Iberia, China, the Near East and the Aegean. Far from being set apart, an apparent anomaly in a broad pattern, the Southeast Asian Bronze Age illustrates how technical knowledge and skill can be used both to set and to attain social goals

REFERENCES

Abbreviations

AAT	Anyang Archaeological Team.
APAT	Anhui Provincial Archaeological Team.
BEFEO	*Bulletin de l'École Française d'Extrême Orient.*
CAG	Changwei Archaeological Group.
CBZC	Cultural Bureau of Zhaoqing City.
CPAMHP	CPAM Hebei Province and the Handan Relics Preservation Station.
CPAMZP	CPAM Zhejiang Province.
EATIA	Erlitou Archaeological Team, Institute of Archaeology, CASS.
EFEO	École Française d'Extrême Orient.
FAD	Fine Arts Department of Thailand.
GATIA	Gansu Archaeological Team, Institute of Archaeology, CASS.
GDWGW	Committee for the Preservation of Cultural Relics in Guangdong.
GPM	Gansu Provincial Museum.
GPMNNC	Gansu Provincial Museum and Northeast Normal College.
GS	Gansu Squad.
GuiPM	Guizhou Provincial Museum.
GuPM	Guangdong Provincial Museum.
GXBWG	Museum of the Guangxi Zhuang Autonomous Region.
GXWGD	Cultural Relics Work Team of the Guanxi Zhuang Minority Autonomous Region.
GZAR	Guangxi Zhuangsu Autonomous Region.
HAI	Hunan Archaeological Institute.
HATIA	Henan Archaeological Team, Institute of Archaeology, CASS.
HPM	Hunan Provincial Museum.
HuAT	Hubei Archaeological Team.
HuPM	Hubei Provincial Museum.
LCR	Office for the Compilation of the Annals of Lechang Cultural Relics.
LDWHJ	Cultural Bureau of Luoding County.
MSP	Museum of Sichuan Province.
NM	Nanjing Museum.
PEFEO	*Publications de l'École Française d'Extrême Orient.*
SATIA	Shandong Archaeological Team, Institute of Archaeology, CASS.
Shanxi-ATIA	Shanxi Archaeological Team, Institute of Archaeology, CASS.
SMRPC	Shanghai Municipal Relics Preservation Committee.
SPCRAC	Sichuan Province Cultural Records Administrative Committee.
VMH	Vietnam Museum of History.
YPM	Yunnan Provincial Museum.
ZPM	Zhejiang Provincial Museum.

AAT, 1979, Excavation of the Yin tombs in the western section of Yin-hsü. (in Chinese). *Kaogu Xuebao*, 1979:27–146.

    1981, The two tombs of the Yin Dynasty excavated at the north of the Xiaotun village in Anyang County. (in Chinese). *Kaogu Xuebao*, 1981:491–518.

Agrawal, D.P. 1982, *The Archaeology of India*. Scandinavian Institute of Asian Studies Monograph Series no. 46, Curzon Press, London.

Aitken, J.J. 1993, *Archaeological Sediments as Artifacts*. PhD thesis, University of Otago.

Allard, F. 1994, Interaction and social complexity in Lingnan during the first millennium B.C. *Asian Perspectives* 33:309–26.

    1995, *The Interaction and social complexity in Lingnan during the late Neolithic and the Bronze Age*. PhD thesis, University of Pittsburgh.

Allard, F., Higham, C.F.W., and Manly, B.J.F. 1995, *A statistical analysis of the Warring States cemetery of Yinshanling*. Unpublished paper.

Allchin, B. and Allchin, R. 1982, *The Rise of Civilization in India and Pakistan*. Cambridge University Press, Cambridge.

An Chin-huai, 1986, The Shang City of Cheng-Chou and related problems. In Chang, K.-C., editor, *Studies of Shang Archaeology*, pages 15–48. Yale University Press, New Haven.

Anon. 1990, List of radiocarbon dates. (in Vietnamese). *Khao Co Hoc*, 75:78–9.

An Zhimin, 1980, The Neolithic archaeology of China: a brief survey of the last thirty years. *Early China*, 6:33–45.

    1982-3, Some problems concerning China's early copper and bronze artefacts. *Early China*, 8:53–75.

APAT, 1982, Excavations at Xuejiagang (in Chinese). *Kaogu Xuebao*, 1982:283–324.

Ardika, I.W. 1987, *Bronze Artifacts and the Rise of Complex Society in Bali*. MA Dissertation, Australian National University.

    1991, *Archaeological Research in Northeastern Bali, Indonesia*. PhD thesis, Australian National University.

Bagley, R.W. 1988, Sacrificial pits of the Shang period at Sanxingdui in Guanghan county, Sichuan. *Arts Asiatiques*, XLIII:78–86.

Balfour, H. 1901, A spear-head and socketed celt in bronze from the Shan States, Burma. *Man*, 77:97.

Bannanurag, R. and Bamrungwongse, A. 1991, A site survey of Ban Chiang culture sites in the Sakon Nakhon Basin, Northeast Thailand. (in Thai). *Silpakon Journal*, 34:38–60.

Bannanurag, R. and Khemnark, P. 1992, *Prehistoric burials at Wat Pho Si Nai, Ban Chiang*. Fine Arts Department, Bangkok.

Bard, S. 1995, Archaeology in Hong Kong. A review of achievement. In Yueng Chung-tong and Li Wai-ling, W. (editors). *Archaeology in Southeast Asia,* pages 383–96. The University Museum and Art Gallery and the University of Hong Kong.

Barnard, N. 1987, Bronze casting technology in the peripheral 'barbarian' regions' – preliminary assessments of the significance of technical variations between these regions and the metallurgy of the *Chung-yuan*. *Bulletin of the Metal Museum*, 12:3–37.

    1991, *Thoughts on the emergence of metallurgy in pre-Shang and early Shang China and a technical appraisal of relevant bronze artifacts of the time*. Unpublished paper read at the Hsia Culture Conference, UCLA, May 1990.

    1996, The entry of cire-perdue investment casting, and certain other metallurgical techniques, (mainly metal-working) into South China and their progress northwards. In Barnard, N. and Bulbeck, F.D., editors, *Ancient Chinese and*

Southeast Asian Bronze Age Cultures. Vol. 1. In press. Southern Materials Center Inc., Taipei.

Barnard, N. and Sato, T. 1975, *Metallurgical Remains of Ancient China.* Nichiosha, Tokyo.

Bar-Yosef, O. and Meadow, R.H. 1995, The origins to agriculture in the Near East. In Price, T.D. and Gebauer, A.B., editors, *Last Hunters – First Farmers: New Perspectives on the Prehistoric Transition to Agriculture,* pages 39–94. American School of Prehistoric Research, Santa Fe.

Battaglia, D.B. 1983, Syndromes of ceremonial exchange in the eastern Calvados: the view from Sudest Island. In Leach, J.W. and Leach, E.R., editors, *The Kula. New Perspectives on Massim Exchange,* pages 445–66. Cambridge University Press, Cambridge.

Bayard, D.T. 1971, *Non Nok Tha. The 1968 Excavations: Procedure, Stratigraphy and a Summary of the Evidence.* Otago University Monographs in Prehistoric Anthropology 4, University of Otago, Dunedin.

    1980, The roots of Indochinese civilization: recent developments in the prehistory of Southeast Asia. *Pacific Affairs,* 53:89–114.

    1984, A tentative regional phase chronology for Northeast Thailand. In Bayard, D.T., editor, *Southeast Asian Archaeology at the XV Pacific Science Congress,* pages 161–8. Otago University Studies in Prehistoric Anthropology 16, Dunedin.

    1992, Models, scenarios, variables and suppositions: approaches to the rise of social complexity in Mainland Southeast Asia, 700 BC–500 AD. In Glover, I.C., Suchitta, P., and Villiers, J., editors, *Early Metallurgy, Trade and Urban Centres in Thailand and Southeast Asia,* pages 13–38. White Lotus, Bangkok.

    1996, Bones of contention: the Non Nok Tha burials and the chronology and context of early Southeast Asian bronze. In Barnard, N. and Bulbeck, F.D., editors, *Ancient Chinese and Southeast Asian Bronze Age Cultures.* Vol. 2. In press. Southern Materials Center Inc., Taipei.

Bayard, D.T. and Charoenwongsa, P. 1983, The development of metallurgy in Southeast Asia: reply to Loofs-Wissowa. *Journal of Southeast Asian Studies,* XIV(1):12–17.

Bayard, D.T., Charoenwongsa, P., and Rutnin, S. 1986, Excavations at Non Chai, Northeastern Thailand. *Asian Perspectives,* 25(1):13–62.

Bellwood, P. 1985, *Prehistory of the Indo-Malaysian Archipelago.* Academic Press, New York.

    1989, The colonisation of the Pacific: some current hypotheses. In Hill, A.V.S. and Serjeantson, S.W., editors, *The Colonisation of the Pacific. A Genetic Trail,* pages 1–59. Clarendon Press,

    1991, Foraging towards farming; a decisive transition or a millennial blur? *The Review of Archaeology,* 11:14–24.

    1992, Southeast Asia before history. In Tarling, N., editor, *The Cambridge History of Southeast Asia,* pages 55–136. Cambridge University Press, Cambridge.

    1993, Cultural and biological differentiation in peninsular Malaysia: the last 10,000 years. *Asian Perspectives,* 32:37–60.

Bellwood, P., Gillespie, R., Thompson, G.B., Vogel, J.S., Ardika, I.W., and Datan, I. 1992, New dates for prehistoric Asian rice. *Asian Perspectives,* 31:161–70.

Bennett, A. 1988, Prehistoric copper smelting in Central Thailand. In Charoenwongsa, P. and Bronson, B., editors, *Prehistoric Studies: the Stone and Metal Ages in Thailand,* pages 125–135. Thai Antiquity Working Group, Bangkok.

    1989, The contribution of metallurgical studies to Southeast Asian archaeology. *World Archaeology,* 20:329–51.

Bennett, A. and Glover, I. 1992, Decorated high-tin bronze bowls from Thailand's prehistory. In Glover, I.C., editor, *Southeast Asian Archaeology, 1990*, pages 187–208. Centre for South-East Asian Studies, University of Hull.

Bernet Kempers, A.J. 1988, The kettledrums of Southeast Asia. *Modern Quaternary Studies in Southeast Asia*, 10:1–599.

Bezacier, L. 1972, *Le Vietnam*. Picard, Paris.

Bintarti, D.D. 1993, *The Bronze Age of Indonesia*. Unpublished paper read at the 34th International Conference of Asian and North African Studies, Hong Kong, September 1993.

Blunden, C. and Elvin, N. 1983, *Cultural Atlas of China*, Phaidon, London.

Blust, R. 1976, Austronesian culture history: some linguistic inferences and their relationships to the archaeological record. *World Archaeology*, 8:19–43.

1985, The Austronesian homeland. A linguistic perspective. *Asian Perspectives*, 26:107–17.

1993a, *Beyond the Austronesian homeland: the Austric hypothesis and its implications for archaeology*. Paper read at a meeting on Austroasiatic languages, Philadelphia.

1993b, *The Austronesian settlement of Mainland Southeast Asia*. Unpublished paper read at the second annual meeting of the Southeast Asian Linguistic Society.

Bock, K. 1883, *Temples and Elephants: the Narrative of a Journey of Exploration Through Upper Siam and Burma*. Sampson, Low, Marston, Searle and Rivington, London.

Boyd, W. 1994, The palaeoenvironment of the archaeological site of Nong Nor, and the implications of a palaeoenvironmental model for the regional archaeology. In Higham, C.F.W., Thosarat, R., Boyd, W., Chang, N., Debreceny, J., Higham, T.F.G., Hogg, A., Mason, G.M., O'Reilly, D., Pailles, C. and Tayles, N. *The Excavation of the Prehistoric Site of Nong Nor, Central Thailand. Report to the National Research Council of Thailand*.

Bronson, B. 1979, The late prehistory and early history of Central Thailand with special reference to Chansen. In Smith, R.B. and Watson, W., editors, *Early South East Asia*, pages 315–36. Oxford University Press, Oxford.

1989, The Archaeology of Mainland Southeast Asia by C.F.W. Higham. A Review. *Antiquity*, 63:854–5.

1992, Patterns in early Southeast Asian metals trade. In Glover, I.C., Suchitta, P., and Villiers, J., editors, *Early Metallurgy, Trade and Urban Centres in Thailand and Southeast Asia*, pages 63–114. White Lotus, Bangkok.

Bronson, B. and Natapintu, S. 1988, Don Noi: a new flaked tool industry of the middle Holocene in Western Thailand. In Charoenwongsa, P. and Bronson, B., editors, *Prehistoric Studies: The Stone and Metal Ages in Thailand*, pages 91–106. Thai Antiquity Working Group, Bangkok.

Brumfiel, E.M. and Earle, T.K. 1987, Specialization, exchange and complex societies: an introduction. In Brumfiel, E.M. and Earle, T.K., editors, *Specialization, Exchange and Complex Societies*, pages 1–9. Cambridge University Press, Cambridge.

Buchan, R. 1973, *The three-dimensional jigsaw puzzle: a ceramic sequence from NE Thailand*. Master's thesis, University of Otago.

Bui Van Liem and Pham Quoc Quan. 1991, Boat coffins burial ground at Minh Duc (Son Binh Province) (in Vietnamese). *Khao Co Hoc*, 76:56–63.

Bui Vinh, 1991, The Da But culture in the Stone Age of Viet Nam. *Bulletin of the Indo-Pacific Prehistory Association*, 10:127–31.

Buranrak and Co. 1994a, *Report on the Excavation of Don Klang*. (in Thai). Fine Arts Department, Bangkok.

1994b, *Report on the Excavation of Non Praw.* (in Thai). Fine Arts Department, Bangkok.

CAG, 1980, A report on the excavation of the Chengzi site in Zuchen County, Shandong Province. (in Chinese). *Kaogu Xuebao,* 1980(3):329–86.

Cartailhac, E. 1879, Review of Noulet, J-B, l'Age de la pierre polie et du bronze au Cambodge d'après les découvertes de M. Moura. *Matériaux de l'Histoire de l'Homme,* X:315–23.

1890, Les bronzes préhistoriques du Cambodge et les recherches de M. Ludovic Jammes. *L'Anthropologie,* 6:641–50.

Casanowicz, I.M. 1922, The collections of Old World Archaeology in the United States National Museum. *Annual Report of the Smithsonian Institution,* 1922:415–98.

Casteleyn, P. 1669, *Distant Voyage to the Kingdoms of Cambodia and Laos.* (in Dutch). Harlem.

Chang, K.-C. 1983, Sandai archaeology and the formation of states in ancient China. Processual aspects of the origin of Chinese civilization.In Keightley, D.N., editor, *The Origins of Chinese Civilization,* pages 495–521. University of California Press, Berkeley.

1986, *The Archaeology of Ancient China.* Yale University Press, New Haven.

1987, Archaeology in southeastern coastal China and the origin of the Austronesians. *Southern Ethnology and Archaeology,* 1:1–14.

Chang, T.-T. 1983, The origins and early cultures of the cereal grains and food legumes. In Keightley, D.N., editor, *The Origins of Chinese Civilization,* pages 65–94. University of California Press, Berkeley.

Chantaratiyakarn, P. 1984, The research programme in the Middle Chi. In Higham, C.F.W. and Kijngam, A., editors, *Prehistoric Investigations in Northeast Thailand,* pages 565–643. British Archaeological Reports (International Series) 231, Oxford.

Chapman, R.W. 1981, The emergence of formal disposal areas for the dead and the 'problem' of megalithic tombs in prehistoric Europe. In Chapman, R., Kinnes, I., and Randsborg, K., editors, T*he Archaeology of Death,* pages 71–81. Cambridge University Press, Cambridge.

1982, Autonomy, ranking and resources in Iberian prehistory. In Renfrew, C. and Shennan, S., editors, *Ranking, Resource and Exchange: Aspects of the Archaeology of Early European Society,* pages 46–51. Cambridge University Press, Cambridge.

Charoenwongsa, P., editor 1987, *Archaeology of the Four Regions.* (in Thai). Fine Arts Department, Bangkok.

1988, The current status of prehistoric research in Thailand. In Charoenwongsa, P. and Bronson, B., editors, *Prehistoric Studies: the Stone and Metal Ages in Thailand,* pages 17–42. Thai Antiquity Working Group, Bangkok.

Chiawanwongsa, P. 1987, *The Archaeological Site of Ban Wang Hi.* (in Thai). Fine Arts Department, Bangkok.

Chiu, S.T. 1993, *Recent excavations at Yung Long.* Unpublished paper read at the 34th International Conference of Asia and North African Studies, Hong Kong, September 1993.

Choosiri, P. 1992, *The Human Remains from the Excavation of Khok Phanom Di.* (in Thai). Fine Arts Department, Bangkok.

Chu Van Tan, 1973, Social differentiation in Hung King period through archaeological material. (in Vietnamese). *Hung Vuong Dung Nuoc,* 3:328–33.

Ciarla, R. 1992, The Thai-Italian Lopburi regional archaeological project, a preliminary report. In Glover, I.C., editor, *Southeast Asian Archaeology, 1990,* pages 111–28. Centre for South-East Asian Studies, University of Hull.

Coedès, G. 1968, *The Indianised States of Southeast Asia*. East-West Centre Press, Honolulu.

Colani, M. 1935, *Mégalithes du Haut-Laos*. (2 vols.). PEFEO, 25–6.

—— 1940, Emploi de la Pierre en des Temps Reculés, Annam-Indonesie-Assam. *Amis du Vieux Hué*, Hanoi.

Coote, V. 1990, Ancient metal mines and mining in Southwest Thailand. In Glover, I.C. and Glover, E., editors, *Southeast Asian Archaeology 1986*, pages 131–7. British Archaeological Reports (International Series) 561, Oxford.

CPAMHP, 1981, The Cishan site in Wu'an, Hebei Province. (in Chinese). *Kaogu Xuebao*, 1981:303–38.

CPAMZP, 1961, Excavations of the Neolithic site of Ma-Chia-Ping, Chia-hsing County, Chekiang. (in Chinese). *Kaogu*, 1961:345–54.

—— 1978, Excavations (first season) at Ho-mu-tu in Yu-Yao County, Chekiang Province. (in Chinese). *Kaogu Xuebao*, 1978:39–94.

Cremaschi, M., Ciarla, R., and Pigott, V.C. 1992, Palaeoenvironment and late prehistoric sites in the Lopburi region of Central Thailand. In Glover, I.C., editor, *Southeast Asian Archaeology, 1990*, pages 129–42. Centre for South-East Asian Studies, University of Hull.

Daeng-iet, S. 1978, Khok Phlap: a newly discovered prehistoric site. (in Thai). *Muang Boran*, 4(4):17–26.

Dao Linh Con and Nguyen Duy Ty, 1993, *Dia Dien Khao Co Hoc Doc Chua*. (in Vietnamese). (in Vietnamese). Nha Xuat Ban Khoa Hoc Xo Hoi, Ha Noi.

de la Loubère, S. 1693, *A New Historical Relation of the Kingdom of Siam*. Tho. Horne, London.

Diep Dinh Hoa, 1978, On the metal artifacts from the beginning of the Bronze Age in Vietnam. *Khao Co Hoc* 75:10–20.

Diffloth, G. 1991, Austro-Asiatic Languages. *Encyclopaedia Britannica Macropaedia*, 22:719–21.

Du Faqing, 1980, The mining of nonferrous metal minerals in ancient China. (in Chinese). *Nonferrous Metals*, 32:93–6.

Du Faqing and Gao Wuxun, 1980, The mining of non-ferrous metals in China prior to the Warring States period. (in Chinese). *Youse Jinshu* 32:93–7.

Earle, T. 1991, The evolution of chiefdoms. In Earle, T., editor, *Chiefdoms: Power, Economy and Ideology*, pages 1–15. Cambridge University Press, Cambridge.

EATIA, 1974, Excavation of the palace remains of the early Shang at Erh-li-t'ou in Yen-shih County, Honan Province. (in Chinese). *Kaogu*, 1974:234–50.

—— 1976, The bronzes and jades recently discovered at Erlitou in Yanshi County, Henan. (in Chinese). *Kaogu*, 1976:259–63.

—— 1980, Excavation of a Shang site at Erlitou in Yanshi, Henan in autumn 1980. (in Chinese). *Kaogu*, 1980:199–216.

FAD, 1990, *Archaeological Sites in Thailand: Volume IV. The Southern Provinces of the Northeast*. (In Thai). Fine Arts Department, Bangkok.

—— 1991, *Archaeology of Don Noi*. (in Thai). Fine Arts Department, Bangkok.

—— 1992, *Archaeology of Pak Mun*. (in Thai). Fine Arts Department, Bangkok.

Finn, D.J. 1936, Archaeological finds on Lamma Island near Hong Kong. Part XI. *The Hong Kong Naturalist*, XI:37–60.

—— 1958, Archaeological Finds on Lamma Island, Near Hong Kong. *Ricci*, Hong Kong.

Finot, L. 1928, Ludovic Jammes, préhistorien. *BEFEO*, 28:473–9.

Fontaine, H. 1972, Nouveau champ de jarres dans la province de Long-Khanh. *Bulletin de la Société des Études Indochinoises*, xlvii:397–486.

Fox, R.B. 1970, *The Tabon Caves: Archaeological Explorations and Excavations on Palawan Island, Philippines.* National Museum of Manila, Monograph no. 1, Manila.

Frost, R.J. 1975, Sha Chau. *Journal of the Hong Kong Archaeological Society*, VI:37–50.

Fuchs, E. 1883, Station préhistorique de Som-Ron-Sen, au Cambodge, son âge. *Materiaux de l'Histoire de l'Homme*, XIII:356–65.

Garnier, F. 1871, Voyage des Hollandais en Cambodge et Laos en 1644. *Bulletin de la Société de Géographie*, II-19:251–89.

GATIA, 1974, Excavation of the remains of Ch'i Chia culture at To-ho-chuang in Yungching County, Kansu Province. (in Chinese). *Kaogu Xuebao*, 1974:29–62.

    1975, The excavation of a Ch'i Chia culture cemetery at Chin-wei-chia in Yung-Ching County, Kansu Province. (in Chinese). *Kaogu Xuebao*, 1975:57–96.

GDWGW, 1963, Zhou dynasty bronze artifacts found in Qingyuan, Guangdong. (in Chinese). *Kaogu*, 1963(2):57–61.

    1964, An eastern Zhou grave in Qingyuan, Guangdong. (in Chinese). *Kaogu*, 1964(3):138–42.

Gilman, A. 1987, Unequal exchange in copper age Iberia. In Brumfiel, E. and Earle, T., editors, *Specialization, Exchange and Complex Societies*, pages 22–9. Cambridge University Press, Cambridge.

    1991, Trajectories towards social complexity in the later prehistory of the Mediterranean. In Earle, T., editor, *Chiefdoms: Power, Economy and Ideology*, pages 146–68. Cambridge University Press, Cambridge.

Glover, I.C. 1976, Ulu Leang cave, Maros: a preliminary sequence of post-Pleistocene cultural development in South Sulawesi. *Archipel*, 11:113–54.

    1989, *Early Trade Between India and Southeast Asia: a Link in the Development of a World Trading System.* The University of Hull Centre for Southeast Asian Studies Occasional Paper No. 16, Hull.

    1990, Ban Don Ta Phet: the 1984–5 excavation. In Glover, I.C. and Glover, E., editors, *Southeast Asian Archaeology 1986. Proceedings of the First Conference of the Association of Southeast Asian Archaeologists in Western Europe*, pages 139–83. British Archaeological Reports (International Series) 561, Oxford.

    1991, The late prehistoric period in west-central Thailand. *Bulletin of the Indo-Pacific Prehistory Association*, 10:349–56.

Glover, I.C., Charoenwongsa, P., Alvey, P., and Kamnounket, N. 1984, The cemetery of Ban Don Ta Phet, Thailand, results from the 1980–1 season. In Allchin, B. and Sidell, M., editors, *South Asian Archaeology*, pages 319–30. Cambridge University Press, Cambridge.

Glover, I.C. and Higham, C.F.W. 1993, *New evidence for early rice cultivation in South, Southeast and East Asia.* Unpublished paper presented to the Prehistoric Society Conference: The Origins and Spread of Agriculture and Pastoralism in Eurasia, London, 24–26 September 1993.

Goloubew, V. 1929, L'âge du bronze au Tonkin et dans le nord-Annam. *BEFEO*, 29:1–46.

    1940, Le tambour métallique de Hoàng-ha. *BEFEO*, 40:383–409.

Goodenough, W. 1982, Ban Chiang in world ethnological perspective. In White, J., editor, *Ban Chiang. The Discovery of a Lost Bronze Age*, pages 52–53. University of Pennsylvania, Philadelphia.

Gorman, C.F. and Charoenwongsa, P. 1976, Ban Chiang: a mosaic of impressions from the first two years. *Expedition*, 8(4):14–26.

GPM, 1960, Excavation of a Neolithic site at Huang-Niang-Niang-T'ai, Wu-wei County, Kansu. (in Chinese). *Kaogu Xuebao*, 1960:53–72.

1978a, Excavation of a Neolithic cemetery of the Pan Shan type at Ti-pa-p'ing in Kuang-ho County, Kansu Province. (in Chinese). *Kaogu Xuebao*, 1978:193–210.

1978b, Excavations of the fourth season (1975) at Huang-Niang-Niang-T'ai in Wu-wei County, Kansu Province. (in Chinese). *Kaogu Xuebao*, 1978(4):421–44.

1980, Tombs of the Banshan type at Huazhaizi near Lanzhou. (in Chinese). *Kaogu Xuebao*, 1980:221–38.

1982, Banshan-Machang tombs at Yuanuangchi, Wuwei, Gansu. (in Chinese). *Kaogu Xuebao*, 1982:199–227.

1983, A group of Warring States bronze artefacts found in Luoding, Guangdong. (in Chinese). *Kaogu*, 1:43–8.

GPMNNC, 1984, Studies on remains of millet and hemp unearthed from a Majiayao culture site in Linjia, Gansu. (in Chinese). *Kaogu Xuebao*, 1984:54–5.

GS, 1960, Excavations at the Ch'i Chia culture sites at Ta Ho Chuang and Ch'in Wei Chia, Lin Hsia County, Kansu. (in Chinese). *Kaogu*, 1960:9–12.

GuiPM, 1986, Excavations at Kele Township, Hezhang County, Guizhou Province. (in Chinese). *Kaogu Xuebao*, 1986:199–251.

GuPM, 1959, The stone implements unearthed at Hsi-Ch'iao-Shan, Nan Hai County, Kwangtung. (in Chinese). *Kaogu Xuebao*, 1959:1–16.

1961, The Neolithic shell mound sites at Tung Hsing, Kwangtung. (in Chinese). *Kaogu Xuebao*, 1961:644–9.

1975, The Warring States grave of Niaodanshan, in Sihui, Guangdong. (in Chinese). *Kaogu*, 2:102–8.

1983, A group of Warring States bronze artifacts found in Luoding, Guangdong. *Kaogu* 1983:43–8.

GuPM and CBZC, 1974, Excavation report of the ancient burial at Beilingsongshan, Zhaoqing City, Guangdong. (in Chinese). *Wenwu* 11:69–77.

GuPM and LDWHJ, 1986, A Warring States grave at Beifushan, Luoding, Guangdong. (in Chinese). *Kaogu*, 3:210–20.

GXBWG, 1973, Bronze artefacts recovered excavated in Gongcheng county, Guangxi. (in Chinese). *Kaogu*, 1973:30–4.

1984, Pre-Qin bronze artefacts recovered from Guangxi in recent years. (in Chinese). *Kaogu*, 1984:798–806.

1988, Short excavation report on the burials at Yuanlongpo, Matou, Wuming County, Guangxi (in Chinese). *Wenwu*, 1988(12):1–13.

GZAR, 1978, Warring States burials at Yinshanling, Pingle. (in Chinese). *Kaogu Xuebao*, 1978(2):211–58.

Ha Van Phung, 1993, Stages of development of Go Mun culture. (in Vietnamese). *Khao Co Hoc*, 85:48–63.

Ha Van Phung and Nguyen Duy Ty, 1982, *Di Chi Khao Co Hoc Go Mun*. Nha Xuat Ban Khoa Hoc Xa Hoi, Ha Noi.

Ha Van Tan, 1980, Nouvelles récherches préhistoriques et protohistoriques au Vietnam. *BEFEO*, 68:113–54.

1991, *From pre-Dong Son to Dong Son: sociocultural changes*. Unpublished paper read at the Conference on the High Bronze Age, Hua Hin, Thailand.

1993, Yazhang plaques in the Phung Nguyen culture sites. (in Vietnamese). *Khao Co Hoc*, 86:16–27.

1994, *The Hoabinhian and before*. Unpublished paper read at the Congress of the Indo-Pacific Prehistory Association, Chiang Mai, January 1994.

Hall, K.R. 1985, *Maritime Trade and State Development in Early Southeast Asia*. University of Hawaii Press, Honolulu.

Hanks, L.M. 1972, *Rice and Man. Agricultural Ecology in Southeast Asia*. Aldine, Chicago and New York.

HAT, 1990, Excavation of an early Neolithic site at Pengtoushan in Lixian, Hunan. (in Chinese). *Wenwu*, 8:17–32.

HATIA, 1982, Excavation of the Meishan site in Linru, Henan Province. (in Chinese). *Kaogu Xuebao*, 1982:427–75.

1984, Excavation of the Neolithic site of Peiligang. (in Chinese). *Kaogu Xuebao*, 1984:23–52.

Hayes, J. 1975, Walter Schofield (1888-1968). In Meacham, W., editor, *An Archaeological Site at Shek Pik*, pages iii–iv. Journal Monograph 1, Hong Kong Archaeological Society, Hong Kong.

He Jiejun, 1986, The Neolithic culture of the Lake Dongting area. (in Chinese). *Kaogu Xuebao*, 1986(4):385–408.

1995, Early Neolithic relics in Hunan. In Yueng Chung-tong and Li Wai-ling, W. (editors). *Archaeology in Southeast Asia*, pages 371–8. The University Museum and Art Gallery and the University of Hong Kong.

Heger, F. 1902, *Alte Metaltrommeln aus Südost Asien*. K. von Hiersemann, Leipzig.

Heine-Geldern, R. 1951, Das tocharerproblem und die Pontische wanderung. *Saeculum*, 2:225–55.

Higham, C.F.W. 1972, Initial model formulation in terra incognita. In Clarke, D.L., editor, *Models in Archaeology*, pages 453–77. Methuen, London.

1977, Economic change in prehistoric Thailand. In Reed, C.A., editor, *Origins of Agriculture*, pages 385–412. Mouton, The Hague.

1983, The Ban Chiang culture in wider perspective. *Proceedings of the British Academy*, LXIX:229–61.

1989, *The Archaeology of Mainland Southeast Asia*. Cambridge University Press, Cambridge.

1995, The transition to rice cultivation in Southeast Asia. In Price, T.D. and Gebauer, A.B., editors, *Last Hunters-First Farmers: New Perspectives on the Prehistoric Transition to Agriculture*, pages 127–55. American School of Prehistoric Research, Santa Fe.

1996, The social and chronological contexts of early bronze working in Southeast Asia. In Volume 2, Barnard, N. and Bulbeck, F.D., editors, *Ancient Chinese and Southeast Asian Bronze Age Cultures*, pages 35–102. Southern Materials Center Inc., Taipei.

Higham, C.F.W. and Bannanurag, R. 1990, *The Excavation of Khok Phanom Di, a Prehistoric Site in Central Thailand. Vol. I: The Excavation, Chronology and Human Burials*. Society of Antiquaries of London, Research Report no. XLVII, London.

Higham, C.F.W. and Bannanurag, R., editors 1991, *The Excavation of Khok Phanom Di, a Prehistoric Site in Central Thailand. Vol. 2: The Biological Remains, Part I*. Society of Antiquaries of London, Research Report no. XLVIII, London.

Higham, C.F.W., Bannanurag, R., Mason, G., and Tayles, N. 1992, Human biology, environment and ritual at Khok Phanom Di. *World Archaeology*, 24:35–54.

Higham, C.F.W. and Kijngam, A. 1984, *Prehistoric Investigations in Northeast Thailand*. British Archaeological Reports (International Series) 231 (1–3), Oxford.

Higham, C.F.W. and Thosarat, R., editors 1993, *The Excavation of Khok Phanom Di, a Prehistoric Site in Central Thailand. Vol. 3: The Material Culture, Part I*. Society of Antiquaries of London, Research Report no. L, London.

Higham, C.F.W. and Thosarat, R. 1994, *Khok Phanom Di. Prehistoric Adaptation to the World's Richest Habitat*. Harcourt Brace, Fort Worth.

Higham, C.F.W., Thosarat, R., Higham, T. F.G., and Hogg, A. 1992, *The Excavation of Nong Nor, 1991–3*. Paper read at the 4th International Conference of the European Association of Southeast Asian Archaeologists, Rome, 28 September–4 October 1992.

Higham, C.F.W., Thosarat, R., Boyd, W., Chang, N., Debreceny, J., Higham, T.F.G., Hogg, A., Hunt, V., Mason, G.M., O'Reilly, D., Pailles, C. and Tayles 1994, *The Excavation of the Prehistoric Site of Nong Nor, Central Thailand. Report to the National Research Council of Thailand.*

Ho, C.-M. 1984, *The Pottery of Kok Charoen and its Farther Context.* PhD thesis, University of London.

1992, An analysis of settlement patterns in the Lopburi area. In Glover, I.C., Suchitta, P., and Villiers, J., editors, *Early Metallurgy, Trade and Urban Centres in Thailand and Southeast Asia*, pages 39–46. White Lotus, Bangkok.

Ho Ping-ti, 1984, The paleoenvironment of North China. *Journal of Asian History*, XL:723–33.

Hoang Xuan Chinh, 1968, *Bao Cao Khai Quat Dot Di Chi Lung Hoa.* (in Vietnamese). Nha Xuat Ban Khoa Hoc Xa Hoi, Ha Noi.

Hoang Xuan Chinh and Nguyen Ngoc Bich, 1978, *Di Chi Khao Co Hoc Phung Nguyen.* Nha Xuat Ban Khoa Hoc Xa, Ha Noi.

HPM, 1959, The Ch'u tombs of Changsha. (in Chinese). *Kaogu Xuebao*, 1959:41–60.

1983, The Neolithic site at Huachenggang in Anxiang County, Hunan Province. (in Chinese). *Kaogu Xuebao*, 1983:427–70.

Huang Jinsen, 1984, Changes of sea-level since the late Pleistocene of China. In Whyte, R.O., editor, *The Evolution of the East Asian Environment. Volume 2. Palaeobotany, Palaeozoology and Palaeoanthropology*, pages 309–19. Centre of Asian Studies, University of Hong Kong, Hong Kong.

Huang Ti and Wang Dadao, 1983, Commentary on the plates. In Rawson, J., editor, *The Chinese Bronzes of Yunnan*, pages 217–41. Sidgwick and Jackson and the Cultural Relics Publishing House, London and Beijing.

Huang Zhanyue, 1986, Pre Qin bronzes unearthed in Guangdong and Guangxi. (in Chinese). *Kaogu Xuebao*, 1986:409–33.

HuAT, 1962, The remains of the Western Chou wood structures at Mao-chia-tsui, Ch'i Ch'un, Hupei. (in Chinese). *Kaogu Xuebao*, 1962:1–9.

HuPM, 1982a, The exploration and excavation of the ancient Chu capital, Jinan City (Part one). (in Chinese). *Kaogu Xuebao*, 1982:325–50.

1982b, The exploration and excavation of the ancient Chu capital, Jinan City (Part two). (in Chinese) *Kaogu Xuebao*, 1982:477–507.

Hu Shaojin, 1984, A brief report on the second excavation of the ancient cemetery at Shibeicun, Chenggong, Kunming. (in Chinese). *Kaogu*, 1984:231–42.

1985, The Dian graves at Tianzimao, Chenggong. (in Chinese). *Kaogu Xuebao*, 1985:507–45.

Hutterer, K.L. 1982, Early Southeast Asia: old wine in new skins? *Journal of Asian Studies*, XLI:559–70.

1991, *The High Bronze Age in Southeast Asia: introductory remarks.* Unpublished paper read at the Conference on the High Bronze Age, Hua Hin, Thailand.

Indrawooth, P., Krabuansang, S., and Narkwake, P. 1990, Archaeological study of Ban Krabuang Nok. *Spaafa Digest*, XI:12–20.

1991, Muang Fa Daed Song Yang: new archaeological discoveries. In Université Silpakon, editor, *Récentes Recherches en Archéologie en Thailande: Deuxieme Symposium Franco-Thai,* pages 98–111. Silpakon University, Bangkok.

Jammes, L. 1891, Les anciennes civilisations de l'Indo-Chine. L'âge de la pierre polie au Cambodge. *L'Anthropologie*, 7:35–52.

Janse, O.R.T. 1931, Un groupe de bronzes anciens propres à l'extrême-Asie
     Méridionale. *Bulletin of the Museum of Far Eastern Antiquities*, 3:99–174.
     1958, *Archaeological Research in Indo-China. Vol. III, The Ancient Dwelling Site of
     Dong-S'on (Thanh-Hoa, Annam)*. Harvard University Press, Cambridge, Mass.
Karlgren, B. 1942, The date of the early Dong-S'on culture. *Bulletin of the Museum of
     Far Eastern Antiquities*, 14:1–28.
Kealhofer, L. 1992, *Holocene environmental sequences in Central Thailand:
     preliminary phytolith data*. Paper read at the 4th International Conference of the
     European Association of Southeast Asian Archaeologists, Rome, 28 September– 4
     October 1992.
Kelly, W.J. 1975, Tung Kwu phase 3. *Journal of the Hong Kong Archaeological Society*,
     VI:51–4.
Ko, T. 1986, *The development of metals technology in ancient China*. Paper read at the
     Conference on the Beginnings of the use of Metals and Alloys, Zhengzhou, 1986.
Kristiansen, K. 1987, From stone to bronze: the evolution of social complexity in
     northern Europe. In Brumfiel, E. and Earle, T., editors, *Specialization, Exchange
     and Complex Societies*, pages 30–51. Cambridge University Press, Cambridge.
Lam My Dung, 1993, Arranged stone works for water exploitation in Quang Tri
     province. (in Vietnamese). *Khao Co Hoc*, 86:67–79.
Laune, M. 1904, Les objects de bronze au région Luang Prabang. In Pavie, A., editor,
     *Mission Pavie Indo-Chine 1879–1895. Études Diverses III. Recherches sur
     L'Histoire Naturelle de L'Indochine Orientale*, page 27. Ernest Leroux, Paris.
LCR, 1989, *Annals of Lechang Cultural Relics*. (in Chinese). LCR, Guangdong.
Le Xuan Diem, 1977, Ancient moulds for casting bronze artefacts from the Dong Nai
     basin. (in Vietnamese). *Khao Co Hoc*, 24:44–8.
Leach, E.R. 1954, *Political Systems of Highland Burma*. Harvard University Press,
     Cambridge, Mass.
Lefèvre-Pontalis, M. 1894, Note de M. Lefèvre-Pontalis. In Pavie, A., editor, *Mission
     Pavie. Explorations de l'Indo-Chine. Archeologie et Histoire*, pages 14–23. Ernest
     Leroux, Paris.
Leong Sau Heng, 1990, A tripod pottery complex in Peninsular Malaysia. In Glover, I.C.
     and Glover, E., editors, *Southeast Asian Archaeology 1986*, pages 65–76. British
     Archaeological Reports (International Series) 561, Oxford.
     1991, Jenderam Hilir and the Mid-Holocene prehistory of the west coast plain of
     Peninsular Malaysia. *Bulletin of the Indo-Pacific Prehistory Association*, 10:150–
     60.
Lepowsky, M. 1983, Sudest Island and the Louisiade Archipelago in Massim exchange.
     In Leach, J.W. and Leach, E.R., editors, *The Kula. New Perspectives on Massim
     Exchange*, pages 467–502. Cambridge University Press, Cambridge.
Lévy, P. 1943, *Recherches préhistoriques dans la region de Mlu Prei*. PEFEO: 30, Paris.
Liang Jingjin, 1978, Bronze artefacts recovered in Guangxi (in Chinese). *Wenwu*,
     10:93–6.
Li Chaozhen and He Chaozing, 1986, The wooden coffin and grave at Dabona,
     Xiangyun, Yunnan. (in Chinese). *Wenwu*, 1986:21–4.
Li Guo, 1994, *Neolithic sand bar sites round the Pearl River estuary area and Hainan: a
     comparative study*. Unpublished paper read at the Congress of Indo-Pacific
     Prehistory Association, Chiang Mai, January 1994.
Li Wenjie, 1986, On the classification and periodization of the Daxi Culture. (in
     Chinese). *Kaogu Xuebao*, 1986(2):131–52.
Li Yan, 1995, A preliminary study on problems relating to early Bronze Age finds in

Guangdong: begin with stone moulds unearthed from Tangxiahuan in Zhuhai. In Yueng Chung-tong and Li Wai-ling, W. (editors). *Archaeology in Southeast Asia,* pages 87–94. The University Museum and Art Gallery and the University of Hong Kong.

Loofs-Wissowa, H.H.E. 1980–1, Prehistoric and protohistoric links between the Indochinese Peninsula and the Philippines, as exemplified by two types of ear-ornaments. *Journal of the Hong Kong Archaeological Society,* IX:57–76.

    1983, The development and spread of metallurgy in Southeast Asia: a review of the present evidence. *Journal of Southeast Asian Studies,* XIV(1):1–11.

Lunet de Lajonquière, E. 1902, *Inventaire Descriptif des Monuments du Cambodge.* PEFEO, 4. Paris

Luu Tran Tieu, 1977, *Khu Mo Co Chau Can.* (in Vietnamese) Archaeology Institute, Ha Noi.

McConnell, J. and Glover, I.C. 1988–1989, A newly found bronze drum from Bali, Indonesia: some technical considerations. *Modern Quaternary Research in Southeast Asia,* 11:1–38.

MacDonald, W.G. 1978, The Bang site, Thailand. An alternative analysis. *Asian Perspectives,* 21(1):30–51.

McNeill, J.R. and Welch, D.J. 1991, Regional and interregional interaction on the Khorat Plateau. *Bulletin of the Indo-Pacific Prehistory Association,* 10:327–40.

Maddin, R. and Weng, Y.Q. 1984, The Analysis of Bronze Wire. In Higham, C.F.W. and Kijngam, A., editors, *Prehistoric Investigations in Northeast Thailand,* pages 112–116. British Archaeological Reports (International Series) 231, Oxford.

Maglioni, R. 1975, *Archaeological Discovery in Eastern Kwangtung.* Journal Monograph II, Hong Kong Archaeological Society, Hong Kong.

Malleret, L. 1959–63, *L'Archéologie du Delta du Mekong.* EFEO, Paris.

Maloney, B.K. 1991, Palaeoenvironments of Khok Phanom Di: the pollen, pteridophyte spore and microscopic charcoal record. In Higham, C.F.W. and Bannanurag, R., editors, *The Excavation of Khok Phanom Di. Volume 2 (part 1): The Biological Remains,* pages 6–140. Society of Antiquaries of London, Research Report no. XLVIII, London.

Mankong, S. 1989, *Noen Ma Kok.* (in Thai). Fine Arts Department, Bangkok.

Mansuy, H. 1902, *Stations préhistoriques de Samrong-Sen et de Longprao (Cambodge).* F.H. Schneider, Hanoi.

    1923, Contribution à l'étude de la préhistoire de l'Indochine. Résultats de nouvelles recherches effectuées dans le gisement préhistorique de Samrong Sen (Cambodge). *Mémoires du Service Géologique de' Indochine,* 10:1.

Mason, G. M. 1994, The shellfish remains. In Higham, C.F.W., Thosarat, R., Boyd, W., Chang, N., Debreceny, J., Higham, T.F.G., Hogg, A., Hunt, V., Mason, G.M., O'Reilly, D., Pailles, C. and Tayles, N. *The Excavation of the Prehistoric Site of Nong Nor, Central Thailand. Report to the National Research Council of Thailand.*

Massie, M. 1894, Note de M. Massie. In Pavie, A., editor, *Mission Pavie. Explorations de l'Indo-Chine. Archéologie et Histoire,* pages 7–13. Ernest Leroux, Paris.

    1904, Catalogue des objects recueillés dans la région de Luang Prabang. In Pavie, A., editor, *Mission Pavie. Explorations de l'Indo-Chine 1879–1895. Études Diverses III. Recherches sur L'Histoire Naturelle de L'Indochine Orientale,* pages 10–16. Ernest Leroux, Paris.

Meacham, W. 1975a, The contribution of Father Rafael Maglioni. In Meacham, W., editor, *Archaeological Discovery in Eastern Kwangtung,* pages 7–13. Journal Monograph 11, Hong Kong Archaeological Society, Hong Kong.

1975b, Schofield and Shek Pik in retrospect. In Meacham, W., editor, *An Archaeological Site at Shek Pik*, pages v–ix. Journal Monograph 1, Hong Kong Archaeological Society, Hong Kong.

1975c, Tung Kwu phase 4. *Journal of the Hong Kong Archaeological Society*, VI:55–66.

1978, *Sham Wan, Lamma Island. An Archaeological Site Study.* Journal Monograph III, Hong Kong Archaeological Society, Hong Kong.

1983, Origins and development of the Yueh Neolithic: a microcosm of culture change on the mainland of East Asia. In Keightley, D.N., editor, *The Origins of Chinese Civilization*, pages 147–75. University of California Press, Berkeley.

1985, On the improbability of Austronesian origins in South China. *Asian Perspectives*, XXVI:89–106.

1991, Further considerations of the hypothesized Austronesian Neolithic migration from South China to Taiwan and Luzon. *Bulletin of the Indo-Pacific Prehistory Association*, 11:398–407.

1993, New C14 dates and advances in establishing a precise chronology for Hong Kong's prehistory. *Journal of the Hong Kong Archaeological Society*, XIII:115–17.

1994, *On the dating of painted pottery in Hong Kong.* Unpublished paper read at the Conference on Painted Pottery, Chinese University of Hong Kong, February 1994.

Merpert, N. and Munchaev, R.M. 1982, An den anfängen der geschichte Mesopotamiens. *Das Altertum*, 28:69–80.

Monkhonkamnuanket, N. 1992, *Ban Prasat. An Archaeological Site.* (in Thai). Fine Arts Department, Bangkok.

Moore, E. 1988, *Moated Sites in Early North East Thailand.* British Archaeological Reports (International Series) 400, Oxford.

1989, Water management in early Cambodia: evidence from aerial photography. *The Geographical Journal*, 155:204–14.

1992, Ancient habitation on the Angkor Plain: Ban Takhong to Phum Reul. Unpublished draft paper.

Moorey, P.R.S. 1988, Early metallurgy in Mesopotamia. In Maddin, R., editor, *The Beginnings of the Use of Metals and Alloys*, pages 28–33. M.I.T. Press, Cambridge, Mass.

Mosaic, 1977, Archaeology shifting east. *Mosaic*, 8:31–7.

Mouhot, H. 1864, *Travels in the Central Parts of Indo-China (Siam), Cambodia and Laos* (2 vols.). J. Murray, London.

Moura, J. 1883, *Le Royaume de Cambodge.* Ernest Leroux, Paris.

MSP, 1981, The third season of excavation at the Daxi site in Wushan County. (in Chinese). *Kaogu Xuebao*, 1981:461–90.

Mudar, K.M. 1993, *Prehistoric and Early Historic Settlements on the Central Plain: Analysis of Archaeological Survey in Lopburi Province, Thailand.* PhD thesis, University of Michigan.

Muhly, J. 1988, The beginnings of metallurgy in the Old World. In Maddin, R., editor, *The Beginnings of the Use of Metals and Alloys*, pages 2–20. M.I.T. Press, Cambridge, Mass.

Murowchick, R.E. 1989, *The Ancient Bronze Metallurgy of Yunnan and its Environs: Development and Implications.* PhD thesis, Harvard University.

Natapintu, S. 1988a, Current research on ancient copper-base metallurgy in Thailand. In Charoenwongsa, P. and Bronson, B., editors, *Prehistoric Studies: The Stone and Metal Ages in Thailand*, pages 107–24. Thai Antiquity Working Group, Bangkok.

1988b, *Ban Lum Khao.* (in Thai). Fine Arts Department, Bangkok.

1991, Archaeometallurgical studies in the Khao Wong Prachan Valley, Central Thailand. *Bulletin of the Indo-Pacific Prehistory Association*, 11:153–9.

1992, *The excavation of Phu Noi*. Paper read at the Fourth Conference of the European Association for Southeast Asian Archaeologists, Rome, October 1992.

Ngo Si Hong, 1980, Binh Chau (Nghia Binh). A newly discovered Bronze Age site on the central Vietnamese coast. (in Vietnamese). *Khao Co Hoc*, 33:68–74.

1983, The second excavation at Lang Vac, (Nghe Tinh). (in Vietnamese). *Khao Co Hoc*, 46:68–74.

Ngo Si Hong and Tran Quy Thinh, 1991, Jar burials at Hau Xa, Hoi An Tower, (Quang Nam – Da Nang provinces) and new knowledge of the Sa Huynh culture. (in Vietnamese). *Khao Co Hoc*, 78:64–75.

Nguyen Ba Khoach, 1980, Phung Nguyen. *Asian Perspectives*, 23(1):23–54.

Nguyen Dich Dy, Dhin Van Thuan, and Tran Dat, 1980, Palynological analysis at Con Co Ngua (Thanh Hoa). (in Vietnamese). *New Archaeological Discoveries in 1980*, 1980:62–4.

Nguyen Duy Ty and Dao Linh Con, 1985, Technique of brass metallurgy at Doc Chua (Song Be). (in Vietnamese). *Khao Co Hoc*, 55:24–30.

Nguyen Giang Hai and Nguyen Van Hung, 1983, Bronze items just unearthed at Co Loa (Ha Noi). (in Vietnamese). *Khao Co Hoc*, 47:21–32.

Nguyen Kim Dung, 1990, The lithic workshop site at Trang Kenh. (in Vietnamese). *Khao Co Hoc*, 74:64–82.

Nguyen Phuc Long, 1975, Les nouvelles recherches archéologiques au Vietnam. *Arts Asiatiques*, XXXI:1–154.

Nguyen Truong Ky, 1991, An outline on pre-Dongsonian sites in the Ca River valley. (in Vietnamese). *Khao Co Hoc*, 76:48–55.

Nitta, E. 1991, Archaeological study on the ancient iron-smelting and salt-making industries in the northeast of Thailand. Preliminary report on the excavations of Non Yang and Ban Don Phlong. *Journal of Southeast Asian Archaeology*, 11:1–46.

1992, Ancient industries, ecosystem and environment. *Historical Science Reports, Kagoshima University*, 39:61–80.

1994, Archaeological meanings of Heger 1 drums newly found in the Mekhong Basin. *Historical Science Reports, Kagoshima University*, 41:9–23.

NM, 1958, The first and second excavations at Pai Yin Yang Yeng, Nanking. (in Chinese). *Kaogu Xuebao*, 1958:7–24.

1965, Excavations (second season) of the Neolithic site at Liulin, P'i Hsien, Kiangsu Province. (in Chinese). *Kaogu Xuebao*, 1965:9–47.

1981, Trial digging of a Neolithic site at Sidun (Tsudun), Wujin, Jiangsu. (in Chinese). *Kaogu*, 1981:193–200.

1983, A Neolithic site at Qingdun in Haian County, Jiangsu Province. (in Chinese). *Kaogu Xuebao*, 1983:147–90.

1984, Excavations of the Sidun site at Changzhou in Jiangsu in 1982. (in Chinese). *Kaogu*, 1984:109–29.

Noulet, J.-B. 1879, L'âge de la pierre polie et du bronze au Cambodge d'après les découvertes de M. Moura. *Archives du Musée d'Histoire Naturelle de Toulouse*, 1:1–34.

O'Reilly, D. 1994, The pottery and bone artefacts from Nong Nor. In Higham, C.F.W., Thosarat, R., Boyd, W., Chang, N., Debreceny, J., Higham, T.F.G., Hogg, A., Hunt, V., Mason, G.M., O'Reilly, D., Pailles, C. and Tayles, N. *The Excavation of the Prehistoric Site of Nong Nor, Central Thailand. Report to the National Research Council of Thailand*.

Osborne, M. 1975, *River Road to China. The Mekong River Expedition, 1866–1873.* Liveright, New York.

Pacey, A. 1990, *Technology and World Civilization.* MIT Press, Cambridge, Mass.

Parker, R.H. 1968, Review Article: Review of Archaeological Excavations in Thailand Vol. 2, Ban Kao, Part 1 by P. Sørensen and T. Hatting. *Journal of the Polynesian Society*, 77(3):307–13.

Parmentier, M.H. 1918a, Anciens tambours de bronze. *BEFEO*, 18:18–30.

1918b, Dépôts de jarres à Sa-Huynh. *BEFEO*, 24:325–43.

Parry, J.T. 1992, The investigative role of Landsat-TM in the examination of pre- and proto-historic water management sites in Northeast Thailand. *Geocarto International*, 4:5–24.

Patte, E. 1932, Le kjökkenmödding Néolithique de Bau Tro près de Dong Hoi, Annam. *BEFEO* 24:521–61.

1932, Le kjökkenmödding Néolithique de Da-but et ses sepultures. *Bulletin de la Service Geologique d'Indochine*, 19(3)

Pavie, A. 1894, *Mission Pavie. Exploration de l'Indo-Chine. Archéologie et Histoire.* E. Leroux, Paris.

1904, *Mission Pavie Indo-Chine 1879–1895. Études Diverses III. Recherches sur L'Histoire Naturelle de L'Indochine Orientale.* E. Leroux, Paris.

Pearson, R. 1974, Pollen counts in North China. *Antiquity*, 48:226–8.

1981, Social complexity in Chinese coastal Neolithic sites. *Science*, 213:1078–86.

Pearson, R. and Underhill, A. 1987, The Chinese Neolithic: recent trends in research. *American Anthropologist*, 89(4):807–22.

Pelliot, P. 1903, Le Fou-Nan. *BEFEO* 2:248–333.

Penny, J. 1984, Fish in the water and rice in the paddy: contributions to studies of the Southeast Asian Iron Age. In Bayard, D.T., editor, *Southeast Asian Archaeology at the XV Pacific Science Congress*, pages 152–60. Otago University Studies in Prehistoric Anthropology 16, Dunedin.

Peterson, W. 1974, Summary report on two archaeological sites in north-eastern Luzon. *Anthropology and Physical Anthropology in Oceania*, 9:26–35.

Pham Duc Manh, 1985, The Long Giao bronze halberds. (in Vietnamese). *Khao Co Hoc*, 53:37–68.

Pham Huy Thong, 1990, Introduction. in Pham Huy Thong, Pham Minh Huyen, N. and Lai Van Toi, editors, *Dong Son Drums in Viet Nam*, pages 262–71. The Viet Nam Social Science Publishing House, Ha Noi.

Pham Huy Thong, Pham Minh Huyen, N. and Lai Van Toi, editors, 1990, *Dong Son Drums in Viet Nam.* The Viet Nam Social Science Publishing House, Ha Noi.

Pham Quoc Quan and Trinh Can, 1982, The pirogue-coffins at Xuan La (Ha Son Binh Province). (in Vietnamese). *Khao Co Hoc*, 44:36–50.

Pham Van Kinh, 1977, Excavations at Ben Do (Ho Chi Minh City). (in Vietnamese). *Khao Co Hoc*, 24:19–21.

Phommanodch, S. 1991, The past of Thung Samrit at Ban Prasat. (in Thai). *Silapakon Journal*, 34:6–21.

Pigott, V. 1992, *The archaeology of copper production at prehistoric Non Pa Wai and Nil Kham Haeng in Central Thailand.* Paper read at the 4th International Conference of the European Association of Southeast Asian Archaeologists, Rome, 28 September–4 October 1992.

1994, *The bronze industry of the Khao Wong Prachan Valley.* Unpublished paper read at the Congress of Indo-Pacific Prehistory Association, Chiang Mai, January. 1994.

Pigott, V.C. and Natapintu, S. 1988, Archaeological investigations into prehistoric copper production: the Thailand Archaeometallurgy Project 1984–6. In Maddin,

R., editor, *The Beginnings of the Use of Metals and Alloys*, pages 156–62. M.I.T. Press, Cambridge, Mass.

1996, Investigating the origins of metal use in prehistoric Thailand. In Barnard, N. and Bulbeck, F.D., editors, *Ancient Chinese and Southeast Asian Bronze Age Cultures*. In press. Southern Materials Center Inc., Taipei.

Pilditch, J.S. 1984, The jewellery from Ban Na Di. In Higham, C.F.W. and Kijngam, A., editors, *Prehistoric Investigations in Northeast Thailand*, pages 57–222. British Archaeological Reports (International Series) 231, Oxford.

1993, The personal ornaments. In Higham, C.F.W. and Thosarat, R., editors, *The Excavation of Khok Phanom Di. Volume 3 (part 1): the Material Culture*, pages 119–76. Society of Antiquaries of London, Research Report no. L, London.

Pirazzoli-t'Serstevens, M. 1974, *La Civilization du Royaume de Dian à l'Époque Han*. EFEO, Paris.

1979, The bronze drums of Shizhaishan, their social and ritual significance. In Smith, R.B. and Watson, W., editors, *Early South East Asia*, pages 125–36. Oxford University Press, Oxford.

1988, Les cultures du Sichuan occidental à la fin de l'âge du bronze et leurs rapports avec les steppes. In Ministère des Affaires Étrangères, Editeur, *L'Asie Centrale et ses Rapports avec les Civilisations Orientales, des Origines a L'Âge du Fer*, pages 183–96. Boccard, Paris.

1992, Cowry and Chinese copper cash as prestige goods in Dian. In Glover, I.C., editor, *Southeast Asian Archaeology, 1990*, pages 45–52. Centre for South-East Asian Studies, University of Hull.

Pisnupong, P. 1993, The Industrial Stone Technology. In Higham, C.F.W. and Thosarat, R., editors, *The Excavation of Khok Phanom Di. Volume 3 (part 1): the Material Culture*, pages 45–104. Society of Antiquaries of London, Research Report no. 1, London.

Pookajorn, S., editor 1984, *The Hoabinhian of Mainland Southeast Asia: New Data from the Recent Thai Excavations in the Ban Kao Area*. Thammasat University Press, Bangkok.

Prishanchit, S. 1988, A preliminary survey of lithic industries in Mae Hong Son, Nan and Uttaradit, Northern Thailand. In Charoenwongsa, P. and Bronson, B., editors, *Prehistoric Studies: the Stone and Metal Ages in Thailand*, pages 81–90. Thai Antiquity Working Group, Bangkok.

Qiu Licheng and Li Xiongkun, 1988, One Warring States burial discovered at Mianyinxu, Wuhua county, Guangdong. (in Chinese). *Kaogu*, 10:959–60.

Qiu Xuanchong, Wang Dadao, Huan Derong, and Wang Han, 1983, Report of the excavation of the ancient cemetery at Wanjiaba, Chuxiong. (in Chinese). *Kaogu Xuebao*, 1983:347–82.

Rajpitak, W. and Seeley, N.J. 1979, The bronze bowls from Ban Don Ta Phet: an enigma of prehistoric metallurgy. *World Archaeology*, 11(1):26–31.

1984, The bronze metallurgy. In Higham, C. F.W. and Kijngam, A., editors, Prehistoric Investigations in Northeast Thailand, pages 102–12. British Archaeological Reports (International Series) 231, Oxford.

Reid, L.A. 1993, Morphological evidence for Austric. Paper presented at the Conference on Austronesian-Mainland Southeast Asian Relations, Honolulu.

Renfrew, C. 1972, *The Emergence of Civilisation*. Methuen, London.

1974, Beyond a subsistence economy: the evolution of social organisation in prehistoric Europe. In Moore, C.B., editor, *Reconstructing Complex Societies: an Archaeological Colloquium*, pages 69–95. American School of Oriental Research, Ann Arbor.

1986, Varna and the emergence of wealth in prehistoric Europe. In Appadurai, A., editor, *The Social Life of Things. Commodities in Cultural Perspective*, pages 141–68. Cambridge University Press, Cambridge.

1994, World linguistic diversity. *Scientific American*, 270:104–10.

Rispoli, F. 1990, *La Ceramica di Non Pa Wai (Lopburi, Thailandia Centrale)*. PhD thesis, Università di Roma.

1992, Preliminary report on the pottery from Tha Kae, Lopburi, Central Thailand. In Glover, I.C., editor, *Southeast Asian Archaeology, 1990*, pages 129–42. Centre for South-East Asian Studies, University of Hull.

Rogers, P.R., Leininger, N.W., Mirchandani, S., van den Bergh, J. and Widdowson, E.A. 1995, *Tung Wan Tsai: A Bronze Age and Han Period Coastal Site*. Antiquities and Monuments Office, Hong Kong, Occasional Paper no. 3.

Rogers, P.R. and Engelhardt, R.A. 1994, *Maritime adaptive strategies. An ethnoarchaeological model for the nature and distribution of archaeological sites*. Unpublished paper read at the Congress of Indo-Pacific Prehistory Association, Chiang Mai, January 1994.

Rostoker, W. and Dvorak, J.R. 1989, Direct reduction to copper metal by oxide-sulfide mineral interaction. *Archeomaterials*, 3:69-87.

Rowlands, M.J. 1971, The archaeological interpretation of prehistoric metalworking. *Antiquity*, 3:210–24.

Rudolph, R.C. 1960, An important Dongson site in Yunnan. *Asian Perspectives*, 4:41–9.

Rutnin, S. 1979, *The Pottery from Non Chai, Northeast Thailand*. Master's thesis, University of Otago.

Ryan, T.F. 1958, Rev. Daniel Finn, S.J. 1886–1936. In Ryan, T.F., editor, *Archaeological Finds on Lamma Island near Hong Kong*, pages 277–8. Ricci, Hong Kong.

SATIA, 1984, The excavation of the Beixin Neolithic site in Tengxian County, Shandong Province. (in Chinese). *Kaogu Xuebao*, 1984:159–91.

Saurin, E. 1963, Station préhistorique à Hang-Gon près Xuan Loc. *BEFEO*, 51:433–52.

1973, La champs de jarres de Hang Gon, près Xuan-Loc (Sud Viêt-Nam). *BEFEO*, 60:329–58.

Schauffler, W. 1976, Archaeological survey and excavation of Ban Chiang culture sites in Northeast Thailand. *Expedition*, 18:27–37.

Schmidt, W. 1906, *Die Mon-Khmer Völker: ein Bindeglied Zwischen Völkern Zentralasiens und Austronesiens*. Braunschweig.

Schofield, W. 1975, An archaeological site at Shek Pik. In Meacham, W., editor, *An Archaeological Site at Shek Pik*. Journal Monograph 1, Hong Kong Archaeological Society, Hong Kong.

Seidenfaden, E. 1922, Complement à l'inventaire descriptif de monuments du Cambodge. *BEFEO*, 22:58–99.

Shanxi-ATIA, 1980, Excavations of a Neolithic site at Taosi in Xiangfen, Shanxi. (in Chinese). *Kaogu*, 1980:18–31.

Shoocondej, R. 1991, *Relationships between prehistoric hunter-gatherers and their environments in the lower Khwae Noi Basin* (in Thai). Report submitted to the Research and Development Institution, Silpakon University.

1994, *Working toward an anthropological perspective on Thai prehistory: current research on the post-Pleistocene*. Unpublished paper read at the Congress of the Indo-Pacific Prehistory Association, Chiang Mai, January 1994.

Sieveking, G. de G. 1954, Excavations at Gua Cha, Kelantan, Part 1. *Federation Museums Journal*, 1 and 2:75–143.

SMRPC, 1980, The second season of excavation at Songze site in Qingpu County, Shanghai. (in Chinese). *Kaogu Xuebao* 19801: 29–58.

Soejono, R.P. 1993, *The role of prehistoric bronze drums in Indonesia.* Unpublished paper read at the 34th International Conference of Asian and North African Studies, Hong Kong, September 1993.

Solheim, W.G. II 1959, Sa-Huynh related pottery in Southeast Asia. *Asian Perspectives,* 3:177–88.

1964, Pottery and the Malayo-Polynesians. *Current Anthropology,* 5:376–84.

1968, Early bronze in Northeastern Thailand. *Current Anthropology,* 9(1):59–62.

1969, Review of Archaeological Excavations in Thailand Vol.2, Ban Kao, Part 1. by P. Sørensen and T. Hatting. *Asian Perspectives,* 12:127–30.

1970, Northern Thailand, Southeast Asia, and world prehistory. *Asian Perspectives,* 13:145–62.

1972, An earlier agricultural revolution. *Scientific American,* CCVI(4):34–41.

1983, The development of metallurgy in Southeast Asia: another reply to Loofs-Wissowa. *Journal of Southeast Asian Studies,* XIV(1):18–25.

Solheim, W.G. II and Ayres, M. 1979, The late prehistoric and early historic pottery from the Khorat Plateau with special reference to Phimai. In Smith, R.B. and Watson, W., editors, *Early South East Asia,* pages 63–77. Oxford University Press, Oxford.

Solheim, W.G. II and Gorman, C.F. 1966, Archaeological salvage program: Northeastern Thailand, first season. *Journal of the Siam Society,* LIV:111–81.

Song Zhimin, 1987, The cist graves of Sichuan and Northwest Yunnan. (in Chinese). *Kaogu Yu Wenwu,* 1987:66–76.

Sørensen, P. 1973, Prehistoric iron implements from Thailand. *Asian Perspectives,* 16:134–73.

1988, The kettledrums from Ongbah cave, Kanchanaburi Province. In Sørensen, P., editor, *Archaeological Excavations in Thailand. Surface Finds and Minor Excavations,* pages 95–156. Scandinavian Institute of Asian Studies Occasional Paper No. 1, Copenhagen.

1992, *A newly discovered Heger 1 drum from Laos.* Paper read at the 4th International Conference of the European Association of Southeast Asian Archaeologists, Rome, 28 September–4 October 1992.

Sørensen, P. and Hatting, T. 1967, *Archaeological Investigations in Thailand. Vol. II, Ban Kao, Part 1: The Archaeological Materials from the Burials.* Munksgard, Copenhagen.

SPCRAC, 1987, The site of Sanxingdui in Guanghan. (in Chinese) *Kaogu Xuebao* 1987(2):227–54.

Spriggs, M. 1989, The dating of the island Southeast Asian Neolithic: an attempt at chronometric hygiene and linguistic correlation. *Antiquity,* 63:587–613.

1991, Considering Meacham's considerations on Southeast Asia. *Bulletin of the Indo-Pacific Prehistory Association,* 11:408–11.

1994, *Chronometric hygiene and colonisation in island Southeast Asia and the Pacific: new data and an evaluation.* Unpublished paper read at the Congress of Indo-Pacific Prehistory Association, Chiang Mai, January 1994.

Spriggs, M. and Anderson, A.J. 1993, Late colonization of Polynesia. *Antiquity,* 67:200–17.

Stech, T. and Maddin, R. 1988, Reflections on early metallurgy in Southeast Asia. In Maddin, R., editor, *The Beginnings of the Use of Metals and Alloys,* pages 163–74. M.I.T. Press, Cambridge, Mass.

Stuiver, M. and Reimer, P.J. 1993, Extended 14C database and revised calib 3.0 (14C) age calibration program. *Radiocarbon* 35:215–32.

Suchitta, P. 1983, Characteristics of ancient pottery in the Mun-Chi basin. (in Thai). *Muang Boran,* 9:85–91.

Sun Shuyun and Han Rubin, 1981, A preliminary study of early Chinese copper and bronze artefacts (in Chinese). *Kaogu Xuebao*, 3:287–302.

Suthiragsa, N. 1979, The Ban Chieng culture. In Smith, R.B. and Watson, W., editors, *Early South East Asia*, pages 42–52. Oxford University Press, Oxford.

Tang Chung, editor, 1994, *Ancient Cultures of South China and Neighbouring Regions*. Chinese University of Hong Kong, Hong Kong.

Tayles, N.G. 1992, *The People of Khok Phanom Di*. PhD thesis, University of Otago.

    1994, The human remains from Nong Nor, Central Thailand. In Higham, C.F.W., Thosarat, R., Boyd, W., Chang, N., Debreceny, J., Higham, T.F.G., Hogg, A., Mason, G.M., O'Reilly, D., Pailles, C. and Tayles, N. *The Excavation of the Prehistoric Site of Nong Nor, Central Thailand. Report to the National Research Council of Thailand*.

Taylor, K. 1991, *Encountering Southeast Asia in Shui Ching Chu*. Unpublished paper read at the Conference on the High Bronze Age, Hua Hin, Thailand.

Thompson, G.B. 1992, *Archaeobotanical Investigations at Khok Phanom Di, Central Thailand*. PhD thesis, Australian National University.

Tong Enzheng, 1977, The bronze daggers of Southwestern China. (in Chinese). *Kaogu Xuebao*, 1977:35–55.

    1991, *The chiefdom characteristics of Dian culture as reflected in the archaeological record*. Unpublished paper read at the Conference on the High Bronze Age, Hua Hin, Thailand.

Tregear, T.R. 1980, *China. A Geographical Survey*. Hodder and Stoughton, London.

Trinh Sinh, 1977, From the stone ring to the bronze ring. (in Vietnamese). *Khao Co Hoc*, 23:51–6.

    1990, Spectrographic analysis of bronze artefacts in Go Mun and Dong Dau cultures. (in Vietnamese). *Khao Co Hoc*, 75:49–59.

    1992, Copper artefacts in the Dong Son culture. (in Vietnamese). *Khao Co Hoc*, 80:55–64.

Trinh Sinh and Ngo Sy Hong, 1980, Some remarks about Lang Ca site (Vinh Phu Province). (in Vietnamese). *Khao Co Hoc*, 36:15–30.

Tsang, C. 1992, *Archaeology of the P'eng-hu Islands*. Academia Sinica. Institute of History and Philology, Special Publication no. 95, Taipei.

Vallibhotama, S. 1984, The relevance of moated settlements to the formation of states in Thailand. In Bayard, D.T., editor, *Southeast Asian Archaeology at the XV Pacific Science Congress*, pages 123–8. University of Otago Studies in Prehistoric Anthropology 16, Dunedin.

    1991, *Bronze-Iron age foundations for the origin of the state of Chenla*. Unpublished paper read at the Conference on the High Bronze Age, Hua Hin, Thailand.

van Liere, W.J. 1979, *The environmental archaeology of the prehistoric site of Non Chai*. Unpublished report.

    1980, Traditional water management in the lower Mekong Basin. *World Archaeology*, 11(3):265–80.

Verneau, M. 1904, Les âges de la pierre et du bronze dans les pays des Bahnars, des Sedangs, de Reungaos et dans l'arrondissement de Bienhoa. In Pavie, A., editor, *Mission Pavie Indo-Chine 1879–1895. Études Diverses III. Recherches sur L'Histoire Naturelle de L'Indochine Orientale*, pages 27–40. Ernest Leroux, Paris.

Vernon, W.W. 1996, The crucible in copper-bronze production in prehistoric Phu Lon, Northeastern Thailand: analysis and interpretion. In Barnard, N. and Bulbeck, F.D., editors, *Ancient Chinese and Southeast Asian Bronze Age Cultures*. In press. Southern Materials Center Inc., Taipei.

Vickery, M. 1986, Some remarks on early state formation in Cambodia. In Marr, D.G.

and Milner, A.C., editors, *Southeast Asia in the 9th and 14th Centuries*, pages 95–115. Research School of Pacific Studies, Australian National University, and Institute of Southeast Asian Studies, Singapore, Canberra.

Vincent, B.A. 1987, The ceramics, in Higham, C.F.W. Maloney, B. Bannanurag R. and Vincent B.A., Khok Phanom Di: the results of the 1984–5 excavation. *Bulletin of the Indo-Pacific Prehistory Association*, 7:148–78.

1988, *Prehistoric Ceramics of Northeast Thailand*. British Archaeological Reports (International Series) 461, Oxford.

VMH, 1965, *Ngoi Mo Co Viet-Khe*. Xuet Ban, Hanoi.

von Dewall, M. 1967, The Tien Culture of South-West China. *Antiquity*, 41:8–21.

1979, Local workshop centres of the Late Bronze Age in highland South East Asia. In Smith, R.B. and Watson, W., editors, *Early South East Asia*, pages 31–49. Oxford University Press, Oxford.

1988, *Cattle imagery and bronze-drum decoration – their social meaning in Dian mortuary art and bronze age ritual traditions*. Unpublished paper read at the International Conference on ancient bronze drums and bronze cultures in Southern China and Southeast Asia, Kunming, Yunnan.

Vu The Long, 1979, Animal remains at Da But site (Thanh Hoa) collected in 1971. (in Vietnamese). *New Archaeological Discoveries in 1979*, 1979:54–6.

Walden, J. 1975, The Reverend Father Rafael Maglioni. In Meacham, W., editor, *Archaeological Discovery in Eastern Kwangtung*, pages 5–6. Journal Monograph 11, Hong Kong Archaeological Society, Hong Kong.

Wang Dadao, 1985, A reconsideration of the Wanjiaba tombs in the light of dating and periodization. *Bulletin of the Ancient Orient Museum*, 7:113–33.

Wang Dadao and Qiu Xuanchong, 1980, Brief report on the excavation of the ancient cemetery at Longjie Shibeicun, Chenggong, Yunnan. (in Chinese). *Wenwu Ziliao Congkan*, 3:86–97.

Wang Kaifa, 1980, Palynological study of Songze site in Qingpu County, Shanghai. (in Chinese). *Kaogu Xuebao*, 1980:59–66.

Watson, W. 1979, Kok Charoen and the early metal age of Central Thailand. In Smith, R.B. and Watson, W., editors, *Early South East Asia*, pages 53–62. Oxford University Press, Oxford.

Watt, J.C.Y. 1968, Archaeological finds in Hong Kong and their cultural implications. *Journal of the Hong Kong Archaeological Society*, 1:10–18.

Weiss, A.D. 1992, *The social context of copper production in Central Thailand: evidence from mortuary and industrial data*. Paper read at the 4th International Conference of the European Association of Southeast Asian Archaeologists, Rome, 28 September–4 October 1992.

Welch, D. 1984, Settlement pattern as an indicator of sociopolitical complexity in the Phimai region, Thailand. In Bayard, D.T., editor, *Southeast Asian Archaeology at the XV Pacific Science Congress*, pages 129–51. Otago University Studies in Prehistoric Anthropology 16, Dunedin.

1985, *Adaptation to Environmental Unpredictability: Intensive Agriculture and Regional Exchange at Late Prehistoric Centers in the Phimai Region*. PhD thesis, University of Hawaii.

Welch, D.J. and McNeill, J.R. 1988–9, Excavations at Ban Tamyae and Non Ban Kham, Phimai region, Northeast Thailand. *Asian Perspectives*, 28:99–123.

1991, Settlement, agriculture and population changes in the Phimai region, Thailand. *Bulletin of the Indo-Pacific Prehistory Association*, 11:210–28.

Wheatley, P. 1983, *Nagara and Commandery*. University of Chicago Department of Geography Research Paper Nos. 207–8, Chicago.

White, J.C. 1982, *Ban Chiang. The Discovery of a Lost Bronze Age.* University of Pennsylvania Press, Philadelphia.

 1986, *A Revision of the Chronology of Ban Chiang and its Implications for the Prehistory of Northeast Thailand.* PhD thesis, University of Pennsylvania.

White, J.C., Vernon, W., Fleming, S., Glanzman, W., Hancock, R., and Pelcin, A. 1991, Preliminary cultural implications from initial studies of the ceramic technology of Ban Chiang. *Bulletin of the Indo-Pacific Prehistory Association,* 11:188–203.

Wichakana, M. 1984, The Analysis of Upper Songkhram Settlement Patterns. In Higham, C.F.W. and Kijngam, A., editors, *Prehistoric Investigations in Northeast Thailand,* pages 546–64. British Archaeological Reports (International Series) 231, Oxford.

 1991, Prehistoric sacrifices at Noen U-Loke. (in Thai). *Muang Boran,* 16(4):69–79.

Wilaikaeo, C. 1988, Archaeological evidence from the Bronze Age in the Kwae Yae River Valley. (in Thai). *Muang Boran,* 14:73–80.

Wilen, R.N. 1989, *Excavations at Non Pa Kluay, Northeast Thailand.* British Archaeological Reports (International Series) 517, Oxford.

Williams, L. 1984, *A new approach to the study of bead-making workshop practices with special reference to carnelian and agate beads from Ban Don Ta Phet, Thailand.* B.A. report, Institute of Archaeology, London University.

Williams-Hunt, P. 1950, Irregular earthworks in Eastern Siam: an air survey. *Antiquity,* 24:30–7.

Wilson, P.J. 1988, *The Domestication of the Human Species.* Yale University Press, New Haven.

Wolters, O.W. 1979, Khmer Hinduism in the seventh century. In Smith, R.B. and Watson, W., editors, *Early South East Asia,* pages 427–42. Oxford University Press, Oxford.

Woods, M. and Parry, S. 1993, An archaeological assessment at Don Dong Muang, Northeast Thailand. *Spafa Journal,* 1993:10–17.

Worman, E.C. 1949, Samrong Sen and the reconstruction of prehistory in Indo-China. *Southwestern Journal of Anthropology,* 5:318–29.

Wu, K., Sun, S., Zhang, S., and Wang, D. 1986, *Bronze drum making techniques in ancient Southwestern China.* Paper read at the second International Symposium on the beginning of the use of metals and alloys, Zhenghou.

Xiong Chuanxin, 1976, A Shang Dynasty bronze *tsun* in the shape of an elephant found at Liling, Hunan Province. (in Chinese). *Wenwu,* 1976:49–50.

Xiong Ying and Sun Taichu, 1964, Report on the excavation of a grave with wooden coffin and bronze casket at Dabona, Xiangun, Yunnan. (in Chinese). *Kaogu,* 1964:607–14.

Xu Hengbin, 1984, The Bronze Age of Guangdong. In Lam, P. Y.K., editor, *Archaeological finds from pre-Qin sites in Guangdong,* pages 58–101. Hong Kong Chinese University Museum Press, Hong Kong.

Xu Pingfang, 1992, *Recent archaeological discoveries and research.* Unpublished paper read at the Symposium on Chinese Archaeology, School of Oriental and African Studies, University of London, November 1992.

Yang Hsi-chang, 1986, The Shang Dynasty cemetery system. In Chang, K.-C., editor, *Studies of Shang Archaeology,* pages 49–63. Yale University Press, New Haven.

Yang Huairen and Xie Zhiren, 1984, Sea level changes in East China over the past 20,000 years. In Whyte, R.O., editor, *The Evolution of the East Asian Environment. Volume 2. Palaeobotany, Palaeozoology and Palaeoanthropology,* pages 288–308. Centre of Asian Studies, University of Hong Kong, Hong Kong.

Yang Shiting, 1985, A preliminary study of the Siqiaoshan Culture. (in Chinese). *Kaogu Xuebao*, 1985:9–32.

Yang Shiting and Cuiyong and Deng Zengkui, 1991, Main results and excavation of the Warring States and Western Han burials at Liyangdun, Fengkai, Guangdong. (in Chinese). In Bowuguan, F. and Yanjiusuo, G.W.K., editors, *Collected Papers in Commemoration of the 30th Anniversary of the Discovery of Hujangyandong Cave*, pages 240–50. Guangdong Luxing Chubanshe, Guangzhou.

Yan Wenming, 1991, China's earliest rice agriculture remains. *Bulletin of the Indo-Pacific Prehistory Association*, 10:118–26.

You-di, C. 1976, *Ban Don Ta Phet: Preliminary Excavation Report, 1975–76*. (in Thai) National Museum, Bangkok.

You Rujie, 1976, A few observations on the rice grains and bone '*si*' unearthed from the fourth layer of the Hemudu site. (in Chinese). *Wenwu*, 8:20–3.

YPM, 1956, The ancient site and cemetery at Shizhaishan, Jinning, Yunnan. (in Chinese). *Kaogu Xuebao*, 1956:43–63.

    1958, Brief report on the excavation of the ancient cultural remains at Haimenkou, Jianchuan. (in Chinese). *Kaogu Tongxun*, 1958:5–12.

    1959, *Report on the Excavation of the Ancient Cemetery at Shizhaishan, Jinning, Yunnan*. (in Chinese). Wenwu Chubanshe, Beijing.

    1977, The Neolithic site of Ta-Tun-Tzu in Yuan-Mo County, Yunnan Province. (in Chinese). *Kaogu Xuebao*, 1977:43–72.

    1981, The Baiyangcun site at Binchuan County, Yunnan Province. (in Chinese). *Kaogu Xuebao*, 1981:349–68.

    1986, Brief report on the excavation of the cemetery at Aofengshan, Jianchuan, Yunnan. (in Chinese). *Wenwu*, 1986:1–20.

Yun Kuen Lee, 1994, *Material representations of status in the Dian culture*. Unpublished paper presented to the 15th Congress of the Indo-Pacific Prehistory Association, Chiang Mai, January 1994.

Yu Su, 1978, Brief report on the excavation of Yüdun. (in Chinese). *Kaogu*, 1978:227.

Zeng Zhaoyu and Yin Huanzhang, 1959, On the Hu Shu Culture. (in Chinese). *Kaogu Xuebao*, 1959:47–58.

Zhang Zengqi, 1964, A grave with a wooden coffin and bronze casket discovered at Dabona, Xiangyun, Yunnan. (in Chinese). *Kaogu*, 1964:369–70.

Zhang Zengqi and Wang Dadao, 1975, Report on the excavation of the ancient cemetery of Lijiashan, Jiangchuan, Yunnan. (in Chinese). *Kaogu Xuebao*, 1975:97–156.

Zhang Zhongpei, 1985, The social structure reflected in the Yuanjunmiao cemetery. *Journal of Anthropological Archaeology*, 4:19–33.

    1987, On the Qijia Culture. (in Chinese). *Kaogu Xuebao*, 1987:153–76.

Zhao Baoquan, Hu Youyan and Lu Benshan, 1988, Ancient copper mining and smelting at Tonglushan, Daye. In Maddin, R., editor, *The Beginning of the Use of Metals and Alloys*, pages 125–9. Massachusetts Institute of Technology Press, Cambridge, Mass.

Zhao Songquiao, 1986, *Physical Geography of China*. Wiley, New York.

Zhao Zhiquan, 1985, On the ancient site of Erlitou. *Annali Istituto Universitario Orientale Napoli*, 45:287–302.

Zhou, S.Z., Chen, F., Pan, B.T., Cao, J.X., Li, J.J., and Derbyshire, E. 1991, Environmental change during the Holocene in Western China on a millennial timescale. *The Holocene*, 1:151–6.

Zhou Benxiong, 1981, The animal remains discovered at Cishan village, Wu'an, Hebei Province. (in Chinese). *Kaogu Xuebao*, 1981:339–47.

Zhou Jiwei, 1981, Report of the examination of ancient rice from the middle and lower Yangzi. (in Chinese). *Yunnan Nongye Xuexi*, 1981(1):1–6.

Zhu Feisu, 1984. Several problems related to the archaeology of Neolithic Guangdong. In Lam, P.Y.K., editor, *Archaeological finds from pre-Qin sites in Guangdong*, pages 30–42. Hong Kong Chinese University Museum Press, Hong Kong.

Zhu Shoukang and Han Rubin, 1981, *A preliminary study of copper smelting at Tonglushan*. Unpublished paper read at the Conference on the Beginning of the Use of Metals and Alloys, Beijing, October 1981.

Zide, A.R.K. and Zide, N.H. 1976, Proto-Munda cultural vocabulary: evidence for early agriculture. In Jenner, P.N., Thompson, L.C. and Starosta, S., editors, *Austro-Asiatic Studies part II*, pages 1295–334. Oceanic Linguistics Special Publication 13, Honolulu.

ZPM, 1978a, Excavations (first season) at Ho-Mu-Tu in Yus-Yao County, Chekiang Province. (in Chinese). *Kaogu Xuebao*, 1978:39–94.

  1978b, A study of the animal and plant remains unearthed at Ho-Mu-Tu. (in Chinese). *Kaogu Xuebao*, 1978:85–108.

—

INDEX